FINANCIAL FAILURE
AND
CONFEDERATE DEFEAT

Douglas B. Ball

UNIVERSITY OF ILLINOIS PRESS
Urbana and Chicago

This book is printed on acid-free paper.

Library of Congress Cataloging-in-Publication Data

Ball, Douglas B.
Financial failure and Confederate defeat / Douglas B. Ball.
p.   cm.
Includes bibliographical references.
ISBN 0-252-01755-2 (alk. paper)
1. United States—History—Civil War, 1861-1865—Finance.
2. United States—History—Civil War, 1861-1865—Economic aspects.
3. Finance, Public—Confederate States of America. 4. Confederate
States of America—Economic policy. I. Title.
E480.5.B35 1991
973.7'1—dc20   90-10831
                                                                  CIP

To my parents, Ruth M. and George W. Ball,
with loving thanks over the ten-year period of
this book's preparation.

Contents

Foreword

No task is more difficult for a Civil War historian than to attempt explanation of the reasons for Confederate defeat. Douglas Ball has compounded the difficulty by attacking the most difficult of the myriad causes alleged through all the years since Appomattox—failure of Southern financial policies. Ball is by no means the first scholar to wander in the Confederate economic bramble patch. Charles W. Ramsdell, perhaps the most thoughtful of Confederate scholars, said in his perceptive *Behind the Lines in the Southern Confederacy* (1944) that mishandled finances constituted the wartime South's greatest weakness. Two students attacked the Confederacy's economic problems in 1901—John C. Schwab, in *The Confederate States of America*, and Ernest A. Smith, in *A History of the Confederate Treasury*.

Since those early efforts, a long, thin line of studies touches on phases of Rebel financial policy—the list would include Frank L. Owsley, *King Cotton Diplomacy* (1931), Samuel T. Thompson, *Confederate Purchasing Operations Abroad* (1935), William Diamond, "Imports of the Confederate Government from Europe and Mexico," *Journal of Southern History* (1940), pp. 470–503, and Richard C. Todd, *Confederate Finance* (1954). Some recent general histories of the Confederacy touch on the topic with trepidation, and then quickly slide on to such easier causes of defeat as military mismanagement, political ineptitude, and lapses in leadership.

"Conventional wisdom" has long held the convenient view that the Confederacy collapsed from myriad causes; those historians who could deduce one more possible cause deserved a gold rung on the scholarly ladder! Indeed, the more complex the melange, the sounder the theory—or so went collegial prejudice. And, considering the normal complexity of historical causes, this view has obvious merit.

Not for Douglas Ball—who comes raucously to the hustings of causation. No mincer of words, Ball believes firmly that the Confederacy had every right to expect success in its quest for independence. He agrees with Charles H. Wesley's thesis in *The Collapse of the Confederacy* (1934) that it was "astonishing that with its resources the Confederacy did not continue the war for a longer period" (p. vii).

Ball analytically examines Southern political and financial leadership and finds both dismal. Jefferson Davis, often a scapegoat in standard studies, is skewered deftly as a financial innocent; his first treasury secretary, Christopher G. Memminger, is shown as a confused, recessive misfit; executive policies reveal either abysmal ignorance of American financial experience or egregious optimism.

With fine impartiality, Ball accuses Davis of dangerous ignorance which he did not try to rectify. He accuses Memminger of woeful incompetence in virtually all fiscal matters. And both he attacks for failing to offer the Confederate Congress sound programs the members could support. These inadequacies, Ball thinks are inexcusable, considering the history of the United States in previous wars. Treasury Secretary Albert Gallatin's experience had considerable relevance, as did that of such other national leaders as John Calhoun and all the previous presidents. He believes that a familiarity with the works of Adam Smith, J. B. Say, Ricardo, and John Stuart Mill offered an adequate background for sound wartime fiscal planning. Southern leaders apparently were either unaware of these classics or simply ignored them.

Certainly enough precedents existed to provide better planning for such programs as blockade-running—which did well, but had far greater potential than the Confederates achieved. Ball feels that in areas where local administrators could develop their own plans, untrammeled by poor national policies, things went well. A case in point is the highly controversial Erlanger loan.

This loan has received much historical attention, with a wide variety of guesses available on exactly how much the Confederacy realized from various foreign markets. Ball performs an important service in his thorough reappraisal of the loan and his careful re-computation of receipts and disbursements.

Financial Failure and Confederate Defeat is a tough, opinionated book. There are times when readers may feel that Ball condemns too vehemently, that some of his opinions are too harsh, his characterizations caricatures. Some of his views are probably wrong, others at least arguable. A few readers will lament his almost "single cause" approach. All of which is to say that this will be highly controversial book, one to provoke comment and contention. But it would be a serious error to ignore this book simply because of the author's dissonance. He has written a book to rank immediately among the important studies of the Confederacy.

Financial Failure and Confederate Defeat will remain important not only because the author brings so many threads together in his assessment of the central role of finances, but also because his work is based on wide-ranging and innovative research. Ball's sources range from the traditional to the arcane to the topical. He brings to his research a special background in banking and finance, a background that has opened sources unused before. Those sources have enabled him to attempt the first systematic assessment of the national budget and gross national product of the Confederate States—both vital contributions. His background, too, gives him unusual understanding of the state of American finances in the 1860s, as well as a special basis for judging policies and policymakers.

Above all, Ball has avoided the worst possible pitfall—he has not succumbed to jargon! Despite his expertise and the obvious intricacies of his subject matter, the author writes forcefully and clearly, assesses boldly, analyzes deftly. He offers invaluable tables of data for the close student, but his narrative marches uncluttered to the end.

This book teaches, irritates, enlightens, and rewards.

—Frank E. Vandiver

Acknowledgments

I am deeply grateful to the many people who contributed their time and effort to this book.

To Mattie Russell of Duke University, and James Rhodes, Hope K. Holdcamper, Donald M. King, and Albert U. Blair of the National Archives, I owe a debt of gratitude for many years' advice, research assistance, and cooperation. I am under deep obligation to C. Vann Woodward of Yale and James Potter in London. For most recent services in reading my work and suggesting revisions leading to publication, I am grateful to Miriam Brokaw, William L. Barney, and Richard Beringer, whose thoughts have greatly improved the book.

I must also thank my father, George W. Ball, for his encouragement and his taking the time to read my manuscript at its various stages of preparation when he already had far too much to do.

Finally, I want to thank Karen Vasudeva, who typed her way through endless revisions, deciphered my handwriting, and all the while kept her irrepressible good humor.

Introduction

After 1865, while Southerners kept repeating the consoling incantation that "the South shall rise again," they concentrated their struggle for white supremacy and home rule within the Union, not outside it. That change in mood and tactics in large part reflected the disillusion of the Southern people with Jefferson Davis; they gave vent to their frustrations by blaming the North's victory on the unpopular and inadequate measures of their fallen president. Only after the healing passage of time did they cease to make Davis their scapegoat. By then, widespread resignation to the idea that a Northern victory had been inevitable, combined with a growing sympathy for Davis's mistreatment by Union jailers, led them to take a more charitable view of their erstwhile leader.

The Excuse of Superior Northern Resources

Although Southerners drew comfort from the assumption of inevitability which cast an aura of romantic heroism over the "Lost Cause," that diagnosis has been subjected to revision. Some scholars have now opted for the hypothesis that the key element explaining the outcome of the Civil War was Southern deficiencies rather than merely the preponderance of Northern power or more astute Union policies. The Confederacy collapsed, it is concluded, because—after four sanguinary years—the people of the South lost the will to make further sacrifices. That was only a symptom of a deeper malaise: the South's failure of will was the bitter product of accumulated military defeats which eroded all hope for success.

The thesis of this book is that these defeats were part of a seamless web; the Confederacy's economic setbacks accelerated and exacerbated the inherent weaknesses in the South's society, which in turn contributed to its military reverses. Thus defeat was, to a significant degree, attributable to the inadequate management of the Confederate finances and economy; the fault, I contend, lay particularly in the flawed policies and inept administration of the Confederate treasury.

That analysis, of course, departs from conventional wisdom. It also differs drastically from the conclusions put forward during the Civil War centennial by four distinguished historians, who in 1960 published a series of essays under the revealing title: *Why the North Won the Civil War*.

Why the South Lost: The Conventional Wisdom

In the opening essay of *Why the North Won the Civil War*, "God and the Strongest Battalions," Richard N. Current attributes the result of the conflict to what General Lee in his farewell address of April 10, 1865 referred to as the North's "overwhelming numbers and resources." Current writes that "it is hard to believe, and impossible to prove, that the Southerners did a worse job with economic affairs than the Northerners would have done in the same circumstances," for the South "could not meet the North on anything like an equal footing." Even more decisive in Current's view was the North's "preponderance in most sources of economic power"—a preponderance so great as to make Southern defeat "all but inevitable." Not only was the South hampered by what Current refers to as the "incubus" of John C. Calhoun, but Current also quotes Charles W. Ramsdell's assertion that "there was not time, while a powerful and determined enemy was crashing at the gates, to reorganize their whole system and, without previous experience, create a complex administration and train administrators. . . ."[1]

Although the South did suffer to some degree from the deficiencies Ramsdell mentions, I would challenge Current's attribution of the North's victory almost entirely to quantitative factors. Mere numerical advantage is not a sufficient explanation. In order to succeed, the side possessing the preponderance of material must also possess a firm will to persevere to victory (which, for example, the United States notably lacked during the Vietnam War).

But had the South not displayed every sign of impending collapse in late 1864, the result might well have been different. By July 1864, despite two years of Southern defeats, the Union seemed on the verge of losing that "firm will" that was a condition to success. Generals Ulysses S. Grant and William Tecumseh Sherman had recently suffered heavy casualties and were making little apparent progress. The Radicals in the Republican party openly advocated dropping Lincoln from their ticket, while the Peace Democrats selected General George B. McClellan to run on an end-the-war platform.

Fearing defeat, Lincoln even drew up a secret memorandum laying out how he and his cabinet colleagues would cooperate with the

incoming McClellan administration. Only when Sherman captured
Atlanta in September did the voters realize that victory was at hand
and reelect the Republicans, thereby assuring Confederate defeat.[2]
Lincoln's reelection, a signal that the war would continue, led to the
prompt collapse of Confederate morale and the dissolution of the
Confederate army.[3]

But if the Union victory was not inevitable, did the South exploit
all its opportunities for success? Those opportunities should not be
underestimated. There is a clear presumption that in 1861, Confederate leaders from Davis on down, unless they were afflicted by a
lemminglike urge for self-destruction, believed that they had a fair
prospect of achieving their independence. As the historian Charles E.
Wesley succinctly put it in the 1930s, one should not "be amazed that
the Confederacy was able to continue the contest for so long a while";
on the contrary, it was, he thought, "astonishing that with its resources the Confederacy did not continue the war for a longer period."
The question Wesley asked was why "the people who were seeking
independence seemed powerless to use the nucleus given them for
the building of a greater resistance."[4]

Historians have offered widely differing answers to this question.
Some, such as Clement Eaton and T. Harry Williams, have cited
serious deficiencies in Confederate military strategy, tactics, and personnel appointments.[5] Archer Jones has pointed out that, in disregard
of the doctrines of the concentration of forces and the counteroffensive
that offered the Confederates a promising course of action, the South
chose for political and military reasons to adopt a policy of cordon
defense (stringing out forces and leaving them vulnerable everywhere)
even though its military leaders knew that such a policy left the South
exposed to defeat.[6]

Some have offered the romantic explanation that the Celtic ancestry
of the South's white population rendered it incapable of sustained
effort and therefore influenced its leaders to opt for gallant frontal
assaults that resulted in disproportionately high casualties and the
destruction of the most loyal and best part of the Confederate army.[7]
Others have suggested that the isolation of the Confederate administration in Richmond and the parochial vision of Robert E. Lee, whose
concerns seldom strayed much beyond the borders of his native state,
led the Confederacy to neglect the area west of the Appalachians, with
disastrous effects.[8]

Equally plausible cases have been offered for other causes of Confederate defeat. Southern indiscipline has been cited as a contributing
factor,[9] while the collapse of Southern morale has also been attributed

to defeats and a belief in divine wrath against the South.[10] Dissension and inefficiency have been explained as resulting from the passionate belief in state's rights, the fear of centralized government, and the pervasive provincialism of the Southerners.[11] Finally, it is claimed that the Southerners had no real issue of substance to justify their secession from the Union; the protection of slavery and local rights were inadequate slogans to inspire men to fight and die for Dixie. When, in the end, the Confederate regime decided to centralize power and incorporate blacks into the army, its supporters interpreted these actions as an abandonment of principle and promptly deserted the cause.[12]

None of the preceding explanations, in and of itself, fully explains the final outcome, however. Errors were undoubtedly made in military policy; the Confederate government's relations with the states indisputably led to counterproductive squabbles, thus giving ironic validity to the Southern reference to this contest as "the War Between the States." The asserted betrayal of the Confederate cause implied in the government's shifting position on slavery is hardly convincing because the government did not seriously consider the freeing and arming of the slaves until late 1864, after the Confederate field armies had begun to melt away. Nor should one put much credence in the then-popular belief that God had deserted the South; had there been more victories, Southerners would, with equal plausibility, have adduced God's favor for the cause and felt that God was on their side.

The South's Inferior Leadership

If none of the foregoing theories fully answers Wesley's question, what is the true explanation for the South's defeat? The answer is, I believe, to be found in the South's failure of leadership. Neither the military nor the civilian authorities displayed the requisite ability to plan or to coordinate policies in one area with those in another. Military policy was characterized by a long succession of errors and mismanagement, patchwork changes in strategy, tactics, and organization which showed little or no understanding of the underlying problem confronting the South.

In retrospect, it is easy to outline a course of action the Confederacy should have taken. One would have expected as the first step that on the outbreak of hostilities in April 1861, Southern leaders would have prepared a careful balance sheet of the resources and liabilities of each side. Such a balance sheet would have shown that the North possessed an overwhelming advantage in the tangible measurements of power: population, money, industrial capability, a navy, and diplomatic recognition abroad. The South clearly did not have the means to break a naval blockade on its own, and it was afflicted by a large and basically disloyal slave population which would probably yield to the Union's blandishments and offers of freedom, provided the presence of federal armies permitted it. If Confederate leaders had any delusions on these points, the Union attacks on the coast and the behavior of the slaves in the summer of 1861 should have given them ample warning.

In view of the inferiority of Southern resources and the obvious inability of Southern armies to protect the whole country, the Southern leadership should have recognized that a well-planned joint Confederate-state effort was needed if the nation was to secure its independence. The breathing space afforded to the Confederacy in 1861 provided vital time to implement policies that would secure the Confederacy's survival, before the storm would predictably break sometime early in 1862.

There was a great deal of work to be done covering the whole range of mobilization, military strategy, economic management, domestic morale, and related issues. Yet the possible courses of action, some of which are indicated in Appendix A, depended upon correct appraisals and prompt actions in many matters. And no less important, each program had to be weighed for its impact on other Confederate policies and the combined programs made into a consolidated package.

The Lack of Consensus on the Proper Means of Conducting Confederate Resistance

No matrix of programs, no matter how astute, could be formulated in the face of inferior leadership and bad planning, particularly when confronted by the fundamental inability of the Confederate citizenry to agree on the nature of the war they were forced to fight. Was secession merely "the conservative revolt,"[13] or was it, as asserted by others, a truly revolutionary experience?[14] Without agreement on this point, there was no way to arouse a sense of deep, emotional commitment. The Confederate government showed revolutionary fervor of a dry, bureaucratic kind, only when, in the interest of survival, it was compelled to take an activist role in solving the country's problems. Yet although secession had become decided policy, the Confederate leadership tended to ignore radicals like Robert A. Toombs and Robert Barnwell Rhett, treating the "fire eaters" as an embarrassment. Hence the confusion of spirit and analysis that got the South off to a bad start.

While the most fervent secessionists thought in terms of revolution, the South's ruling elite viewed themselves as the protectors of a highly satisfactory status quo. For them, secession was not an effort to over-throw the social system or to strike out on a radical path. As they saw it, the North, with its restless taste for change and experimentation with communism, atheism, and abolitionism, contained the true revo-lutionaries. Southern leaders denounced such aberrations as proof of the "failure" of Northern society. The Confederate editor Edward A. Pollard, who denigrated the revolutionary tendencies of the North, boasted in 1862 that "The South, in the midst of a war of independence, a war waged not to destroy, but preserve, existing institutions was recurring to the past, and proposing to revive conservative ideas rather than to run into new and rash experiments."[15]

Although Southern public opinion probably agreed with such senti-ments, they proved a critical impediment to Confederate success. The persistent refusal of the Southern leaders to recognize the radical and revolutionary character of their regime accounts for their pervasive lethargy and their preoccupation with the appearance of respectability as typified by the hasty adoption of a permanent constitution. It casts light also on their imprudent rush to locate the permanent seat of government at Richmond, when practical experience during the American Revolution suggested the use of a provisional capital, mov-able at will. Ideal spots would have been Atlanta or Columbia, both of which were beyond the easy reach of federal armies. Such a capital, unlike Richmond, would have provided easy access to every front and avoided isolation at the northernmost end of the South's supply lines, where the government bureaucracy competed with the army for ra-tions. Comfortably located in a well-supplied region, the government could have avoided the alarms and excursions that characterized its physical insecurity in Richmond and concentrated on its task of con-ducting the defense of the country.[16]

Confederate confusion about the revolutionary character of the regime proved a pernicious indulgence in several regards. The same haste with which less essential matters were decided needed to be better employed on getting key laws enacted before the conflicting class interests of the planter and the yeoman groups could become polarized. Whether it touched on conscription, impressment, or taxa-tion, the legislation of the Confederacy, after 1861, was fashioned by a planter class that put its parochial interests well before those of the Lost Cause.[17] Although the planters had initially forged the Confeder-acy to preserve their economic, social, and political power, not to mention their property interest in slaves, they had no intention of altering their accustomed routines, war or no war. The Confederacy was, in their eyes, merely an instrument for preserving their interests, and one which they thought would cost them little or nothing. Thus they suffered all the greater shock when the Confederate government in Richmond insisted that they too must make sacrifices, and their disenchantment was complete when they found that the government, despite its ill-considered assurances, was unable to protect them from Union armies.[18]

Above all, the refusal to recognize revolution as the basis of its existence thrust the Confederacy into an untenable position of trying to wage an exclusively conventional war against a foe on his own terms and on ground of his choosing. The South was seriously hobbled by this curious case of cognitive dissidence.[19]

An Improperly Managed Treasury

No programs, whether those suggested or those actually adopted, stood a good chance of success unless the treasury was in a position to furnish funds for their accomplishment. It is therefore extraordinary that in *Why the South Lost the Civil War* (1986), Richard E. Beringer, Herman Hattaway, Archer Jones, and William N. Still, Jr., assert that "economic shortcomings did not play a major role in Confederate defeat," although they do concede that Confederate taxes were inadequate and that "some shortages and significant economic weaknesses did affect the Confederate War effort."[20] Nowhere do they acknowledge what seems clear from the evidence, that a bankrupt treasury played a significant role in Confederate defeat.

Another historian, James M. McPherson, in his *Battle Cry of Freedom* (1988), has discussed the whole subject in a concise but necessarily superficial six pages of text.[21] One wonders if the revolt against Marxian economic determinism has perhaps gone to the opposite extreme of downgrading the importance of economic influences as they pertain to the American Civil War.

By contrast, such diverse earlier historians of the Confederacy as Ramsdell, Eaton, and Pollard have offered a variety of contradictory answers to those offered by Beringer, Hattaway, Jones, and Still. Ramsdell, a lifelong Confederate scholar, declares that the greatest single weakness of the Confederacy was in the handling of its finances.[22] Eaton argues that "the inability of the Government to mobilize its resources went far to explain the economic deterioration of the Confederacy." He lists a series of Confederate failures and describes the government's currency and taxation programs as disastrous. "Such errors can, of course, be extenuated by the prevailing delusion of a short war and by the people's strong laissez-faire concepts of Government."[23] A participant in the events about which he wrote,

Pollard declared that the overthrow of the Confederacy was due to "the absence of any intelligent and steady system in the conduct of public affairs. . . . " Although Current attempts to controvert this position, an analysis of the Confederacy's financial and economic programs strongly supports Pollard's view.[24]

Inadequacy of Economic Policies and Leaders

Insofar as the Confederate government failed in the key areas of financial and economic policy, it was not unique. War finance is a subtle and sophisticated business that tests the wisdom and determination of its executors. Successful fiscal and economic policies are the logical product of disciplined thinking and coordinated actions, not a matter of chance or hasty improvizations. Effective policies reflect more than industry and insight; they depend heavily on the accuracy with which executive officers assess the strengths and weaknesses of their nation.

It requires special qualities of leadership and executive skill to meet the economic, monetary, and fiscal needs of a revolution and to establish the machinery of a new treasury—qualities the Confederacy lamentably lacked. President Davis was an innocent in the area of public finance. Nor was he an effective administrator; certainly he failed either to supervise or support his secretary of the treasury in his dealings with a timid Congress. Moreover, in his messages to Congress, Davis continued to radiate an unfounded optimism until January 1863, a major tactical blunder because the members of Congress were eager to find in his upbeat statements an excuse to defer not only taxation but also other unpopular but necessary economic measures.

The ability of the executive to guide the Congress was limited. Ever since Thomas Jefferson's time, United States presidents had been widely viewed as passive executors of congressional policy. Their only chance to exert a positive influence on legislation was when they made recommendations in the State of the Union message. Except on rare occasions during the Confederacy, Davis failed to use the technique of federalist presidents, who had addressed Congress in person, lobbied the congressmen, or appealed for public support to assure the enactment of vital measures. When on one occasion Davis did visit with a congressional committee dealing with the term of service in the army, he finally managed to dispel the notion that one Southerner was equal to two or more Northerners. Despite his success on that occasion, he seldom repeated the practice, so it is not surprising that the Congress, left to its own devices, compiled a poor record.[25]

Davis made another misjudgment, which had an adverse impact on the Confederacy's prospects of survival, when he appointed Christopher Gustavus Memminger as secretary of the treasury. The characteristics required for the chief designer and administrator of the Confederacy's financial policies included a detailed knowledge of relevant historical experience and an understanding of why some past policies had succeeded and others had failed; an acquaintance with contemporary economic and financial theory and practice; a flexibility of approach; a capacity to learn from experience; and a willingness to risk innovation in a situation that had only limited precedents. In short, a successful finance minister had to ask the right questions and provide informed and reasoned answers. And, in a democratic society, he also needed a talent for convincing the legislature of the need to translate his proposals into law.

Secretary Memminger seldom proved equal to any of these tests: his marginal acquaintance with the economic literature of the era limited his ability to analyze problems, while too often he was ineffective in getting others to see his side of a question. Even on occasions when he correctly diagnosed both the disease and the remedy, he seemed reluctant to press the president for support and maladroit in his efforts to persuade Congress that what he wanted was reasonable and necessary.

But weakness and mismanagement were not the only reasons that Congress failed to support the executive. Its members seemed to have shared the public's ignorant optimism, while doctrinal self-righteousness reinforced their disinclination to stand up to pressure groups. Their invariable reaction was to delay unpopular measures then, belatedly, to enact a series of half-hearted and contradictory laws.

Because many congressmen had ambivalent feelings about the Confederacy, they withdrew their support when the going got rough. All but the most zealous shied away from a policy of "blood, sweat, and tears," fatuously preferring to believe the widespread boast of many a courthouse speaker, that such blood as might be shed could be wiped up by a pocket handkerchief. When, late in the day, the legislators discovered their error, they took refuge in the Macawber-like hope that something would turn up, either a quick victory or foreign intervention. By the time Congress had to concede that such events were not going to occur, it was too late to initiate sensible measures. Moreover, even when the draft, effective taxes, and other such measures were proposed late in the day, they tended to find support only among those congressmen whose districts had been or were about to be overrun. Those whose constituents were not in immediate danger and still had something to lose could not bring themselves to make sacrifices.[26]

If the Confederacy were to head off the interrelated problems of class conflict, loss of territory and security, the demoralizing need to traffic with the enemy for essentials, and a feeling that the Confederacy's survival was incompatible with the interests of the Southern people, prompt legislation was needed to avert internal disintegration. The blockade had to be mastered and goods brought in, planters had to be assured of a market for their crops, and yeomen, who were providing the bulk of the troops, had to be materially bolstered by the purchase of their crops and their morale sustained with aid to soldiers' families. In addition, they needed a reassurance that conscription and impressment legislation would fall without discrimination on all in accordance with their means. In sum, in order to engender and maintain a spirit of nationalism, the Confederate government needed to do at home what it did abroad—carry out a public information program to create an identity of interest between itself and its audience.

Because executive programs and legislative enactments are not formulated in a vacuum, however, the Confederacy's choice of economic policies was more than a matter of personalities. It was also a function of the policymakers' historical experience, their grasp of economic theory and its application to war finance, and, finally, the constraints imposed by the Southern people's basic assumptions, past experiences, and habits of thought. That function was particularly evident in fiscal and monetary policy, where there were ample precedents for the use of paper money rather than taxes to mobilize resources from the private sector in wartime. Near disasters in earlier wars—Colonial, Revolutionary, and even the War of 1812—had proved that this was a practice to be scrupulously avoided, not slavishly copied. Yet as Southern conservatism encouraged procrastination, the Confederacy tended to await the arrival of a crisis before beginning to deal with it in spite of the fact that by then irretrievable damage had been done.

Belief in a Short War

One explanation for the South's proved incapacity for reacting incisively to foreseeable events was that the Southern population shared the historically disproved assumption, common at the beginning of most wars, that the struggle would be concluded quickly. Such a roseate view was reinforced by a chauvinistic tendency to appraise Southern élan as far more important than the North's discounted material resources.

Still, the growing Northern acceptance of abolitionist principles should have warned even the most obtuse Southerner that the creation of the Confederacy irretrievably committed the South's social and political ideals to the arbitration of the sword. Even so, many politicians, including President Davis, failed to conform their actions to their rhetoric. Thus Davis wrote only a few weeks before his death in 1889: "It is a fact of ineffacable record that *I publicly and always predicted a long and bloody struggle.* It would have been inexcusable want of perception if I had shared the hopes of men less favored with opportunities for forming correct judgments, in believing with them, that secession could be or would be peacefully accomplished" (emphasis added).[27]

The need for action in the face of a long war finds an echo in Davis's message to Congress of November 18th, 1861, when he observed that "if we husband our means and make a judicious use of our resources, it would be difficult to fix a limit to the period which we could conduct a war against the adversary we now encounter."[28] But if Davis had indeed foreseen the character and duration of the war, where were the comprehensive legislative proposals or the consistently pursued executive actions that would have translated these admirable sentiments into effective and timely programs? Certainly the president's actions do not show much evidence of foresight or any recognition of Southern vulnerabilities. Moreover, while most Southerners thought that time was on their side, few understood that positive actions were needed to sustain their frail cause until the time element would work to their advantage.

The lack of recognition of the need for prompt and vigorous action was further reflected in the business-as-usual election of Alexander H. Stephens as vice president. Perceptive Confederate leaders, such as Postmaster General John H. Reagan, opposed his selection at the time and later reflected that "it was the first time I had known of a people embarking in a revolution and selecting as one of their leaders a person known to be opposed to it."[29] That comment emphasizes one fatal flaw in the makeup of the Confederacy—the absence of any public insistence on selecting leaders fiercely determined to overcome all obstacles to Southern independence, regardless of public convenience or cost.

Inconsistency of thought and action found further doctrinal expression in the dogmatic faith in "King Cotton." A key tenet of Southern faith was that the prosperity of Europe depended on the regular receipt of cotton shipments; thus, it was argued, the South could, by attempting to curtail those shipments by an embargo, compel Euro-

pean governments to come to the South's assistance. But that contention never became fully accepted government policy, remaining one of
the mounting aggregation of unresolved issues that contributed to
Southern ineffectiveness. Thus, in spite of much wishful boasting
about the effects of the blockade, Confederate leaders continued to
display their habitual disdain for systematic analysis and pursued
contradictory policies. Not only did they fail to take account of the
trade information then available, but they also did not consult, or act,
on the reports of the South's agents in Europe. The result, as might
have been expected, was pervasive and persistent confusion.

First, although fully aware that few European ships engaged in
direct trade with the Southern ports, the government in 1861 did not
adopt any programs to induce such traffic. Second, although anxious
to win European favor and dubious about the King Cotton doctrine,
the cabinet failed to halt the vigilance committees in their embargo
schemes, thereby giving tacit approval to such activities. Here were
examples of where South's inability to analyze problems and select
reasoned and consistent answers proved damaging.

The intellectual confusion that pervaded the top echelon of the
Confederate government was aggravated by the Southern predilection
for legalistic abstractions.[30] Instead of concentrating all available resources to secure victory, Southerners of every class dissipated their
energies arguing what level of government, if any, should manage
the economy or whether the national regime should adhere strictly
to the then-popular selective application of laissez-faire. In the end,
governmental intervention was accepted, but too late in the day.

Concentration on the letter of the law, while disregarding its underlying realities, was illustrated by the Confederate attitude toward the
blockade. James Mason and John Slidell, the South's envoys to Great
Britain and France, had, among their other instructions, orders to
present proof that the federal blockade of the Southern coast was not
"effective" within the meaning of the Treaty of Paris (1856). Based on
that finding, they concluded that the blockade was not binding on
neutrals (i.e., Great Britain and France); therefore, the neutral powers
were obligated to disregard it.[31]

Such an attitude showed an egregious failure to recognize that, as
the world's foremost naval power, Great Britain had a vested interest
in blockades, whether "effective" or not. Nor did Southern leaders
show any awareness that it was quite irrelevant to declare a blockade
illegal, for even those who might share their views were not, as
Southerners seemed to assume, under any obligation to take action
on their behalf. Had the Southerners put less reliance on legalistic

chimeras, they might more effectively have concentrated on the practical means of smuggling goods through the blockade.

A further example of the Southerners' provinciality can be found in an interview of former Governor Henry A. Wise of Virginia by John B. Jones, the author of *A Rebel War Clerk's Diary* (1866). Jones warned Wise that the North was united and would fight and also that a blockade of the Southern coasts had been proclaimed. Wise, ignorant of the Northern mood, dismissed war as unlikely and felt that a blockade was impossible because it was against international law. "He had no idea that the Yankees would dare to enter upon such enterprises in the face of an enlightened world." Yet Wise backed secession because of the threat of Republican violations of the Constitution and the laws. Why, then, did he think they would scruple to trample on international laws as well?[32]

This legalistic attitude found further reflection in the letters of administration opponents and even Secretary Memminger himself. So devoted were they to their principles that they felt it would be dishonorable even to bend, never mind suspend, them for the duration of the war. As a result, when confronted by a need to change with the circumstances, they consciously chose to put at risk all of their principles rather than sacrifice any of them. Such a course of action was not principled statesmanship as they fondly imagined; rather, it was the product of fatuity and folly and rendered all their efforts futile.

Explanations of Phenomena

There are almost as many explanations for such actions as there are potential expositors. Executive reluctance to move quickly in key matters has been defended, or at least excused, on the ground that the Davis administration undertook only those measures that stood some chance of being passed and avoided potentially counterproductive struggles with the Congress. Yet one of the purposes of the Confederate Constitution's grant to the president of a single six-year term was to encourage executive independence and the pursuit of the national interest, unswayed by electoral considerations.

Moreover, so far as economic matters are concerned, no evidence suggests that President Davis or Secretary Memminger modified their programs to meet congressional objections. On the contrary, they expected Congress to do what they wished, and a tally of votes shows that Congress for the first three years generally cooperated with rigorously pursued executive objectives. Why, therefore, was it too much for the Southern people to expect that when their generals died by the dozen leading their men into battle, their civilian leaders should show moral courage and stop skulking in the safety of the political rear? In short, it was the duty of the president to request what he felt necessary and let the responsibility for inaction fall upon the Congress.

A second argument in defense of the Davis administration was that the executive branch was far more successful in those areas such as armaments-making or railroad management, where Congress played little or no role, than in economic matters such as trade regulations and taxation, where the Congress held stage center. Indeed, Ella Lonn, in *State Socialism in the Confederacy* (1928), Ramondo Luraglhi, in *Rise and Fall of the Plantation South* (1978), and Emory M. Thomas, in *The Confederacy as a Revolutionary Experience* (1971) and *The Confederate Nation* (1979) all point out the same thing: enterprising and competent Confederate and state officials, not to mention private persons, were remarkably successful in creating new resources and exploiting old assets to arm, clothe, feed, and transport the army. Incompetent executive officers, notably in the demonstrated mismanagement of so many matters under the control of the secretary of the treasury and having to do with the routine operations of his department, could be as damaging as a negligent Congress.

Finally, it has been asserted that in matters such as taxation the Confederate magnates, in and out of Congress, were reluctant to undertake controversial measures for fear of alienating the lower orders whose loyalty to the cause they questioned. Yet, when it came time to enact draft regulations or to vote direct taxes on property, wealthier Southerners did not hesitate to look after their own short-sighted interests regardless of the welfare of the country or the effect that their actions might have on popular unity. A program on the part of the planters to shoulder the burdens of the war proportionate to their interests would have done more to promote national cohesion than any other action they might have taken. In short, they had to set an example if they were to continue as leaders. The combination of these selfish special interests aided by executive incompetence resulted in patchwork programs based upon the pusillanimous, dilatory philosophy that contributed so heavily to the final catastrophe.[33]

In the succeeding chapters, I shall attempt to analyze why the Southern leaders failed so lamentably in the design and execution of their financial and economic policies. In chapter 1, I shall examine the wisdom and effectiveness of the South's effort as conditioned not only by the limited magnitude and quality of its material resources, but also and even more important, by the education and competence of its leaders. What training and experience in public finance did these men have? How had the intellectual atmosphere in the antebellum period affected their thinking, and what were their basic assumptions? Indeed, what was the Southern historical experience from colonial times to 1860? And, in addition to the lessons that might have been learned from the past, what were the theoretical propositions of men like Calhoun, whose views should have formed the basis of an intelligent, conservative, but innovative system of public finance?

The next four chapters (chapters 2–5) are devoted to an analysis of the Confederacy's attempts to solve the problems posed by the blockade, cotton, and the shortage of foreign exchange (chapter 2), debt management (chapter 3), currency policies (chapter 4), and finally the South's fiscal program (chapter 5). As such, these chapters are directed exclusively to those areas of public policy under the Treasury's control.

Chapter 6 will seek to demonstrate that the deficiencies in Confederate policy detailed in the preceding chapters can be at least roughly quantified. If, as some prior historians and postwar Southerners have contended, the outcome of the war was virtually foreordained, then the study of Confederate finance would be simply a diversion into antiquarianism. But I do not believe that thesis, and indeed I shall seek to show through the process of counterfactual history, and using methods adopted by Wesley Mitchell in *A History of the Greenbacks* (1960), that the South would, by adopting proper measures before the fall of 1864, have suffered nothing like the degree of economic and military deterioration that did in fact befall it. Nor would that result have been merely of academic interest. Had the South not collapsed in 1864, one may reasonably surmise that Lincoln might have lost the election of 1864, and that a Democratic president and Congress might have "let the erring sisters depart in peace."

In undertaking this study in policymaking with its implications in regard to modern public finances, I am fully aware that others have trod parallel paths in seeking to analyze Southern financial and economic policies. The first serious studies were made by John Christopher Schwab in *The Confederate States of America* (1901) and Ernest Ashton Smith in "A History of the Confederate Treasury" (1901). More recent is Richard Cecil Todd's *Confederate Finance* (1954). Although these sources have unquestioned value, each suffers certain deficiencies. Schwab's book jumps from topic to topic on a chronological basis, while Todd's solid book, although organized by subject and more detailed, is marred by a narrowness of vision. Moreover, as pioneers in the field, Smith, Schwab, and Todd confined themselves largely to narration and description; they made little effort to try to ascertain *why* Confederate officials did what they did, or *why* the Confederacy did not manage its affairs more efficiently. Indeed, Schwab and Todd explicitly assume that no matter who was secretary of the treasury[34] or what laws were passed[35] the result would have been the same.

When I concluded that the descriptive approach to Confederate finance had not yielded the answers that I felt were needed to address Wesley's question about why the South proved unable to mobilize its resources, I turned my attention to matters previously ignored. I was of course fully aware of the unfairness of assessing the South's performance in the light of contemporary knowledge of economic literature. I quickly discovered, however, that Southern leaders had available an adequate level of economic knowledge and practice that could have usefully guided them in formulating a Confederate financial policy. Both the public and the Confederate leaders were familiar with the writings of Adam Smith, J. B. Say, Ricardo, and John Stuart Mill, as well as the economic thoughts of America's presidents, secretaries of the treasury, other prominent leaders such as Calhoun, and Southerners like James Dunwoody Brownson DeBow.

Although I did not initially expect that this book would cast much new light on what had been taken for granted as the facts of Confederate finance, nevertheless, I made certain discoveries that to my mind challenge—and indeed disprove—conclusions reached by earlier writers. For example, it had long been the conventional wisdom that the bulk of the South's specie holdings were mopped up with the bonds issued under the Act of February 28, 1861, and the coin shipped abroad to pay for military supplies. But my examination of the government correspondence and the treasury account books disclosed that a comparatively small amount of coin was used for that purpose. Indeed, Secretary Memminger deliberately avoided taking coin from the banks, thus permitting the coin reserves of the Tennessee and the Louisiana banks to fall into the hands of the enemy. Most remittances were made by bills of exchange on already existing credits held by Southern banks and citizens.

An examination of the foreign operations of the Confederacy discloses a more satisfactory result than has heretofore been suggested. Even after eliminating refunded monies and duplicate expenses, total foreign receipts amounted to double the amount that S. B. Thompson cites in his book *Confederate Purchasing Operations Abroad* (1935). This was due partly to the fact that the Erlanger loan was vastly more productive than Schwab, and later Frank Owsley in *King Cotton Diplomacy* (1931), assert.

In addition, the correspondence of Secretaries Memminger and

Judah P. Benjamin casts grave doubts on Owsley's contention that there was an official cotton embargo in the fall of 1861. Not only did the Confederate officials persistently thwart any such program, but public support in the form of the resolutions of planters' conventions and state legislatures was also directed not at an embargo but at a Confederate government monopoly of cotton exports to assure an adequate supply of arms and munitions. In short, the Southern people demanded that blockade runners should import necessities if they were to receive cotton.

The resulting picture is very different from the forlorn scene that Schwab and Todd depict. The Confederate government had it well within its power to prolong its resistance to a point where independence or at least a compromise peace might have been achieved. Thus, President Davis was too immersed in the routine details of military affairs to concern himself with conditions on the home front, Secretary Memminger was more concerned with appearances and legal fictions than substance and reality, and the Confederate Congress saw no reason why it should incur the wrath of the planter and mercantile classes by enacting effective taxation and trade regulations. The result was, as Pollard complained, the utter absence of any coherent or steady system of public finance. If one were to render a coroner's jury verdict on the cause of the Confederacy's demise, one would in practical terms have to rule that death was due to willful and reckless negligence.

NOTES

1. Richard N. Current, "God and the Strongest Battalions," in *Why the North Won the Civil War*, ed. David Donald (Baton Rouge: Louisiana State University Press, 1960), pp. 15–16; Charles W. Ramsdell, *Behind the Lines in the Southern Confederacy* (Baton Rouge: Louisiana State University Press, 1944), p. 120.

2. Stefan Lorant, *The Presidency: A Pictorial History of Presidential Elections from Washington to Truman* (New York: Harper and Row, 1952), pp. 255–56, 264–65. A shift of eighty-three thousand popular votes would have given McClellan the election. See pp. 264–65 for photograph of Lincoln's written prediction of his supposedly impending defeat.

3. Richard E. Beringer, Herman Hattaway, Archer Jones, and William N. Still, Jr., *Why the South Lost the Civil War* (Athens: University of Georgia Press, 1986), p. 480. One may assume from this that Southerners realized that Lincoln's reelection meant that the North was to persevere in the war and, with nothing but defeats to show for their efforts, the troops saw no purpose in continuing.

4. Charles E. Wesley, *The Collapse of the Confederacy* (Washington, D.C.: Russell and Russell, 1934), pp. vii and x.

5. P. G. T. Beauregard, "The First Battle of Bull Run," in *Battles and Leaders*, ed. Robert U. Johnson and Clarence S. Buel (New York: Century Company, 1884–88), pp. 222–26; Clement Eaton, *Jefferson Davis* (New York: Free Press, 1977), pp. 175, 232; T. Harry Williams, "The Military Leadership of North and South," in *Why the North Won the Civil War*, ed. Donald, pp. 27–47.

6. Archer Jones, *Confederate Strategy from Shiloh to Vicksburg* (Baton Rouge: Louisiana State University Press, 1961), pp. 18-22. Davis feared slave desertions to the enemy and the desertion of Southern soldiers, but made no effort to clear off the slaves from vulnerable border areas or to explain the strategy of the South to the troops.

7. Grady McWhiney and Perry D. Jamison, *Attack and Die: Civil War Military Tactics and the Southern Heritage* (University: University of Alabama Press, 1982), p. 8.

8. Frank E. Vandiver, *Rebel Brass: The Confederate Command System* (Baton Rouge: Louisiana State University Press, 1986), pp. 25–26. In light of the Southern view that the Confederacy was too big to be governed effectively (a view not entertained in the North), the rush to move the capital from Montgomery to Richmond, thereby increasing the distance between the government and most of the country, was inexplicable.

9. David Donald, "Died of Democracy," in *Why the North Won the Civil War*, ed. Donald, pp. 89–90.

10. Beringer et al., *Why the South Lost*, pp. 268–93, 336–67.

11. Ibid., pp. 202–35, 443–57. See also Frank L. Owsley, *States Rights in the Confederacy* (Chicago: University of Chicago Press, 1925), pp. 1–4; and Jesse T. Carpenter, *The South as a Conscious Minority 1789-1961: A Study in Political Thought* (New York: New York University Press, 1930), pp. 34–36.

12. Beringer et al.,*Why the South Lost*, pp. 64–81, 380–81, 439–40.

13. Clement Eaton, *A History of the Southern Confederacy*, 7th ed. (New York: Macmillan, 1954), p. 259.

14. Emory M. Thomas, *The Confederacy as a Revolutionary Experience* (Englewood Cliffs: Prentice-Hall, 1971), pp. 133–35.

15. Edward A. Pollard, *The First Year of the War* (Richmond: West and Johnston, 1862), pp. 84–85. This is repeated in slightly different form in Pollard, *The Lost Cause* (New York: D. Appleton, 1867), p. 178. See also George Fitzhugh, *Cannibals, All—or Slaves without Masters*, ed. C. Vann Woodward (Cambridge: Harvard University Press, 1960), pp. 7–9.

16. The Confederate Treasury Note Bureau and the printers were relocated to Columbia, S.C., with exactly these benefits in view, so that the application of similar considerations to the rest of the government seems reasonable enough.

17. Paul D. Escott, "The Failure of Confederate Nationalism: The Old South's Class System in the Crucible of War," in *The Old South in the Crucible of War*, ed. Harry P. Owens and James J. Cooke (Jackson: University Press of Mississippi, 1983), pp. 15–28. See also Stanley Lebergott, "Why the South

Lost: Commercial Purposes in the Confederacy, 1861-1865," *Journal of American History* 70 (June 1983):60–64.

18. Lawrence N. Powell and Michael S. Wayne, "Self-Interest and the Decline of Confederate Nationalism," in *The Old South in the Crucible of War*, ed. Owens and Cooke, pp. 29–45.

19. Robert L. Kerby, "Why the Confederacy Lost," *Review of Politics* 35 (July 1973):326–45.

20. Beringer et al., *Why the South Lost*, pp. 11–12.

21. James M. McPherson, *Battle Cry of Freedom: The Civil War Era* (New York: Oxford University Press, 1988), pp. 437–42.

22. Ramsdell, *Behind the Lines*, p.viii.

23. Eaton, *A History*, p. 235.

24. Current, "God," pp. 14–15; and Pollard, *The Lost Cause*, p. 489.

25. John M. Reagan, *Memoires with Special Reference to Secession and the Civil War*, ed. Walter F. McCaleb (New York: Neal Publishing, 1906), p. 117.

26. Thomas B. Alexander and Richard E. Beringer, *The Anatomy of the Confederate Congress: A Study of the Influence of Member Characteristics on Legislative Voting Behavior 1861–1865* (Nashville: Vanderbilt University Press, 1972), pp. 139–65, 201–35.

27. Jefferson Davis, "Lord Wolseley's Mistakes," *North American Review* 149 (October 1889):475.

28. James D. Richardson, ed. *A Compilation of the Messages and Papers of the Confederacy: Including the Diplomatic Correspondence, 1861–1865* (Nashville: United States Publishing, 1906), vol. 1, p. 140; see Message of November 18, 1861.

29. Reagan, *Memoires*, p. 109.

30. The fact that Vice President Stephens's official memoires of the Civil War are entitled *A Constitutional View of the Late War Between the States* demonstrates the legalistic concerns of the Southern leaders at the expense of practical realities.

31. Hunter to Mason, September 23, 1861, *War of the Rebellion: A Compilation of the Official Records of the Union and Confederate Navies*, 30 vols. (Washington, D.C.: Government Printing Office, 1894–1927), ser. 2, vol. 3, pp. 257–64.

32. Escott, "The Failure of Confederate Nationalism," pp. 15–28; John B. Jones, *A Rebel War Clerk's Diary at the Confederate States Capital*, 2 vols. (Philadelphia: J.B. Lippencott, 1866, repr. New York: Hermitage Bookstore, 1935), vol. 1 (April 22, 1861), p. 25.

33. Escott, "The Failure of Southern Nationalism," pp. 15–28.

34. John Christopher Schwab, *The Confederate States of America 1861–65: A Financial and Industrial History of the South During the Civil War* (New York: Charles Scribner's Sons, 1901), p. 14; see also Ernest Ashton Smith, "A History of the Confederate Treasury," Southern History Association Publication no. 5 (1901):1–34.

35. Richard Cecil Todd, *Confederate Finance* (Athens: University of Georgia Press, 1954), p. 17.

CHAPTER ONE

Material, Intellectual, and Personnel Limitations of Confederate Financial Policy

Material Limits of Southern Capacities

Wherever they turned their eyes, the South's leadership faced a daunting task. By practically every measurable standard, the resources available to them to wage a war were inferior to those of the North. Even with slaves included, the overall Southern population was outnumbered two to one by the Union's; hence the tremendous importance of securing the support of the border states of Kentucky and Missouri (table 1).[1]

Among the first items to command the attention of Southern officials was the South's capacity to feed its people and army under siege conditions. Although the South in the years before 1860 had moved toward self-sufficiency in foodstuffs,[2] surplus wheat[3] and meat-producing areas were located in the border states, with additional beef cattle in isolated areas of Texas and Florida.[4] Given the heavy demands of transient armies and refugee populations, the danger of local famines were such as to inspire a desire to continue to look to the North as a source of supply.[5] The loss of the border-state areas proved to be a great trial to the government[6] and threw it back on the inadequate resources of the Deep South.[7]

Another source of actual food shortages lay in the incompetence of the Confederate Commissary Department, headed by Colonel L. B. Northrop.[8] Because of the Commissary Department's ineptitude, the government imported more than 4,300 tons of meat through the blockade,[9] and meat was imported into Texas, even though the ranchers' corrals were reportedly crowded with cattle.[10]

While the treasury had no direct responsibility for the operations of the Commissary Department, Secretary Memminger did sensibly attempt to aid its operations by encouraging a shift from the production of staples to foodstuffs. But his inflationary monetary policy, coupled with the failure to tax adequately, aborted the initiative by encouraging cotton growing, subsistence agriculture, and hoarding.[11]

The efficient distribution of food was further inhibited by the inade-

Table 1. Contribution of the Border States* to the Confederacy

	Total Confederacy ($)	Border States ($)	% of Both
Land values ($ million)	2,372.9	1,162.7	49
Horses	2,885,082	1,550,344	54
Beef cattle†	9,089,877	1,752,802	19
Pigs	22,799,887	9,585,581	42
Sheep	5,743,906	3,998,632	70
Wheat (bu)	44,065,000	30,453,000	69
Oats (bu)	28,782,000	20,714,000	72
Corn (bu)	419,613,000	23,360,000	57
Potatoes (bu)	46,634,000	13,011,000	28
Tobacco (hogsheads)	436,859	300,515	69

Sources: Bureau of the Census, *Agriculture in the United States in 1860* (Washington, D.C.: Government Printing Office, 1864); Richard D. Goff, *Confederate Supply* (Durham: Duke University Press, 1969), pp. 27–29 ff.

*Virginia, Kentucky, Missouri, and Tennessee.
†In addition, Texas held 40 percent of the Confederacy's cattle supply (3,623,382 cattle).
This dangerous aggregation of assets in the exposed border areas and in peripheral areas such as Texas and Florida spelled trouble for the Confederates. The Confederate Subsistence, Ordnance, and Quartermaster departments were well aware of these figures, but nonetheless failed to make any serious effort to use the fluid situation in 1861 to draw on border state resources or to make contingency plans in the event of their loss.

quacy of the South's transportation system. Steamboat lines existed largely as feeders for the ports, while the primitive roads proved an obstacle course for Confederate and invading Unionist alike. Southern railroads were short of rolling stock and because they had been designed to promote exports, they did not constitute an effective system for internal trade. There were several gauges of track, and even where two railroads used the same gauge, rolling stock often could not move from one railroad to the other. In Richmond, Petersburg, and Augusta, for example, teamsters had prevented a junction of the railroads. Southern railroads also had isolated pockets in Texas, Florida, and Mississippi. To his credit, Jefferson Davis took a special interest in these problems; it was under his leadership that a third Virginia-North Carolina connection was built, a connection made with Florida, and half the Alabama-Mississippi gap closed.[12]

Nor were the deficiencies in the design of the network by any means the whole problem. Railroad spare parts facilities were limited, and Southern shops constructed only nineteen locomotives in the year 1859–60. The quantity of railroad iron coming out of Southern mills was inadequate even for replacement purposes, and it was thus vitally necessary that spare parts be procured from abroad.[13]

In addition to dealing with the railroad problem, the government needed to survey the quantity and quality of the South's draft animals, which were urgently required for the cavalry, artillery, and supply system. Unfortunately, the South's available draft animals (table 1a) included a disproportionate number of mules in the Cotton Belt,[14] a fact that Eugene V. Genovese has attributed to the mule's greater ability to survive slave abuse.[15] Whatever the cause of this concentration, most horses were massed in the border states and Texas. It should thus have been clear that in the contingency of a protracted war, and before the Union could strike in 1862, quartermasters must sweep the border states clean of every available horse.

No less discouraging from the long-range point of view were the South's deficiencies as an industrial producer. Most of the goods it manufactured were processed staples. Textile and shoe production were adequate to keep only a small percentage of Southern people clothed and shod. Bridging the gap would require heavy imports through the blockade.[16]

An important element in the treasury's planning depended on the strength of the Southern banks. These well-capitalized institutions and their branches had a 25 percent reserve behind their demand liabilities. The high level of reserves was a function of conservative banking practices necessitated by the illiquidity of the banks' loans. Effective mobilization of this pool of foreign exchange and specie could have made a substantial contribution to the Confederate war effort (table 2).[17]

Finally, more than 40 percent of the Southern gross national product was tied up in the production of staples (table 3). Because Adam Smith had stated that a staple-producing economy provided a poor basis for war finance,[18] a shrewd manager of the Confederate treasury would have drawn two reasonable conclusions. The first should have been that the Southern economy had to be supported by facilitating exports and suitable imports. This in turn required that only essential goods should enter the South, which implied a need to regulate foreign commerce. That, however, did not diminish the need for the government to make a crash effort early in the war to procure ships and cargo space for public use and to assure exports to pay for the imports.

The second point that a wise secretary of the treasury would have recognized was that a staple economy would be in the best position

Table 2. Banking Statistics*

Area	Number of Banks and Branches	Capital Paid In (Millions)	%	Capital Per Bank
North	1,338	$308.0	73.0	$230,194
South	221	92.0	21.8	416,290
Border	83	21.9	5.2	263,855
	1,642	$421.9	100.0	$910,339

	Loans (Millions)	%	Specie	%	Circulation	%
North	$507.7	73.4	47.7	57.1	125.2	60.5
South	143.0	20.7	27.2	32.5	60.5	29.2
Border	40.8	5.9	8.7	10.4	21.4	10.3
	$691.5	100.0	83.6	83.6	207.1	100.0

	Deposits (Millions)	%	Quick Ratio Demand Liabilities to Specie	
North	$197.5	77.8	6.79 to 1 or 14.7% reserve	
South	47.2	18.6	3.96 to 1 25.3%	
Border	9.1	3.6	3.51 to 1 28.5%	
	$253.8	100.0	5.51 to 1 18.1%	

*Based on 1860 Census, *Manufactures.*

to bear heavy taxation at the beginning of a war before enemy incursions had depleted resources. To encourage a shift from cotton to food crops, it was necessary to tax property rather than income (which was much too easy to conceal) in order to force farmers to participate in the money economy. But Secretary Memminger's principles, deeply rooted in Southern thought and tradition, made many of these economically dictated actions unpalatable.

Intellectual Limitations of Southern Policy

The experience of the Southern leaders in the management of the economic and financial affairs of the Confederacy must be judged in the light of the knowledge available to them at the time—not only through economic writings but also through experience in past situations of conflict. If, viewed by present-day standards, the economic

Table 3. Southern Gross National Product

1.	Fogel and Engerman estimate	$1,114,500,000
	(less Missouri and Kentucky)	297,300,000
	Total Southern GNP	$ 817,200,000
2.	Lerner approach	
	Cotton	$277.6 million
	Tobacco	21.4
	Sweet potatoes	36.0
	Wheat	33.0
	Potatoes	2.8
	Corn	166.7
	Oats	7.8
	Hay	7.5
	Rye	1.6
	Sugar cane	18.9
	Rice	2.2
	Value of animals slaughtered	81.6
	Manufactures	155.5
	Sundry	10.0
		$820.6 million

Sources: Robert William Fogel and Stanley L. Engerman, "The Economies of Slavery," *The Reinterpretation of American Economic History*, ed. Fogel and Engerman (New York: Harper and Row, 1971), table 8, pp. 335–36; see also Eugene M. Lerner, "Southern Output and Agricultural Income, 1860–1880," in *The Economic Impact of the American Civil War*, ed. Ralph Andreano (Cambridge, Mass.: Schenkman Publishing, 1967), p. 121.

literature that Southerners could readily consult seems primitive, leaders still had access to economic writings that offered effective solutions for their problems. Unhappily, the Southern intellectual atmosphere tended to stifle the study of public finance. So it is not surprising that, in the bitter exchange of recriminations that followed the disaster of 1865, the antagonists should have overlooked substantial evidence that showed how the treasury's bankruptcy had hobbled the government and fostered military and economic collapse.

War is by definition a trial of strength and will between opposing forces, and one way of examining the effectiveness of the Confederacy's economic and financial policies can be accomplished by comparing them with the equivalent policies pursued in the North. The difference is sharply apparent. Even after allowing for the greater resources available to the Union, one must conclude that the federal congressmen approached their task far more competently than did their opposite numbers in the South.

Availability of Economic Literature

The years preceding 1860 had, in the South, been marked by little intellectual adventure—in part because the defense of the South's "peculiar institution" was a pervading hindrance to free inquiry.[19] Intolerance, by 1860, led Southern universities to impose strict standards of belief, which included not only a fidelity to slavery, but also religious orthodoxy (preferably Protestant) and an undeviating adherence to the free-trade principles of Smith, Say, Ricardo, and Mill. At least in the eastern portion of the South, deviant opinion with regard to this trinity of issues was tantamount to treason compounded by heterodoxy and moral turpitude.[20]

The teaching of economics in the South—indeed throughout the United States—was sketchy at best. All too often the subject was assigned to a professor who taught several other subjects or to a minister who used economic principles to reinforce or illustrate the tenets of revealed religion. Because the works of Smith, Say, Ricardo, and Mill were regarded as too recondite for students, there was a tendency to settle for popularized works by less skilled expounders such as Francis Wayland's *Elements of Political Economy* (1837).[21]

Serious Southern economists were an endangered species constantly under the threat of extinction. For example, in 1825, George Tucker, a professor of political economy at the University of Virginia, was sharply attacked when it was rumored that his students were reading Daniel Raymond's protectionist *Thoughts on Political Economy*. The conservative free-trade Richmond *Enquirer* set up a hue and cry for Tucker's dismissal on the ground that no texts other than the writings of Say, Ricardo, and Smith should be used at the university.[22] Disgusted, Tucker gave up his professorship at Charlottesville in 1845 and moved to Philadelphia, where society was more tolerant of his mildly protectionist views.[23]

Later Virginian economists, such as George Frederick Holmes and George Fitzhugh, were so preoccupied with justifying the South's position on slavery that neither contributed much to the literature of currency management or governmental finance.[24] Holmes at least went to the trouble of corresponding with Memminger in late 1863 regarding the desirability of establishing a bureau of statistics to help guide the formulation of policy, although nothing came of the idea.[25]

Another group of Southern economic thinkers was the Carolinian contingent, originally led by Thomas Cooper, president of the University of South Carolina from 1819–34.[26] Despite the pressures toward conformism, two of his successors, William Gregg and James Dunwoody Brownsen DeBow, veered from the course of orthodoxy and by 1860 were ardent advocates both of slavery and a protective tariff. Gregg, who later advised Secretary Memminger on taxation, was biased toward protectionism, primarily because he owned a textile mill. It was his contention that tariffs would stimulate the development of Southern resources and hence were necessary to enable the South to develop commercial, as well as political, independence. He also broke precedent by hiring Southern whites as mill workers,[27] a proceeding abhorrent to Memminger, who feared that whites in Southern factories would be a prime recruiting ground for the abolitionists.[28]

The other Carolinian protectionist, DeBow, was the editor of *DeBow's Review* and chief clerk in charge of the 1850 census. He drifted westward to New Orleans, where he came under the patronage of Maunsel White, who established at the University of Louisiana a chair of commerce and statistics, with DeBow as its first occupant. Yet DeBow's lectures failed to attract many students.[29] That was unfortunate because DeBow rejected the parochial views of the region in his course bibliography and included the works of protectionists.[30] Like Gregg, DeBow also advocated Southern industrialization.[31] But during the Civil War, DeBow's talents were largely wasted as a produce loan agent, when his energy and abilities were sorely needed in Richmond.

The last member of the Carolinian school was Jacob Newton Cardozo, a Southern Loco-Foco. Although DeBow argued that "Cotton is King," Cardozo asserted correctly that cotton production was outstripping consumption.[32] This view was reaffirmed in several articles which could have served as a basis for attacking the King Cotton doctrine.[33] Yet Cardozo exercised no influence on Confederate policy, for he opposed both impressments and effective taxation.[34]

If Southern economists before 1860 wasted their energies on discussions of the tariff as a mode of taxation and bank notes as a currency, Confederate politicians occupied their time to no greater profit. Thus an unskilled Congress was called upon to elect a president, and the president to appoint a secretary of the treasury—with no one having much comprehension of what was required of either.

In electing Jefferson Davis as president, the Provisional Congress probably picked the best man available. He brought to his post solid administrative experience in the United States War Department, personal participation on the battlefield as a colonel, and a considerable capacity for hard work. Moreover, although nominally resident in

Mississippi, Davis from 1815–35 had lived in Kentucky or West Point, either attending schools or pursuing a career as an army officer. Thus, his formative years were spent outside of Mississippi, and Davis never developed the same narrow, parochial loyalties as other politicians who ranked loyalty to their states well ahead of their devotion to the Lost Cause.[35] He was well aware of the South's economic deficiencies, and he recognized the possibility of a prolonged war.

Still he had fatal deficiencies as a chief executive. Few men had had an easier political career. With the way paved for him by his brother, Joseph, Davis's life had largely been politics without tears. His later effectiveness suffered from this effortless progress because Davis had missed the tempering process that results from the need to make the compromises most officeholders find necessary. He had thus failed to develop the suppleness, tact, and finesse required of a president.

Davis was charming within his own family circle and could be quite effective with small groups.[36] On the other hand, to Senator R. M. T. Hunter, his secretary of state, he was curt to the point of rudeness, and he tended to lecture large groups.[37] At the same time, he was inordinately sensitive to criticism and wasted valuable time writing letters of self-justification. He also had a weakness for sycophants in selecting colleagues. As even his second wife, Varina Howell, observed soon after they first met, "he impresses me as a remarkable kind of man, but of uncertain temper, and has a way of taking for granted that everybody agrees with him when he expresses an opinion. . . ."[38]

Davis was not unique in that willfulness. Taken as a group, Southern politicians were a petulant lot; the master-slave relationship seemed to create men incapable of mastering their own passions. Thus, although Southerners expected others to be ingratiating, they were not only insulting, but also indifferent to, or unaware of, their boorishness.[39]

If the new president was a man of strongly held opinions, his economic views were not original but typical of both the time and the place. As will be seen, although Davis favored direct taxation in theory, he settled in practice for a tariff for revenue. When secretary of war, he had advocated that the United States government build a transcontinental railroad,[40] so it was natural that as president of the Confederacy he favored the building of lines to link portions of the Southern railroad system.[41] Even he acknowledged that the construction of railroads by the government was only permissible as a necessary means of prosecuting a war.[42] Accordingly, he strongly opposed the peacetime purchase by the United States of the Louisville and

Portland Canal.[43] He also adopted the restrictive view that government purchases should be limited exclusively to the needs of the several departments and that the Post Office should be self-sustaining. Contradictorily, Davis had no objection, in 1840, to a proposed federal special interest subsidy to himself as a cotton grower.[44]

But Davis made no pretense of being an economist; rather, he thought of himself primarily as a soldier. He had spent his formative years and practically all of his public career associated in one way or the other with the military.[45]

Only on one occasion did Davis play a prominent role in an economic controversy. The Union and the Planters banks of Mississippi had been founded with capital raised by the sale of state bonds which the banks were supposed to service. When the banks defaulted, the owners of the bonds sought recourse against the state of Mississippi. In denying their claims Davis, writing in the *London Times*, justified the state's refusal to pay the Union Bank bonds on the ground that they were unconstitutionally issued and thus null and void. However Davis admitted Mississippi's liability for the Planters Bank bonds and tried to get the debt paid. His position on this widely discussed issue was one factor among several leading to his defeat in the race for governor in 1850.[46] The incident returned to haunt him during the Civil War, when federal supporters in Europe revived the story, using his ambivalence on the repudiation issue in an effort to prevent the sale of Confederate bonds.

In light of President Davis's basic lack of experience in economic questions, his choice of a secretary of the treasury was important in determining the shape and direction of Confederate finance. Here accident played a central role. The president had originally planned to offer the post of secretary of the treasury to Robert Toombs, a senator from Georgia, and to give the post of secretary of state to Robert Barnwell. But the indolent Barnwell declined the honor and suggested that the South Carolina delegation would like the treasury offered to Christopher Gustavus Memminger. Accordingly, Davis reshuffled his cabinet, putting Toombs in the State Department and giving Memminger the treasury.[47] But whether Memminger was really the choice of the South Carolina delegation is at least doubtful. That indefatigable diarist Mary Boykin Chesnut reported gossip that Memminger was foisted off on Davis by Barnwell alone and that the rest of the delegates were mortified when the appointment was announced.[48]

As certain snobbish critics were to point out later, Memminger was an immigrant—one of the two naturalized first-generation Americans in Davis's original cabinet. Born in the Kingdom of Wurttemburg in

1803, he was, by 1805, an orphan in Charleston. At fifteen he attracted the attention of former Governor Thomas Bennett, who took him into his home and sent him through college. In due course, Memminger became a citizen, and, in 1824, was admitted to the South Carolina bar.[49]

Originally a staunch Unionist, he had, in 1830, published a satirical tract called *Book of Nullification* in which he ridiculed the fire-eating activities of Congressman Robert Barnwell Rhett, who later served with Memminger in the Provisional Congress.[50] That did not, however, prevent Memminger's election as a Charleston alderman (1834) nor as an Assembly delegate (1835). As a member and later chairman of the Education Committee, he played an innovative role in securing for Charleston the benefits of a public school system and an increase in state support for higher education.[51] By the late 1850s Memminger had become an ardent secessionist and was disenchanted with the Union.[52]

Imbued with the Protestant work ethic and high moral standards, Memminger entered upon public office with a seriousness of purpose and such a firm dedication to religious principles that Edward A. Pollard thought him "a zealot in religion, who had a strange passion for controversial theology."[53] Memminger was also depicted as a strict Sabbatarian,[54] although that seems inconsistent with his later insistence that the treasury note printers should work on Sundays.[55] The secretary's rigid personality soon led to clashes with his subordinates. Philip Clayton, the assistant secretary, was fired for entertaining his friends with non-business discussions, while Robert Tyler, the register of the treasury, was threatened with dismissal for not signing enough bonds and wandering around the hallways.[56]

Unhappily the secretary's personality difficulties were not limited to his own department. His insistence that people make appointments, rather than casually drop by, stirred up talk of "red-tape-ism" and "royal customs,"[57] while he had repeated run-ins with his cabinet colleagues. He quarreled with Postmaster General John H. Reagan over the disbursement of the Post Office's gold; he upbraided the secretaries of war and navy for their failure to pay their bills with bonds and their tendency to make massive unheralded demands upon the Treasury.[58] Secretary of War George W. Randolph was so provoked by Memminger's strictures about military actions that he made it a practice to support his subordinates in their quarrels with the treasury.[59] Randolph's successor Secretary James Seddon thought Memminger "an ass," while Seddon's chief clerk, Robert G. H. Kean, described him as "a man of smartness, finesse but tricky, shifty, and narrow." Toombs also thought poorly of him, while Gazaway Bugg Lamar, the Georgia banker, found the secretary's predilection for "little technical constructions" in financial matters annoying. The adverse opinion of Memminger was summarized by General Josiah Gorgas, who noted that "Mr Memminger treats others with rudeness, and is . . . dogmatic, narrow minded and slow . . . whenever I leave Mr. M. after an interview, I feel somehow as tho' I had been trying to do something very much out of the way, so injured and *put upon* does he represent himself."[60]

Whatever else can be said of the man, he did not lack the courage of his convictions. In 1835, when 117 out of 118 members of the South Carolina legislature denied free Negroes the right to land in South Carolina, Memminger's was the only vote against the resolution.[61] Totally lacking in humor outside his circle of friends, he also lacked the technique of polite refusal; it was a personality flaw that greatly complicated his relations with the Congress.

Even had Memminger been charm personified, his lack of financial training and experience were an insuperable handicap. His only exposure to government finance had been as a member and later chairman of the South Carolina House Ways and Means Committee in the 1850s, overseeing a state budget in balance and a real estate tax system that had not undergone a reassessment since 1840. Memminger had thus never seen a modern system of property taxation in action.

No less serious was his stilted concept of currency and banking, influenced by his long experience as a director of the Planters and Mechanics Bank. In 1839, he put through the South Carolina legislature an act forfeiting the charter of any bank that might thereafter suspend specie payments. Although this act was generally considered to be a display of force that everyone could safely ignore, Memminger meant business. Thus when the Bank of Charleston and the State Bank suspended specie payments late in 1839, he brought quo warranto proceedings against them. In vain, opposing counsel, led by James L. Petigru, argued that "it is not by keeping their paper in, but by keeping their paper out, that the banks confer a benefit upon the community under such circumstances." Memminger's reply was strictly legalistic. The fact that there were bank suspensions elsewhere was irrelevant. Indeed, he contended that had the banks paid out their coin, the suspension could have been avoided. Although Memminger won a judgment against the State Bank, the legislature reversed the court's ruling, declaring: "nor was it supposed to be required by the public interest, that the forfeitures should be enforced, even against such banks as had been judicially declared subject to it."[62]

Memminger's tendency to exalt doctrine while ignoring reality is further illustrated in 1848 when, imbued with the notion that a state had no business running a bank, he sought to force the liquidation of the Bank of the State of South Carolina. Because the bank's earnings were a key factor in paying off South Carolina's debts, he was defeated after a prolonged fight.[63]

What the South's financial predicament called for in 1861 was a secretary of the treasury gifted in analysis, impatient with wishful thinking, flexible in mind, unfettered by state's rights shibboleths, capable of imaginative thought, and sufficiently tactful and persuasive to extract necessary legislation from a resistant Congress. It was no task for an ignorant, blunt, laissez-faire zealot bemused by legalisms.

Whether the choice of a better man would have altered the fate of the Confederacy must remain a matter for conjecture. Yet there is reason to believe that had Davis adhered to his original plan of appointing Toombs or had selected George Alfred Trenholm as secretary of the treasury in 1861, the final result might have been different. Toombs may have been afflicted by a drinking problem and tended toward insubordination, but drunk or sober he was a popular and respected figure, capable of neutralizing some of the state's rights opposition to Davis. He was also inclined to vigorous, even radical measures, including the early levying of heavy taxes.[64]

Trenholm, who reluctantly succeeded his friend Memminger in July 1864, had much in common with his predecessor. He too was orphaned at an early age, but by hard work coupled with the strictest integrity achieved wealth and a seat in the South Carolina Assembly in 1852. There the similarities ended. Memminger pursued a legal career, whereas Trenholm was a distinguished merchant. With his business background he was a practical-minded secessionist who measured success in terms of tangible results. If he encountered obstacles, he sought ways around them.

In addition to having a more positive intellectual approach, Trenholm, unlike Memminger, was genial and charming. Even the quarrelsome Henry Foote thought well of him.[65] Because Trenholm realized the importance of public relations, he tried, like Hamilton, to neutralize opposition by taking the Congress into his confidence.[66] Still more important, he was a foe of the King Cotton doctrine and played an active role in making treasury notes receivable throughout the Confederacy. Although he was reluctantly prepared to consider aid for the planters, he showed far more enthusiasm for blockade-running on the government's account and accumulating coin for debt service purposes. Trenholm's weakness on taxation would have been nicely complemented by the appointment of DeBow as commissioner of internal revenue. DeBow's unrivaled knowledge of economics and past advocacy of direct taxes would, when combined with Trenholm's talents, have produced a team capable of getting effective legislation through Congress.[67]

In addition to Memminger's deficiencies, the Confederate Congress proved a serious impediment to an effective economic policy. On the surface, at least, the men serving on the finance committees in Richmond were an able and distinguished group. Men such as Robert Toombs (senator from Georgia and first Confederate secretary of state), R. M. T. Hunter (speaker of the House and senator from Virginia, chairman of the Confederate Senate Finance Committee, and second Confederate secretary of state), Colin J. McRae (an Alabama cotton factor and Confederate agent in Europe), and Francis Strother Lyon (a congressman, commissioner of the Bank of the State of Alabama, and chairman of the House Ways and Means Committee in 1864) should have been as effective as their Northern counterparts and ought to have inspired equal confidence. Yet the Lincoln administration proved able to generate greater enthusiasm for its measures than did the Davis administration. Why?

At least part of the answer may lie in the absence of a loyal opposition in the South. The disappearance of the Whig party left a one-party system with politics more a matter of personalities than of issues. Lacking an opposition party, those who opposed the Davis administration had no vehicle through which to formulate and build support for alternative policies. As a result, only the administration programs were discussed or voted upon.[68] This problem was rendered worse by the fact that there was no bona fide administration faction in the Congress. Even the friends of the administration did not view the president's policies as party measures, the success or failure of which would reflect on their group as a whole.[69]

The absence of these prerequisites for effective democratic government meant that the opposition could harass the administration without having to offer anything better. Vice President Alexander H. Stephens and Toombs tried to bridge this gap by inserting into the Permanent Constitution a proviso that cabinet officers might appear on the floor of Congress to explain the operations of their departments and to solicit support for their proposals.[70] This system had worked well in the Provisional Congress, where Stephens, Toombs, Hunter, Memminger, and Reagan had sat. It had allowed Memminger to amend bills to conform with his own thinking. However, the Permanent Congress never gave effect to Stephens's constitutional provision and, after the Provisional Congress ended, Memminger's influence visibly declined.

The Provisional Congress in 1861–62 represented a unique window of opportunity. This legislative convention was atypically filled with appointed local notables, many of whom had no interest in seeking reelection. Had Davis and Memminger realized this difference from any likely elected Congress that would follow it and had they been prepared to seize the opportunity, they could have used this receptive body to enact innovative measures, especially in fiscal matters, before the larger slaveholders lost their enthusiasm for the war and blocked laws that impinged on their own special interests.[71]

That should not have been difficult to manage, and there was no need to manufacture an economic policy out of whole cloth. Anyone could have drawn guidance from historical experiences and the theoretical writings well known to Southerners at the time.

The Historical Background of Confederate Monetary, Fiscal, and Economic Policy

Experience during the years preceding the American Civil War was important in shaping the empirical and theoretical aspects of Confederate policy. During those years Americans had to find answers to the questions of who should provide a sound currency, and how the government should raise its revenues. A brief exposition of the American historical experience and theoretical background of these subjects may help identify those events and propositions that cast light on wartime practices and suggest possible solutions to the problems faced by the Confederacy. Thus the following discussion will focus on sometimes atypical thinking from 1607–1860 and will deemphasize the more conventional subject matter that received attention during the period.

Because the South was so conservative and disinclined to accept innovations, and because a large part of its government's personnel had had Washington positions, the Confederates were deeply influenced by the events of the past. They were well aware of the historical struggle for a sound currency; the battle between hard money and paper; and the dispute between the supporters of bank note issues and a government currency from 1607 to 1860. They were also conversant with the details of United States debt management from 1775–1860 and quite conscious of the errors of the past.

Because the South financed the war largely through the issuance of currency, one of the more important chapters in the complicated annals of Confederate finance is the story of how it managed its money. To understand the evolution of Confederate monetary policy, the following discussion will review accumulated experience since the earliest days of the American Republic. Thereafter, it will turn to the various issues and options considered by the South: creation of a central bank with power to issue currency, the direct issue of currency by the central government, and the continued circulation of state issues.

The American Paper Money Experience, 1690–1860

American monetary thought and practice were deeply conditioned by the peculiar difficulties the Americans faced in settling and developing a continent. During the time they were colonial subjects of Great Britain, they had suffered from traditional colonial economic problems: a shortage of capital, an adverse balance of trade, and the unfavorable terms of trade that afflict any producer of raw materials in exchanging them for manufactured goods. In most years there were always more demands for money than limited domestic resources could provide, and that in turn necessitated a policy of reserving coin for foreign transactions while, at home, alternative currencies were experimented with as imperfect substitutes.

Lacking an ample and stable currency[72] and faced with a specie shortage, colonists first sought to augment their limited resources by clandestine trade; then they resorted to competitive devaluations, which the British stopped in 1709.[73] The colonists next improvised alternate monies. In the South, tobacco was monetized; later the tobacco was deposited in warehouses and circulating receipts issued.[74] During the Civil War, Mississippi reverted to this system and emitted cotton-based state treasury notes. Colonial land was also "coined" by issuing currency secured by mortgages.[75]

The usual means of meeting the currency crisis from 1690 on was to issue colonial bills of credit. Although paper money was denounced as a "Second South Sea Bubble,"[76] only its excessive issue during the Revolution checked its further use and revived a specie currency. This inspired the constitutional provision granting the central government the monopoly to strike coins.[77]

Yet the mere adoption of the Constitution did not mean that the United States would exclusively use a specie currency. The Founding Fathers had not anticipated that the three state banks then extant would be multiplied by hundreds, and, in any event, even after 1853, with the Subsidiary Coinage Act and the California gold strikes, the United States' economy still required a sound paper currency.[78] Thus, the period from 1789 to 1860 was also marked by endless debate about paper money and experimentation with its use as the most important element of the currency.

One Possible Solution: A Central Bank of Issue

One solution to the problem of creating a stable paper currency lay in the chartering of a central bank. In 1791, Alexander Hamilton, in keeping with Adam Smith's doctrines, espoused the establishment of the First Bank of the United States.[79] Both that bank (1791–1811) and the Second Bank (1816–36), while emitting a sound currency of their own, displayed certain weaknesses which made the adoption of such a system impractical for the Confederates.[80]

First, the notes of the Banks of the United States were representative money whose value and quantity were controlled by their instant redemption in coin,[81] and thus a specie-paying central bank would need to possess an immense cash reserve. A Southern central bank would otherwise simply have been another bank issuing irredeemable currency in competition with the government. Second, any prolonged treasury deficit would destroy the bank's control of the state banks because it could not "force home" their notes without impairing government bond sales. Moreover, because the notes of the United States Banks, the Free Banks, and later the National Banks, were all collateralized to some degree by government bonds, such bills were obviously little better than the bonds that secured them.

Nor were these the only realities Southern politicians had to face in determining a course of action. The untidy end of the Second Bank of the United States amid revelations of mismanagement and political corruption discredited the very idea of a central bank.[82] In view of the fact that a former United States president, John Tyler, sat in the Provisional Confederate Congress, it might have made some sense to revive his idea of an "Exchequer Bank," a forerunner of the Federal Reserve system. But a Confederate Reserve Bank was probably a deferrable initiative.[83]

A Second Alternative: A Government Currency

The years 1789–1860 were marked by three booms followed by bank suspensions, panics, and depressions. Unsound banking practices abounded and, by the end of the antebellum period, there was general agreement that the note issue privileges of the state banks clearly needed either stringent reforms or complete abolition. Objections to the state bank note currency system[84] and the attempts at reforming its obvious abuses[85] were finally resolved by the National Banking Act of 1863 and the Act of March 3, 1865, whereby the federal Congress taxed such notes out of existence. The idea of eliminating the notes of state-chartered banks[86] through the device of a tax had been prefigured by the Act of August 2, 1813, which had taxed all bank notes at a rate of 1 to 2 percent without challenge in the courts.[87] A similar concept was proposed by Albert Gallatin in 1831, when he observed that Congress had the power to use stamp duties to carry out the implied obligation of creating a uniform currency.[88]

Because the very idea of a bank currency had fallen into disrepute, the obvious alternative was that federal authorities should issue money on their own credit. The idea of a government currency went back to 1690, when Massachusetts won the distinction of being the first government in the Western world to issue bills of credit under its own name. Colonial issues had been used to pay war expenses, cover peacetime deficits, or provide loans to promote agriculture and industry.[89] In accordance with the conventional wisdom of the day, these notes were generally non-interest bearing and given legal-tender status. Yet, by the time of the Civil War, the federal and Confederate Congresses, after earnest debate, reached opposite decisions on whether anything but specie should be made mandatorily receivable for private obligations.[90]

Until the 1950s, scholars assumed that most responsible pre-Civil War American statesmen abhorred paper money. They noted that the Founding Fathers at the Constitutional Convention had made their position clear by prohibiting state issues[91] while pre-Civil War writers such as William Gouge colored their descriptions of the colonial issues by including them in the same wildcat currency class as the bank notes they were denouncing.[92] But the men of 1776 had their own reasons for opposing bills of credit. They had seen the Continental Congress finance the bulk of its expenses by issuing bills of credit, and they had seen such issues reach a total of $241.5 million and became a byword for worthlessness.[93]

Between October 1776 and September 1777, the Congress's attempts to float loans were only partially successful. As long as there was coin, borrowed abroad to meet interest payments at home, bond sales grew to $63 million. But when specie payments were suspended in March 1782, bond sales and prices collapsed.[94] Part of the difficulty stemmed, of course, from the fact that the Continental Congress, as a convention of ambassadors, could do little to sustain the value of its issues.[95] The Congress's efforts in the 1780s to replace the old notes with a new currency bearing 5 percent interest failed. A resentful public refused to accord to the "new tenor" notes anything like their expected value in coin. The Confederates had to learn all over again in 1864 that it is easier to maintain the value of a currency from the outset than to restore public confidence in a government's promises after a period of runaway inflation.

If the Continental Congress's lack of fiscal powers compelled it to resort to fiat money inflation as a particularly vicious form of taxation, the state governments could not use the same plea. The war got in the way of fiscal responsibility, particularly in the South; Virginia and the Carolinas alone accounted for more than half of the state issues during the Revolutionary War.[96]

The Philadelphia Convention and Government Currencies

Committed to reform the monetary abuses of the Confederation, the federal Constitutional Convention flatly prohibited state bills of credit, whether legal tender or otherwise.[97] A specific clause allowing the federal government to issue bills of credit was crushingly defeated, but so, quite inconsistently, was a flat prohibition against federal note emmissions.[98] By its ambiguous actions the convention clearly intended to leave a note-issuing power available to the federal government while discouraging its casual use.

These votes were, for some years, not fully understood. Even the men at the convention may not have grasped the full implications of their ambiguous actions in regard to a federal currency. In any case, Madison, in his old age, reversed views expressed during his presidency and denied that the federal government had the power to issue currency. In early 1862, this opinion of his last years was solemnly quoted in the federal Congress by the opponents of the legal-tender law.[99]

But the idea of a government currency lived on after 1787. As early as 1803, Jefferson wrote to Albert Gallatin, his secretary of the treasury, suggesting the use of government notes. Later, he expounded his ideas to his son-in-law, John W. Eppes, chairman of the House Ways and Means Committee. He reiterated his belief that what was needed was the revival of a treasury note currency, the suppression of the state bank notes, and a direct internal tax.[100]

The War of 1812 was, in time-honored fashion, financed largely through government issues of bonds and treasury notes. When bond sales faltered, the treasury first issued interest-bearing notes of high denomination, then non-interest-bearing notes clearly meant for circulation. Emboldened by the popular acceptance of these notes, which were received everywhere at par without exchange charges, Secretary of the Treasury George M. Dallas in 1815 proposed a permanent

$10 million government currency.[101] President Madison echoed such views, asserting that if Congress did not charter a new national bank, it might consider whether a government currency should be issued as a medium of exchange.[102]

Other proponents of a government currency proposed a "bank" issue redeemable in coin or United States 6 percent bonds; "national notes" payable only in 4 percent U.S. bonds; or a "local currency" (government notes) which would have the inestimable virtue of remaining in circulation, panic or no.[103]

But it was reserved for the president and directors of the Bank of the State of South Carolina to produce one of the most effective expositions in favor of a government currency. Commenting on the state of the currency at the time of their report (November 1819), the bank's officers declared that "a paper currency. . . should be issued exclusively by the Government of that society." President Stephen Elliott of the bank attacked the specie standard as a currency only for peacetime with a tendency to depress the entire economy. Because paper had always been the real standard of value in America, the time had come to create a stable paper currency upon which the government could base an intelligent system of war finance. Specie, with its tendency to disappear when most needed, would never do as a currency.[104]

The crises of 1814–21 and 1837–41 created an eager audience for such proposals. In 1829, President Jackson proposed a treasury note issue in lieu of the Second Bank's notes, as did Secretary Levi Woodbury in 1837.[105] In 1841, even opponents of Tyler's Exchequer Bank made no objection to the government currency it would issue.[106]

Still more surprising were the views of Calhoun and Rhett of South Carolina. In the panic of 1837, the government was embarrassed by the defaults of the "pet" banks. In the difficult period that followed, Calhoun made several important speeches. In commenting on the treasury note bill on September 19, 1837, he argued that the government must provide the nation with a sound, but non-legal-tender currency. Because treasury notes bearing interest would be held closely as investments, he opposed them as he did any currency which had to be paid on demand or even at a future day. Instead, Calhoun contended that his proposed currency should be redeemed either by receiving it for taxes or by making it fundable in government bonds. He closed his remarks by firmly asserting the government's duty to assist economic recovery, a sentiment with which President Van Buren disagreed.[107]

Calhoun amplified his thoughts the next year in his speech on the Independent Treasury Bill on March 22, 1838. Reiterating his opposition to government promissory notes in any form, he castigated Daniel Webster for trying to turn state bank notes into a government-sponsored currency.[108] Calhoun had earlier rebuked Webster on October 3, 1837 for his attack on a government currency. On that occasion, Calhoun had pointed out that what had made the Continental currency objectionable (the absence of government taxing power) no longer pertained. Government treasury notes, fundable at par into bonds, would make it possible to dispense with "public loans" of the type current in 1812–14, which had cost the nation millions. Moreover, Calhoun dismissed the alleged danger of depreciation by asserting that reputable state bank notes had maintained their value after the general suspension of May 1837 and that so long as a bank (or the government) had claims against the key money dealers in the community, its notes would be generally received and paid out.[109] The ideas expressed in Calhoun's speeches in 1837–38 were, strangely enough, adopted by the Union (except for the legal tender proviso) but only partially copied by the Confederates, who spoiled their effectiveness by not only setting unrealistic due dates but also neglecting to furnish the required fiscal underpinning.[110]

Rhett, a second South Carolinian, was a U.S. Representative in 1837 who subsequently served as a member of the Confederate Provisional Congress. Unlike Calhoun, Rhett was not content merely to propose the issue of non-interest-bearing treasury notes; he actually moved to amend a treasury note bill in accordance with his and Calhoun's views.[111] Not surprisingly, on October 17, 1837, the House voted down Rhett's motion 137 to 81. In view of this measure's radical character, Rhett must have been very persuasive to garner 37 percent of the vote. Forty-one of eighty-three Southern members from the future states of the Confederacy—most from the gulf states—voted for the measure. The border states were strongly opposed. Those favoring the measure included Rhett himself and Lyon; opposing Rhett was Hunter. Being persistent, Rhett renewed his effort on May 13, 1838, but was unsuccessful.[112]

Despite the steady economic recovery after 1841, the case for a national currency continued to be vigorously debated. George Tucker published an article in 1842 proposing that the government issue a currency redeemable in coin.[113] A roughly similar idea was floated in 1849 in the *Bankers Magazine and Statistical Review* by an anonymous writer who advocated treasury notes payable at New York. The key feature of both proposals was their redemption-on-demand provision, which the United States government later adopted for the demand notes of 1861 and the legal-tender United States notes in 1879. In support of his proposal the anonymous author cited Secretary of the Treasury John C. Spencer, who reported that the public used treasury notes for domestic exchange, even after the votes ceased to draw interest. New York was selected as the redemption point because no cities had credit balances with it except New Orleans and Mobile. Thus notes issued elsewhere would gravitate to New York, with a healthy effect on the domestic exchanges.[114]

Another advocate of a government currency, Stephen Colwell, suggested that specie be demonetized and that the government should issue a limited amount of non-interest-bearing treasury notes of small denominations.[115] To prevent an over-issue, the amount in circulation was to be regulated by the ebb and flow of the exchanges, in keeping with John Stuart Mill's dicta.[116]

Thus, by 1860, a government currency had been advocated by Presidents Jefferson, Madison, Jackson, and Tyler; by Treasury Secretaries Gallatin, Dallas, Jones, Crawford, Rush, Woodbury, Ewing, and Spencer; and by other men of the stature of Calhoun, Rhett, Tucker, and Colwell. It was not therefore surprising that when war came in 1861, both sides promptly resorted to government note issues.

The South's Experience with State Currencies, 1789–1860

The Southern experience with state currencies from 1789–1860 provides an insight into the question why the South permitted the states to issue bills of credit from 1861–65. Part of the problem was that the state notes issued before 1789 continued to circulate for years thereafter. For example, Georgia notes were still used as currency into the 1830s.[117]

In addition, from 1789 to 1860, the states of the American Union, particularly, but not exclusively in the South, emitted a considerable amount of new currency. Apart from Texas, which issued notes in its capacity as an independent nation (1837–45)[118] and Florida, which as a territory presumably did so with the tacit acquiescence of Congress, five other Southern states circulated notes. North Carolina was the worst offender, issuing $262,000 of fractional currency from 1814–25 to buy bank stock.[119] Alabama issued notes in 1819–23, to pay salaries and furnish $30,000 of fractional currency for its merchants.[120] Mississippi used some $5, $10, $20, and $50 auditor's warrants in 1841 as bridge financing while the legislature was scrambling to secure funds with which to operate the state government. Kentucky put out a few treasury notes to meet its obligations to some railroads and turnpikes in the late 1840s. Although there were legal objections to these bills, no one made a major issue of them. But this was not true of the Missouri notes, which provided a test case, *Craig v. Missouri.*

The Craig case came about in 1831, after Missouri established loan offices and lent loan office bills. Craig, one of the borrowers, refused to pay on the ground that such notes were unlawful state bills of credit and appealed his case to the United States Supreme Court. In the Court's opinion, Chief Justice John Marshall defined a bill of credit as a direct obligation of a state, issued in currency denominations, not bearing a current market rate of interest, and payable at a future day. Whether such notes were or were not a legal tender was irrelevant.[121]

That decision would have seemed to rule out the issues of banks owned wholly by a state or the emissions of city and county governments. However, the federal government maintained a passive stance until the Civil War, while such issues flourished.[122] In view of this attitude, the South's resort to state notes and the failure to prohibit local government issues cannot be a cause for astonishment.

Sources of Finance Available to the Confederacy

The most vital challenge to the masters of Confederate finance was to decide how to find the revenues to fund the Confederate struggle. Here, the options considered ranged widely from customs dues to direct taxation, based on an earlier experience with direct taxes, and to the possible lessons to be learned from foreign governments in formulating Confederate taxation. Finally, there was the sage advice of Calhoun available to Confederate leaders.

Because American governments until the early twentieth century, except under extraordinary conditions, derived the bulk of their revenue from customs dues in one form or another,[123] the tariff was perforce the most frequently discussed tax source in the period leading up to the Civil War. Customs dues were the preferred mode of raising revenue for one simple reason: smuggling aside, they could be collected with relative ease and a minimum of economic dislocation. Moreover, because only merchants dealt on the whole with the customs officer, the costs of the system could be better disguised in the increased cost of goods than direct taxes extracted by a revenue officer from a wide body of the citizens.[124]

Yet customs dues were not without their drawbacks. First, there was always a temptation to adjust tariffs primarily to keep out foreign goods and thereby protect domestic producers from unwelcome foreign competition. Although this clearly benefited those protected, it denied others the opportunity to buy in the cheapest or best quality markets. Because throughout the period the South exhibited most of the features of a colonial economy, producing raw materials and buying manufactured goods, Southerners opposed a protective tariff as a rule, while favoring what they piously called "a tariff for revenue only."

A second notable deficiency of customs revenues was that they fluctuated in response to the volume of imports. Not only did they rise and fall perversely in times of boom or panic, but they also could dry up completely were the nation at war with a naval power. For example, during the War of 1812, the Congress doubled the tariff rates in 1812, only to see receipts plummet from $13 million in 1813 to $6 million in 1814. It was that experience which led Gallatin to observe that "in time of peace [tariffs] were ample to maintain a war establishment, but in time of war they were hardly adequate to meet the expenses of a peacetime establishment."[125]

A variant on the customs dues system was a system of export duties. Such duties were to be found in eleven of the thirteen colonies but were prohibited in the federal Constitution at the insistence of the Southerners.[126] They had several reasons for opposing export levies, for the South was even then the prime exporter of produce in the United States and were such taxes employed it would largely have to bear the burden of supporting the federal government. Fears were also entertained that export dues would penalize the products of slave labor or be used for regulatory purposes, again to the South's disadvantage. In addition to these concerns, there was earnest debate over whether it would be possible to pass on the cost of export duties to European consumers or whether, in the end, Southerners would be forced to pay the levy in the form of lower prices for their produce.

Because the Republic of Texas was the only Southern government with any recent experience with export duties (there had been a modest levy on cotton),[127] the King Cotton advocates felt they could charge what they pleased and their opponents had no practical reading on the subject. As a result, the suitability of export duties as part of a Southern Confederacy's taxing powers had to be thrashed out in the Confederate Provisional Congress.

Direct Taxation

Direct taxation, chiefly taxes on property or income, had existed to a greater or lesser degree in all the colonies, but faced with public resistance, Southern colonies shunned direct taxes as much as possible, even at the cost of a lamentable level of public services.[128] Such caution was fully merited, for when Governor William Tyron induced the North Carolina legislature to grant a poll tax to build himself a palace at New Bern, the result was a revolt in 1771 that involved serious casualties and expense to the colony.[129] As a result of this attitude, the Revolutionary War had been largely fought by monetary means. As one legislator put it: "Do you think, gentlemen, that I will consent to load my constituents with taxes when we can send to our printer and get a wagon load of money, one quire of which will pay for the whole?"[130]

After the Revolution, direct taxation was divided between state and federal systems. State tax schedules were as various as the states themselves. Those disposed to carry on internal improvements, such as North Carolina, levied taxes on land, personal property, and luxury goods such as gold watches, musical instruments, and carriages. But regardless of the objects of taxation, state prewar rates were low. For example, Virginia charged a modest 3/10 of 1 percent, while Georgia rates ran at l/10 of 1 percent. Legislators also fought bitter battles over whether slaves were to be taxed on a specific rate or on an ad valorem basis. Generally speaking, the demand for ad valorem rates was bitterly resisted by the planters. Yet by 1860 even the specific duties bore an increasing relationship to slave values.[131]

Federal direct taxation, except for customs dues, was seldom experienced, and in 1861 there must have been few with any memory of it. As provided by the Constitution, direct taxes were to be apportioned among the states according to their original representation in Congress or a decennial census. In accordance with a special compromise on that point, slaves were to be taxed at only three-fifths of their value.[132]

During the Constitutional Convention, there had been a sharp debate over how such taxes should be collected. Despite the conspicuous failure of several states during the Revolution to honor the requisitions made on them, Luther Martin proposed that the requisition system be retained and that federal tax-gatherers should be sent among the people only if a state failed to comply. This proposal was voted down, yet Martin triumphed in the end, for the states continued to collect federal real estate taxes for the treasury until 1865.[133]

Federal direct taxes from 1791–1816 came in two forms: excise taxes and property taxes. The excises, best known for the tax on whiskey and the rebellion it provoked, produced an average of about $700,000 a year from 1792–1802, with collection costs representing nearly 20% of the revenue thus produced.[134] By 1807, all such revenues had been repealed, and the machinery for their collection dismantled.

Because excises had produced nothing like the hoped-for revenue, recourse was had to two direct property tax levies, one in 1798 for $2 million and a second one in the War of 1812. The 1798 tax chiefly fell on houses, but there was a 50-cent-per-head poll tax on slaves and a land tax which each state assessed as it thought fit. Collections were slow, and the bulk of the tax was not paid into the treasury until 1802.[135]

Even though war was declared on Britain in June 1812, the Congress, deluded by the expectation of a speedy triumph, voted no new taxes. In March 1813, when the 12th Congress adjourned without taking action, President Madison summoned the 13th Congress into special session and told its members that the time for procrastination was over.[136] The Congress grumpily responded with a tax package, the collection of which was put off until 1814. In 1814, with the situation deteriorating, the direct taxes were extended to one year after the end of the war. By 1817, after the taxes were abolished, only $15.2 of $17.1 million levied had been received.

The slowness in collection largely reflected the need to reestablish the internal revenue apparatus that Gallatin had improvidently dismantled, a problem Calhoun noted in his speech on direct taxation in 1816. Gallatin himself later agreed with Calhoun, noting that a program of direct taxes required the prompt organization of the tax machinery by selecting officers as far as possible in advance and immediately furnishing appointees the forms and instructions necessary to carry out their duties. While the new staff was being assembled in 1814, the cost of collection reached 7.8 percent of the gross proceeds. By 1817, with a more experienced staff in being, this amount had been reduced to 4.8 percent.[137]

This precedent impressed DeBow, the Southern economist. Writing on direct taxes in 1857, he observed that if internal taxes were maintained long enough, collection expenses would decline; indeed, they would ultimately fall below the comparable cost of maintaining customs houses. In support of this argument he cited figures issued by the British treasury in 1797 showing that the Crown had spent 6.15 percent of gross receipts to collect customs as against only 3.6 percent to collect direct taxes.

Furthermore, DeBow observed that during the War of 1812, Congress had permitted the states to assume the tax laid on them by the federal government. Thus in 1814, Virginia, Kentucky, South Carolina, and Georgia all paid the taxes owed by their citizens. By 1815, only South Carolina and Virginia continued to assume the tax, while in the confusion, Louisiana avoided paying anything.[138] This experience demonstrated that if direct taxes were to be effectively collected from the people, large or multiple levies were necessary; otherwise the states would simply augment the wartime inflation by borrowing the money necessary to pay the tax. But the Confederates ignored this lesson.

The Discussion of Direct Taxes, 1830–60

In the years following the War of 1812, although there was no new direct federal taxation, there was at least some discussion of the subject. After retiring as secretary of the treasury, Gallatin declared that since democratic governments had the bad habit of waiting until after the outbreak of hostilities before doing anything effectual about taxes, they were destined for embarrassment and disaster until they could take needed measures. To offset the delay, Gallatin suggested that a direct federal levy be grafted on to the state systems to avoid tedious assessments and accelerate collections.

Finally, Gallatin laid down principles to determine the amount of direct taxes to be collected. To compute the required taxes, he proposed that all government expenditures should be broken into two categories: war expenses and regular expenses. By deducting the estimated revenues yielded by current taxes from the estimated regular expenses and war debt service charges (based on the amount of estimated funded debt outstanding at the end of each year), one could arrive at the total amount of additional taxes required.

Displaying his customary keen perception, Gallatin noted that, although treasury notes were an indispensable mode of raising revenue, particularly during the earlier phases of a war, they were a one-shot weapon. Once the channels of circulation had been filled, the method could be used again only by retiring treasury notes then outstanding through taxation or funding.[139] In advancing such views, Gallatin was consciously or unconsciously repeating the orthodoxies of Adam Smith, who had observed that the necessary delay in the collection of new taxes will almost certainly necessitate government borrowings.[140] But not everyone was prepared to face the prospect of accumulating large debts. Jefferson, for example, had written that "It is a wise rule . . . in a Government . . . never to borrow a dollar without laying a tax in the same instance for paying the interest annually, and the principal within a given term. . . . "[141]

Along the same line, Jefferson had earlier written "That we are bound to defray its [the War of 1812] expenses within our own time, and unauthorized to burden posterity with them, I'm supposed to have been proved in my former letter. . . . " But, he conceded, "the modes which are within the limits of right, that of raising within the

year its whole expenses by taxation, might be beyond the abilities for
our citizens to bear." The obligation of one generation not to burden
its successor led Jefferson to conclude that all debts should be paid
within twenty years.[142] The same attitude was shared by Senator
Thomas H. Benton of Missouri, who declared "that every generation
should bear its own burdens and not cast them upon posterity." [143]

Even as the War of 1812 receded into history, direct taxation was
not ignored. In supporting direct taxes on June 22, 1840, Rhett noted:

> It has been said that this bill has a tendency to accumulate taxes on the
> people, to increase the expenses of collection, and produce embezzle-
> ment and waste. I think its influence is directly the contrary. . . . Gentle-
> men who are seized with the horrors at the object of requiring a tax
> directly from the people . . . are perfectly willing that the same tax
> should be taken from them by a customs-house officer. It is not the tax,
> then, but the manner of getting it which awakens their sympathies. If
> it is taken indirectly—by stealth . . . their democracy is vastly gratified;
> but to take it or receive it directly—openly from the people, excites their
> patriotic sensibilities to a damning excess. . . . [144]

In 1844, Rhett was still an advocate of direct taxes, asserting that
direct taxes and free trade were the essential concomitants of liberty.
He admitted that direct taxes were not going to be adopted by Congress in peacetime, but one day people would realize that such taxes
would do much to reform the government.[145] Support for these views
came from Congressmen Boyce of South Carolina, Campbell of Kentucky, and various editors who discussed it during the 1850 Southern
Convention at Knoxville.

During an 1857 congressional debate on the tariff, several of the
future Confederate leaders expressed their views on the tariff versus
direct taxes. Jefferson Davis went on record as saying "I look upon all
duties imposed on imports . . . as a most expensive mode in which
a given amount of money can be raised. It imposes a large amount of
tax upon the consumers which does not go into the public Treasury
and because of the indirect manner in which the money is raised, it
encourages profligacy of expenditure. I think, therefore, the whole
system is a bad one. . . . So far as any discrimination is made, let . . .
the burdens of Government fall more upon property and less upon
consumption."

The future Confederate president then went on to argue that the
rich could well afford to pay heavy duties on luxury goods. He preferred ad valorem duties, although he conceded that they could lead
to fraudulent valuations and other chicanery at the customs house.
Specific duties, he felt, were at variance with proper tax distribution

practices and, although he did not say so, such duties fell hardest upon goods which the South wanted.[146]

Toombs agreed with Davis "that the true basis of taxation is on property; and the reason why it has been departed from is, that in . . . all Governments, the financial question is the great question. Believing myself that the best way of levying the revenues of this Government is by indirection—by duties on imports and not by direct taxation; and then I agree with my honorable friend from Virginia; for, like him, I do not wish to resort to any other mode than indirect taxation."[147]

Yet rather inconsistently, Toombs demonstrated his ambivalent feelings on the whole subject a few days later by offering an amendment to eliminate the appropriation for customs houses. As he stated: "If the people knew the uses to which they were put, the abuses of the present system of collecting the revenue, they would with one accord abolish it, and resort to direct taxation."[148]

The man whom Toombs styled "my honorable friend from Virginia" was Hunter, who only the day before had clashed with Senator Jacob Collamer, a Republican from Vermont. Collamer had said: "I view free trade and direct taxation as identical: and the Senator said he was for that bill because it was a step to free trade." To which Hunter had replied: "I certainly said I was for the bill because it was a step towards free trade; but I have always disclaimed any wish . . . to confine this Government to direct taxation. On the contrary, I expressed then, as I do now, the opinion that the revenue of this country should be derived from customs imposed with a view to a revenue and not protection. . . ."[149]

Why this illogical preference for tariffs as against direct taxes? Could not the Southern congressmen see that direct taxes would drastically shift the burden of supporting the Union onto the North? Or were they too pusillanimous to let the voters calculate how much the government cost them? What *is* certain is that the Southerners contended that taxes should in theory fall on property (wealth) and not consumption; that the tariff was unduly burdensome; and that the customs house system was expensive and conducive to government extravagance. Yet when the congressmen faced the Confederate fiscal problem, instead of setting up a system of direct taxes, they preferred to continue the politically convenient tariff system.

Foreign Developments in Direct Taxation and War Finance

If the Americans had spent little time examining the utility of direct taxes and the necessity of underpinning a war effort by fiscal means, the same could not be said for Britain. Southerners like DeBow were well aware that between 1793 and 1815 David Ricardo had vigorously attacked the British system of taxation and funding. A sinking fund, so Ricardo averred, merely served as a pool of funds into which irresponsible politicians dipped to cover deficits. Heavy war taxes would "Let us meet our difficulties as they arrive and keep our estates free from permanent encumbrances, of the weight of which we are never truly sensible till we are involved in them past remedy."[150]

During the Crimean War, William Gladstone, the chancellor of the exchequer, was, like Smith, strongly opposed to war loans, if only because they encouraged light-hearted plunges into war and extravagance.[151] As Gladstone put it: "It is impossible for the Government . . . to give an absolute pledge . . . that the expenses of the War shall be borne by additions to taxation; but it is possible for us to do this: to put a stout heart upon the matter . . . and so long as the supplies necessary for the service can be raised within the year . . . we will not resort to the system of loans."[152] In fact, because of a change in ministries, this pledge proved impossible to keep. Nevertheless, 44 million out of 77.5 million pounds of expenses were paid by the famous 1 shilling 2 pence on the pound income tax.[153]

That development roused the English pamphleteers. John Cairnes, an abolitionist economist, strongly backed the chancellor upon the ground Ricardo cited; that is, during the war years between 1793 and 1815, the British government's expenses had been 1,254 million pounds and its revenues 1,081 million. Yet the revenue deficiency of 173 million pounds had resulted in a net increase in the public debt of 482 million, because of the sale of consols at only 7 shillings 6 pence on the pound. Such a discrepancy suggested "that the method of meeting the expenses of war by Government loans . . . stands condemned on moral, economical and financial grounds."[154]

Another British observer, Professor George K. Richards, noted that "It . . . [the loan system] obviates much of that opposition and discontent which have to be encountered when the money is exacted in the shape of taxes; it makes the path of financial policy plain and smooth. But . . . it is this very feature of the loan-system which constitutes its danger. The delusive facility of borrowing is the temptation which lures nations, as it does individuals, to their ruin."[155] Richards conceded that it was easier for a professor to get on a podium and suggest such a policy; it was a great deal harder for a minister "who has to consider in what shape the taxes can be imposed, to justify his choice against all objectors, and all interests affected by these, and finally to carry his propositions into law."[156]

Neither in practice nor as an advocate did Secretary Memminger or the Confederate Congress prove to be the equal of either Gladstone or the professors.

The Wisdom of John C. Calhoun

If the Southern leaders failed to absorb or act on the wisdom of the economic writings available to them, they also turned their backs on the lessons of the War of 1812 as expounded by one of the South's most perceptive statesmen, John C. Calhoun. In that war, the young United States had faced difficulties remarkably similar to those confronting the Confederacy more than fifty years later.

Not only was the United States' coast blockaded by a foe possessing naval superiority, but its more vulnerable ports were also assailed. The resulting diminution of international trade affected customs dues, the chief source of the central government's fiscal revenues. Because the government had abolished direct taxes, it was driven to massive borrowing at a discount and later to the use of treasury notes intended to serve as a currency. Added to this was the fact that bulky staple produce was cut off from foreign markets while high-priced luxury goods were slipped by the blockaders; thus the country was drained of coin and foreign exchange to pay for imports.

Economic decline coupled with military defeats led to the suspension of bank specie payments and a flooding of the country with an irredeemable paper currency. Inflation mounted astronomically while farmers, stuck with unsalable and rotting crops, had little incentive to harvest still more worthless produce. At the same time, with the coastal trade cut off and with no usable roads, internal transportation of produce or manufactured goods was gravely hampered, further depressing morale and the economy.

Impressed by these experiences and anxious not to see their repetition, Calhoun in 1816 delivered two speeches. The first of these, "The Motion to Repeal the Direct Tax," was on January 31, 1816; and the second, on "The New Tariff Bill," was delivered in the House of Representatives on April 6, 1816. In his magisterial statements, Calhoun recounted the experiences through which the country had just passed and his reflections upon them. Taken together, these addresses provided what could have been, and in fact were partially used as, an almost made-to-order program for the Confederacy in 1861. These speeches go far to disprove Richard N. Current's opinion that Calhoun was an "incubus"; rather, as Richard Hofstadter put it, he was "the Marx of the master class."[157]

Calhoun began his reflections on war finance by laying down certain broad principles; he then derived specific proposals from them. Based on the United States' unfortunate experiences during the War of 1812, Calhoun concluded that under 1816 conditions, a war with a naval power would lead to a repetition of the evils endured only four years before. The corrective military and economic steps which he believed necessary to alleviate this state of affairs were forthrightly described.

First, Calhoun declared that in order to fight a great naval power with any success, the United States required a substantial navy. A navy was the most effective means to defend the long coast line and offered, moreover, the additional advantage of permitting attacks on the commerce of the enemy, thereby relieving pressure on the coast. Second, since the government must expect the occupation or attempted seizure of the ports, and since there were neither men nor money enough to garrison every threatened point, internal communications (roads and canals) had to be created so that goods and a central pool of troops could be speedily moved from one point to another. Third, in order to maintain and render them efficient, the militia forces of the country had to be called up and kept on duty for at least a year. In addition, Calhoun asserted, their ranks should be augmented by conscription, needed to raise a large force and to apportion fairly the duty of defending the country. Fourth, since a blockade would cut off the armed forces from arms, clothing, and other supplies, the government in time of peace, by tariff or other means, must encourage the manufacture of military goods. Nor should it be content to await passively the actions of private enterprise; it must, if necessary, act on its own account to procure the necessary supplies either domestically or from abroad.[158]

Fifth, if government revenues were dependent on customs dues, they would be greatly diminished in a war with a maritime power. Thus, if the government relied on such revenue-raising methods in wartime, it would not be long before there was a financial crisis. In a state of hostilities, that crisis might arise too quickly for the government to organize the necessary internal revenue machinery in time. Therefore, a staff of tax collectors and the imposition of direct taxes must be commenced at an early day, even if the rates were very low. It would then be easy to increase the revenues by augmenting the rates, as the situation required.

Sixth, Calhoun argued that it was the government's duty to furnish the nation with a sound currency. Since coin always disappeared when needed, he argued that a government treasury note currency was clearly the best substitute. He objected strongly to a currency which either bore interest or was payable at any fixed day; rather, value should be based primarily on the notes being receivable for public dues. A corollary of his view was that Congress must assure that sufficient taxes were levied to compel everyone to keep and use such notes. And should taxes be insufficient, Calhoun suggested that such a government currency should be fundable into government bonds at par, thereby dispensing with the "loan system" which had caused sales at heavy discounts during the War of 1812. Such a government currency, unlike any issue of bank notes, would be receivable throughout the country at par, thereby eliminating the domestic exchange charges applied to bank notes distant from their place of issue.

Calhoun made one other collateral point which, while not specifically of an economic character, remains as pertinent today as to the time in which he uttered it. He suggested that people were very often in advance of their representatives in accepting measures necessary for the welfare of the country. Thus, he argued, the congressmen could lead their constituents by explaining to them what was required and thus gain their support. True leadership required that the people be taken into the government's confidence.[159]

Such leadership was vitally necessary because anything approaching Calhoun's plan involved a serious departure from past practices, particularly as they related to public attitudes toward the central government, laissez-faire economic concepts, and taxation. Clearly the government was going to have to assume vastly greater powers than people were accustomed to, and those powers were bound to affect a wide range of economic interest groups. No less surely, the public was going to require considerable preparation for the tax burden that must be imposed upon it if there was not to be a fiat-money-inspired inflation or a crushing and unnecessary increase in the size of the funded debt.

In the actual event, although the Confederate government failed to make the best use of Calhoun's program, it did adopt, almost of necessity, many of its elements. For example, it placed the railroads under government control and built key linking lines to speed the movement of troops and goods.[160] It procured armaments, and arrangements were made for sufficient domestically made munitions so that no battle was lost for lack of them.[161] It even organized a propaganda effort abroad that, at a cost of less than $75,000, created a significant pro-Confederate sentiment in Britain, whereas before the war, the South had been in very poor repute.[162] The Confederacy also created a reasonably modern selective service system in April 1862.

In the financial and economic spheres, the government was also active. In 1864 it bought ships to run goods through the blockade and enacted regulations prohibiting the import of unnecessary luxuries, thus leaving outbound cargo space for Confederate use. In 1861, the Congress created a national treasury note currency fundable into bonds and initiated a system of internal direct taxes.

Yet most of these actions shared one common deficiency. They were usually undertaken too late to affect the outcome of the war materially, and because the measures were only half-hearted and adopted often on a patchwork basis rather than as part of a systematic whole, they proved far less effective than they could and should have been. In chapter 2, I will examine the key economic areas under the government's authority and the disastrous policy blunders that characterized each.

NOTES

1. Bureau of the Census, *Population of the United States in 1860* (Washington, D.C.: Government Printing Office, 1864), pp. 590–95.

2. Robert William Fogel and Stanley L. Engerman, *Time on the Cross: The Economics of American Negro Slavery*, 2 vols. (Boston: Little, Brown, 1974), vol. 1, pp. 109–15.

3. H. M. Spofford to President Davis, April 17, 1862, in *War of the Rebellion: A Compilation of the Official Records of the Union and Confederate Armies*, 70 vols. (Washington, D.C.: Government Printing Office 1880–1901), ser. 1, vol. 53, p. 802. H. M. Spofford, provost marshal at New Orleans, reported that the Union capture of the area between the Cumberland and Tennessee rivers had cut New Orleans off from its wheat supply and that neither Texas nor western Louisiana had surplus wheat to send; Charles S. Sydnor, *Slavery in Mississippi* (New York: Appleton-Century, 1933), pp. 30–39.

4. L. B. Northrop (Commissary General CSA) to President Davis, August 21, 1861, in *Jefferson Davis, Constitutionalist: His Letters, Papers, and Speeches*, 10 vols., ed. Dunbar Rowland (Jackson: Mississippi Department of Archives and History, 1923), vol. 5, pp. 124–26. See also Edward Younger, ed., *Inside the Confederate Government: The Diary of Robert Garlich Hill Kean* (New York: Oxford University Press, 1957), p. 214.

5. Bureau of the Census, *Agriculture in the United States in 1860* (Washington, D.C.: Government Printing Office, 1864), pp. 185–87.

6. Ibid., pp. 184, 192.

7. Eugene V. Genovese, *The Political Economy of Slavery: Studies in the Economy and Society of the Slave South* (New York: Pantheon Books, 1966), pp. 106–18. See specifically table 3.

8. Clement Eaton, *A History of the Southern Confederacy* (New York: Macmillan, 1954), p. 140. The problem was exacerbated by the need to move surpluses by rail to the armies and by the accumulation of refugees at points such as

Richmond, bloating the population at a time when the city was cut off from its hinterland.

9. Frank E. Vandiver, ed., *Confederate Blockade-Running through Bermuda, 1861–65* (Austin: University of Texas Press, 1947), pp. 109–48, xxxix.

10. Samuel B. Thompson, *Confederate Purchasing Operations Abroad* (Chapel Hill: University of North Carolina Press, 1935), p. 125.

11. Circular of October 15, 1861, *Reports of the Secretary of the Treasury of the Confederate States of America 1861–1865*, ed. Raphael P. Thian (Washington, D.C.: Privately published, 1878), p. 51.

12. Robert C. Black, II, *The Railroads of the Confederacy* (Chapel Hill: University of North Carolina Press, 1952), pp. 1–25; see also the system map on the book's back cover; George E. Turner, *Victory Rode the Rails* (New York: Bobbs-Merrill, 1953), pp. 33–38, 148–53. The Northern system suffered from some of the same difficulties, but the North had the capacity to correct them. See also Thomas Weber, *The Northern Railroads in the Civil War 1861–1865* (New York: Kings Crown Press [Columbia University], 1952), pp. 25–41.

13. Bureau of the Census, *Manufactures of the United States in 1860* (Washington, D.C.: Government Printing Office, 1865), cixxxviii.

14. Bureau of the Census, *Agriculture in 1860*, pp. 184, 192.

Table 1a. Draft Animals

	Area*	1860	Percent	Per Capita
Horses	Total North	4,549,606	61.1	.23
	Total South	2,025,726	27.2	.23
	Border	859,956	11.7	.32
Mules and	Total North	186,539	14.0	.01
Asses	Total South	903,768	68.1	.10
	Border	236,627	17.9	.09
Total Draft	Total North	4,736,145	54.1	.24
Animals	Total South	2,928,494	33.4	.33
	Border	1,095,983	12.5	.41

Based on: U.S. Census, *Agriculture.*

*North: All states other than the nominal members of the Confederacy north of
      Virginia and east of Ohio.

South: The eleven effective states of the Confederacy.

Border: Kentucky and Missouri.

15. Genovese, *Political Economy of Slavery*, p. 114.

16. Bureau of the Census, *Manufactures in 1860*, pp. 705–11, 715–18.

17. Bureau of the Census, *Statistics of the United States (Including Morality, Property, etc.) in 1860* (Washington, D.C.: Government Printing Office, 1866), pp. 292–93; for the potential Border State contribution see table 3.

18. Adam Smith, *An Inquiry into the Nature and Causes of the Wealth of Nations*, ed. Edwin Cannon (New York: Modern Library, 1937), p. 862.

19. Clement Eaton, *The Freedom-of-Thought Struggle in the Old South* (New York: Harper Torch Book, 1964), pp. 162–215.

20. Louisa C. McCord, "Justice and Fraternity," *Southern Quarterly Review* 15 (July 1949):357. See also George Fitzhugh, *Cannibals, All—or Slaves without Masters*, ed. C. Vann Woodward (Cambridge: Harvard University Press, 1960), pp. 9, 213–16, 228–30. Also, Robert Toombs to Alexander H. Stephens, April 21, 1863, in "The Correspondence of Robert Toombs, Alexander H. Stephens, and Howell Cobb," *Annual Report of the American Historical Association for the Year 1911*, ed. Ulrich B. Phillips (Washington, D.C.: Government Printing Office, 1913), pp. 615–16. Toombs reports that he has lost his copy of Ricardo's *Principles of Political Economy* and asks that another be procured.

21. Joseph Dorfman, *The Economic Mind in American Civilization 1806–1865*, 2 vols. (London: George G. Harrap, 1947), vol. 2, pp. 635–710.

22. *Richmond Enquirer*, July 1, 1825. Even Jefferson had tried to censor the textbooks at the University of Virginia.

23. Dorfman, *Economic Mind*, vol. 2, p. 87.

24. Ibid., pp. 920–34.

25. Holmes to C. G. Memminger, November 2, 1863, in *Correspondence with the Treasury Department of the Confederate States of America, Part 5, 1861–1865*, ed. Raphael P. Thian (Washington, D.C.: Privately published, 1880), pp. 194–95.

26. Eaton, *Freedom-of-Thought*, pp. 304–8.

27. Dorfman, *Economic Mind*, vol. 2, pp. 850–52. See also Katherine Bruce, *Virginia Iron Manufacture in the Slave Era* (New York: Century, 1931), pp. 224–30.

28. C. G. Memminger to William Gregg, April 28, 1849, in Thomas T. Martin, ed., "Correspondence of William Gregg," *Journal of Southern History* (August 1945):414.

29. Clement Eaton, *The Mind of the Old South* (Baton Rouge: Louisiana State University Press, 1967), pp. 69–89.

30. James Dunwoody Brownsen DeBow, "Professorship of Public Economy, Commerce and Statistics in the University of Louisiana," *DeBow's Review* 4 (November 1847):414.

31. James D. B. DeBow, "Productive Energies and Spirit of Massachusetts," *DeBow's Review* 4 (November 1847):459.

32. "The Growth and Consumption of Cotton," *Charleston Courier*, May 31, 1845.

33. "Supply and Consumption of Cotton, Present and Perspective," *DeBow's Review* 22 (April 1857):342.

34. Jacob N. Cardozo, *The Plan for Financial Relief, Addressed to the Legislature of Georgia and Confederate States Congress as Originally Published in the Atlanta Southern Confederacy* (Atlanta: J. H. Seals, 1863), pp. 1–37.

35. Burton J. Hendrick, *Statesmen of the Lost Cause: Jefferson Davis and His Cabinet* (New York: Literary Guild of America, 1939), p. 16. See also Hudson Strode, *Jefferson Davis, American Patriot 1808–1861* (New York: Harcourt Brace, 1955), vol. 1, pp. xvii–xix.

36. Strode, *Jefferson Davis*, vol. 1, pp. xvi–xvii.

37. Edward A. Pollard, *Life of Jefferson Davis with a Secret History of the Southern Confederacy* (Philadelphia: National Publishing, 1869), pp. 150–51.

38. Strode, *Jefferson Davis*, vol. 1, p. 126.

39. John Hope Franklin, *The Militant South, 1800–1861* (Cambridge: Harvard University Press, 1956), pp. 33–62. See also Charles H. Wesley, *The Collapse of the Confederacy* (Washington, D.C.: Russell and Russell, 1934), p. 49.

40. Strode, *Jefferson Davis*, vol. 1, pp. 323–24.

41. Executive Message of November 18, 1861, in *A Compilation of the Messages and Papers of the Confederacy: Including the Diplomatic Correspondence, 1861–1865*, 2 vols., comp. James D. Richardson (Nashville: United States Publishing, 1906), vol. 1, p. 139.

42. Executive Message of December 17, 1861, in *A Compilation*, comp. Richardson, vol. 1, pp. 151–53.

43. Rowland, *Jefferson Davis*, vol. 4, pp. 207–9.

44. Ibid., pp. 30–34; see also Strode, *Jefferson Davis*, pp. 106–24.

45. Hendrick, *Statesman*, pp. 24–43.

46. Davis to the editor of the *Mississippian*, August 29, 1849, as quoted in *Bankers Magazine*, November 1852 pp. 363–70. See also Strode, *Jefferson Davis*, vol. 1, pp. 123–24.

47. Jefferson Davis, *The Rise and Fall of the Confederate Government*, 2 vols. (1881, repr. New York: Thomas Yoseloff, 1958), vol. 1, pp. 241–42.

48. Entry of February 29, 1864, Mary Boykin Chesnut, *A Diary from Dixie*, ed. Ben Ames Williams (Boston: Houghton, Mifflin, 1949), p. 385. The entry does not occur in the C. Vann Woodward edition of her diary, and so may or may not be accurate.

49. Henry D. Capers, *The Life and Times of C. G. Memminger* (Richmond: Everett Waddey, 1893), pp. 7–33.

50. Christopher G. Memminger, *The Book of Nullification* (Charleston: No imprint, 1830), pp. 1–31.

51. Capers, *Life*, pp. 110–44, 395.

52. Hendrick, *Statesman*, p. 191; Memminger was out of the legislature from 1852–54.

53. Pollard, *The Life of Jefferson Davis*, pp. 174–75.

54. John B. Jones, *A Rebel War Clerk's Diary*, 2 vols. (Philadelphia: J. B. Lippincott, ed., 1866, repr. New York: Hermitage Bookstore, 1935), vol. 1, p. 54.

55. Thian, ed., *Correspondence with*, p. 345.

56. Capers, *Life*, pp. 325–27. See also C. G. Memminger to President Davis, June 26, 1863, "Miscellaneous Correspondence with the Confederate Treasury," Record Group 365, National Archives.

57. Joseph Gregoire de Roulhac Hamilton, ed., *Papers of Randolph Abbott Shotwell* (Raleigh: North Carolina Historical Commission, 1929), vol. 1, p. 382.

58. C. G. Memminger to G. W. Randolph, secretary of war, March 27, 1862, in *Correspondence with*, Thian.

59. George W. Randolph to C. G. Memminger, July 28, 1862, in Hartman Papers, New York Historical Society.

60. Younger, ed., *Inside the Confederate Government*, pp. 98, 130; Ulrich B. Phillips and Edwin B. Coddington, "The Activities and Attitudes of a

Confederate Businessman: Gazaway B. Lamar," *Journal of Southern History* 9 (February 1943):10; Clement Eaton, *A History of the Southern Confederacy* (New York: Macmillan, 1954), p. 235.

61. Capers, *Life*, p. 190. He opposed this measure because it lay beyond the competence of the legislature, not from any interest in the blacks per se.

62. South Carolina Legislature, *The Bank Cases Voted by Order of the State Legislature, December 19, 1843* (Charleston: James Leystock Walker, 1843), pp. 46, 243–44.

63. For the bank's defense see Franklin Harper Elmore, *Defense of the Bank of the State of South Carolina: In a Series of Letters to the People of South Carolina* (Columbia: Palmetto State Banner Office, 1850), pp. 1–120.

64. Toombs could also be stubborn as a mule, as when he kept on planting cotton instead of changing over to foodstuff as local pressures dictated.

65. *Charleston Mercury*, July 23, 1864.

66. Foote had helped drive Memminger from office by a resolution of censure on May 27, 1864, *Journal of the Congress of the Confederate States of America, 1861–1865*, 7 vols. (Washington, D.C.: Government Printing Office, 1904–5) vol. 7, pp. 109–10.

67. Rembert W. Patrick, *Jefferson Davis and His Cabinet* (Baton Rouge: Louisiana State University Press, 1961), pp. 234–43.

68. Wilfred Buck Yearns, *The Confederate Congress* (Athens: University of Georgia Press, 1960), pp. 218–35. See also Thomas B. Alexander and Richard E. Beringer, *The Anatomy of the Confederate Congress: A Study of the Influence of Member Characteristics on Legislative Voting Behavior, 1861–1862* (Nashville: Vanderbilt University Press, 1972), pp. 201–35.

69. David M. Potter, "Jefferson Davis and the Political Factors in Confederate Defeat," in *Why the North Won the Civil War*, ed. David Donald (Baton Rouge: Louisiana State University Press, 1960), pp. 113–14.

70. Charles Robert Lee, *The Confederate Constitutions* (Chapel Hill: University of North Carolina Press, 1963), p. 147; Yearns, *Confederate Congress*, pp. 228–29.

71. Alexander and Beringer, *The Anatomy of the Confederate Congress*, pp. 74–105. See also the table on p. 226 that shows that only a minority of those having estates over $80,000 were prepared to levy the needed taxes in 1863, whereas a majority of those having under $80,000 favored taxes.

72. Andrew MacFarlane Davis, ed., *Colonial Currency Reprints 1682–1751*, 4 vols. (Boston: Prince Society, 1910–11), vol. 2, pp. 3, 15–16; vol. 3, pp. 68, 219, 309; William J. Schultz and M. R. Caine, *Financial Development of the United States* (Englewood Cliffs: Prentice-Hall, 1939), pp. 14, 20–22.

73. Schultz and Caine, *Financial Development*, pp. 3, 23, 267. See also E. James Ferguson, "Currency Finance: An Interpretation of Colonial Monetary Practices," *William and Mary Quarterly* ser. 3, 10 (1953):160; William M. Gouge, *A Short History of Paper Money and Banking in the United States* (New York: B and S Collins, 1835), p. 10.

74. Francois Jean Chastellux (Marquis de), *Travels in North America*, 3 vols. (New York: White, Gallagher, and White, 1827, repr. Chapel Hill: University of North Carolina Press, 1963), vol. 2, p. 131.

75. Act No. 1, Act of January 29, 1863, in *Laws and Joint Resolutions of the Last Session of the Confederate Congress (November 6, 1864–March 18, 1865). Together with the Secret Acts of the Preceding Congresses,* ed. Charles W. Ramsdell (Durham: Duke University Press, 1941), pp. 164–65, Act. No. 70, Act of April 30, 1863, pp. 166–67; see also *Laws of the State of Mississippi; Passed at a Regular Session of the Mississippi Legislature* (Jackson: Cooper and Kimball, State Printers, 1862), ch. 14, pp. 59–66. Act approved December 19, 1861.

76. "An Essay Concerning Silver and Paper Currency," in *Colonial Currency,* ed. Davis, vol. 3, pp. 221–26. See also "A Discourse Concerning the Currencies of the British Plantations in America etc.," vol. 3, pp. 309–29 (see also p. 69), and Anonymous, "The Second Part of the South Sea Bubble," vol. 2, in ibid., vol. 3, pp. 304–31.

77. Charles C. Tansill, ed., *Documents Illustrative of the Formation of the Union of the American States,* 69th Cong., 1st sess., doc. 398 (Washington, D.C.: Government Printing Office, 1927), pp. 27–37; Wayte Raymond, ed., *The Standard Catalogue of the United States Coins from 1652 to Present Day* (New York: Wayte Raymond, 1947), pp. 114–38.

78. A. Barton Hepburn, *History of Currency in the United States* (New York: Macmillan, 1915), pp. 273–96, 301–3. Act of August 2, 1813 (taxed state banknotes), A. T. Huntington and Robert J. Mawhinney, comps., *Laws of the United States Concerning Money, Banking and Loans, 1778–1909,* National Monetary Commission, Senate, 61st Cong. 2d sess., doc. 480 (Washington, D.C.: Government Printing Office, 1910), pp. 293, 326, 136. See also Act of August 6, 1846 9 Stat. L. 59 ch. 90 (reestablished the Independent Treasury), p. 293; Act of August 2, 1813, 3 Stat. L. 79 ch. 53 (taxed state banknotes), p. 326; and Act of July 7, 1838 5 Stat. L. 309, ch. 212 (restrained the issue of notes of less than $5).

79. Alexander Hamilton, *Papers on Public Credit, Commerce and Finance,* ed. Samuel McKee, Jr. (New York: Columbia University Press, 1934), pp. 54–59.

80. Bray Hammond, *Banks and Politics in America from the Revolution to the Civil War* (Princeton: Princeton University Press, 1957), p. 326.

81. Smith, *The Wealth of Nations,* pp. 308–9.

82. Hammond, *Banks and Politics,* pp. 208–9; Walter B. Smith, *Economic Aspects of the Second Bank of the United States* (Cambridge: Harvard University Press, 1953), pp. 233–63.

83. M. Grace Madeleine, *Monetary and Banking Theories of Jacksonian Democracy* (Philadelphia: Dolphin Press, 1943), pp. 132–34.

84. Fred L. Israel, ed., *The State of the Union Messages of the Presidents 1790–1860* (New York: Chelsea House Publishers, 1967), pp. 942–47.

85. Hammond, *Banks and Politics,* pp. 680–85. See also George D. Green, *Finance and Economic Development in the Old South, Louisiana Banking 1804–1861* (Stanford: Stanford University Press, 1972), pp. 127–35.

86. Jefferson to Gallatin, December 1803, in *The Writings of Thomas Jefferson,* 10 vols., ed. Paul L. Ford (New York: G. P. Putnam's Sons, 1897), vol. 8, p. 285.

87. Huntington and Mawhinney, *Laws,* p. 293. The law lasted until 1816.

88. Albert Gallatin, "Banks and Currency," in *The Writings of Albert Gallatin,*

4 vols., ed. Henry Adams (Philadelphia: J. B. Lippincott, 1879), vol. 3, pp. 324–25.

89. Gouge, *A Short History*, p. 7; Schultz and Caine, *Financial Development*, pp. 13–14, 28–29; Ferguson, "Currency Finance," pp. 153–80.

90. Benjamin Franklin, "Vindication of the Provincial Paper Money System" (1767), in *The Complete Works of Benjamin Franklin etc.*, 10 vols. ed. John Bigelow (New York: G. P. Putnam's Sons, 1887), vol. 4, pp. 79–94; Ferguson, "Currency Finance," pp. 160, 177; Elisha R. Potter, "A Brief Account of Emissions of Paper Money Made by the Colony of Rhode Island," in *Colonial Currency*, ed. Davis, vol. 3, pp. 102–5. *Bank* simply meant a note issue, not a financial institution.

91. Max Farrand, *The Making of the Constitution* (New Haven: Yale University Press, 1913), pp. 423, 471.

92. Lloyd W. Mints, *A History of Banking Theory in Great Britain and the United States* (Chicago: University of Chicago Press, 1945), p. 153.

93. Davis R. Dewey, *Financial History of the United States* (New York: Longmans, Green, 1934), p. 36.

94. Dewey, *Financial History*, pp. 36, 45–46.

95. Schultz and Caine, *Financial Development*, pp. 68–69; Dewey, *Financial History*, pp. 39–40.

96. Ralph V. Harlow, "Aspects of Revolutionary Finance, 1775–1783," *American Historical Review* 35(October 1929):68. Virginia issues amounted to $7,066,660 and £44,850,000. North Carolina issues amounted to $125,000 and £13,690,000. South Carolina issues amounted to $13,995,348 and £2,262,000.

97. Tansill, ed., *Documents*, pp. 628–30.

98. Ibid., pp. 555–57.

99. *Congressional Globe*, January 29, 1862, 37th Cong., 2d sess. (Washington, D.C.: Congressional Globe Office, 1862), pp. 549–51.

100. Jefferson to Gallatin, December 13, 1803, in *Writings*, ed. Ford, vol. 8, p. 285; Jefferson to John W. Eppes, June 24, 1813, ibid., vol. 9, pp. 391–93; Jefferson to Eppes, September 11, 1813; ibid., p. 399; ibid., p. 391.

101. Message of February 20, 1815 to J. W. Eppes, chairman of House Ways and Means Committee, in George M. Dallas, *The Life and Writings of Alexander James Dallas* (Philadelphia: J. B. Lippincott, 1871), p. 271.

102. Message of December 5, 1815 in *State of the Union*, ed. Israel, vol. 1, p. 137.

103. Justus Erik Bollmann, *Plan of an Improved System of the Money Concerns of the Union* (Philadelphia: William Fray, Printer, 1816), pp. 1–52; Isaac Bronson (Aristides), *A Letter to the Secretary of the Treasury on the Commerce and Currency of the United States* (New York: C. S. Van Winkle, 1819), pp. 22–28; Jefferson to Law, November 6, 1813, in *Writings*, ed. Ford, vol. 9, p. 433; Thomas Law, *Report of the Proceedings of the Committee Meeting in Washington on April 2, 1829 and Its Memorial to Congress Praying for the Establishment of a National Currency* (Washington, D.C.: Way and Gordon, 1824), pp. 12–14.

104. South Carolina Legislature, *A Compilation of All the Acts, Resolutions, Reports and Other Documents, in Relation to the Bank of the State of South Carolina,*

Affording Full Information Concerning that Institution (Columbia, S.C.: A. S. Johnston and A. G. Sumner, 1848), pp. 376, 380; see also Gouge, *A Short History*, pp. 40–41. Gouge attributed this thinking to the English Anti-Bullionists.

105. Message of December 8, 1829, in *State of the Union Messages*, ed. Israel, vol. 1, p. 313; Larry Schweikart, *Banking in the American South from the Age of Jackson to Reconstruction* (Baton Rouge: Louisiana State University Press, 1987), p. 46.

106. Speech of Robert J. Walker (Mississippi), Thursday, September 2, 1841, in *Congressional Globe*, 27th Cong., 1st sess., vol. 10, p. 260.

107. John C. Calhoun, *The Writings of John C. Calhoun*, 6 vols., ed. Richard K. Cralle (New York: D. Appleton, 1854–59), vol. 3, pp. 82–86, 90. See also Martin Van Buren, 4th Annual Message in *State of the Union Messages*, ed. Israel, p. 555; James R. Morrill, *The Practice and Politics of Fiat Finance, North Carolina in the Confederation, 1783–1789* (Chapel Hill: University of North Carolina Press, 1969), pp. 57–91. Morrill contradicts Calhoun's view that there was no depreciation by saying that the depreciation ranged from a 25 percent discount up to 33 percent. The state recognized a 20 percent reduction, later.

108. Cralle, ed., *Writings*, pp. 304–7.

109. Ibid., pp. 110–11, "Speech on the Bill to Separate the Government from the Banks," pp. 122–24.

110. Duff Green, *Facts and Suggestions Relative to Finance and Currency Directed to the President of the Confederate States of America* (Augusta: J. T. Paterson, 1864), pp. 5–8.

111. *Congressional Globe*, 25th Cong. 1st sess., vol. 5 (Washington, D.C.: Blair and Rives, 1837), pp. 113–14.

112. Ibid., pp. 151–52.

113. George Tucker, "The Currency," *Hunt's Merchant's Magazine and Commercial Review* 6 (May 1842):433–39.

114. Report of the Secretary of the Treasury, *Congressional Globe*, 28th Cong., 1st sess. (Washington, D.C.: Blair and Rives, 1844), pp. 8–9; Anonymous, "A National Currency," *Bankers Magazine and Statistical Review* 4 (December 1849):421–29.

115. Stephen Colwell, *The Ways and Means of Payment: A Full Analysis of the Credit System with Its Various Modes of Adjustment* (Philadelphia: J. B. Lippincott, 1859), pp. 624–26.

116. John Stuart Mill, *Principles of Political Economy with Some of Their Applications to Social Philosophy* (London: Longmans, Green, 1909), pp. 543–46.

117. John Jay Knox, *History of Banking in the United States* (New York: B. Rhodes, 1903), pp. 571–72.

118. William C. Gouge, *The Fiscal History of Texas Including an Account of Its Revenues, Debts and Currency, from the Commencement of the Revolution in 1834 to 1851–2 with Remarks on American Debts* (Philadelphia: Lippincott, Grambo, 1852), pp. 270–72.

119. Branston Beeson Holden, "The Three Banks of the State of North Carolina 1810–1872," Master's thesis, University of North Carolina, 1934, p.

44, quoting "Message of Governor Stone to the Legislature 1810," *The Star,* Raleigh, November 22, 1810.

120. William H. Brantly, *Banking in Alabama 1816–1860* (Birmingham: Birmingham Printing, 1963), vol. 1, pp. 66–67.

121. John Marshall, *The Writings of John Marshall Late Chief Justice of the United States upon the Federal Constitution* (Boston: James Munroe, 1839), pp. 390–404.

122. Neil Caruthers, *Fractional Money: A History of the Small Coins and Fractional Paper Currency of the United States* (New York: John Wiley and Sons, 1930), pp. 160–67. Such notes were forbidden by the Act of July 17, 1862.

123. See Bureau of the Census, *Historical Statistics of the United States, Colonial Times to 1957* (Washington, D.C.: Government Printing Office, 1960), pp. 712, 722.

124. Schultz and Caine, *Financial History,* pp. 17–18, 40–41. See also Edward C. Kirkland, *History of American Economic Life* (New York: F. S. Crofts, 1932), p. 121.

125. Schultz and Caine, *Financial History,* p. 141.

126. Tansill, ed., *Documents,* pp. 552–55, 584–88.

127. Gouge, *Fiscal History,* pp. 281–82.

128. Schultz and Caine, *Financial History,* pp. 16–40.

129. Ibid., pp. 204–5; Helen Hill Miller, *The Case for Liberty* (Chapel Hill: University of North Carolina Press, 1965), pp. 204–25.

130. Speech of R. Barnwell Rhett, September 29, 1837 (quoting a Revolutionary legislator), *Appendix to the Congressional Globe,* 25th Cong., 1st sess. (Washington, D.C.: Blair and Rives, 1837), p. 151.

131. Report of July 24th, in *Reports,* ed. Thian, p. 23; also, Douglas B. Ball, *Virginia Currency 1861–5* (Hampton: Multiprint Press, 1972); George Reubler Woolfolk, "Texas and Slavery in the Ante-Bellum South," *Journal of Southern History* 26 (May 1960):180–200.

132. Tansill, ed., *Documents,* pp. 364–71. No similar understanding existed in the Confederate Congress when the subject came up in 1863, the Confederate Constitution copying the federal one verbatim, including the 3/5 clause on slaves.

133. Ibid., pp. 583–84.

134. E. H. Scott, ed., *The Federalist and Other Contemporary Papers on the Constitution of the United States* (New York: Scott, Fresman, 1894), pp. 117, 161–64. Articles 21 and 30 written by Hamilton.

135. Scott, ed., *The Federalist,* pp. 105–10.

136. Message of September 20, 1813, in *State of the Union Messages,* ed. Israel, vol. 1, pp. 129–33.

137. Ibid., pp. 138–41; Gallatin, *Writings,* p. 539. See also Alexander Balinsky, *Albert Gallatin's Fiscal Theories and Policies* (New Brunswick: Rutgers University Press, 1958), pp. 230–32.

138. "Direct Taxes," *DeBow's Review* (May 1857):650–53.

139. Gallatin, *Writings,* vol. 3, pp. 537–53.

140. Smith, *The Wealth of Nations,* p. 862.

141. Jefferson to Eppes, June 24, 1814, in *Writings,* ed. Ford, vol. 9, pp. 389–91. Jefferson, like Hamilton before him, died with his estate nearly bankrupt.

142. Jefferson to Eppes, September 11, 1813, in ibid., pp. 395–98.

143. Senator Thomas H. Benton, ed., *Abridgement of the Debates of Congress from 1789 to 1856 from Gales and Seaton's Annals of Congress,* 16 vols. (New York: D. Appleton, 1860), vol. 13, p. 605.

144. *Appendix to the Congressional Globe,* 26th Cong., 1st sess. (Washington, D.C.: Blair and Rives, 1840), pp. 650–51.

145. *DeBow's Review,* May 1857, pp. 649–50.

146. Appendix June 20, 1860, *Congressional Globe,* Special Session of the Senate 36th Cong., 1st sess. (Washington, D.C.: John C. Rives, 1860), pp. 3187–189.

147. Appendix, *Congressional Globe,* 35th Cong., 1st sess., May 25, 1858 (Washington, D.C.: Rives Office, 1858), p. 446.

148. *Congressional Globe,* 35th Cong., 1st sess., June 12, 1858 (Washington, D.C.: Rives Office, 1858), pp. 2290–292. See p. 93 for his pro-tariff views.

149. Ibid., May 24, 1858, p. 384.

150. David Ricardo, "Essay on the Funding System," in *The Works of David Ricardo* (London: John Murray, 1888), pp. 528, 538–41.

151. Francis W. Hirst, *Gladstone as Financier and Economist* (London: Ernest Benn, 1931), pp. 160–63. See also Smith, *The Wealth of Nations,* p. 872.

152. John E. Cairnes, *On the Best Means of Raising the Supplies for a War Expenditure* (Dublin: Hodges and Smith, 1854), p. 16. For a Confederate acquaintance with Gladstone, see *Correspondence with,* ed. Thian, pp. 158–59.

153. Arthur Redford, *The Economic History of England 1760–1860* (London: Longmans, 1960), pp. 199–200. See also Hirst, *Gladstone,* p. 165.

154. Cairnes, *Best Means,* pp. 15–16.

155. George K. Richards, *Two Lectures on the Funding System and on the Different Modes of Raising Supplies in Time of War* (London: James Ridgeway, 1855), pp. 51, 53.

156. Richards, *Two Lectures,* p. 69.

157. Richard Hofstadter, *The American Political Tradition and the Men Who Made It* (New York: Vintage Books, 1948), pp. 68–92.

158. Calhoun, *Writings,* vol. 3, pp. 142–44; 147–49.

159. William A. Berkey, *The Money Question: The Legal Tender Paper Monetary System of the United States* (Grand Rapids: W. W. Hart, 1876), p. 59. Berkey quotes Calhoun repeatedly to back up his opposition to the law requiring the redemption of United States legal tender notes in coin after January 1, 1879.

160. Black, *The Railroads of the Confederacy,* pp. 95–123; 148–63.

161. Frank E. Vandiver, *Ploughshares into Swords: Josiah Gorgas and Confederate Ordnance* (Austin: University of Texas Press, 1952), pp. 55–271.

162. Charles P. Cullop, *Confederate Propaganda in Europe 1861–1865* (Coral Gables: University of Miami Press, 1969), pp. 29–45. Henry Hotze organized an effective effort in his "Index"; a domestic information program could have been even more to the point.

CHAPTER TWO

Cotton, the Confederate Economy, Blockade-running, and Confederate Financial Operations Abroad

On April 15, 1861 the Confederates faced an array of interrelated problems, each of which required mutually reinforcing solutions. But for such a program to be conducted rationally, the Confederate leaders had to face the implications of the reality that they presided over a staple products economy dependent on foreign markets both for the sale of its produce and the purchase of arms and the necessities of life. If the domestic economy was to be maintained and provide the requisite support for the war effort, the crops must be harvested and the produce shipped to Europe where it could be sold for cash. That in turn required laws regulating commerce and the organization of a blockade-running operation. Purchasing blockade-running ships and weapons in turn required a rigorous plan for borrowing domestic foreign exchange reserves and floating a foreign loan as bridge financing until produce exports should reach a satisfactory level. Delay in carrying out coordinated actions in each of these areas might forfeit the chance to do anything useful to preserve the economy.

If President Jefferson Davis, Secretary Christopher G. Memminger, and other Confederate statesmen had analyzed the South's predicament thoroughly, they might have realized this, and, by examining the options available to the North, Great Britain, and France, they could have shaped policies that not only had a fair prospect of success, but also avoided many of the adverse reactions which their actual policies, or lack of policy, provoked.

Such a strategy in turn depended on assumptions about whether the war would be long or short. In 1861, opinion in the South assumed a short war in spite of the weight of historical experience which proved the contrary. But such unrealistic expectations have been routine for centuries. Yet President Davis claimed later to have been under no such illusion. He knew that the South was short of almost everything needed for mobilization. He therefore ought to have known that he had no chance of achieving a quick decision against the much stronger Union.[1] Moreover, he was well aware that the South's early achievement of military successes was imperative to sap the North's will to stay the course. Because it was possible but unlikely that the Republicans would lose control of Congress after only one military campaign in 1862, it was probable that the South might have to hold its own until the 1864 election, when Lincoln and the Republicans stood a serious danger of losing control of the presidency or the Congress. Such a loss could have a major impact on the outcome of the war, for it seemed likely that the Democrats would run on a peace platform. If they won, particularly at a time when the Union was becoming war weary, they would refuse to continue the war—provided, of course, that the South could convince the Northern electorate that victory was no longer worth the enormous costs of achieving it.

Could the South be saved the anguish of a long war through recognition by, or the intervention of, foreign powers? Southern opinion was divided on this topic. Some felt that the mere fact that the South had set up a government entitled it to recognition, and that recognition would compel the United States to give up its war of aggression. Some even assumed, without bothering to gather any evidence on the actual state of British and French public opinion on the subject, that recognition would flow from affinities between the South and Western Europe and an offer of free trade.

A second school, clinging to an equally superficial, unexamined belief in King Cotton, assumed that foreign intervention and diplomatic recognition would be the inevitable consequence of a Union blockade that would cut off Western Europe's cotton supply and thereby compel foreign intervention. Failing an effective Northern interdiction effort, the South might itself, through a cotton embargo, secure recognition before any cotton was furnished to Europe.

The French ambassador in Washington and the French consul in New Orleans encouraged both of these schools. Robert Bunch, the British consul in Charleston, gave Robert Barnwell Rhett to understand that recognition would soon be forthcoming. Further developments such as the neutrality proclamation in Great Britain, the surreptitious aid furnished in the form of ships, arms and the Erlanger loan, also promoted such thinking, and the optimistic glow persisted until the end of 1863, when the last hope of intervention and recognition faded.

A minority of Confederates, led by Vice-President Alexander H. Stephens and the first secretary of state, Robert Toombs, were of a different opinion. Although hoping for recognition, Toombs admitted that that event must await the passage of "time or our decided success gives assurance of our power to maintain ourselves." Stephens came even nearer the mark when he noted that neither Britain nor France had affection for any part of the United States; that it was in their economic and political interest to promote a war which promised profitable arms sales to both sides; and that it was certain that the warring states would be so weakened that they would be unable to interfere with British and French designs in the Western Hemisphere. Thus the Confederacy's best policy was to exploit whatever benefits and surreptitious help it could obtain from Europe but not to let itself become beholden to any power. Instead, the Confederacy should look to its own resources and wage the most vigorous war possible. Victory, or an unyielding defense that might compel the United States to surrender its claims to the Southern states, offered the South the surest and safest means of becoming an acknowledged member of the family of nations.

President Davis's views were as ambivalent as those of the Southerners generally. He shared the general view that the mere fact that he was the de facto ruler of an extensive territory entitled him to recognition. He shared Stephens's fears that the British, as they had in the case of Texas in 1836, might try to make recognition conditional on the abolition of slavery. He was also anxious to avoid any imputation of weakness and defeatism.[2] As Secretary of State R. M. T. Hunter interpreted Davis's views in terms that foreshadowed later Wilsonian self-determination; "whilst he [Davis] neither feels nor affects an indifference to the decision of the world upon these questions . . . he does not present their claim to a recognized place among the nations of the earth from the belief that any such recognition is necessary to enable them to achieve and secure their independence."[3] Hunter was even more emphatic in early 1862, when he wrote to John Slidell, Confederate commissioner in France, "But at the same time you will declare that we seek no such interventions. . . . You will also take care to explain that we do not doubt our abilities to achieve our own independence and to free our soil from the invaders' tread."[4]

If one takes Hunter's statements at face value, Davis refrained from asking for intervention because he was honestly persuaded that the South could win without outside help and because he feared that overt efforts to secure intervention might be interpreted as a confession of weakness. Or Davis himself may never have been able to distinguish his own prideful hopes from reality. Yet a careful analysis would have disclosed just how slight were the prospects of intervention.

Both Davis and Secretary of State Judah P. Benjamin felt that setting up a government automatically entitled them to recognition, and recognition would result in strong moral pressure on the North to stop the war.[5] Both men also assumed that Lincoln's blockade was not "effective" within the meaning of the Treaty of Paris (1856), and that the other signatories were therefore obligated to see to it that this blockade was not enforced. Yet it was soon clear that foreign governments did not accept these premises. Davis complained bitterly that "the commerce of the world . . . [is] subject to the caprice of those who execute or suspend it at will."[6] Nor after reading the reports of his diplomats in Europe could Davis have retained any illusions on this score; Confederate envoys were much annoyed that their demonstration of the ineffectiveness (and hence illegality) of the blockade was answered in France by inquiries about why cotton was not arriving in French ports.[7] Nor did they receive any greater satisfaction from Great Britain, where the foreign secretary refuted their arguments by stating that "Her Majesty's Government are of the opinion that, assuming that the blockade is duly notified, and also that a number of ships is stationed and remain at the entrance of a port, sufficient really to prevent access to it or create an imminent danger of entering it or leaving it . . . the fact that various ships may have successfully escaped through it . . . will not of itself prevent the blockade from being an effective one by international law."[8]

But even if the blockade per se did not result in intervention, many Southerners felt that the need for cotton would compel Europe to come to their aid, for the advocates of the King Cotton doctrine presumed that a cotton famine would spell ruin for the French and British economies. Such a doctrine, of course, assumed that other cotton-producing countries would not increase production, that unemployed cotton textile workers would be unable to find other occupations, and that revolution would ensue if cotton were not procured. Yet these presumptions were merely wishful thinking, directly at variance with the contemporary evidence.

First, John C. Calhoun had noted in 1827 that the South was not the only grower of cotton; it was merely the most efficient producer. Thus, should Southern production be curtailed,[9] other producers would attempt to take over the South's markets. This prediction was partially borne out during the war, when non-American cotton deliveries to Europe rose from 1.9 million bales in 1862 to 2.7 million bales in 1864.[10]

In addition, Europe in 1861 had a glut of cotton; one writer estimated that three hundred million pounds of manufactured cotton lay unsold above and beyond the usual stocks held by clothing shops and textile mills.[11] This ninety days' sales supply was augmented by record raw cotton stocks.[12] Although the average number of bales normally held in April was 400,000, April 1861 saw 955,000 bales in inventory, with a further increase to 1.1 million bales in June.[13] Even in December 1861, there were still more than seven hundred thousand bales on hand.[14] Under these circumstances, it is not surprising that the mills laid off workers at the end of 1861, long before raw cotton stocks were exhausted or the price of cotton fabrics rose in July 1862.[15]

A more provident Confederate government could have discovered these significant facts; it should also have been aware that the cotton industry's importance had declined after the early 1850s, so that although there were still four million textile employees, they made up 14 percent, not 20 percent, of the workforce (table 4.) Moreover, 80 percent of the five hundred thousand textile workers were concentrated in Lancashire.[16] Given this bunching of voters, their limited representation in Parliament (twenty-eight seats) and the fairly even Conservative (twelve) versus Liberal (sixteen) division of that delegation, one can see why the textile industry was in no position to change the government's neutral posture.[17] Indeed, it is a devastating commentary on the quality of Confederate thinking that the instructions of William Yancy, a commissioner in Europe, did not order an inquiry

Table 4. Cotton in the British Economy, 1853–61*

Year	Cotton Goods Exported		Raw Cotton Exports		Total Cotton Exports	
	Value/% of Total Exports		Value/% of Total Exports		Value/% of Total Exports	
1853	32,713	33.1	2,000	2.0	34,713	35.1
1859	46,497	35.8	4,000	3.1	50,497	38.9
1860	50,218	36.9	5,000	3.8	55,318	40.7[†]

	Workers in the Cotton Industry	% of Population in the Cotton Trade
1853	4,000	19.0
1859	—	—
1860	4,000	14.6

Sources: Frank L. Owsley, *King Cotton Diplomacy* (Chicago: University of Chicago Press, 1931), pp. 6–9; *The Merchant's Magazine and Commercial Review*, July 1861, pp. 2–5.
* All cotton figures in thousands of pounds; other numbers in thousands.
† Based on exports and local consumption figures, there was an eight-month stock of cotton goods on hand at the end of 1860.

on these subjects or a discreet polling of Parliament to ascertain its views on intervention.[18]

British dislike of slavery and a crop failure in 1861 that made Britain dependent on the North for grain[19] were other factors that mitigated against intervention. So too did the attempted cotton embargo, which the British quite properly resented. But the worst failure of Southern leaders was their inability to calculate the variety of responses available to the British. Although a cotton famine promised hardship for the textile trade, a war with the United States threatened Britain with heavy casualties, massive expense, the loss of British investments in the United States, and the exposure to attack of much of the British merchant marine. Nor could the government ignore the danger to Canada, which Samuel Flagg Bemis was wont to describe as Britain's hostage to America.[20]

At no time did the Southerners analyze these facts, nor did it occur to them before 1862 that the British could forestall a revolution by increasing Poor Law relief and private charity to ameliorate the effects of unemployment. Although expensive, such a program was a bargain when compared with the potential costs of a war with the United States. Moreover, if there was to be war, Britain had a choice of allies. As Abraham Lincoln put it: "I am quite sure that a sound argument could be made to show them [the British] that they can reach their aim [cotton procurement] more readily . . . by aiding to crush this rebellion than by giving encouragement to it."[21]

In other words, the British could assist the Union blockade, cut off Confederate supplies, and do everything possible to sustain the Union. Had Britain done so, the Confederacy would have collapsed sooner, cotton would have once more flowed to British mills, the United States would be put in Britain's debt, and the odious institution of slavery would be abolished. Instead of recognizing these balancing factors, Southerners focused their hopes on British grievances against the Union. These included irresponsible talk in the North about seizing Canada as compensation for the loss of the Gulf States; Britain's annoyance about a string of American diplomatic triumphs at its expense; and, finally, anger at the discrimination against British goods in the Morrill Tariff of 1861.[22]

But for the South to capitalize on these opportunities, it would have had to dispatch to Europe its permanent representatives (James Mason and John Slidell) in March, not November 1861, and Southerners would have had to approach their problems with an open mind unimpressed by vacuous slogans.

For reasons no historian seems to have explored, Americans have always had a misplaced faith in the efficacy of embargoes; thus the Confederates' fallacious confidence in the power of economic warfare to shape the policies of other nations had deep roots in American history. It is true that the first non-importation agreement in the Colonies (1764–65) was successful in getting the stamp duties repealed. But thereafter, embargoes proved almost uniformly unsuccessful. A second boycott failed in 1770 when British merchants profited so well from a Russo-Turkish war that few of them noticed more than a slight diminution in their business. The Townsend duties were repealed largely because of English objections to a tax on British exports to the Colonies. As for the third non-importation agreement of 1773, it only drove the annoyed merchants into supporting Britain's colonial program.[23]

Nor did Jefferson's trade embargo of 1808–9 persuade the French or British to halt their spoliations of American shipping. Jefferson had first proposed such a scheme to Washington in 1794, arguing that the only way of obtaining justice from the English lay in distressing their commerce.[24] Had the Southerners been more cognizant of history, they would have remembered that although many in Britain had opposed the policies of their government that had provoked the embargo, "the Ministry stood its ground, the people gritted their teeth, and the Orders [in Council] were enforced. . . ."[25]

In addition, for all their admiration for British institutions, Southerners seemed to specialize in antagonizing the English. Davis's failure to control the committees of public safety, which were inhibiting cotton exports, infuriated friendly British consuls such as Bunch in Charleston, who wrote that "so far as the legislation of the South goes, there is no obstacle in the way of a foreign vessel which may run the blockade. But . . . a very serious and probably insuperable impediment is to be found in . . . the uncontrollable will of an irresponsible community, which sets itself up above all law and supersedes constituted authority wherever it thinks fit to assume the management of office."[26]

William Howard Russell, the *Times* correspondent, was no less angry when he wrote of his displeasure and that of Bunch "to find that no considerations were believed to be of consequence in reference to England except to a material interest, and that those worthy gentlemen regarded her as a sort of appendage of their own cotton kingdom."[27]

The French consuls were equally emphatic in resenting Southern attitudes. Alfred Paul, who headed the consulate at Richmond, scoffed at the King Cotton doctrine; he thought the South would have more trouble getting along under blockade than would the rest of the world, even assuming a cotton shortage. Count Mejan, a friend of the South and the consul at New Orleans, was also irked at the various steps taken to prevent cotton from reaching the wharves and thus being exported.[28]

The actions of the Southerners did not escape the notice of Europeans, who resented measures clearly intended to coerce them. Moreover, foreign opinion was important; in a trial of economic strength, the South, with an unbalanced economy and a need for basic raw materials and manufactured goods, was much weaker than Europe. The South should, therefore, have followed the advice of one Treasury Department correspondent who urged that it stop seeking foreign help and rely on its own resources in achieving Southern independence.[29]

In the fall of 1861 Southern statesmen should have recognized that postponing important regulatory and economic decisions in the expectation of foreign intervention risked Southern defeat if the hoped-for aid failed to materialize. Instead, the South should look to its own carefully exploited resources and avoid dependence on foreign powers, as Stephens and Toombs had advocated.

A Minimal Confederate Foreign Operation Program

As was seen in chapter 1, Calhoun had warned that unless precautionary measures were taken, the strain produced by a blockade would rapidly crack a staple economy. Had the Confederate government possessed anything approaching a realistic vision of its possible future, and a practical, nondoctrinaire view of its predicament, it might well have taken the following urgent steps in the spring of 1861:

> The dispatch of permanent envoys to Europe to gather information for government planning.
> The posting to London of an assistant treasurer to oversee the government's foreign finances and purchasing operations.
> The appointment of a European banker (preferably in London) to hold the Confederacy's funds.
> The purchase of all domestically owned foreign exchange.
> The flotation of a substantial foreign loan.
> The development of a systematic program for the use of cotton.
> The acquisition in Europe of steamers to transport government goods to and from the Confederacy.

Although the South did, in the end, take all these actions, its efforts were half-hearted—and far too late to save the economy.

The Treasury Department and the Appointment
of a Sole Government Agent Abroad

For reasons that are hard to understand, the secretary of the treasury was very slow to undertake the appointment of a government agent in Europe. As the government's principal financial officer, he was the logical person to supervise the procurement and disbursement of government funds. Yet Memminger—a man of limited bureaucratic ambition—was content to let the secretaries of war and navy handle their foreign operations with minimal intervention from the treasury.[30] That does not mean the problem passed unnoticed. On November 14, 1861, Secretary of State Hunter appointed Henry Hotze as "Commercial Agent" in London.[31] Although denominated a "commercial agent," Hotze's chief duties, as Hunter made clear in his instructions, were to keep the Confederate government informed about the state of public opinion in Britain and to try to mold that opinion in a pro-Southern manner.[32]

Because Hotze was to be immersed in propaganda operations, Memminger in 1862 selected James Spence, another Confederate representative, to serve as financial agent. This appointment, made at the suggestion of Mason, the Confederate commissioner to Britain,[33] was inspired by the need to sell Confederate cotton warrants abroad. But no businessman,[34] Spence proved unable to market the bonds entrusted to his care.[35] Because he was also incapable of getting along with the Confederates' French bankers,[36] Memminger, at Secretary of State Benjamin's urging, used the pretext of Spence's antislavery views to dismiss him.[37]

In the spring of 1863, Secretaries Memminger and Benjamin decided that Colin J. McRae, an erstwhile member of the Provisional Congress and a planter involved in various manufacturing schemes, should be sent to France to manage the foreign loan.[38] When, after protracted delay, he arrived in France on May 14, 1863, he found the Confederacy's affairs in a high state of confusion. But McRae was not made sole agent until September 1863.

In the meantime, Mason had tried, on his own authority, to bring some order to the Confederacy's European operations. To this end he invited all the Confederate agents in England—Spence, Major Caleb Huse (Ordnance Department), Major J. B. Ferguson (Quartermaster Department), Captain J. D. Bulloch and Lieutenant North (Navy), and Charles K. Prioleau (Fraser, Trenholm and Company)—to a meeting at which a uniform policy on bond sales and cotton certificates was hammered out. But they were still not able to achieve adequate coordination of their disparate departmental interests, and when the secretaries of war, navy, and treasury appealed to the president, he turned the matter over to Secretary Benjamin for arbitration.[39] By then it was late in the day.

A treasury representative in Europe by the late summer of 1861 could have negotiated a foreign loan and supervised and coordinated ship purchases as well as the operations of the War and Navy Departments. By submitting estimates of future needs from Bullock and Huse, he could have forewarned Secretary Memminger of the magnitude of impending overseas expenditures. But because the treasury learned of such expenditures slowly and in a piecemeal fashion, contractual obligations remained shrouded in mystery until bills suddenly came due. Thus, far from being able to predict the Confederacy's foreign exchange needs with any precision, Memminger was rushed from crisis to crisis.

The situation was chaotic not only with regard to government procurement, but also government credit. A host of unregulated agents hawked their contracts in London, Manchester, or Liverpool in competition with one another. As a result, while the secretary was preoccupied with effecting petty economies at home, millions were thrown away abroad. For example, a Missourian named Chiles agreed to furnish merchandise at Matamoros, Mexico, in exchange for 9.18 million pounds of middling fair cotton, at 20 cents a pound. Although Chiles was foolish enough to pay $1.84 million for his goods, he still emerged with a profit of $2.75 million. Had the business been handled (as it ought to have been) by Major Huse, the government ordnance representative, the goods could have been bought on the government's own account for only $650,000 and there would have been $3.94 million left over for other expenditures.[40]

The Search for a Confederate Depository in Europe

Once having selected an agent, the Confederacy needed a banking house to serve as a depository. To some degree, Secretary Memminger's choice was already made because from April 1861 he had employed the South Carolina firm of John Fraser and Company, together with its branch, Fraser Trenholm in Liverpool.[41] To formalize that relationship, Memminger belatedly offered a resolution "authorizing the Secretary of the Treasury to transfer certain Government funds," and the resulting law was signed by President Davis on November 26, 1861. But the act, reflecting the timid scope of Memminger's vision, only authorized him to deposit $2 million with a foreign banker,[42] whereas the Confederacy had already sent $4.6 million abroad and more money was urgently required.

Acting under this legislative authority, the secretary leisurely concluded an agreement with Fraser, Trenholm and Company on January 16, 1862.[43] Fraser, Trenholm was a large and competent mercantile house with substantial cotton and shipowning interests, but the government also needed the services of a London merchant banker—which were not procured until early 1863.

Confederate Foreign Exchange Purchases

Memminger showed the same ineptitude in planning his purchases of foreign exchange, for he overlooked the facts that the banks of New Orleans possessed half of the South's foreign exchange reserves, and those conformed to a seasonal pattern.[44] Prewar statistics disclose that foreign exchange reserves peaked in April, then declined sharply thereafter. The refusal of the New Orleans banks to suspend specie payments after April 12, 1861, cost the South at least $4 million of coin and foreign exchange, most of which went North.[45]

But Secretary Memminger paid no attention to this established pattern of foreign exchange availability. He began his spasmodic exchange purchases in the spring of 1861, when £120,000 was sent to the Ordnance Bureau and Navy Department agents Huse and Bulloch in England. Another wave of buying came in the fall and winter of 1861–62, by which time Huse and Bulloch had received approximately £950,000.

When the Confederate treasury resumed its foreign exchange purchases in October 1862, sterling drafts were scarce. Whereas bills of £10,000 or more had once been available, the treasury was now reduced to buying drafts for £40. Moreover, even by mid-May 1862, exchange was selling at a 100 percent premium for treasury notes, whereas gold could be bought with treasury notes at only a 33 percent premium. The price differential proves both a need to find funds to make remittances abroad coupled with an inability, because of the blockade, to ship gold to Europe, which was the traditional answer to such a problem.[46]

Instead of continuing its task of procuring funds for the government, the treasury capriciously withdrew from the market, advising the War and Navy Departments to fend for themselves.[47] In the meantime, Secretary Memminger directed that some of the coin seized from the New Orleans banks and deposited at Augusta, Georgia, be shipped to Fraser, Trenholm in Liverpool.[48] Notifying John Fraser and Company in Charleston of his intentions, Memminger asked Mason in London to float a loan secured by this coin.[49] Since there were no takers, Memminger had no choice but to risk sending the coin through the blockade in the fall of 1862.

With very incomplete records, it is difficult to tell how much coin was actually shipped abroad during 1862. But, judging by the reports of Henry Savage, the depository at Wilmington, the sums were substantial.[50] Small intermittent shipments were recorded in 1863,[51] but massive transactions began in 1864, before cotton shipments could provide the necessary funds. Official correspondence regarding the coin dispatched to Europe shows that shipments in August and September alone amounted to $800,000 with $1.5 million a reasonable estimate for the whole year (table 5).[52]

In addition to sterling exchange and gold shipments,[53] there were bills payable in French francs. In July 1862, J. K. Sass, president of the Bank of Charleston, suggested that the government buy francs, because the demand for francs was smaller than that for sterling and the premium was correspondingly less.[54] The bulk of the francs procured was bought from John A. Lancaster Company, almost certainly as an advance on produce sold to the French government's tobacco monopoly.

But these expedients could not indefinitely support the Confederacy. Shipments of coin exposed vital resources to capture and removed coin from the Confederacy, where it was needed. Moreover, heavy governmental purchases of foreign exchange increased the government's expenditures and the resultant inflation. By early 1863, the Confederate government had to find another source of foreign exchange.

Table 5. Confederate Coin Disbursements

1. Used to meet current expenses	$1,600,000
2. Paid-out interest on bonds of February 28, 1861, etc.	1,600,000
3. Miscellaneous gold expenditures, post office, and sundries	400,000
4. Sundry drafts drawn by the Bank of Louisiana on lent coin	67,000
5. Coin shipped abroad	3,000,000*
6. Coin exchanged for Confederate treasury notes to meet government expenses in early 1865.	2,100,000
Total	$8,767,000

* About $1 million was not paid in coin, but by purchase of foreign exchange with specie funds.

The Confederate Foreign Loans

The obvious answer to the need for funds was to float a foreign loan. A substantial foreign loan would promote arms purchases and also permit effective blockade-running. For a modest £10,000, the Confederates could build ships of four hundred tons with a nine-foot draft and eleven knots' speed.[55] These ships could bring in military supplies and also civilian goods that could be sold at a handsome premium for coin, foreign exchange, or treasury notes.

There were additional benefits in becoming a debtor. By creating a class of European creditors with a vested interest in its survival, the Confederacy could greatly enhance its leverage on the British and French governments. Rather than lose their investments, not only might the creditors apply pressure to their own governments, but they might even be willing to lend still more money. It was a tactic effectively used by Hjalmer Schacht on behalf of Germany in the 1930s.

It is hard to know why Secretary Memminger failed to float a foreign loan early in the war because he advocated just such a step in his report of May 1, 1861, when his desire to seek credits in foreign markets was impelled by the feeling that no domestic loans would be forthcoming until the 1861 cotton crop was sold.[56] Memminger had urged the Congress to grant him authority to sell $50 million of bonds "at home or abroad," and by the Act of May 16, 1861, Congress permitted the sale of bonds for foreign exchange[57] without any proviso regarding their place of sale.[58]

But, although the secretary had toyed with the idea of offering the February 28, 1861 Act bonds in New York,[59] he made no effort to dispose of the May 16 bonds in Europe. Narrowly interpreting the law on the assumption that anything not specifically authorized was prohibited, the secretary misallocated his precious supply of treasury notes buying bills of exchange, leaving the foreign bond market untapped.

Ironically enough, the fall and winter of 1861–62 were, from the viewpoint of the money market, an ideal time for a Confederate loan in Europe. The discount rates of the Bank of England and the Bank of France ranged from 2.5 to 3 percent.[60] Borrowing conditions were exceptionally favorable in late 1861 because of the gold influx from the United States, and because of Southern successes at Manassas, Springfield, Belmont, Bowling Green, and Ball's Bluff.[61] But such luck could not hold, and when a loan was finally floated in early 1863, would-be creditors were put off by the loss of New Orleans, Kentucky, Missouri, northern Arkansas, and western Tennessee.

The First Stage: The Effort to Sell Domestic Bonds Abroad

It was not until the summer of 1862 that, to cover its mounting European deficit, the Confederate treasury first forwarded its domestic coupon bonds for sale abroad. The secretary had proposed this in a letter to the president, urging that Confederate bonds be sold in Europe at 50 cents on the dollar (if necessary) or else hypothecated (mortgaged) to the contractors as collateral security.[62]

But within less than two months the secretary reversed himself, denying to Slidell that he had authority to sell bonds abroad,[63] that all bonds must be sold at par, and that he urgently needed every available bond to meet his domestic obligations. Because Congress had just passed the Act of October 13, 1862, putting a time limit on funding some $200 million of notes into 8 percent bonds, Memminger's oversight in requesting a new bond issue to augment the inadequate supply on hand proved singularly awkward. But even leaving that technical faux pas out of the picture, the secretary clearly erred in his legalistic view that sales of the bonds were restricted to the home market. It was true the funding clauses of the Act of August 19, 1861 as amended required that such bonds could not be exchanged for treasury notes at less than par. However, that requirement could easily have been complied with by selling treasury notes to the Europeans in exchange for coin, and then converting the notes at par into bonds.[64] What was wanting was a fervent desire to sell bonds abroad combined with a willingness to dispense with inconvenient legalisms—or to find ways around them. In retrospect, one wonders if these objections' prime purpose was to rationalize the secretary's inaction.

The amount of bonds forwarded to Europe cannot be verified. Major Ferguson took $1 million with him in the fall of 1862, and during 1862–64, another $6 million may have been shipped abroad.[65] Such bond shipments reached $10 million by 1864, when tax-free bonds of the Act of February 17, 1864 were remitted to Fraser, Trenholm and Company[66]

The efforts to sell these bonds proved signally barren of results, and there is only one reference to their acceptance as collateral on a debt in 1864.[67] This failure was in part attributable to Spence's lack of enterprise and the absence of any arrangement for paying the European creditors' coupon interest in coin.

The Second Stage: The Erlanger Loan

The proposals which led to the Erlanger loan of £3 million came from two sources. First, the Confederate government had offered creditors "cotton warrants" which promised the delivery of cotton priced at 5 pence per pound at certain specified ports, at a time when cotton was selling in Europe at 15 pence a pound. But Secretary Memminger's reason for offering the purchaser a 200 percent profit was not solely a calculated inducement to secure credit. Rather, the price was set at that rate because five pence was equal to 28 cents, the domestic price of cotton in Confederate treasury notes, thereby preventing the purchaser from going to the Confederacy and purchasing cotton directly at a lower price.[68]

Second, impressed by the pervasive corruption in the Court of Napoleon III, Slidell concluded that bribery might encourage the political recognition of the Confederacy. In addition, Slidell may also have been influenced in selecting a banker by the personal consideration that his daughter was engaged in a romance with the son of the Franco-German financier Baron Emile Erlanger. To avoid any suspicion of personal bias, Slidell emphasized in reporting Erlanger's proposal to Secretary Benjamin, an old Louisiana friend, that he had been approached by Erlanger rather than the other way around and that "I should not have gone so far as I have in recommending these propositions . . . had I not the best reason to believe that even in anticipation of its acceptance a very strong influence will be enlisted in our favor.[69]

What was Slidell hinting at? Given the sleazy moral standards of the regime, he presumably meant only one thing: that the profit to be made from this loan would serve as an incentive for French intervention. Nor was this so fantastic as it now may sound; after all, it was the pretext of collecting debts owed to a Swiss banker named J. B. Jecker that had led the French to invade Mexico in 1861.[70]

There is no reason to believe that the venality implicit in this transaction in any way offended the worldly Benjamin. Earlier in the year, he had asked Slidell to tender the French a $12.5 million subsidy to break the blockade.[71] If the French had intervened, even Erlanger's terms would have been a bargain. But as Benjamin put it:

> the agents of Messrs. Erlanger & Co. arrived a few days before the receipts of your dispatches; and notwithstanding our desire to ratify the outline of the contract drawn up in Paris, the terms were so onerous that [it would not] have been possible to obtain the sanction of Congress. *It was plain . . . that . . . the contract was really one for the purchase of cotton, and that cotton would be demanded for the whole amount. . . .*
> Your intimation of political advantages likely to be derived from the loan possessed great weight, though not as much as if you had felt at liberty to express yourself more definitely. *We finally agreed, in view of that intimation, to make a sacrifice. . . .*[72] (Emphasis added.)

In a letter to Mason in London, Benjamin repeated these points, but went on to add that "there is no desire or intention on our part to effect a loan in Europe. . . . We want only such very moderate sums as are required abroad for the purchase of war-like supplies and for vessels, and even that is not required because of our want of funds, but because of the difficulty of remittance."[73] This letter suggests that the Richmond authorities were completely divorced from reality, for by that time they were almost £1 million behind in their European payments.

The final terms of the Erlanger loan were better than those originally offered. There was a 7 percent coupon (not 8 percent) and the Confederacy was to receive £2,160,000 (72 percent) not 61 percent on the face amount of £3 million. But the proceeds were not to be received until September 23, 1863.[74] This by no means atypical payment schedule opened the way, as will be seen, for default and cost the Confederacy more than £500,000.

Erlanger's terms were not unique. Merchant bankers had traditionally insisted on a 2–5 percent commission on the principal amount of the bonds, a 1 percent service charge for debt service, and the imputed interest on money subscribed but not yet paid to the foreign government. Nor was it in accord with the then-current practice to "shop around" for a better bargain.[75] Under the circumstances, therefore, the Confederates had no cause for complaint.

But whether this loan was such a great success as Judith Fenner Gentry has suggested is open to question.[76] What she has overlooked, in an otherwise astute evaluation, is that the Erlanger loan, unlike *any* of the other flotations she cited, was *not* a straight debt issue. Rather, as Benjamin pointed out, it was a secured loan convertible on demand by the holder into cotton at 6 pence the pound when cotton in Europe was worth 24 pence the pound. In order to cash in on this bargain, a bondholder had to exchange his bonds for cotton certificates signed by Mason, send an agent with the certificates to Richmond, present them to the treasury, take possession of the cotton, and get it aboard a ship leaving the Confederacy. Even allowing for a 30 percent (£30,000) fee for insurance, shipping, and agency costs, an investment of £22,500 (£25,000 face value in bonds) would gross £100,000 for a £47,500 net profit even if the cotton were captured or sent to the bottom of the sea! That more people did not immediately cash in their bonds for cotton was probably due to an overweening confidence in a Confederate victory.

The suggestion that Benjamin handled the negotiations because Memminger was incompetent is not sustained by the available evidence.[77] Benjamin was probably selected not only because he spoke fluent French, but also was cynical enough not to lose his equanimity while rejecting the shady proposals of the French bankers. The same could not be said for Memminger, who discovered that Erlanger's agents had visited the treasury and offered Edward Elmore, the treasurer, a job with their organization at $6,000 a year in gold, three times his nominal salary in Confederate money. Elmore rejected this offer, and the secretary chose to construe this demarche as a thinly veiled bribe. His indignation at such conduct did not make striking a deal any easier.[78]

The Actual Working of the Erlanger Loan

Subscription books for the Erlanger loan were opened on March 18, 1863, with the bonds priced at ninety. Although the issue at first went to a premium, the revival of stories connecting Jefferson Davis with Mississippi's repudiated bonds resulted in a sharp price break.[79] The impact for the Confederacy was material. Although in the original contract, drawn in Paris, Erlanger had agreed to buy the whole issue, the revised Richmond contract required that Erlanger take only £300,000, or 10 percent, of the loan. Thus in order to deter the subscribers from forfeiting their subscriptions, Erlanger demanded that the Confederates conduct a price-support operation.

Unfortunately, at this crucial juncture, McRae had still not arrived in London, so Spence, Mason, and Slidell had to decide on a course of action. They were singularly ill-equipped for the task; in addition, Slidell was dealing with his son-in-law. More sophisticated men might have been more cautious, but the Confederates' ability to resist Erlanger's proposition was weakened by the fact that the Treasury, War, and Navy Department agents were clamoring for funds, and no alternative financial expedient was available.[80]

A tabulation of what it cost the government to make a market for the Erlanger bonds is shown in table 6. If Mason's intention was to

Table 6. Erlanger Loan Support Purchases

	Date	Face Value (£)	Cash Value (£)
Purchases	April 7–24, 1863	1,388,500	1,234,785.75
Sales	April 8–10, 1863	26,000	23,438.75
Net		1,362,500	1,211,347.00

Source: John B. Bigelow, *Retrospections of an Active Life* (New York: Baker and Taylor, 1909), vol. 1, p. 626. Purchases ranged from 87 to 91⅝, with the average 88.93; sales par was 90.

prevent contract defaults, price support at ninety until April 9 might have made sense. Few subscribers would have thrown away £50 to save £10. But to drive the price of the bonds above £90, where all the subscribers could unload at a quick profit, was tempting fate. Moreover, Mason ought to have insisted on bond sales when the market price exceeded £90, in order to recover the funds invested.[81]

Taking into account bond hypothecations, sales subsequent to the original offering, and the Erlanger penalty of £100,000 in cash for failing to dispose of the whole issue within the time specified, the net proceeds less interest and principal charges amounted to £1.78 million ($8.6 million), a much higher sum than the $2.5 million Schwab estimated.[82]

It has been contended that the sale of these bonds was hindered by the absence of a Confederate government monopoly of the cotton supply or the exclusive right to export cotton from the Confederacy. By the end of 1863, the price of cotton in treasury notes had sunk to only 2 pence sterling versus the 6 pence rate offered in the bonds. But, although the price decline did indeed take place, it occurred too late to block the bond sales, and no fixed rate for cotton could be expressed on the bonds that would avoid the problem unless the price was ridiculously low. Moreover, at a time when cotton was selling for twenty-four pence per pound in England, a £1,000 bond promising the delivery of forty thousand pounds of cotton in the Confederacy worth £4,000 could scarcely be viewed as a bad investment. The subsequent decline in the market price of the Erlanger bonds therefore reflected not the low Southern price of cotton, but the South's fading prospects of survival coupled with the growing realization that, with the capture or closure of the Southern ports, it was becoming increasingly doubtful whether the cotton could be gotten out of the country, even if the bonds were converted.[83]

Confederate Cotton Policy

Of all the decisions facing the Confederate cabinet, one of the most important was its policy toward cotton. Here the cabinet faced two distinct but related problems. As a matter of domestic policy, it was desirable that the cotton planters obtain cash for their crops. As a matter of trade policy, the government needed to use the Confederacy's cotton to pay for imports. For both reasons, the Confederate government ought to have acquired cotton and controlled its shipment. The Provisional Congress took the initiative in dealing with the Confederate produce problem in the Act of May 16, 1861. That legislation provided that the bonds were to be "sold for specie, military stores, or for the proceeds of sales of raw produce or manufactured articles to be paid in the form of specie or with foreign bills of exchange."[84]

An amendment was offered to the bill which would have allowed the planters to exchange their cotton directly for bonds. But Secretary Memminger let this opportunity slip by. Indeed, had he, Postmaster General John M. Reagan, and McRae (a member of the finance committee) shifted their votes, a cotton purchase program would have been adopted by a vote of five states to one, with two divided.[85]

One can readily understand floating a loan for coin or military supplies, and certainly Congress was aware of the need for credits abroad—hence the proviso about foreign exchange. But why insert a seemingly irrelevant clause about the "proceeds of sales of raw produce or manufactured articles"? As a body largely composed of lawyers, Congress clearly inserted such a phrase because the secretary was supposed to find some way of converting staples into cash or foreign exchange. Moreover, while the Act of August 19, 1861 revoked the cited clause of Act of May 16, Congress still provided that the secretary of the treasury might exchange bonds for the proceeds of the sale of raw produce. Memminger was also allowed to defer the date by which the produce must be sold to meet the subscription deadline.

From these clauses we may reasonably deduce that despite the undercurrent favoring an embargo, Congress intended that the planters could sell their cotton and subscribe to the loan.[86] Also, it seems clear that the planters were quite willing to sell their crops to the government.[87] Indeed, Walker Brooke of Mississippi had moved that the Committee on Finance inquire into the advisability of adopting a system of finance based on subscriptions of produce to be sold on the account of the government, and the net amount to be paid over to the subscribers in treasury notes or bonds.[88] Secretary Memminger seems to have been thinking along roughly the same line when he wrote to Francis S. Lyon of Alabama that "The planters may sell the portion contributed by their own agent, and they merely order the net proceeds to be paid over to the Government for Confederate bonds. . . ."[89] In a letter to George A. Trenholm, Memminger's friend and successor at the Treasury Department, the secretary further amplified his thinking in regard to this produce loan: "I thought it best to leave the crops to be sold by the private agent of each planter rather than have Government agents to hold large amounts of cotton and dispose of them without responsibility to the owners.[90] While there is no reply from Trenholm extant, the secretary's point was answered indirectly by Lyon, who wrote, "I think you will either have to cause the sales to be made in this country for coin . . . or to accept the plan of shipping and having it sold abroad under your own direction."[91] That, of course, was what the secretary did not wish to do.

A few days later, Charles T. Lowndes of Charleston suggested a government advance of one-third to two-thirds on the value of the cotton crop.[92] The secretary answered this proposal on July 3, saying that a government loan on the crop in conjunction with, but not in exclusion of, the subscription of the proceeds of the crop might be possible provided that the planters paid the government a sufficient rate of interest to compensate for the expense involved. The secretary proposed to pay for the crop by issuing notes bearing 7.30 percent interest, which he assumed would be held for investment and would thus not add to the mounting inflation. In effect, the secretary was proposing to assume the position of the planters' creditor,[93] although he officially reiterated that the Congress had authorized him to take only the proceeds of sales.[94]

In response to a letter from General W. W. Harllee in which it was asserted that "bonds based on cotton are the best we can have," Memminger wrote on July 9, "I perceive from its contents that in writing your first letter you have not distinguished the cases of the Government borrowing and lending . . . *I entirely agree with you that . . . we ought to do what we can to enable the country to get along, if the blockade continues*; and I am endeavoring to mature a plan for lending the credit of the Government to the planters in the shape of an advance of Treasury notes based upon the value of cotton" (emphasis added).[95]

The secretary was still of the same mind at the end of the month,[96] and he continued so through August, although he refused to concede that the situation required even contingency planning. "If the blockade, or any other cause, should postpone the sale, the subscriptions, of course, would remain suspended. . . . For myself *I am inclined to favor an advance, but that is so much out of the usual course of Government that until the necessity arises it is unnecessary to bring forward a plan*" (emphasis added).[97]

While the secretary from May to August 1861 was bombarded by various schemes which would have the government lend money on cotton, buy cotton, or borrow cotton in exchange for bonds, several themes characterized all the treasury's correspondence. The first was the public perception that Confederate action was urgently needed because the magnitude of the problem exceeded any private or state capacity to deal with it. Second, the public expected their government to mobilize cotton and other produce for the support of their cause. And third, the secretary was warned from almost every corner of the land that if the blockade persisted and the staple produce of the South remained unsold, planters would be without funds to pay their debts or taxes, and the whole economy would be crippled.[98]

This overwhelming preponderance of opinion would have caused most men to court popularity by devising a cotton-buying or borrowing program. But Secretary Memminger resisted such considerations, even though he was sorely tempted to go along with them. His innate distaste for government meddling in the economy found full confirmation in the advice he received on this subject from James D. Denegre. Denegre, the leader of the New Orleans bankers, viewed with alarm and disapproval any plan that would curtail the banks' profitable near-monopoly of the cotton loan business. He insisted that the government not involve itself in such matters, particularly as the blockade would not last long enough to discommode the planters.[99]

Nine years after the war, in answering General Joseph Johnston's criticisms, Memminger fell back on a different defense: that the cotton crop could only have been procured by force, gift, or purchase. As the first means was immoral and the second impracticable, could the crop be purchased? Memminger's response was that "There was not to be found in the whole Confederacy a sheet of bank-notepaper on which to print a note. . . . It is within the memory of the printers of these notes, that months elapsed before bonds or notes could be engraved and printed; and these constituted our entire currency. How, then, was the cotton to be paid for?"

Without doubt the secretary had reason for concern as he spent a frantic September and October 1861 trying to augment treasury note production. But he had, as will be discussed in chapter 3, made several blunders that had crippled the entire security printing program.[100] Even so, a more imaginative and enterprising man might have acquired the Southern staple crops by emitting interim receipts redeemable in bonds or tax receivable for the years 1861–62. These could have been easily prepared at any stationer. But the use of such certificates presupposed a force of tax collectors and a substantial fiscal revenue, neither of which the secretary had made much effort to induce Congress to provide him.

Still worse, although he admitted the need to procure produce loan subscriptions, the secretary vetoed anything but a volunteer program on the ground that salaried personnel would be suspected of self-interest. As a result, large areas were left unsolicited. Still worse, even in those areas where there were agents, the men varied greatly in their zeal, efficiency, and adherence to department procedures. Moreover, there was no follow-up on the subscriptions, the department, in the confusion, having only the vaguest knowledge of who its agents were or what they were doing.[101]

Yet within two months the secretary had one of his recurring changes of heart, recognizing that "many portions of the country . . . have not been reached, and it is desirable to make proper arrangements for an organization of the entire country. . . ." Accordingly, he asked J. D. B. DeBow to carry out such a program.[102] By January 1862, DeBow reported that he had reduced the chaos to the point where actual collections could begin. Yet once again Secretary Memminger's contradictory pronouncements and policies proved insufficient and tardy. The misunderstandings over the meaning of the produce loan's terms and the discovery that neither cash nor bonds were to be forthcoming in exchange for produce quickly chilled the widespread enthusiasm for the whole program. Planters began to cancel their subscriptions and made every effort to dispose of their cotton at home or abroad on their own account.

To stop this, the secretary appointed Robert Tyler, the register, head of the Produce Loan Bureau while at the same time issuing regulations to put DeBow's proposals into effect. As conceived by the secretary, there were to be agents at New Orleans, Mobile, Montgomery, Augusta, Charleston, and Richmond,[103] but none in the Trans-Mississippi region. These agents were to give subscribers interim certificates and remit the proceeds to the nearest depository.[104] At the same time, the secretary reluctantly decreed that the agents were to receive $1,000 on the first $100,000 collected, with a maximum commission of $4,000 to any one agent.[105]

Confronted by public discontent and confusion in October 1861, Memminger sought to head off criticisms by sending the produce loan commissioners a circular. The commissioners were to assure the subscribers that only cash would be taken and that subscription payments would be deferred until the produce could be sold at a fair price. The government would not force any planter to make distress sales. He also emphasized that "the subscriptions are quite as valuable to the Government during the blockade as after it." Aware of the disenchantment of the planters, the secretary sought to mollify them further by stating that "No power is granted to any department to lend for the relief of any interest. Even the power of Congress in relation to money is confined to borrowing, and no clause can be found which would sanction so stupendous a scheme as purchasing the entire crop with a view to aid its owners."

Discreetly glossing over the fact that he was the author of this constitutional impediment (chapter 5), Memminger asserted that a government advance on cotton would cost at least $100 million, not to mention another $25 million for other staples. The government, he asserted, needed every treasury note it could get and should not exchange them for planters' useless promissory notes or produce.

For the future, the secretary felt that the planters must concentrate upon producing grain and meat that would enable the South to feed itself, while for their immediate needs they should look to the banks, which should lend to the planters the funds they had previously used to purchase Northern exchange. Finally, "it is far better that each class of the community should endeavor to secure its own existence by its own exertions. . . . Delay in these efforts, occasioned by vague expectations of relief from the Government . . . may defeat that which is yet practicable."[106]

The secretary's views vividly exemplify the imprecision of his calculations in addition to the invalid premises and the obsession with legalisms that characterized his thinking. Consider his first assumption that he would have to buy $125 million in produce. President Davis had implicitly denied this expectation in his message of July 20, 1861, to the Congress: "In the single article of cotton the subscriptions to the loan proposed by the Government cannot fall short of fifty millions of dollars. . . ."[107] The president's remarks were not an independent assessment, but merely an echo of Memminger's report of the same date.[108]

The extent to which this expectation was exaggerated became clear when DeBow filed his preliminary report. Far from the $50 million predicted by the president six months before, DeBow calculated that receipts might amount to 450,000 bales of cotton, which (after allotting $1 million for the cash and minor items received) would place the total value of the subscriptions at about $21.25 million.[109] That proved a sound prophecy. Approximately $15.8 million was collected on the old subscriptions and $4.7 million on those made after 1862, so that the aggregate realization from the scheme was only $20.5 million. And, further discrediting Memminger's claims, the Confederate government purchased the bulk of its cotton with bonds, not with treasury notes.[110]

Even on his favorite terrain of legalisms, the secretary did not seem very sure-footed in condemning with equal vehemence lending to farmers and the borrowing of cotton. The constitution certainly put a crimp on government lending, but the Congress still had the express power to borrow without any proviso about the form which the proceeds of a loan would take. If Congress, as in fact it did, could use bonds to buy arms, transportation, or food for the army, why was it barred from buying cotton with bonds and selling the cotton in Europe for weapons?

Nor was there much merit in Memminger's contention that the banks were best able to help the planters. The banks had indeed bought exchange in the past, but only by borrowing the funds in New York. With those credit facilities gone, the only way the banks might secure the funds to lend was by increasing their note issues. Even leaving aside a bank note shortage,[111] that action was undesirable because bank issues, unlike treasury notes, could not be controlled by taxation. The banks could retire their own notes only by securing payment of the debts owed to them, which in turn depended on the end of the blockade. If the secretary feared inflation, the last thing he should have done was to encourage monetary expansion by the banks that had suspended specie payments.

The Produce Loan of April 14, 1862

As is often the case with the weak, Memminger's policies were subject to constant revision and reversal. Having opposed the purchase of cotton with bonds in the fall and early winter of 1861–62, he belatedly proposed such a measure in his report of March 14, 1862, when he observed that "large sums must be paid abroad for purchase of arms . . . The cotton and tobacco crops . . . can probably now be used with advantage for the same purpose. The holders of cotton . . . may be induced to close their subscriptions . . . by delivering to the Government . . . at the market . . . the produce which they have subscribed. . . . If Congress should see fit to attempt the experiment, the effort will be made to carry it into execution."[112]

Congress responded to this quite reasonable request by permitting Memminger to accept, for bonds, agricultural produce up to the value of $35 million.[113] Under this authority, the Produce Loan Office in 1862 bought another four hundred thousand bales of cotton for $30.3 million.[114] Later, government purchases reached 430,724 bales aggregating $34.5 million. The tithe tax, so Secretary Trenholm estimated later, yielded another fifteen thousand bales.[115]

In making these acquisitions the government was compelled to spend more than if it had availed itself of the opportunity in 1861 to purchase cotton at 7 to 8 cents per pound (for New Orleans middling), as had been suggested at the time by those citizens who wrote to the treasury.[116] In backing such purchases, one correspondent echoed widespread public sentiment when he wrote that "It may be feared that the people would complain that the Government would become a speculator. . . . This is one feature in the plan that recommends it to us. We would have the Government realize at least $60 million clear profit, enough to pay a large portion of the war debt. . . ."[117]

Instead of realizing a net profit through an accretion in value of cotton, the government's expenses more than offset the gain.[118] Moreover, sales were aborted because the treasury chose to deem the quantity of cotton under effective control as too small for it to guarantee delivery of any fixed amount.[119] By deferring his purchases for six months Memminger paid 70 percent ($14 million) more than would otherwise have been necessary.[120] Confirmation on this point can be found in study of the price indices drawn up by John C. Schwab (1901) and Eugene Lerner (1954). According to them, cotton prices until November 1861 were only about 7 cents per pound. Thereafter, there was a steady rise in price to 1863. Meanwhile, price differentials developed between blockade-running cities like Wilmington and interior cities where the crop had less prospect of a market.[121] It seems likely that the comparatively low price for Confederate government cotton[122] is attributable to the substandard quality of the cotton and the fact that it was improperly baled.[123]

It has been argued that the Confederate regime's failure to obtain cotton at reasonable prices was caused by the greed and self-interest of the planters who refused to sell to the government.[124] Although one cannot deny the selfishness of the cotton-growers, or their waste of scarce manpower on growing cotton when food was needed, they cannot be blamed single-handedly for the government's failure to control the cotton crop. A seizure of the crop with a view to monopolizing it was (as Secretary Memminger correctly pointed out) clearly inexpedient. The real problem was that Secretary Memminger had sent contradictory signals regarding the government's intentions for six months, had left the taking of subscriptions solely in volunteer hands, had delayed asking Congress for legislation to buy the produce with bonds for eight months, and had exhorted and indeed forced planters to engage in self-help. Furthermore, by failing to regulate exports to the government's advantage until 1864, planters were given ample incentive to ship their cotton out of the country. Under these circumstances, the limited success of the Confederate cotton procurement program and the lack of planter cooperation are scarcely to be marveled at.

The Confederate Government Cotton and the Blockade

It was one thing for the Confederate government to secure a supply of cotton but quite another to use that cotton in an effective manner. The government's ability to do so depended on several variables—whether its leadership withheld or exported cotton, and how, if necessary, to send cotton out of the country. Each of these questions required major decisions in which Memminger should surely have played a key role.

In *King Cotton Diplomacy* (1931), Frank L. Owsley has argued persuasively that many Southerners saw a possible embargo of cotton shipments as an instrument for compelling Great Britain to become a Confederate ally. He alludes to the planters' widespread practice of withholding cotton from the ports, editorial demand for an embargo, and the reports of foreign consuls in proof of the proposition. We shall also see that various states, from a real or ostensible concern about accumulating valuable produce at vulnerable ports where it might be captured or destroyed, urged planters to keep their cotton on their plantations. But it is one thing to assert the existence of an embargo mentality and quite another to prove that the Confederate government was a party to such a scheme.

So far as the president was concerned, Owsley deduces that Davis favored an embargo because he was "a firm believer in the power of cotton to bring British and European intervention on behalf of the South . . . although Davis was too discreet to blurt out. . . an arrogant confession of faith. . . ."[125] This assertion is based on the memoirs of Varina Howell Davis, who depicted her husband and his advisors as being so sure of the devastating effects of a cotton shortage in England that diplomatic recognition would necessarily follow.[126]

Yet does Davis's assessment of the British economic distress that might result from withholding cotton prove that he was promoting an embargo? Such an embargo would presuppose a consistency of purpose and execution of policy at no time evident in Confederate financial history. Moreover, an examination of the Davis papers fails to establish any connection between the president and the embargo, although Owsley, Burton J. Hendrick, and others try to explain away the absence of such evidence to an alleged, implicit conspiracy of silence. Thus, Hendrick and Owsley argued that "The Confederate Government could not brazenly lay an interdict on the transportation of its staple. . . . Debates on this subject . . . were ostentatiously printed in the newspapers, and these accounts—of course by intention—found their way into the English press. Such proposed legislation was useful as a threat, but the bills were never passed—Davis and his Cabinet saw to that."[127]

It seems unlikely, however, that Jefferson Davis was sufficiently Machiavellian to encourage an embargo which he was simultaneously telling the Congress to table. Even if he were, the Provisional Congress, although well disposed toward him, was not in his pocket, nor could he lobby against sudden amendments from the floor. Moreover, public discussion of a cotton embargo was too widespread to be concealed, and in fact it created a negative attitude among the British. Nor were the French taken in. For instance, M. Thouvenal, the French foreign minister, reportedly asked why "if so many vessels had broken the blockade how it was that so little cotton had reached neutral ports."[128]

Slidell explained to the French that turpentine offered a greater profit than cotton. Yet an examination of wholesale prices in Fayetteville, North Carolina, discloses that during the fall of 1861, the price of turpentine averaged about 18 cents per gallon.[129] At this rate, turpentine was valued at approximately 2 1/4 cents a pound compared with cotton at 8 cents. Slidell's claim was, it can be assumed, a smoke screen which the French consuls in the South could have quickly penetrated.

The Cabinet's and the Congress's View of the Embargo

Although the second secretary of war, Judah P. Benjamin, was cited by Owsley as a fervent partisan of King Cotton,[130] his predecesor LeRoy P. Walker wrote that "Mr. Benjamin proposed that the government purchase as much cotton as it could hold, at least 100,000 bales, and ship it at once to England. With the proceeds of a part of it he advised the immediate purchase of . . . guns and munitions. . . . The residue of the cotton was to be held as a basis for credit. For, said Benjamin, we are entering on a contest that may be long and costly."[131] Secretary of War Benjamin tried to put his earlier proposals into practice. He advocated cotton shipments from Texas to Europe via Matamoros,[132] and he told the governors of Florida and Louisiana to stop interfering with cotton exports.[133]

But Secretary Memminger's views wobbled. In July 1861, he was convinced that foreigners would break the blockade.[134] Reversing himself in early October 1861, he ordered James T. Miller, the collector at Wilmington, to allow vessels loaded with naval stores to clear the port. Yet Benjamin ordered their departure deferred until he was satisfied that they would not be captured.[135]

The next month, in response to a letter from Beverly Tucker asking for assurance that cotton could be exported to pay for government supplies, Memminger wrote:

> I beg leave to inform you that the Government *has never sanctioned any opposition to such return cargoes,* and it seems to me that where objection has been made by individuals or local boards, it has been under a mistaken view of the true policy of our Government, and will not be persevered in. I have the pleasure of informing you that at Savannah, where some difficulty arose, it has been removed, and the "Bermuda" has sailed with a cargo of cotton. *The only limitation of which has been recognized by the Government has been in the shipment of Naval stores and articles of contraband of War* (emphasis added).[136]

There is evidence that Memminger opposed a cotton embargo in his intervention to prevent other agencies from imposing one. Thus in April 1862, John Fraser and Company, the Charleston firm of which the future secretary of the treasury George A. Trenholm was the principal partner—and which had earlier written Attorney General Benjamin voicing its opposition to a cotton embargo[137]—asked Memminger to stop vigilantes in New Orleans from interfering with the sale of specie and foreign exchange.[138] In reply, the secretary concurred with the firm's "opinion that vigilance committees are not proper agents to regulate commerce. . . ."[139] He then wrote Governor F.W. Pickens about the South Carolina Council's cotton embargo:

> I very much regret this measure has been adopted by the Executive Council, as in the view of this Department it is not within the Constitutional range of State Authority. . . . If the object of the order be to prevent the shipment of cotton, with a view to the coercion of foreign Governments, I respectfully submit that the foreign relations of the Government should be left to the regulation of the Confederate Government, to which the constitution has entrusted them.
>
> If Congress should see fit to lay an embargo on cotton, then its export would be unlawful; *but until then it is the right of every shipper to export the same to any neutral Port, and in the present condition of things such shipments can not but in my opinion be otherwise than beneficial to our country* (emphasis added).[140]

Trenholm, Owsley notwithstanding, wholeheartedly supported Memminger's position. Indeed, a mutual friend wrote that he had not consulted Trenholm because "Mr. Trenholm . . . advocates the policy of supplying Europe with cotton without requiring the recognition of our independence, or furnishing us with goods in exchange." Trenholm's views were shared by the Commerical Convention, which met at Macon, Georgia, on October 17, 1861. In a unanimously adopted resolution it was "Resolved, that in order to encourage the importation of articles necessary in the present exigency of the country, return cargoes ought to be furnished to all vessels introducing commodities within the Confederate States from European Nations. . . ."[141]

Nor, apparently, were Trenholm's views exceptional. After the outbreak of war, Congress debated a bill to prohibit the export of cotton except through the ports of the Confederacy. All efforts to require an absolute prohibition were defeated; in fact, an amendment offered on the floor by the Texas delegation explicitly allowed cotton to be exported via Mexico. If a majority of the congressmen had opposed exporting cotton until the British granted recognition, passage of this legislation is incomprehensible. In insisting on channeling shipments through Southern ports Congress sought to cripple the New England textile industry, not that of Britain.[142]

Secretary Benjamin, in a letter to Slidell, was at great pains to emphasize that no embargo existed. As he put it: "It is known that strenuous efforts have been made by the agents of the United States to create abroad the impression that this Government refuses to permit the exportation of the products of the country with a view to extort from the necessities of neutral powers that acknowledgement of our independence which they would otherwise decline to accord . . . Europe is without cotton, because Europe does not choose to send for cotton, *and we have no means of sending it*" (emphasis added).[143]

In view of the urgent need for exports and the desirability of the administration substituting its control over interstate commerce in lieu of that imposed by vigilantes, why didn't President Davis trump Northern propaganda claims of a Southern embargo by issuing a proclamation explaining the government's policy and banning interference with cotton shipments? It is doubtful whether fear played a role, for Davis was not one to court popularity. It was more probable that he was beset by indecision, particularly as unorganized interference was not as effective as its proponents liked to pretend. For instance, in spite of Rhett's claim that his newspaper, the *Charleston Mercury*, had prevented cotton shipments in 1861–62,[144] the local collector of customs, W. F. Colcock, reported 6,870 bales of cotton shipped between October 1, 1861 and March 31, 1862.[145]

Incredibly, Secretary Memminger opposed keeping cotton positioned near the ports for shipment abroad on the grounds of popular disapproval and the absence of foreign vessels to take it away. Even more perplexingly, he claimed that only a minimal effort should be made to break the blockade because successful cotton exports would provoke increased efforts to seal the ports (as if the federal navy was not already exerting itself to the utmost to achieve that goal).[146]

Moreover, the futility of a bona fide embargo policy was demonstrated at the outset. In May 1861, Yancy wrote from Europe that "the government of England simply waits to see which shall prove the stronger" and "it is sincere in its expressed desire to be neutral."[147] Further confirmation on this point came during the *Trent* affair, when he observed: "if Mason and Slidell are given up, the Government here will endeavor . . . to observe a frigid neutrality towards us—that is, will lean to the United States on the blockade and diplomatic issues, and postpone or refuse recognition."[148]

Bad news along the same line belatedly came from Mason, who confirmed Yancy's gloomy prognosis:

> As regards the . . . cotton supply, which we had supposed would speedily have disturbed the level of their neutral policy, this state of things manifestly exists: The constantly increasing supply of cotton. . . has so stimulated the manufactories that the blockade found the markets overstocked with fabrics. . . .
>
> True that more than one-third of the mills have been stopped, and the rest working only on half time; still the owners find it to their account not to complain and they silence the working classes by sufficient alms in aid of parish relief, to keep them from actual starvation. . . .[149]

With the British workers bought off with poor relief funds and with manufacturers depleting excess textile stocks, the South could not use restrictions on cotton to induce British intervention. The Confederacy was, therefore, thrown back on its own resources. As a coup de grace to Confederate hopes, Mason reported that the British assumed an early end of the war and, on that account, saw no need for intervention.[150]

The Confederate Government's Shipping Policies

The shortage of vessels in which the government's cotton might be shipped resulted from errors of omission and commission during the earliest days of the Confederacy. On February 26 or 27, 1861, Trenholm, together with some Charleston friends, entered into negotiations with a Mr. Barry from England to promote direct trade between the South and Europe. To secure government support for this program, the elder Trenholm sent his son, William, to Montgomery to brief Memminger on the scheme proposed by John Fraser and Company. Although there is some confusion over whether there might have been two visits, one in March and the other in May of 1861, William Trenholm, General P.G.T. Beauregard (who met young Trenholm on a train to Montgomery), and Secretary Memminger all remembered that two propositions were laid before the cabinet. One was a scheme for direct trade between Charleston and Liverpool, and the other called for the establishment, under government guarantee, of a steamboat line between Charleston and the West Indies. As Memminger put it later: "I was most earnest in advocating these early shipments, in that I actually brought young Mr. Trenholm to Montgomery to advocate before the cabinet, the establishment of two lines of Steamers to run to some intermediate Depot at Bermuda and Havannah for the purpose of accumulating cotton and munitions of War."[151]

Although the secretary had "formally advocated this plan" and "it met with my cordial approval," it was voted down by the cabinet.[152]

Trenholm's version of events was only slightly different, and it is corroborated by Beauregard's memory of what Trenholm had told him in 1861. Trenholm asserted that he had urged the cabinet to undertake the purchase of seven steamers of the Orient Line and to use them for blockade-running to the West Indies. As he described the scene: "No discussion took place in my presence but from questions put to me I have always been under the impression that few if any of those present realized . . . the scope and importance of the measures laid before them."[153]

Apparently Trenholm had a subsequent meeting or meetings with Secretary of the Navy Mallory and Secretary of War Walker. Walker, a strict constructionist, opposed the scheme because, in his view, it was not proper for a government to own a shipping line. Mallory believed that the draft of the ships (eleven feet) was too deep for most Southern harbors, and he also had doubts about ships made of iron.[154]

In view of the fact that the secretaries of navy and war opposed the scheme and that it was supported by the secretary of the treasury and probably then-Attorney General Benjamin, the attitudes of Secretary of State Toombs, Postmaster General Reagan, and particularly President Davis were crucial. Toombs was a King Cotton advocate who betrayed a lack of sensitivity when he urged the Confederate commissioner to Britain to make a "delicate allusion" to the probability of a cotton shortage that "might not be unkindly received by the Minister of Foreign Affairs. . . ."[155] One can assume that the postmaster general may have favored the proposal since his votes in the Provisional Congress supported an embargo on trade, except where it was on the government's account.[156] Thus, the position of Davis, the only person whose vote really counted, was critical. Given his opposition to the public ownership of transportation facilities, and the lack of action on Memminger's suggestions, one is safe in assuming that it was Davis who killed these proposals.

Yet it was vital that action to organize blockade-running and enact import controls be taken immediately. An examination of table 7 shows that despite a high volume of foreign trade with the South, the amount of customs collected in New York proves that there was little direct trade with the Southern ports except via New York. Thus, the first priority was the procurement of a blockade-running fleet of a hundred ships to establish direct trade with Europe and to overcome the problem noted by Benjamin and Trenholm.

Second, it would take time for Fraser, Trenholm and other firms to organize private efforts, and Calhoun had argued that the government

Table 7. Trade Figures by Port in 1860*

Port	Exports	Imports
New York	$ 80.0	$231.3
Other Northern ports	71.5	95.3
Total North	151.5	327.0
Charleston	16.0	2.0
Savannah	2.4	.8
Mobile	27.0	.6
New Orleans	108.2	20.6
Other Southern ports	28.9	3.0
Total South	182.5	27.0
Total U.S.A.	$337.0	$354.0

Customs Collections by Major Port (1860)	
New York	$ 34.9
New Orleans	3.1
Total South	4.0
Total North	48.3
Total U.S.A.	$ 52.3

Sources: Census Bureau *Abstract 1951*, pp. 853–213; U.S. Bureau of the Census, *Historical Statistics of the United States Colonial Times to 1957* (Washington, D.C.: Government Printing Office, 1957), pp. 543, 712.

* All figures in millions of dollars.

Average rate about 17.7 percent because 15 percent of goods were not dutiable.

should not count merely upon free enterprise to furnish the needed services; direct government resources must be used, if necessary, to secure the desired result.

Third, blockade-running for private parties would become profitable only when the supply of cotton in Europe and imported goods in the Confederacy had been exhausted and prices had risen. By then, the Southern foreign exchange reserves would have been expended, the economy undermined, and the blockade rendered increasingly effective.

Fourth, given the announced policy of blockade and port seizures and the impossibility of defending the whole coastline, the passage of time would mean that several ports would have been lost, thus making it possible for the Union to intensify its surveillance of the ports still in Confederate hands.

Fifth, the best time for getting the 1861 crop out of the South lay between September 21, 1861 and March 21, 1862, when the nights were longer than the days. To defer action until 1862 would mean that only a modest level of exports could be achieved before the winter of 1862–63, when conditions would be significantly less favorable.

Yet despite these incontrovertible goads to action, the secretary did nothing. His hope for foreign intervention, his preference for laissez-faire, and his lack of tenacity in urging his colleagues to change their minds were destined to sabotage every effort to solve the South's trade problems.[157]

Efforts to Secure Foreign Exchange by Hypothecating Cotton

In early 1862, confronted by the dire need for funds abroad, Secretary Benjamin wrote to E. J. Forstall, the Baring Brothers' representative in New Orleans, inquiring whether Forstall could not arrange to advance the Confederacy $1 million in sterling. In addition to paying interest charges and commissions, the Confederacy was to pledge "such a number of bales of cotton as might be . . . sufficient to cover the advance. . . ." The government would pay the storage and insurance expenses but, for obvious reasons, the cotton was to be kept out of the vulnerable ports until peacetime. The cotton would then be shipped, and the lenders would enjoy brokerage fees on top of their other profits.[158] Because Baring Brothers were bankers for the federal government in London, they rejected this approach. Nor was Secretary Memminger any more successful in his direct efforts to pledge cotton abroad.[159] It was, therefore, just as well that he had already started another approach to meet his foreign credit needs.

The Act of November 26, 1861, which allowed the secretary to deposit funds abroad, also permitted the secretary to keep the Confederacy in funds by shipments of produce. Writing to John Fraser and Company, he asked them whether the *Fingal* at Savannah could be loaded with cotton and turpentine for the government's account. Apparently the Charleston firm was to buy the produce for the treasury in order to keep the department clear of any imputation of commodity speculation.[160] But because the *Fingal* was bottled up in Savannah, the cotton had to be sold off.[161]

In the meantime the search continued for cotton to ship on the government's account. on November 24, for the second time, Congress, by nine states to two, rejected a proposal to buy produce with bonds. The secretary was absent at the time and thus missed an opportunity to secure such a plan's adoption.[162] Meantime, Benjamin, now secretary of war, tried to get Memminger to arrange cotton shipments from Texas to Matamoros, Mexico.[163] But as noted earlier, no arrangements were ever made to procure government-owned cotton in Texas.[164] Then Memminger threw cold water on a similar proposal from Don Jose Oliver[165] on the ostensible grounds that cotton purchases were impossible and that he could not put a procurement plan into operation.[166]

At this point John Fraser and Company offered the secretary a charter for the *Mackinaw* with a cargo of two thousand bales of upland cotton and four hundred bales of Sea Island cotton. After paying the cost of the cargo ($150,000) and the shipping costs ($50,000), the government should still have been able to sell the cotton in Liverpool for a profit of $100,000 payable in sterling—or, in view of the rise in cotton prices by mid-1862, perhaps nearer $200,000. There was also the possibility of obtaining the *John Ravenal* on similar terms.[167]

By coincidence, on the very day this proposal was forwarded to Richmond, Secretary Memminger wrote Trenholm asking if the government could not buy some Sea Island cotton near the Savannah railroad with bonds, or if absolutely necessary, treasury notes, for the purpose of shipping it abroad.[168] He also wrote John Fraser and Company directly, asking them to procure vessels for government use and to consult with Isaac Bennett, the produce loan agent in Charleston, about getting the subscribers to that loan to take bonds for their cotton. If cotton was not to be procured in that manner, then cotton should be bought with bonds on the open market.[169]

Unfortunately, the secretary had waited too long. Those who might have taken bonds eagerly six months before now insisted on payment in treasury notes. Suddenly changing his mind about using treasury notes to buy cotton, the secretary rejected the offer of the *Mackinaw*.[170]

In a remarkable letter to DeBow, he defended this action, asserting that although the purchase of produce with bonds was highly desirable, treasury notes should not be used, even if that meant buying no cotton at all. Quite obviously, the secretary, despite vaulting exchange rates, did not realize the urgency of securing foreign exchange.[171]

Nor was he apparently aware that, with the price of raw cotton rising in Europe as the inventory of cotton goods was exhausted, and with a high exchange premium within the Confederacy, the government could buy cotton with notes, ship it abroad, and sell at a handsome profit. For example, if the secretary had taken up the John Fraser offer on the two ships, it would have cost $400,000 in notes. Yet he stood to receive $564,000 in gold if the cotton arrived in Britain safely! With about £115,000 available, he could use £40,000 to buy back the notes he had expended on the purchase and still have nearly £75,000 to pay his bills abroad.

It was a lamentable example of short-sightedness, which was further highlighted when the secretary of the navy a few days later asked for $2 million in foreign exchange. Memminger replied with a nonsequitur that £30,000 was on hand, "which is probably sufficient for contingencies."[172] Thus until 1864, the only cotton shipped on the treasury's account was one cargo of 428 bales sent via the *Economist*.[173]

Confederate Regulation of Foreign Commerce

Having allowed his chance of shipping cotton to lapse by mid-1862, the secretary showed no concern that he now had cotton but no means of shipping it. The obvious alternative was for the government to claim the right to charter a certain amount of each ship's cargo outward bound; yet that collided with the secretary's doctrinal obsessions. His principles did not permit him to approve the idea that those who shipped cotton abroad should be required (as they were in South Carolina and Louisiana) to bring back military supplies. Evidently the secretary thought that the shipment of cotton should be divorced from the importation of supplies on the ground that the combination of the two would be injurious to both.[174] This was indeed curious reasoning. Ships had to come through the blockade to pick up the cotton, so why shouldn't they bring items of common necessity and use with them?

Nor was the idea of leaving blockade-running to the uncontrolled greed of free enterprise confined to Memminger, as Slidell made clear: "So long as we had any reason to hope that practical illustrations of inefficiency of the blockade might lead to a denial by European powers of its obligatory force it was wise to hold out every inducement to individual enterprises to multiply those illustrations."[175] Only the South's obsessive addiction to doctrine can explain why Memminger was content to stand idly by while government cotton rotted at home and blockade-runners imported nonessential luxuries. It was not until late 1863 that the secretary and other Confederates inaugurated a better way to handle the situation.

As early as January 1862, at least one correspondent had pointed out to Benjamin that something would have to be done about the Confederate economy. Key industries were breaking down and essential manufacturing projects were being thwarted for lack of spare parts or key components. Should not the government, so the writer thought, exercise its unquestioned power over foreign commerce to compel shipowners to bring in the right kind of goods?[176]

Slidell wrote in 1863 to suggest such an approach.[177] As McRae summed it all up, the government must effect the following:

> First. To revoke or annul all contracts in Europe, in which profits or commissions are allowed. . . .
>
> Second. That there should be one contracting or purchasing officer each for the War and Navy Departments in Europe.
>
> Third. That there should be one general agent for Europe, who should have the entire control of the credit of the Government abroad, with large discretionary powers.
>
> Fourth. That the Government should take the exports and imports into its own hands, and no cotton, tobacco or naval stores should be allowed to leave the country except on Government account or for account of holders of produce bonds.[178]

Evidently Confederate officials came to the same conclusion since President Davis, together with Secretaries James Seddon, Benjamin, Memminger, and Mallory, all favored McRae's scheme.[179]

McRae's idea, the so-called "New Plan," was remarkably successful. By "an Act to impose regulations upon the foreign commerce of the Confederate States and to provide for the public defense,"[180] the export of Southern staples was prohibited except under the regulations provided by the president. Likewise "an Act to prohibit the importation of luxuries or articles not necessities or of common use" eliminated some of the less useful aspects of blockade-running.[181] The new regulations governing trade, as laid down by the president, provided:

> First. That every vessel owned by private persons shall be considered on every voyage as chartered to the Confederate Government for one-half of her tonnage, outward and inward.

Second. That all private owners of cargo exported from the Confederacy shall bring in return supplies equal to one half the proceeds of their expected cargo.

Third. That the several states shall remain at liberty to charter the other half of each vessel. . . .[182]

These regulations had already been partially in effect for several months, because the War Department required that all vessels "devote one-third of their tonnage to use of the Government."[183] The Treasury, Navy, and War Departments had also, on April 14, 1863, submitted a plan to President Davis for the systematic purchase and transportation abroad of tobacco, cotton, and naval stores.[184] To fund the operation, Congress appropriated $20 million, while Lieutenant Colonel Thomas L. Bayne was put in charge of the operation.[185]

As might have been expected, the new regulations infuriated the blockade-running groups, who objected to the curtailment of their profits. Some firms deliberately kept their ships idle in order to bring pressure on the government, and when the government refused to capitulate, several groups threatened to transfer their vessels to state control. In furtherance of this scheme, they induced Congress to pass a bill that would have exempted from the regulations any vessel chartered by the states. In vetoing this measure, President Davis made clear that the states must be satisfied to import goods either on ships they owned or on ships whose chartered cargo space they had to divide with the Confederate government.[186]

Meanwhile in Europe, McRae was busy. Working closely with J. D. Bulloch, the senior naval officer, McRae borrowed money through Fraser, Trenholm and Company and contracted for the purchase of fourteen steamers.[187] If one includes this contract,[188] the four steamers owned by the Ordnance Bureau, and the three-quarters government interest in the five steamers operated by William G. Crenshaw, McRae's program would have put twenty-seven steamers at the government's disposal in early 1865. This program of ship acquisitions was given special impetus by the compulsory sale of the Confederate's iron-clad war vessels in Britain and France for £357,000.[189]

The regulation requiring that shipmasters assign the government one-half of the cargo space of their ships, coupled with an increased number of government vessels afloat, resulted in the shipment of 10,412 bales of cotton, only 1,037 bales of which was captured.[190] By December 10, Secretary of War Seddon was able to report that more than twenty-seven thousand bales of cotton had been shipped, and that this cotton was worth approximately $5.3 million.[191] These exports, primarily of cotton (table 8), played an important role in the government's finances.

Confederate Cotton and Foreign Exchange Operations in Retrospect

Why had it taken the Confederates so long to settle on a fixed plan which, had it been adopted two years earlier, might have saved the South from defeat? The most serious impediments to a sensible program resulted from a doctrinal aberration and a tactical misjudgment: a rigid commitment to laissez-faire on the part of Secretary Memminger coupled with his belief in a war of short duration. Thus, planning was

Table 8. Confederate Foreign Exchange Purchases

Year	Sterling Exchange Value (£)	($–CSA)	Franc Exchange Value (Frs.)	($–CSA)	Merchandise Sales (£)
1861	705,800	3,393,960	—	—	—
1862	767,850	6,096,329	973,000	444,760	7,444
1863	300,786	1,824,395*	10,904	10,904	—
1864–65	—	—	—	—	1,660,000‡
	1,786,436	11,314,684	993,000 (£40,000)	455,364	1,667,444

Year	Loan Flotations (£)	Gold Shipments (£)
1861	—	—
1862	—	90,000
1863	1,443,978	10,000
1864–65	690,000†	300,000
	2,133,975	400,000

Total foreign exchange revenues: £6 million or $29.2 million; about double the sum suggested by Thompson, that is, $14,750,000.

* The decline in rate was probably due to late payments for 1861 exchange.

† Included £200,000 general credit from Alexander Collie and Company; £150,000 from J. K. Gilliat and Company based on the pledging of $1 million of 8 percent bonds as collateral. £40,000 of six months credits were also secured by Huse.

‡ Includes $3 million or £600,000 from Texas 1863–65. Most sales were of cotton, with only a few cargoes of tobacco or naval stores thrown in to meet contracts.

jostled into the background until the need for it became manifest in mid-1863.

A more forceful and less doctrinaire secretary of the treasury would have faced reality and stood his ground. He would have rebelled instinctively against entrusting the government's purchasing operations to a collection of independent baronies operating in conflict with one another. Without an overall agent, there was no way to estimate and consolidate future needs or to devise a central plan to meet them. Although he recognized the necessity for a foreign loan, his dilatoriness in appointing either an agent or a banking house to supervise it crucially delayed a bond flotation while paving the way for the unfortunate Erlanger loan. Content to buy for the day's needs only, he failed to accumulate an adequate contingency reserve of foreign bills of exchange, and when purchases became difficult, he withdrew from the market, leaving the War and Navy Departments to their own devices.

Yet the damage from these blunders might have proved of only marginal account had the secretary developed a coherent cotton policy. Although realizing the need for planter liquidity, he was so anxious to avoid any imputation of a government subsidy that he forgot that the treasury's interests were tied inextricably to those of the planters. Had he bought cotton early, he could have used bonds. But he listened too complaisantly to the New Orleans bankers, and by the time he was ready to purchase with bonds, the owners of the available cotton supply wanted treasury notes. When he found he could purchase cotton only with treasury notes, his fear of currency inflation led him to miss the chance to procure foreign exchange by buying cotton for sale abroad. In examining the record one looks in vain for any sign of his understanding of the vital connection between the economic health of the planters, cotton shipments and the external credit of the government. Rigorously compartmentalizing these interdependent problems, the secretary, by his exaltation of legal dogmas over practical realities, rendered a successful solution impossible.

The same sad verdict must be passed on his handling of ship procurement and treasury control of foreign commerce. Failing to convince the cabinet of the need for a government-owned shipping line, he declined even to take advantage of the facilities offered to him by John Fraser and Company. With the initiative in other hands, the secretary in 1863 was left in the ignominious position of ratifying arrangements imposed on him by the secretary of state.

By 1865, the disaster needlessly inflicted on the country had become all too evident. While the domestic economy lay prostrate with the railroads and industry slowly grinding to a halt for lack of parts, the Confederate government faced a shortage of ready means abroad. Had the "New Plan" been adopted in a more timely manner, and had "cotton been exported on its own account, instead of, for the most part, private speculators, the Confederate Government might have dispensed with foreign loans, might have bought its warlike stores at the lowest cash prices and supplied its citizens with commodities of prime necessity at a moderate advance on cost."[192] It was an epic saga of what should have happened.

NOTES

1. Jefferson Davis, *The Rise and Fall of the Confederate Government*, 2 vols. (1881, repr. New York: Thomas Yoseloff, 1958), vol. 1, pp. 471–83; see also Letters of W. Goodman to Alex M. Clayton, May 5 and 7, 1861, in *Correspondence with the Treasury Department of the Confederate States of America*, part 10: *1861–1865*, ed. Raphael P. Thian (Washington, D.C.: Privately published, 1880), pp. 95–98. Goodman reports the massive Union preparations, the unity of public opinion, the hostility to the South of Lord Lyon, the British Ambassador, and so forth. He asked that his letters be sent to President Davis.

2. Henry Blumenthal, "Confederate Diplomacy: Popular Notions and International Realities," *Journal of Southern History* 32 (May 1966):151–71; see also "Texas Diplomatic Correspondence," in *Annual Report of the American Historical Association 1911*, ed. Ulrich B. Phillips (Washington, D.C.: Government Printing Office, 1911), vol. 2, pp. 135–36; vol. 3, pp. 1000–1001.

3. Hunter to James M. Mason, September 23, 1861, in *A Compilation of the Messages and Papers of the Confederacy: Including the Diplomatic Correspondence, 1861–1865*, 2 vols., comp. James Richardson (Nashville: United States Publishing, 1906), vol. 2, p. 94.

4. Hunter to Slidell, February 8, 1862, in *A Compilation*, comp. Richardson, vol. 1, pp. 172, 174–75; Message of January 12, 1863, ibid., vol. 1, p. 287.

5. Ibid., p. 287.

6. Message of November 18, 1861, ibid., vol. 1, pp. 142–43.

7. Slidell to Hunter, February 11, 1862, *War of the Rebellion: A Compilation of the Official Records of the Union and Confederate Navies*, 30 vols. (Washington, D.C.: Government Printing Office, 1874–1927), ser. 2, vol. 3, no. 1, pp. 336–42.

8. Ibid., pp. 379–84.

9. John C. Calhoun, *The Writings of John C. Calhoun*, 16 vols., ed. Richard K. Cralle (New York: D. Appleton, 1854–59), vol. 3, pp. 20–21.

10. "Commercial History and Revenue Supplement," *The Economist*, March 11, 1865. Compiled from the British Board of Trade Reports.

11. Robert Arthur Arnold, *The History of the Cotton Famine from the Fall of Sumter to the Passing of the Public Works Act* (London: Saunders, Otley, 1864), pp. 40–47, 79–83.

12. *Merchant's Magazine and Commercial Review* (July 1863):4–5.

13. Ibid., p. 10.

14. *The Economist*, December 31, 1864; June 7, 1865.

15. John Watts, *The Facts of the Cotton Famine* (London: Grimpkin Marshall, 1866), diagram opposite unnumbered front page, pp. 366–67.

16. *Hunt's Merchant's Magazine* (July 1861):13.

17. Mary Louise Ellison, *Support for Secession; Lancashire and the American Civil War* (Chicago: The University of Chicago Press, 1972), pp. 226–27, table 9.

18. Instructions of March 16, 1861, in *A Compilation*, comp. Richardson, vol. 2, pp. 3–8.

19. S. Poppenham, M.D., to Memminger, January 27, 1862, in *Correspondence with*, ed. Thian, pp. 480–82.

20. Samuel Flagg Bemis, *A Diplomatic History of the United States* (New York: H. Holt, 1936), pp. 364–81.

21. First Annual Message, December 3, 1861, in *A Compilation*, comp. Richardson, vol. 6, p. 45.

22. Brian A. Jenkins, *Britain and the War for the Union*, 2 vols. (Montreal: McGill-Queen's University Press, 1980), vol. 2, p. 1.

23. Arthur M. Schlesinger, Sr., *The Colonial Merchant in the American Revolution, 1763–1776* (New York: Frederick Ungar Publishing, 1957), pp. 82–84, 236–39, 538–40. Heavy American wheat shipments in 1774 cushioned the British merchant class against non-importation much the same way that British textile mill owners were protected against a cotton famine by large cotton stocks.

24. Jefferson to George Washington, May 14, 1794, in Thomas Jefferson, *The Writings of Thomas Jefferson*, 10 vols., ed. Paul L. Ford (New York: G. P. Putnam's Sons, 1897), vol. 8, p. 150.

25. Lewis Martin Sears, *Jefferson and the Embargo* (Chapel Hill: University of North Carolina Press, 1927), p. 271.

26. Bunch to Russell, December 13, 1861, British Foreign Office Papers, "America, Dispatches," vol. 781, part ii. See also Richard I. Lester, *Confederate Finance and Purchasing in Great Britain* (Charlottesville: University of Virginia Press, 1975), pp. 11–17.

27. William Howard Russell, *My Diary, North and South*, 2 vols. (London: Bradbury Evans, 1863), vol. 1, pp. 170–71.

28. Gordon Wright, "Economic Conditions in the Confederacy as Seen by the French Consuls," *Journal of Southern History* 7 (May 1941): 195–214.

29. Poppenham to Memminger, in *Correspondence with*, ed. Thian; see also Lester, *Confederate Finance*, pp. 24–25.

30. Raphael P. Thian, ed., *Correspondence of the Treasury Department of the Confederate States of America 1861–65* (Washington, D.C.: Government Printing Office, 1879), pp. 608–9; Memminger to Mallory, March 22, 1864, in *War of the Rebellion: A Compilation of the Official Records of the Union and Confederate Armies*, 70 vols. (Washington, D.C.: Government Printing Office, 1880–1901), ser. 4, vol. 2, pp. 236–37.

31. Walker to Hotze, August 31, 1861, in *War of the Rebellion: Navies*, ser. 2, vol. 3, p. 117; see also ser. 4, vol. 1, p. 597; Hunter had earlier made Hotze a War Department purchasing agent.

32. Hunter to Hotze, November 14, 1861, ibid., pp. 283–84.

33. Mason to Benjamin, May 2, 1862, ibid., ser. 4, vol. 3, pp. 401–2.

34. Spence to Mason, April 28, 1862, ibid., pp. 403–5.

35. Ferguson to Col. A. C. Myer, quartermaster general, April 18, 1863, ibid., vol. 2, pp. 556–57.

36. Memminger to McRae, September 15, 1863, in *Correspondence of*, ed. Thian, p. 521.

37. Memminger to Spence, September 15, November 24, 1863, ibid., pp. 524, 578.

38. Memminger to McRae, February 3, 1863, ibid., pp. 412–13.

39. Seddon to McRae, September 26, 1863, *War of the Rebellion: Armies*, ser. 4, vol. 2, pp. 824–27.

40. Ibid., pp. 982–86. The excuse given for such contracts was the shortage of government funds and the impropriety of government ownership or operation of a blockade-running business.

41. Memminger to John Fraser and Company, April 15, 1861, in *Correspondence of*, ed. Thian, p. 62.

42. *War of the Rebellion: Armies*, ser. 4, vol. 1, p. 756; see also *Journal of the Congress of the Confederate States of America, 1861–65*, 7 vols. (Washington, D.C.: Government Printing Office, 1904–5), vol. 1, pp. 473, 475, November 21–22, 1861.

43. Memminger to John Fraser and Company, January 10, 18, 1862, in *Correspondence of*, ed. Thian, pp. 250, 258; see also John Fraser and Company to Memminger, January 13, 1862, ibid., pp. 467–68.

44. John C. Schwab, *The Confederate States of America etc.* (New York: Charles Scribner's Sons, 1901), pp. 124–25.

45. *Banker's Magazine* 41 (December 1859):724–25; Raphael P. Thian, *Reports of the Secretary of the Treasury of the Confederate States of America 1861–1865* (Washington, D.C.: Private published, 1878), p. 44, see table 10.

46. Thian, *Reports*, pp. 83–84; see also "Letters and Telegrams of the Secretary's Office, February 23, 1861–July 3, 1861, Miscellaneous Correspondence May 2, 1862 to October 11, 1862," Record Group 109, ch. 10, vol. 163, National Archives; "Record of Civil Warrants of the Confederate Treasury February 23, 1861–December 31, 1861," ch. 10, vol. 252; "Record of Civil and Miscellaneous Warrants of the Fiscal Year 1861–2," ch. 10, vol. 221; "Record of Civil Warrants January 1, 1863–December 31, 1863," ch. 10, vol. 257; "Record of Civil Warrants January 1, 1864–April 30, 1864," ch 10, vol. 261. These sources report purchases of bills of exchange, their amount, and the cost in treasury notes.

47. Memminger to Seddon, December 15, 1862, *War of the Rebellion: Armies*, ser 4, vol. 2, pp. 236–37.

48. Memminger to T. S. Metcalf, October 17, 1862, in *Correspondence of*, ed. Thian, p. 366.

49. Ibid., pp. 366–67; Memminger to John Fraser and Company, October

17, 1862, ibid., pp. 372–74; Memminger to J. M. Mason, October 24, 1862, ibid.

50. Memminger to Metcalf, October 17, 1862, ibid., p. 366.

51. Table 16, Henry Savage to Memminger, July 25, 1863, in *Correspondence with*, ed. Thian, p. 122.

52. William D. Nutt (acting treasurer, CSA) to Memminger, May 23, 1864, ibid., p. 434; Henry Savage to E. C. Elmore (treasurer, CSA), July 16, 1864, ibid., pp. 515–16; H. Savage to Trenholm (secretary of the treasury), October 4, 1864, ibid.

53. Interim certificate, formerly in the author's possession, dated October 15, 1861: £100,000 ($500,000) on the Bank of Charleston.

54. Sass to Memminger, July 9, 1862, "Letters Received by the Secretary of the Treasury 1861–5," Record Group 365, National Archives.

55. Mallory to Bulloch, August 8, 1862, *War of the Rebellion: Navies*, ser. 2, vol. 2, p. 235. Larger and faster ships like the "Banshee" cost three times as much.

56. Report of May 1, 1861, in Thian, *Reports*, p. 3.

57. Ibid., p. 11; see also James M. Mathews, ed., *Public and Private Laws of the Confederate States of America, Passed at the First and Second Congresses 1862–4* (Richmond: R. M. Smith, 1864); James M. Mathews, *The Statutes at Large of the Provisional Government of the Confederate States of America . . .* (Richmond: R. M. Smith, 1864), 2nd sess., ch. 24, pp. 117–18.

58. Act of May 11, 1861, Mathews, *Provisional Government Laws*, ch. 2, p. 108.

59. Memminger to G. B. Lamar, April 11, 1861, in *Correspondence of*, ed. Thian, p. 58.

60. R. G. Hawtrey, *A Century of the Bank Rate* (London: Longmans, Green, 1938), pp. 282–83, 302.

61. Hawtrey, *A Century*, p. 297. On the other hand, secession principles raised fears regarding the certainty of payment. *London Times*, April 10, 1861 and April 17, 1861.

62. Memminger to Davis, September 13, 1862, in *Correspondence of*, ed. Thian, p. 352.

63. There were 8 percent bonds of the April 8, 1862 loan that were specifically saleable abroad, but the secretary had evidently forgotten their existence.

64. Henry D. Capers, *The Life and Times of C. G. Memminger* (Richmond: Everett Waddey, 1893), p. 359. Because the secretary was accepting treasury notes at par worth 33 cents in gold for bonds at home, the 50 cent rate should have been a bargain.

65. Memminger to Robert Tyler (Register of the Treasury) October 23, 1862, Capers, *Life and Times*, p. 372; see also Memminger to Robert Tyler, October 29, 1862 ($2 million), ibid., p. 376, and Memminger to Tyler, November 4, 1862 ($4 million on the War Department's account), ibid., p. 380; see table 15.

66. Ibid., p. 686, Memminger to Tyler, July 5, 1864 (Memminger ordered $3 million of bonds sent to Fraser Trenholm and Company.), ibid., p. 686; see

also Trenholm to C. J. McRae, August 2, 1864, ibid., pp. 706–7; Trenholm to Messrs. Fraser, Trenholm and Company, August 1, 1864, ibid., pp. 707–9.

67. McRae to Seddon, July 4, 1864, *War of the Rebellion: Armies*, ser. 4, vol. 3, p. 525.

68. Memminger to Mallory, January 5, 1863, in *Correspondence of*, ed. Thian, pp. 403–4; see also Memminger to G. A. Trenholm, November 11, 1862, ibid., pp. 384–85.

69. Slidell to Memminger, October 28, 1862, in *A Compilation*, comp. Richardson, vol. 2, pp. 339–40. Many in France also realized that the success of the French enterprise in Mexico depended upon the Confederacy's survival.

70. Burton J. Hendrick, *Statesman of the Lost Cause: Jefferson Davis and His Cabinet* (New York: Literary Guild of America, 1939), p. 306.

71. Benjamin to Slidell, April 12, 1862, in *A Compilation*, comp. Richardson, vol. 2, pp. 228–29.

72. Benjamin to Slidell, January 15, 1863, ibid., vol 2., pp. 405–7.

73. Benjamin to Mason, January 15, 1863, ibid., p. 399.

74. Thian, *Reports*, pp. 98b–98c.

75. Leland Hamilton Jenks, *The Migration of British Capital to 1875* (London: Thomas Nelson and Sons Ltd., 1963), pp. 47–49, 272–80. The bankers always attributed loan failures to their clients' bad credit; success they attributed to their own brilliance; see also *Westminster Review* 52 (November 8, 1839):213. Many Britons made a point not to buy the securities of the slave states, a ban that would have presumably limited the market for Confederate bonds.

76. Judith Fenner Gentry, "A Confederate Success in Europe, the Erlanger Loan," *Journal of Southern History* 36 (May 1970):157–88.

77. Hendrick, *Statesman*, pp. 222–23.

78. Claude E. Fuller, *Confederate Currency and Stamps 1861–5* (Nashville: Parthenon Press, 1949), p. 50.

79. *War of the Rebellion: Navies*, ser. 2, vol. 3, pp. 721–30; see also John Bigelow, *Recollections of an Active Life*, 5 vols. (New York: Baker Taylor, 1901–13), vol. 1, *1812–1863*, p. 642; and Robert J. Walker, *Jefferson Davis and Repudiation* (London: William Ridgeway, 1863), pp. 1–58.

80. Mason to Benjamin, February 5, 1863, in *A Compilation*, comp. Richardson, vol. 2, p. 421.

81. Bigelow, *Recollections*, vol. 1, pp. 622–27.

82. Gentry, "Confederate Success," pp. 167–72. Professor Gentry says that Erlanger paid a penalty of £100,000 in bonds. The original contract called for £140,000 in bonds that at 71 (at forfeiture time) were worth £100,000 cash, the sum Erlanger paid. This is confirmed by Gentry's own bond sales figures; see National Archives Record Group 365, entry 323 (Box 96); and Schwab, *Confederate States*, p. 35.

83. Stanley Lebergott, "Why the South Lost: Commercial Purposes in the Confederacy, 1861–1865," *Journal of American History* 70 (June 1983):69–70. The Confederate profit on these bonds was practically total, since only a small fraction of these were paid off.

84. Mathews, ed., *Provisional Government Laws*, p. 117.

85. *Journal of the Congress* 1 (May 14, 1861): 227.

86. Mathews, ed., *Public and Private Laws*, p. 177.

87. W. S. Lyles to Memminger, July 24, 1861, in *Correspondence with*, ed. Thian, pp. 222–25; see also Almawzon Huston to Memminger, June 16, 1865, ibid., p. 140.

88. *Journal of the Congress*, vol. 1, p. 186.

89. Memminger to F. S. Lyon, May 24, 1861, in *Correspondence of*, ed. Thian, pp. 91–92. An identical letter was sent to Robert M. Patton in Florence, Alabama.

90. Memminger to Trenholm, June 6, 1861, ibid., p. 95.

91. Lyon to Memminger, June 24, 1861, in *Correspondence with*, ed. Thian, pp. 153–54.

92. Memminger to Lowndes, July 3, 1861, in *Correspondence of*, ed. Thian, p. 141.

93. Memminger to James Williamson, July 3, 1861, ibid., p. 142.

94. Harllee to Memminger, July 3, 1861, "Letters Received by the Secretary of the Treasury 1861–5," Record Group 365, National Archives.

95. Memminger to Harllee, July 9, 1861, in *Correspondence of*, ed. Thian, pp. 147–48.

96. Memminger to Edward G. Palmer, July 30, 1861, ibid., p. 168.

97. Memminger to Wright, September 6, 1861, ibid., p. 185.

98. Letters from F. S. Lyon to C. J. McRae, May 13, 1861, ibid., p. 98; letter from C. T. Lowndes to Memminger, June 13, 1861, ibid., p. 133; letter from James F. White and J. W. Drake to Jefferson Davis, July 13, 1861, ibid., p. 211; letter from J. H. Dent to Memminger, July 17, 1861, ibid., p. 228; letter from L. P. Spyker to Memminger, July 21, 1861, ibid., p. 236; letter from Edward Delony to Memminger, August 30, 1861, ibid., p. 304.

99. Denegre to Memminger, June 15, 1861, ibid., p. 103. In the letter Denegre claimed that an aid program would be too expensive, that the states were the only governmental bodies with the authority to undertake such activities, and that the Confederacy should not undertake "new responsibilities."

100. Memminger to the editor, March 17, 1874, *Charleston Courier*, March 28, 1874. Cotton was paid for in early 1862 by produce loan certificates made up by the Richmond stationers, and the same could have been used six months earlier had there been any disposition to do so. Capers, *Life and Times*, p. 351; Thian, ed., *Correspondence with*, vol. 1., pp. 169–227.

101. Memminger to E. A. Nisbet, and W. B. Johnston, June 17, 1861, in *Correspondence of*, ed. Thian, p. 104.

102. Memminger to J. D. B. DeBow, August 3, 1861, ibid., pp. 169–77. The North had no equivalent problem because there were more government agents already available and no need to buy produce to relieve a blockaded economy. Secretary Salmon P. Chase did hire the Jay Cooke banking firm, which in turn employed agents in all the main towns to sell bonds. Memminger, with fewer big pools of cash to tap, needed to create such an organization much sooner.

103. Memminger to Archibald Roane (chief clerk of the produce loan),

January 21, 1862, ibid., p. 259. For a fascinating account of one federal agent's efforts to seize the Confederate cotton after the war for the Union, see Richard C. O'Connor, *Ambrose Bierce: A Biography* (London: Victor Gollenez, 1968), pp. 46–56.

104. Memminger to B. C. Pressley (assistant treasurer at Charleston), January 28, 1862, in *Correspondence of*, ed. Thian, pp. 260–61. Why no agents were appointed for Texas, with its access to neutral Mexican ports, is unknown, but Memminger evidently was unable to work with the Texas congressional delegation or Postmaster General Reagan and therefore, having no independent sources of information, felt unable to do anything. If so, he should have asked President Davis for help.

105. Memminger to Tyler, January 3, 1862, ibid., pp. 247–48. "The unfortunate temper which Congress exhibits" slowed up the agents' pay for four months.

106. Memminger to the Commissioners, October 15, 1861, ibid., pp. 213–16.

107. Richardson, comp., *A Compilation*, vol. 1, p. 123.

108. Report of July 20, 1861, in Thian, *Reports*, p. 14.

109. DeBow to Memminger, January 16, 1862, ibid., p. 48.

110. A. Roane to Memminger, November 30, 1863, ibid., p. 216. Memminger's claims about the impracticability of borrowing or purchasing the cotton crop have been uncritically accepted by later authors such as Schwab, *The Confederate States*, p. 234, and Lester, *Confederate Finance*, p. 91.

111. Denegre to Memminger, October 2, 1861, in *Correspondence with*, ed. Thian, p. 350.

112. Thian, *Reports*, pp. 65–66.

113. Act of April 21, 1862 in *Public and Private Laws 1862–4*, ed. Mathews, p. 47.

114. Archibald Roane to Memminger, November 30, 1863, in Thian, *Reports*, p. 217.

115. Trenholm to R. M. T. Hunter, Report of November 10, 1864, ibid., p. 386. The government's nominal cotton holdings were therefore 850,000 bales.

116. Thian, ed., *Correspondence with*, p. 134; C. T. Lowndes to Memminger, June 13, 1861, ibid., p. 204; William G. Smedes to Jefferson Davis, July 10, 1861, ibid., pp. 203–5; James F. White and J.W.W. Drake to President Davis, July 13, 1861, ibid., p. 211.

117. Ibid., p. 212.

118. 1st Cong., 1st sess., "An Act making appropriations to carry into effect 'an Act authorizing the exchange of bonds for articles in kind. . . '" April 21, 1862, in *Public and Private Laws 1862–4*, ed. Mathews, p. 50; see also Thian, ed., *Correspondence of*, pp. 360–63.

119. Memminger to S. R. Mallory (secretary of the navy), October 9, 1862, in *Correspondence of*, ed. Thian, p. 362.

120. Roane to Memminger, November 30, 1863, in Thian, *Reports*, p. 217.

121. Schwab, *The Confederate States*, pp. 312–13; see also Eugene Lerner, *Money, Prices and Wages in the Confederacy 1861–5* (Chicago: Privately mimeo-

graphed by the author, 1954), pp. 95–125, Appendix 2:"Wholesale Prices in Four Southern Cities: Augusta, Wilmington, Fayetteville and Richmond."

122. Lerner, *Money Prices*, p. 152. The price was 18 cents a pound with bagging, formerly bought in Kentucky, in short supply.

123. "Regulations as to the Purchase of Produce . . .," in *Correspondence of*, ed. Thian, pp. 297–99. For government efforts to procure rope and bagging for government cotton, see also Memminger to Henry Savage (Depository, Wilmington, N.C.), January 16, 1864, ibid., p. 570. For a letter of Belgian Consul Laurent de Give dated November 15, 1862, reporting the low quality of cotton generally, see *Journal of Southern History* 3 (November 1927):484–89.

124. Lebergott, "Why the South Lost," pp. 74–75. Lebergott cites a refusal to sell cotton for bonds in 1861; no offer to that effect was made by the Confederate regime until 1862.

125. Frank L. Owsley, *King Cotton Diplomacy: Foreign Relations of the Confederate States of America* (Chicago: University of Chicago Press, 1931), pp. 19–20, 27–32; see also Lester, *Confederate Finance*, p. 13.

126. Varina Howell Davis, *Jefferson Davis: A Memoir by His Wife*, 2 vols. (New York: Bellford, 1890), vol. 2, pp. 161–64.

127. Hendrick, *A Statesman of the Lost Cause*, p. 210. Hendrick copies Owsley's claims on this score; Owsley, *King Cotton*, pp. 31–33.

128. Slidell to R. M. T. Hunter, February 11, 1862, in *A Compilation*, comp. Richardson, vol. 2, p. 181.

129. Lerner, *Money*, pp. 118–19.

130. Owsley, *King Cotton*, p. 43.

131. Pierce Butler, *The Life of J. P. Benjamin* (Philadelphia: G. W. Jacobs, 1907), p. 234.

132. Benjamin to Memminger, December 2, 1861, *War of the Rebellion: Armies*, ser. 4, vol. 1, p. 774. Benjamin asked Memminger to place cotton in the hands of a War Department agent under the provisions of the Act of November 26, 1861.

133. Ibid., pp. 836–37; Thomas O. Moore (governor of Louisiana) to Benjamin, January 9, 1862, ibid., ser. 4, vol. 1, p. 633; vol. 2, p. 57.

134. Memminger to Harllee, July 3, 1861, in *Correspondence of*, ed. Thian, p. 148. The grounds on which this view rested were not explained.

135. William T. Browne, assistant secretary of state, to James M. Mason, October 29, 1861, in *A Compilation*, comp. Richardson, vol. 2, pp. 108–9; see also Benjamin to B. G. Joseph R. Anderson (Tredegar Works owner), October 8, 21, November 15, 1861, in *War of the Rebellion: Armies*, ser. 4, vol. 1, pp. 768–70.

136. Memminger to Tucker, November 5, 1861, *Christopher Gustavus Memminger Papers*, MSS Department, University of North Carolina, Chapel Hill; see also Edwin B. Coddington, "The Activities and Attitudes of a Confederate Businessman: Gazaway B. Lamar," *Journal of Southern History* 9 (February 1943): 22.

137. John Fraser and Company to Secretary of War Benjamin, September

30, 1861, *War of the Rebellion: Armies,* ser. 4, vol. 1, p. 633. Benjamin was attorney general in September 1861 and became secretary of state in February 1862.

138. John Fraser and Company to Memminger, April 5, 1862, in *Correspondence with,* ed. Thian, pp. 507–8.

139. Memminger to John Fraser and Company, April 9, 1862, in *Correspondence of,* ed. Thian, pp. 282–83.

140. Memminger to Pickens, April 15, 1862, ibid., pp. 287–88.

141. C. T. Lowndes to Memminger, July 15, 1861, in *Correspondence with,* ed. Thian, p. 214; also, *DeBow's Review,* November 1861, p. 462.

142. *Journal of the Congress* vol. 1, pp. 250–51, May 20, 1861; see also Mathews, ed., *Public and Private Laws,* 2d sess., pp. 152–53. New England's mills took one million bales a year.

143. Benjamin to Slidell, April 8, 1862, in *A Compilation,* comp. Richardson, vol. 2, pp. 221–22. Cotton acquisition was a goal of the Union army and more particularly the navy; cotton captured within five miles of a waterway would be sold for prize money. See also Ludwell Johnson, *Red River Campaign: Politics and Cotton in the Civil War* (Baltimore: Johns Hopkins University Press, 1958), pp. 101–4.

144. *Charleston Mercury* (cited in the New York *Herald* of January 12, 1863).

145. W. F. Colcock to General Thomas Jordan (no date), in *War of the Rebellion: Armies,* ser. 4, vol. 2, p. 562. The resistance to cotton shipments seems to have faded after July 1, 1862, judging by the rapid growth per ship of the number of bales taken.

146. Memminger to Governor Pickens, April 15, 1862, in *Correspondence of,* ed. Thian, p. 288, see note 147 for Confederate knowledge of British cotton stocks; see also the *Richmond Examiner,* February 26, 1862.

147. Yancy and Rouse to Robert Toombs, secretary of state, May 10, 1861, in *A Compilation,* comp. Richardson, vol. 2, p. 20.

148. Yancy to Hunter, December 31, 1861, ibid., p. 136.

149. Mason to Hunter, March 11, 1862, ibid., pp. 197–99.

150. Senator Thomas Semmes of Louisiana came to a similar conclusion. Richmond *Enquirer,* March 13, 1862.

151. Memminger to Jefferson Davis, September 25, 1877, in *Jefferson Davis, Constitutionalist,* ed. Dunbar Rowland (Jackson: Mississippi Department of Archives and History, 1923), vol. 3, pp. 25–27; see also Capers, *Life and Times,* pp. 348–57; Schwab, *The Confederate States,* pp. 233–34. The *London Times,* April 15, 1861, reported a scheme whereby the Lairds, the CSA shipbuilders, and A. M. Weir, a London shipowner, were to raise half the money needed for a direct Charleston-Liverpool shipping line.

152. Memminger to Davis, September 27, 1878, in Capers, *Life and Times,* p. 288.

153. Trenholm to General Beauregard, September 18, 1878, ibid., pp. 302–3. William Trenholm later served as United States comptroller of the currency (1885–89).

154. Trenholm to Memminger, ibid., pp. 301–2. Toombs apparently mixed up the two propositions. Mallory later reversed himself with an iron-clad warship program.

155. Toombs to the Commissioners, March 16, 1861, in *A Compilation,* comp. Richardson, vol. 2, p. 8.

156. *Journal of the Congress* 1 (August 28, 1861):432; (February 12, 1862):807.

157. Stanley Lebergott, "Through the Blockade: The Profitability and Extent of Cotton Smuggling, 1861–1865," *Journal of Economic History* 41 (December 1981):867–88. Lebergott suggests that blockade-running was not as profitable as was believed at the time, and that those who made one successful voyage were content to quit while they were ahead.

158. Benjamin to Forstall, January 17, 1862, *War of the Rebellion: Armies,* ser. 4, vol. 1, pp. 845–46; D. T. Bisbie to Benjamin, January 16, 1862, ibid., pp. 843–45.

159. Memminger to J. D. B. DeBow, February 17, 1862, in *Correspondence of,* ed. Thian, p. 264.

160. Memminger to Messrs. John Fraser and Company, November 21, 1861, ibid., pp. 232–33.

161. *War of the Rebellion: Navies,* ser. 2, vol. 2, pp. 127–33; Thian, ed., *Reports,* pp. 85–87.

162. *Journal of the Congress* 1 (November 24, 1861):479, 484.

163. Benjamin to Memminger, December 2, 1861, *War of the Rebellion: Armies,* ser. 4, vol. 1, p. 774.

164. G. H. Gidding to Benjamin, January 11, 1862, ibid., pp. 840–41; see also de Give to the Belgian Foreign Minister, November 15, 1862 (note 123). De Give reports that British speculators were having no trouble getting cotton out of Texas via Matemoros, when Memminger was declaring that shipments were impossible.

165. Oliver to Memminger, February 8, 1862, in *Correspondence with,* ed. Thian, pp. 484–86.

166. Memminger to Oliver, February 17, 1862, in *Correspondence of,* ed. Thian, p. 264.

167. John Fraser and Company to Memminger, March 24, 1862, in *Correspondence with,* ed. Thian, p. 500.

168. Memminger to George Trenholm, March 7, 1862, in *Correspondence of,* ed. Thian, p. 269.

169. Memminger to John Fraser and Company, March 24, 1862, ibid., pp. 272–73.

170. John Fraser and Company to Memminger, March 29, 1862 (in answer to a telegram to them of March 28), in *Correspondence with,* ed. Thian, p. 506.

171. Memminger to DeBow, April 5, 1862, in *Correspondence of,* ed. Thian, pp. 280–81.

172. Memminger to Mallory, April 16, 1862, ibid., p. 288; see also Edward Elmore, treasurer, CSA, to John Boston, CSA Depository at Savannah, February 26, 1862 (Confederate Museum, Richmond, Va.). Elmore at Memminger's

behest, queried Boston for buying £556.80 too much foreign exchange, when Memminger should have been delighted to get the extra funds.

173. Thian, *Reports*, pp. 85–87.

174. Memminger to F. W. Pickens (governor of South Carolina), April 15, 1862, in *Correspondence of*, ed. Thian, p. 287; *War of the Rebellion: Armies*, ser. 4, vol. 1, pp. 836–37.

175. Slidell to Benjamin, April 4, 1863, John T. Pickett Papers, vol. 2, no. 59, Washington, D.C.: MS Div., Library of Congress.

176. R. Sales to Benjamin, January 2, 1862, *War of the Rebellion: Armies*, ser. 4, vol. 1, p. 829.

177. Slidell to Benjamin, June 12, 1863, Pickett Papers, vol. 2, no. 37.

178. McRae to Memminger, October 7, 1863, *War of the Rebellion: Armies*, ser. 4, vol. 2, pp. 983ff.

179. Seddon to McRae, September 26, 1863, ibid., pp. 824–27.

180. Mathews, ed., *Public and Private Laws*, 1st Cong., 4th sess., ch. 24, p. 81.

181. Ibid., ch. 23, p. 79.

182. *War of the Rebellion: Armies*, ser. 4, vol. 3, p. 554.

183. Ibid., p. 954.

184. Benjamin to Memminger, Seddon and Mallory, September 15, 1863, ibid., ser. 2, vol. 3, pp. 897–99.

185. Bayne to Seddon, May 2, 1864, ibid., ser. 4, vol. 3, p. 370.

186. Richardson, comp., *A Compilation*, vol. 1, pp. 466–69, veto June 10, 1864.

187. McRae to Seddon, July 4, 1864, *War of the Rebellion: Armies*, ser. 4, vol. 3, p. 525; see also James D. Bulloch, *The Secret Service of the Confederate States in Europe*, 2 vols. (New York: J. Putnam Sons, 1884), vol. 2, pp. 237ff.

188. *War of the Rebellion: Armies*, ser. 4, vol. 3, pp. 529–30.

189. Bulloch to Mallory, August 25, 1864, *War of the Rebellion: Navies*, ser. 2, vol. 2, p. 711. The funds derived from the sale of the iron-clads were used for the blockade-runners.

190. Bayne to Trenholm, November 1, 1864, *The Trenholm Papers*, Portfolio 1, Library of Congress.

191. *War of the Rebellion: Armies*, ser, 4, vol. 3, p. 930.

192. *The Index*, December 24, 1863, p. 552 (written by Henry Hotze).

CHAPTER THREE

Debt Management Policies

Without a treasury yet in being or any funds to deposit in it, the congressmen assembled in Montgomery lacked the means to pay even their own expenses. As a temporary makeshift, the convention, on February 9, 1861, accepted the offer of a $500,000 treasury note loan from Alabama. Although otherwise well-informed Confederate historians continue to confuse the promise with the fact,[1] neither the records of Alabama nor of the Confederacy show any indication that this loan was ever made. Nor was any help forthcoming after June 1, 1861 from the Post Office, for when the Confederates took it over, that body was spending four times its revenues. Fortunately, some cash was obtained when the Confederates took charge of mints and customs houses.[2]

On taking office on February 21, 1861 Secretary Memminger thus faced a discouraging prospect. Although nominally a department chief, he was without a staff or offices. To be sure, former Treasury Department personnel from Washington had arrived, bringing with them books and forms thereby assuring an invaluable continuity of personnel and bureaucratic routine. Moreover, providentially, all customs house and mint employees had stayed at their posts. Memminger was therefore free to organize his office with a minimum of interviews and patronage problems.

As a first step, the secretary hired as his chief clerk Henry D. Capers, a lawyer and a fellow South Carolinian, who possessed at least some competence in rudimentary housekeeping. On February 22, Capers, on behalf of the Treasury Department, moved into a dirty, unfurnished office building. He swept and mopped the floor and filled the room with desks, chairs, a counter, stationery, inks, and even mats. On Monday, February 25, the Department of the Treasury opened for business.

The department's first customer was a Captain Deas from DeKalb County, Georgia. As neither Capers nor the secretary had enough cash to pay Deas's requisition, they left him waiting and went to the Central Bank of Alabama, where the secretary floated a loan on his personal credit.[3] It was an act of improvisation that set the tone for treasury operations during the balance of the Confederacy's existence.

While the secretary was thus preoccupied, the Congress passed an

"Act to raise money for the support of the Government and to provide for the defense of the Confederate States of America." This law authorized the President to borrow up to $15 million to fund the appropriations made by Congress (Appendix B).[4]

The mere passage of authorizing legislation did not mean money in hand for the treasury. The solicitation of loan subscriptions required six to eight weeks, and meanwhile the secretary's bank account could not support the government. Congress, therefore, passed the Act of March 9, 1861, authorizing the issue of up to $1 million of one-year 3.65 percent treasury notes (Appendix C).[5]

With the advent of war, the secretary's task assumed larger dimensions and created new realities. He had just spent seven weeks recruiting a staff, and it was clear that a war could multiply his work by a substantial factor. A more realistic man would have foreseen a contest of uncertain duration involving unknown but substantial expense. Past experience (chapter 1) suggested that until the internal revenue machinery could be activated, the initial phase of the war would need to be financed largely by borrowing. Thus treasury notes and bonds would be the government's primary source of revenue for most of 1861.

Considerations Jointly Affecting Management of the Funded Debt and the Confederate Currency

Before Memminger's management of the funded debt can be analyzed in this chapter and of the currency in the next, his solutions to two basic problems should be examined. He first had to get government securities printed; and once that mechanical hurdle was overcome, he had to procure specie to underpin his bonds.

The Printing Problem

One of the constraints facing the secretary was the limited number and productive capacity of Southern security printing establishments. If he were to procure the necessary notes and bonds, he had to augment fundamental resources essential to their effective performance, that is, skilled workers, paper, inks, steel plates, lithograph stones, and presses. It would require a book in itself to recount the secretary's long and harried experiences with Confederate printers, for, as will be shown, he never adopted a consistent program for getting the printers to produce what was needed on time.

In the crucial initial phase that lasted until December 1862, the secretary showed great reluctance to intervene more than tangentially in the printers' businesses. This reflected Memminger's experience as a banker. In peacetime, bankers' dealings with printers were limited to the placement and payment of orders. Had the South possessed the printing establishments located in the North, that approach might have been feasible. But local printers had such meager resources that the secretary had to lend them money, recruit their workers, and procure supplies from abroad. In mid-1862, Memminger briefly toyed with the idea of establishing a government printing office but settled for closer supervision of the contractors. The result was a slow but steady elimination of the inefficient firms, until by 1865 only two printers were left.

The Government and the Printers

Following the passage of the Acts of February 28 and March 9, 1861, the Confederate treasury placed orders for registered bonds and treasury notes with bank-note firms in New York. In order to put such confidential business beyond the reach of the Union, contracts were also signed for the coupon bonds authorized on February 28, 1861, to be printed in New Orleans by the branch of the American Bank Note Company (ABNCo) and by John Douglas. But even after dividing the order, these local contractors fell seriously behind schedule.[6]

In an effort to solve the printing problem, Secretary Memminger then solicited the assistance of the American Bank Note Company's main office in New York, asking it to furnish men and material for a Confederate security printing firm. But why did ABNCo cooperate with the proposal? One reason may be that the 90 percent share of the Southern bank-note market held in 1861 by "The Association"[7] gave that firm a powerful incentive to hedge its bets. If ABNCo did not accommodate the South, then the business would go by default to the National Bank Note Company of New York, which had already printed some Confederate treasury notes and was eagerly waiting in the wings.

Another reason for ABNCo's continued dubious relationship with the South was that, like other firms in New York, its management contained rebel sympathizers. Among these was probably its president, Tracy Edson, who had formerly been resident head of the New Orleans branch. His resignation in January 1863 was the price the company paid for a continuation of its contract to print federal currency.

In its centennial book published in 1958, the company's historian argued that because ABNCo assumed that the Union would be peaceably dissolved, the Confederacy was a "legitimate source" from which orders might be routinely accepted. But, after the president's blockade proclamation, Edson instructed the New Orleans resident manager, Samuel Schmidt, not to aid the rebels. Yet, categorical as this language might now appear, Schmidt did not close his office. Instead, he changed the branch office name to "Southern Bank Note Company," and about a year later, on July 4, 1862, once again resumed contact with his northern partners.[8]

Although the company's official account cannot be faulted for factual errors, it fails to include the whole truth. For example, after the affair at Fort Sumter, the company completed and shipped to Montgomery books of registered bonds.[9] Meanwhile, back at the New Orleans branch, Schmidt signed two contracts with the Confederate treasury (on May 13 and May 24, 1861), promising to deliver one plate of interest-bearing notes on June 27, and three plates of notes of non-interest-bearing notes in July. Delivery on the first plate was delayed two months, two plates were more than five months late, and one never was completed.[10]

In spite of the assurances of James D. Denegre, president of the Citizen's Bank, the alarmed Confederate treasury sent William Reyburn to New Orleans in July 1861. He promptly reported that although he had received many promises, he personally put little faith in any of them. Reyburn proposed, therefore, that some of Schmidt's work be given to another printer. When the delays continued, the secretary ordered Schmidt's shop sequestered as the property of an alien enemy.[11]

Why all the delays? In December 1861, Memminger learned from John Douglas, a competitor of Schmidt's, what ABNCo admitted in its centennial history: Schmidt was neglecting his Confederate work in order to fill orders for the New Orleans banks, including Denegre's.[12] Confronted with Schmidt's willful neglect, Secretary Memminger selected Thomas A. Ball, a stockbroker, to set up a new bank-note engraving firm. Armed with the proceeds of a $5,000 treasury warrant, Ball went to New York,[13] where he was introduced by an unnamed ABNCo officer to an Irishman named Edward Keatinge. Ball and Keatinge formed a partnership with William Leggett (another ABNCo employee), but because a vigilance committee had intercepted their materials in Louisville, Kentucky, the opening of the firm was delayed until October 1861.[14]

Failing to obtain effective assistance from ABNCo, the treasury took hasty inventory of the distressingly small roster of available printers. Although Douglas had competently handled other tasks assigned to him, he refused to leave New Orleans to become head of a government engraving plant in Richmond. Jules Manouvrier, a long-time New Orleans lithographer, had negligently bound up his notes only in brown wrapping paper before sending them to Richmond. When the packages were broken into in Petersburg, his contract was cancelled because of security violations on September 13, 1861.[15]

Against the backdrop of these disappointments, the treasury had no option but to hire the Richmond lithographic firm of Hoyer and Ludwig. Given the problems involved, Ludwig produced the notes of the Act of May 16, 1861 in a surprisingly short time. But, because he did not turn his attention to the notes of the Act of August 19, 1861 until November, the treasury was deprived of more than $78 million of its authorized resources.

Other problems arose. To speed the effort to meet the treasury's needs, Ludwig printed a disproportionate number of $100 and $50 bills. In the May 16 issue, such notes constituted 58 percent of the $17 million emitted, compared with the 16 percent they represented in the U.S. 1974 currency of $5 and over. This excess of large-denomination notes led dealers to charge 5 percent commissions for making change.[16]

The Banks Come to the Rescue

The shortage of $5 and $10 bills, which rendered the government unable to pay its drafts, was quite apparent to Confederate bankers. Accordingly, on August 31, 1861, South Carolina and Georgia banks offered to lend their low-denomination notes to the Confederacy at 5 percent interest, repayable in treasury notes. Although Memminger declined this offer on the advice of the Finance Committee, he fell so far behind meeting his requisitions that on October 20, 1861, he did borrow $10 million in $5, $10 and $20 bills.[17]

To speed note production, the treasury asked the War Department to detail lithographers serving in the army for duty with printing establishments. In addition, the secretary hired other contractors to scour the South for bank-note paper, inks, and presses,[18] while the government installed agents in each shop to supervise security arrangements, break wildcat strikes, reject shoddy work, and thwart attempts at bill-padding.[19] Closer supervision also prevented the printers from inflating their bills with superfluous plate charges[20] by making several designs of the same denomination. Finally, disillusioned with the contracting system, the treasury in early 1862 sent an agent, Major Benjamin F. Ficklin (erstwhile quartermaster of Virginia), to England with orders to procure materials and skilled workers for a government establishment. Meanwhile, the treasury hired other contractors in the hope that competition might improve printer efficiency.[21]

Government Supervision 1862–63

The spring of 1862 proved momentous for the printing establishments. The capture of New Orleans in April resulted in the loss of the local printers, because the treasury, ignorant of the gloomy warnings coming into the War Department, had postponed until too late their removal to less vulnerable points.[22] At the same time, the government relocated the Richmond printing establishments in a supposedly safer site at Columbia, South Carolina.

The removal to Columbia and the arrival of the Scottish lithographers whom Major Ficklin had hired in London provided the government alternative possibilities for action.[23] Because the Scots' contracts stipulated that they should work only for the treasury, Secretary Memminger had the opportunity to gather all the workers and government-owned materials into a Southern Bureau of Engraving and Printing, thereby eliminating the contractors. In advocating an exclusively government-run operation, Joseph D. Pope, the chief clerk of the Columbia Treasury Note Bureau, warned the secretary that "I do not think that we will mend the matter a great deal by putting three or four contractors in one house and calling them a Government establishment. They would quarrel still, and perhaps worse than ever. . . . To counteract all of this, I would . . . propose that a real Government establishment be inaugurated (for long after a peace these notes will have to be used), and to this end . . . material [be imported] in sufficient quantities to put the Government beyond the control of contractors. . . ."[24]

Why did the secretary reject Pope's views? First, as a hard-money Jacksonian Democrat, Memminger abhorred a peacetime irredeemable government currency and planned to fund all the notes into bonds after the war. The fact that the treasury would be saddled with heavy interest expenses and the public deprived of the benefits of a uniform national currency seemed to carry little weight with him. A government printing office would simply encourage the continued use of the treasury notes; therefore it had to be avoided.

Even more important was his concern for the "rights" of the printers; Memminger could not "with any propriety" break up any printer's shop "even if the public should seem to gain thereby."[25] In other words, the printers' proprietary interest took precedence over public welfare. Yet the printers' contracts could have been lawfully terminated on thirty days' notice, and the government could have repossessed its property that had been lent to the printers and given it to someone else. One is once again confronted by the question of whether Memminger's inaction was a function of misplaced legal principle or only a reluctance to act.

In any case, Memminger instead appointed Joseph D. Pope, an old South Carolina friend and former war tax collector, as chief clerk of the Columbia Treasury Note Bureau and armed him with full powers. Pope spent his entire tenure (April 1862 to April 1863) trying to get the contractors under control.[26] When not preoccupied with printing and shipping millions of bonds and notes, he was busy with short-circuiting the contractors' plots, settling street brawls, quashing false treason charges before the South Carolina Council, summoning troops to force drunken strikers back to work, thwarting an arson attempt, and writing letters to the contractors (especially Colonel Blanton Duncan) ordering them to stop stealing each others' workers, bank-note paper, ice, and ink.[27]

Yet, in spite of the contractors' united opposition to reform, progress was made. Starting in the fall of 1862, the Charleston firm of Evans and Cogswell became a contractor, and it gradually superseded every other firm but Keatinge's, which handled the engraving work.[28] At about the same time, using the talents available to him in Keatinge and George Dunn, a Scots lithographer, Pope consolidated currency designs so that starting with the issue dated "December 2, 1862," each denomination had only one design.[29] Moreover, the once-crude notes were now printed from intaglio steel or copper plates, or vastly improved lithographic stones.

But once again the treasury was too late; the multiplicity of note types and their crude workmanship paved the way for a flood of counterfeits from Tennessee that created a panic in the fall of 1862.[30] The pandemonium was augmented when the secretary recalled all the Hoyer and Ludwig notes, thereby discrediting anything with their imprint. As a result, everyone refused such notes, and $22 million had to be redeemed with interest-bearing 7.30 percent treasury notes or call (payable on demand) certificates at 6 percent. But $130 million of such notes remained in circulation, and the distrust felt for them insidiously spread to the government's other issues.

The secretary once again exacerbated the problem by his efforts to manage the Columbia Bureau's operations down to the smallest detail. He ordered the curtailment of production even though the army's pay was then in arrears, lamely explaining this mistaken order on the grounds that he wanted to avoid creating a note reserve that would increase printing expense.[31]

The whole system collapsed when the Act of February 17, 1864 required a mass funding operation coupled with a currency exchange. Because the printers simply could not produce the treasury notes and bonds needed for exchange purposes and the government's expenses, by 1865 the treasury was short $300 million in notes to pay its creditors.[32]

Analysis of Memminger's Approach

In retrospect, it would appear that the secretary's management of the printers involved a strange amalgam of laxity and severity. On the one hand, he looked on complacently while the printers became involved in counterfeiting schemes and the proliferation of competitive currencies.[33] On the other hand, the secretary's penny-pinching on the prices paid for work forced printers to operate on very narrow margins after early 1863. This encouraged them to find every possible means of cutting corners and also to take on more profitable side business with states, banks, and scrip issuers to the detriment of the government's work. By February 1865, petty haggling over printing bills had so alienated Keatinge that he abandoned his equipment in Columbia, South Carolina, leaving it for the federal forces to capture.[34] Had the secretary promptly posted a clerk in New Orleans, he could have forced Schmidt, Manouvrier, and Douglas to merge their shops, share their manpower and equipment, meet their schedules, and stop their outside business. Such an agent could also have packed Manouvrier's notes, thereby preventing the Petersburg theft. The Confederates never found the golden mean.

But even superlative management could not have extended the printers' maximum production capacity much beyond $60 million in notes and $20 million in bonds per month. That meant that the secretary had to design his programs around this limitation while insisting on effective taxation and treasury note funding. Yet by letting three years pass without any source of revenue but treasury notes, the secretary created an inflation that forced government expenditures above the level at which the printing presses could meet the demand. The secretary's failure to attack this simple management and mechanical problem that lay entirely within his power of correction materially contributed to Confederate defeat.

The Fruits of Memminger's Neglect

Contrary to the claim advanced by Richard Beringer et al. that "economic shortcomings did not play a major role in Confederate defeat,"[35] it can be demonstrated that the Confederacy's overthrow was materially assisted by Memminger's coddling of the printers and his tendency to pay off claimants based on their proximity to his office. A prime example of this tendency can be found in the Confederate West, where, starting in 1861, the Trans-Mississippi section of the country was lumped into one military department to include the territory between the Mississippi River and the Appalachians. As a distant part of this immense command, such cash and supplies as came from Richmond seldom crossed the river. Thus, during the mobilization period in 1861, the Trans-Mississippi area was practically forgotten; the local state and Confederate authorities, aided by private citizens, had to promise payment in Confederate bonds in order to procure arms, food, and clothing. By May 1862, the Quartermaster Bureau west of the river had only received $4 million; because no records were kept, it was impossible to discover to whom these funds were disbursed. In spite of efforts made by the officers sent to Richmond to bring the situation to the treasury's and War Department's attention,[36] the troops' pay was six to nine months in arrears and, by mid-1863, arrearages reached an average of a year. In the absence of cash, subsistence had to be procured by disingenuous appeals to the kind-hearted or by thefts and seizures. Such procedures demoralized both the civil and the military populations.

On May 28, 1862, General P. G. T. Beauregard appointed General Thomas C. Hindman as commander of the Trans-Mississippi. But with the exception of some old weapons, the new commander was furnished with nothing to defend the region. Stopping off at Memphis just before it fell, Hindman providently extorted a forced loan of $1 million from western Tennessee banks to obtain funds. But on his arrival in Arkansas he found no army, no supplies, no arms, a panic-stricken, mutinous Arkansas state government, and a Confederate currency which, for lack of taxes, was being refused. He did his best to make the Trans-Mississippi self-sufficient by proclaiming martial law and undertaking many key supply actions. He could have done a lot more had the treasury furnished him with funds, so he reported. But the funds needed were not forthcoming, and, on the evidence now available, Hindman's defeat at Prairie Grove (December 3–6, 1862) seems directly attributable to a dearth of cash with which to arm, clothe, and pay his men, half of whom, as a result, had deserted or had to be left behind.[37] Thus by the late winter of 1862–63 when General Grant was laying the foundations for his Vicksburg campaign, the Trans-Mississippi forces had melted away to a nominal twenty-five thousand present out of a hundred thousand on the rolls, and the new commander, E. Kirby Smith, was left with no field force worthy of the name.

Grant promptly exploited that lamentable weakness by marching down the right bank of the Mississippi, crossing the river at Grand Gulf, and attacking Vicksburg from behind. At that critical juncture, General Smith was unable to assemble a mere four-thousand-man force to relieve the beleaguered defenders of Port Hudson; nor could he even muster the manpower to drive a herd of cattle across the Mississippi to the hungry Vicksburg garrison. Thus on July 6, 1863, the Confederacy was cut in half.[38]

Had Secretary Memminger had more vigor and paid more attention to detail, he would have recognized these difficulties and sought to solve them. Given the uncertain communications lines of the time, the treasury should have established an assistant treasurer's office west of the Mississippi River (as it eventually did late in 1864), furnished that office with a staff, and, at the same time, removed the New Orleans printing offices to some safe place such as Shreveport. Yet the secretary took no action. As he wrote after Vicksburg: "It is true that the loss of the Mississippi River is a very serious injury to our cause; but . . . all evils have some counter-poise. The one in this case is, that all the old currency in circulation on the other side of the Mississippi is cut off from affecting this side. Scarcely any of the new currency [of $200 million issued] reached that side, and if we were rid of the old on this side we could get along for another year."[39] Memminger failed to acknowledge—or perhaps even to realize—that the loss of Vicksburg, Port Hudson, and the Mississippi Valley were in part attributable to his failure to remit funds west of the Mississippi River.

But even though aware of the disaster caused by the "loss of the Mississippi River," Memminger continued to neglect the Trans-Mississippi Department. From July 1863 to April 1864 only $27 million in notes and $18 million in bonds reached that area. By December 1864, only $20 million in new currency and $27 million in new securities had arrived there. Unpaid debts and requisitions totaled a disproportionately high $82 million out of $313 million owed in early 1865.[40] Nor, as will be discussed in chapter 4, was this the only contribution of the treasury to the weakening of the Confederate defenses in the Mississippi Valley. From the point of view of the treasury, the Trans-Mississippi seems to have been out of sight and out of mind.

Unfortunately, this was not the only occasion on which the secretary's policies promoted the disintegration of the army; his mismanagement also effected a decline in public morale. As Robert G. H. Kean, chief clerk of the War Department, observed, the public was discontented "for want of payment of dues and the worthlessness of it when obtained."[41] Moreover, Memminger's failure to produce and distribute funds in a timely manner also left the Confederate army east of the Mississippi unpaid, without food, clothing, or shelter. Admittedly, given the primitive transportation facilities of the era, the movement of funds from one place to another involved serious difficulties. Yet, the delay in paying the soldiers, and in increasing their pay in proportion to the inflation, left no surplus for remittances home. That in turn occasioned pathetic appeals to the soldiers by their families. Because Confederate propaganda emphasized that the troops were fighting to defend their homes, such a state of affairs (combined with the absence of any system of leave) provided an almost unanswerable justification for desertion. At the same time, funds shortages and the inflation forced the use of impressment and dried up supplies, making a bad situation worse.[42]

Indeed, the shortage of funds was made disastrously more acute by the hyperinflation created by other treasury blunders and proved a pervasive problem for the entire Confederate establishment. While there were occasional delays in getting through congressional appropriations, most of the problem lay in the Treasury Department. Colonel Josiah Gorgas in the Ordnance Bureau was crippled for lack of funds.[43] The Engineer Bureau persistently complained about the absence of funds and, during the crucial summer of 1864, shortages became acute for the entire army. By December 1864 Secretary of War James Seddon complained to Secretary Trenholm, noting that the situation had never been good, but now the lack of funds was producing desertion and the stoppage of supplies, transport, and the department's work in general.[44]

State efforts to furnish troops from their territory with essentials needed for their health or comfort (items not furnished by the bankrupt Confederate army) as well as to aid soldiers' families forced states to issue notes and have bonds printed by the same firms that worked for the Confederacy. Thus the same printing capacity that could and should have been used to prevent the problems the states sought to alleviate was diverted to state and local use. Printers were induced to accept the business by its greater profitability compared to the stinginess of Secretary Memminger and his dictated contracts.[45]

The Need to Find a Solid Foundation for the Confederate Debt

The foundation of any government's borrowing program rests ultimately on its treasury's fiscal revenues. But even the most rigorous system of taxation would not permit the Confederacy to dispense with loans. In view of the absence of a public debt and the initial public confidence in victory, the secretary's first task should have been to concentrate on the procurement of funds to service the public debt.

In the nineteenth century, the usual mode of paying interest was in specie, a medium of payment that assured that bond prices would never sink below the estimated number of future payments less the current discount rate. Bond values could also be sustained by payments made in foreign exchange or commodities, both subject to fluctuations in value.[46] Payments in treasury notes would be helpful only if the interest was paid at their specie value. If note prices fell in terms of coin (almost a certainty under wartime conditions), interest payments in notes at par would crimp bond sales because no note-holder would want to buy bonds payable only in increasingly worth-less treasury notes.

As events evolved, the Confederacy initially opted for a program of coin payments. But the Confederacy defaulted on its coin payments and after July 1862, made payments in notes. Efforts to find an alternate basis of support in the form of bonds payable in cotton failed, as did subsequent efforts (the Act of February 17, 1864) to make bond coupons the equivalent of specie.

The First Approach: A Specie Foundation

At the time the Congress assembled in Montgomery, all but a few banks in Alabama and all those in Louisiana had suspended specie payments. This meant that those having payments to make to the government would no longer tender coins, and thus the government could not maintain coin payments from current revenues. Nevertheless, when Secretary Memminger took control of the federal government's assets, he did acquire a supply of coin (table 9) amounting to approximately $1.6 million. Because he made no arrangements with the banks for bridge financing to conserve that precious resource, it was dissipated in the spring of 1861 to meet current expenses.[47] Yet it was imperative for the government to mobilize all specie available from existing stocks. Secretary Memminger had a chance to pursue that objective when he served public notice on March 16 of his intention to request bids for $5 million in February 28, 1861 Act bonds. Subscribers were required to pay 5 percent down and the balance by May 1—all in specie. To ensure that the public had the maximum inducement to subscribe, the secretary persuaded prominent citizens to serve as commissioners for the loan.[48]

Although that appeal produced downpayments for $8 million of the bonds, it proved easier to subscribe than to pay the balance due. The suspended banks would not part with their coin, and coin in

Table 9. Confederate Specie Revenues*

1. a. Confiscation of U.S. cash assets	$ 200,000
b. Confiscation of the mints	500,000
c. Federal customs duties	700,000
d. Post office revenues	300,000
	$ 1,600,000
2. Coin drawn from the banks under the Act of February 28, 1861	ca. $ 1,630,000[†]
3. New Orleans coin loan	$ 1,000,000
4. Seized from the Citizens Bank of Louisiana (May 1862)	$ 500,000
5. Seized from the Bank of Louisiana (October 1862)	$ 2,521,000
6. Seized May 10, 1864	
a. From Louisiana State Bank	$ 630,000
b. From Merchants Bank	110,000
c. From the Mechanics and Traders Bank	251,000
d. From the Crescent Bank	162,000
e. From the Canal Bank	500,000
7. Miscellaneous gold coin loans	240,000
8. Richmond City gold coin loan (March 1865)	300,000
Total	$ 8,954,000[‡]
Total specie in the Confederate banks, 1861	$26,000,000
Total gold coin in circulation	18,500,000
Subsidiary silver coin	18,000,000
	$62,500,000

Sources: Thian, ed., *Reports* and *Correspondence with, 1861–65.*
* Percentage of specie used by the Confederate government: 14 percent.
† Includes about $1 million used to purchase foreign exchange.
‡ The surplus of acquisition over expenditure is represented by the balance of the Virginia bank gold finally returned to the banks after its recovery from the Confederate government.

private hands was scattered in small hoards. That put the secretary in a quandary. If he accepted payment in suspended banks' notes at par he risked a loss from depreciation, so he decided provisionally to take specie-paying notes at par and other notes below par, which explains the "premiums paid" in the secretary's financial reports.[49]

In the end, the secretary settled on another plan. His scheme called for the banks that had suspended to redeem at par in coin any of their notes used in payment for the bonds. Because that amounted, in effect, to a partial resumption of specie payments, the banks balked. They were reluctant to part with their coin, particularly when the state governments made legalization of their suspensions contingent on coin loans to themselves for defense purposes.[50]

Secretary Memminger first advanced his redemption scheme in a letter to R. R. Cuyler, president of the Central Railroad and Banking Company of Georgia. Noting the bank notes' depreciation and the necessity of taking specie for the bonds, the secretary requested that Cuyler's bank adopt a resolution to pay coin on its subscribed notes. Soothingly, Memminger assured Cuyler that "coin will in fact be wanted to a very small amount . . . ," and that he would deposit all funds received with the bank and use only notes, not coin, to pay the government's bills.[51]

What the secretary implied was that the loan of February 28, 1861 was only nominally for coin. Apparently it had not occurred to him that a coin reserve was needed and that his proposal was simply a device for circumventing the Sub-Treasury Act that required coin payments.[52] Indeed, the secretary had already decided to suspend the Sub-Treasury Act, first as it pertained to specie payments and second with regard to the requirement that all deposits be made with the treasurers or the depositories, most of whom were customs collectors. That irregular action, taken without Congress's prior approval, effectively took the treasury off the gold standard.[53]

The Myth of $26 Million in Coin

A myth has persisted that the Confederate government held more than $20 million in coin.[54] Although treasury records disclose that specie was not accounted for as a distinct item, Thian suggests that before final default in September 1862 the Confederate government disbursed about $1.6 million in coin in debt service on its bonds.[55] By early December 1861, the treasury was short of coin and was asking New Orleans bankers for a loan.

In the course of Memminger's correspondence with Denegre, the secretary dealt not only with the immediate problem of coin procurement but also the theoretical principles that ought to govern payment of the public debt. While he declared that the government's credit must be maintained and that coin payments on the debt were thus indispensable, he still had credits with the New Orleans banks nominally payable in coin that he wished to keep as a reserve. Could he borrow another $1 million?[56]

In reply, Denegre agreed that the government's credit had to be maintained but questioned whether coin payments would have that effect. The public would clearly know that the treasury was borrowing to pay its interest and the coin was being exchanged for notes on the open market at a hefty premium. Besides, Denegre claimed that public confidence in the banks would be undermined by the withdrawal of so much coin from their vaults. Having downplayed the importance of specie payments, Denegre then contradictorily warned Memminger that "if the Government ever stopped paying the interest in coin, it would have the worst possible effect on its credit. . . ." What Memminger should do regarding interest payments Denegre did not say.[57]

The correspondence deserves analysis. The financial community probably knew, as Denegre suggested, that the government was paying the interest by borrowing. But even by his admission, fear of an ultimate suspension of payments was a lesser evil than payments made in rapidly depreciating treasury notes. Moreover, the fact that the bond-holders were selling their coin on the open market would presumably restrain the growth of the specie premium while rendering the bonds more attractive in terms of treasury notes (i.e., a 9.6 percent versus an 8 percent yield). Nor was Denegre morally entitled to censure others for squandering the Southern coin reserves. For, despite "the remonstrances of the secession leaders and in disregard of threatened violence," not to mention several Confederate laws, the New Orleans banks, including Denegre's, had paid off their Northern creditors in coin and foreign exchange after hostilities began.[58]

Denegre was on firmer ground when he asserted that stopping specie payments would have a devastating effect on Government credit. In March 1862 (table 10), the February 28, 1861 bonds priced at $107 in paper were worth only $70 in gold. When specie payments were suspended, many people wrote to complain about the government's bad faith.[59] As a result, bond prices plunged so that by September 1862 the price was only $101.50 in treasury notes that were worth about $41 in gold.

Following Denegre's letter, Duncan F. Kenner, a member of the Provisional Congress, arrived in New Orleans. Evidently, Kenner secured Denegre's reluctant consent to a loan, for in a letter of December 28, 1861, Denegre shifted positions. He claimed that because people did not want to buy bonds, coin payments were of little help. Deposits in the New Orleans banks, he noted, had risen more than $8.5 million in the three months following the New Orleans bank suspension (September 16, 1861), yet bonds remained unsold. Denegre therefore suggested an issue of 6 percent notes redeemable six months after the restoration of peace. However, at the secretary's suggestion, Congress had already opted for 6 percent call certificates.[60]

The Confederate Specie Supply after February 1, 1862

Although Secretary Memminger had acknowledged that specie payments were an important part of the government's program, he made no serious effort to augment his coin reserves. He was so confident that peace would be achieved by July 1862 that he assured Dene-

Table 10. Bond Prices of the Loan of February 28, 1861,
in Terms of Gold and Treasury Notes*

		Gold ($)	Treasury Notes ($)
1861	October	86	97
1862	January	82	103
	March	70	107
	April	67	94
	August	79	118
	September	41	102
1863	January	36	109
	April	17	96
	July	22	200
	October	11	160
1864	January	8.9	178
	April	5.1	114
	July	5.3	114
	October	5.7	152
1865	March	2.0	121

Sources: The Richmond *Examiner, Enquirer,* and *Dispatch,* 1861–65; Schwab, *CSA* depreciation table.
* Average monthly prices; par = $100.

gre that less than half of the $1 million lent to the treasury would be needed.[61]

The New Orleans bankers were more perspicacious. They saw the federal fleet accumulating downriver preparing for an attack and concluded that the federal assault would capture the city. To thwart any Confederate seizure of their coin in advance of that event, they abruptly announced a resumption of specie payments in March 1862. Thomas O. Moore, the governor of Louisiana, saw through this scheme and wrote President Davis on March 18 to suggest counter-measures. The governor proposed that he force the banks to retain coin in their vaults until the Confederate government declared martial law—after which it would be easy to secure the coin by a forced loan.[62]

The secretary seemed unalarmed and was content to ask the governor to keep the coin in the bank's vaults.[63] But by April 24, 1862, more energetic councils had belatedly prevailed. By then—but far too late— Davis was prepared to seize the coin and while the secretaries of war and the treasury were still trying to coordinate their measures, New Orleans fell.[64] Not only did the Confederacy lose its largest city, but also $8 million of gold and silver coin still in the banks' vaults.

Had he been more astute, Secretary Memminger would have realized that the New Orleans banking community was pursuing its own interests, not those of the Confederacy. It had shown that tendency in its commerce with the enemy, sabotage at the Mint,[65] and by the refusal of the New Orleans bankers to buy bonds. Moreover, the need to prevent valuable products from accumulating at the ports had already been a matter of widespread public discussion and legislation.[66] The powerful displays of federal naval superiority in 1861 had led several states to authorize their banks to remove their headquarters to safer places in the interior.[67]

Nor did the government lack warning of the perils which confronted New Orleans.[68] General Mansfield Lovell, the local commander, had sent repeated warnings about the inadequate local defenses and the disaffection of his unpaid, ill-armed, and mutinous troops. Taken in connection with the heavy bombardment of Forts Jackson and Phillips starting on April 17, 1862, Memminger had ample cause for alarm. Yet, in marked contrast to his orders to the public depositories to move their coin into the interior in case of danger, he did nothing. Once again his misplaced scruples and his tendency to give the rights of private persons and corporations precedence over the survival of the Confederacy were to cost the South dearly.[69] Because of his inaction, April 24 found the bankers with more than one hundred and fifty tons of specie on hand. Because the military was commandeering all available transport, the bankers did well to escape with approximately ten tons of gold, worth $5 million.[70]

Most New Orleans banks left officers and directors behind to continue business as usual,[71] but their scheme of trying to ingratiate themselves with both sides was so transparent that it failed in its objective. For example, in New Orleans, Benjamin F. "Beast" Butler put such pressure on the banks, that to placate him, they agreed to bring back their gold surreptitiously.[72] This time, however, the Confederate government was awake. Apprised of the scheme on October 7, 1862, Secretary Memminger wrote to President Davis requesting authorization to seize the coin. A compromise was arranged whereby the Bank of Louisiana yielded its coin to the Confederate government, taking either bonds or treasury notes at the current exchange rate. The specie was then transferred from Columbus, Georgia, to Thomas S. Metcalf, the depository at Augusta, Georgia.[73] Shortly thereafter, $500,000 of coin from the Citizens' Bank was seized by General Beauregard and turned over to Thaddeus Sanford, the depository at Mobile, Alabama.[74] A final seizure, on May 10, 1864, of coin belonging to five Louisiana banks yielded approximately $1,650,000. By these activities, the War Department acquired approximately $4.7 million in coin.[75]

Far from having amassed the $26 million claimed by Schwab, the treasury seems to have procured less than $8.65 million—more than half by seizures. Small additional sums were secured through petty coin loans ($260,000) and purchases, and another $300,000 later obtained from the Richmond banks.[76] On this basis (table 9), the Confederacy seems to have secured only an aggregate of $8.95 million, or 14.3 percent of the available supply, scarcely an impressive performance.

Confederate Specie Disbursements

Yet the Confederate government did not use even this small specie supply very efficiently. It has already been indicated that $1.6 million in coin received from customs dues and confiscated federal assets was spent in the business-as-usual atmosphere prevailing in early 1861. In addition, another $1.6 million was used to service the public debt before the specie suspension in September 1862 (table 5).

The treasurer faced other needs for coin disbursements. Postmaster General John M. Reagan appealed over Memminger's head to the president, who ordered the secretary to provide Reagan with $50,000 worth.[77] Memminger resented the order bitterly, for coin was precious and its expenditure to be carefully husbanded. This sentiment is reflected in a letter to John Harley, chief collector of the war tax in Mississippi. The secretary explained that with the large specie premium and the lowest treasury note in the denomination of $5, the government would lose large sums when giving change in coin. Therefore, no such change was to be given except for coin payments.[78]

The Richmond banks' gold was either expended in President Davis's flight to Georgia or returned to the banks; therefore, the fate of the Louisiana banks' coin must still be determined. The acquisition of that specie could not have come at a more convenient time because the foreign exchange reserves of most banks were exhausted. The government did not negotiate a foreign loan until early 1863, thus the only way the Confederate government could cover its overdrafts in Europe was by shipping coin or selling it for the foreign exchange of those banks that would not take bonds or treasury notes. Coin, made up in packages of $25,000 to $100,000, was shipped in the fall of 1862. Such shipments were revived in late 1864 and continued until early 1865 when Wilmington was captured.[79] From the treasury's incomplete correspondence, it would appear that in 1864 alone, $1.7 million in gold coin was shipped, of which about $1.5 million reached Europe, $127,750 was captured, and $50,000 was rescued by the purser of the wrecked *Lynx* and safely brought back to Wilmington.[80]

From these facts we may estimate that $2 million in coin was sent abroad. Therefore, Schwab's claim that $15 million was sent abroad is clearly erroneous, although Thompson and later Todd seem to accept this conclusion without independent investigation.[81]

By February 1865, with the Columbia printing plants broken up or captured, what remained of the government's coin was urgently required to meet day-to-day expenses. Although some people still paid their taxes and even donated $2 million to the treasury,[82] these revenues could not supply General Lee's army for a single week. In a memorandum written on March 5, 1865, Judge John A. Campbell, the assistant secretary of war, pointed out that during the preceding three weeks the Confederate government had exchanged $1 million in coin for treasury notes, and that only $500,000 in coin was left. These coin sales explain the decline in the gold premium in Richmond in March of 1865. When that supply was exhausted, the treasury, with congressional approval, seized the Richmond banks' coin. Thus the Confederate treasury expired in the same circumstances in which it had been born—it was living off the confiscated assets of others.[83]

The Government's Specie Program

It is apparent in retrospect that the Confederate government's specie program was notably deficient. By failing to get bridge financing before the war began, the government wasted its early specie revenues on current expenses. In addition, it deliberately let lapse the opportunity to acquire specie through the loan of February 28, 1861. Thus, the $26 million of coin in Southern banks, which Schwab noted "was no inconsiderable source of strength to the Southern cause . . . was not taken full advantage of."[84] At least $2.2 million of coin in Tennessee and $7.8 million in New Orleans fell into the hands of the enemy. On this basis, the Union got 16 percent of the entire Confederate coin supply, the Confederacy 14 percent, and the banks retained 14 percent; 56 percent of the coin remained untapped in private hands. While intellectually recognizing that specie was the ultimate store of value, Secretary Memminger was content in this matter, as in so many others, to buy for the current day's needs only.

But the Confederate government's improvidence in that important aspect of public policy was not due merely to a lamentable absence of a sense of urgency. Another reason for inaction was a profound reluctance to tamper with the banks' property rights, even to the point that no serious effort was made to remove valuable specie supplies to safer locations. Only because military authorities lacked Memminger's unseemly diffidence for the bankers did the treasury net as much coin as it did.

Another serious blunder was the failure to undertake any program to extract specie from the general public. It is true that the export duty was payable in coin, but this revenue was inadequate even to pay the interest of the February 28, 1861 bonds. Moreover, by the Act of March 9, 1861, Congress inaugurated a policy of making treasury notes receivable for customs dues. The idea of reversing that policy to create a coin revenue was first broached in Congress on April 4, 1863, when P. W. Gray, a congressman from Texas (later treasury agent in the Trans-Mississippi) offered a resolution instructing the Ways and Means Committee "to inquire into the expediency of providing for the security of the currency of the Government, by declaring that . . . the said duties, and also imports and taxes . . . shall be made payable only in certificates or coupons for interest on the funded stock or bonds of the Confederate States, or in specie." Only by the Act of February 17, 1864 did Congress belatedly adopt the program.[85]

Had the government levied specie taxes and borrowed the banks' coin and foreign exchange early in the war, the treasury would have been in a much stronger position. Preempting the existing supply of foreign exchange would have tided the Confederacy over until a loan could be negotiated in Europe. Even more important, a store of specie would have made possible the payment of interest in coin on selected bond issues. Specie-paying bonds, with inflation-proof interest, would have encouraged funding and allowed bond sales at a premium in treasury notes, thus checking the rise in the public debt.

Northern Debt Management

The problems faced by the Confederacy were not unique; the United States also needed to finance a major war, but it found more effective solutions. When, in December 1861, New York banks suspended specie payments, the House of Representatives responded in February 1862 by authorizing the issue of $150 million of legal-tender notes and an issue of funding bonds. Although the Senate inserted an amendment requiring the interest of the bonds to be paid in coin, it also provided specie revenues by requiring that customs dues should be paid only in coin. Moreover, it authorized the secretary of the treasury to purchase or borrow coin on the best available terms.

Many of the arguments that Denegre had advanced against coin payments were echoed on the floor of the House in Washington when the amended bill was returned. To embarrass those who supported paying interest in specie, the chairman of the Ways and Means Committee, Thaddeus Stevens of Pennsylvania, moved an amendment to pay the troops in coin. The motion was beaten, and to Stevens's bitter disappointment, the House, by narrow margins, adopted the Senate program.[86]

Because the federal government persevered with this program during the entire war, the market value of one federal bond issue provides a clue about what might have happened had the Confederate government pursued a similar course. The 6 percent bonds of 1858 due in 1868 were similar to the February 28, 1861 Confederate loan; both were callable, medium-term loans. Under the impact of the secession crisis, the average price of the U.S. bonds in 1861 reached a low of 86 (par being 100). Then, in 1862, amid a bank suspension and a currency bloated by greenbacks, bond prices fell to 64 in coin; by 1864, the bonds were selling at 54 in coin and 125 in paper. Their sales price in specie offered a liberal return through capital appreciation.[87]

By comparison, the Confederate 8 percent bonds of February 28, 1861, with specie payments not yet suspended, were still quoted in August 1862 at 79 (table 10). Then prices dropped to 41 in September 1862 when specie payments went into default, and by January 1864, they were selling in coin for under $9. Had coin payments been continued, Confederate bonds would have gone to a paper premium and funding could have been effected at a premium, thereby reducing the nominal amount of the debt.

The Confederate Attempt to Base the Currency upon Cotton

The Act of August 19, 1861 inaugurated a period in Confederate finance that lasted a year. Under that act, the Congress created a treasury note currency, fundable in twenty-year, 8 percent bonds, with interest payable in specie. By doing so, the government tried to prevent an overissue.[88] But as Memminger disingenuously explained away his own negligence later: "We issued Treasury notes without interest, and then offered to exchange them for bonds whose interest was paid in coin. . . . Unfortunately, the blockade was accepted by neutral powers, and our just expectations were disappointed. The specie of the world could not flow in upon us, and *when ours was exhausted we were compelled to pay interest on our bonds in Treasury notes.* The foundation of the system was thus lost" (emphasis added).[89] A similar view was expressed by the Senate Committee on Finance in January 1864, to which Senator Thomas J. Semmes of Louisiana added: "When, therefore, it became obvious that this [coin payment] could not be done . . . it ought to have been understood . . . that the necessity had arisen to place the finances upon a different foundation."[90]

The need "to place the finances upon a different foundation" arose in 1862, but it took nine months for the Confederates to formulate a tentative approach to the problem by offering to pay cotton interest on the bond coupons emitted under the Act of April 30, 1863. Under the provisions of that loan, the secretary was authorized to issue $100 million of 6 percent, twenty-year bonds, with interest and principal payable at the pleasure of the government, either in specie or in cotton. If the government paid in cotton, that commodity was to be delivered to the ports of New Orleans, Mobile, Savannah, Charleston, Wilmington, Richmond, or Norfolk. Because the price of cotton at the time was about 23 pence a pound,[91] and the coupons were each equal to five hundred pounds of cotton priced at 6 pence sterling, any bondholder able to export cotton would—in theory at least—realize a handsome profit.

In urging newspaper editors to tout this loan to the public, the treasury declared that "at present market rate . . . the actual interest received by the holder is equal to 18 percent." Moreover, as the "purchase money is now paid in Confederate notes" the buyer stood to gain "all the advantage resulting from investment of Treasury notes in a specie security." Thus the "bonds possessed an intrinsic value greatly exceeding any security yet offered by the Confederate Government."[92] Reviewing the merits of "the new cotton loan" the Charleston *Mercury* declared that "Compared with other stock or bond issues it is far superior. . . . The $15,000,000 loan pays 8% only. It cannot rise higher. . . . The bonds now issued will give an interest to be paid in a mode which absolutely fixes its value, for it must be paid at once, in coin or cotton. . . ."[93] But although editors sedulously promoted the loan, the secretary, on opening the sealed bids on July 20, found that the best bid was for double the face value of each bond in paper, while at a subsequent auction on August 5, the premium bid over face in treasury notes was only 30 percent to 51 percent. Accepting the 50 percent premium as typical, the secretary ordered the bonds sold at $1,500 each.[94]

In spite of the secretary's efforts, he disposed of only $8,393,000 in bonds, with $4,285,000 of premiums paid. The disappointing result could scarcely be attributed to a shortage of treasury notes when $700 million were outstanding. Rather, it suggests that by the summer of 1863, many financiers regarded the Confederacy's days as numbered and did not expect to receive more than one payment (June 1, 1864) from which they might make a slight profit. Thus they were willing to lay out only $1,500 in paper (worth about $187.50 in coin) for the opportunity to receive $255.66 (one year's cotton interest). Still, in spite of the potential profits and the further decline of the currency in terms of gold before December 1, 1863, when sales were cut off, there was no rush to subscribe.[95]

This lack of enthusiasm reflected a calculation that the Confederate government habitually broke its promises and that little, if any, cotton would be paid. That view is confirmed by Archibald Roane, chief of the Produce Office, who reported that only 607 bales were used to pay the interest on the bonds during 1864.[96]

Because the coupons of the bonds also called for payment in coin, it is possible that some bonds were paid in specie to discourage investors from pressing for payment. But evidence also exists that the government offered to pay only 5 cents in treasury notes per pound on the cotton ($25 or $1.50 in coin) on a coupon promising $60 in coin or cotton worth more than $250.[97] Quite clearly the investors were thoroughly disenchanted by June of 1864 when the cotton bonds were quoted at only paper par (which by then was worth only $50 in specie).[98]

Basing the Confederate Monetary System on a Specie Equivalent

The abandonment of a cotton-based funding system did not mark the end of Secretary Memminger's search for a new foundation for his monetary program. In his report of December 7, 1863, he argued that if Congress would only authorize a $500 million loan together with taxes payable in coin or in bond coupons (like the February 28, 1861 loan), "a foundation in the nature of a specie value would be secured. . . ."[99]

In the Act of February 17, 1864, Congress accepted this proposal; section 6 provided a $500 million bond issue to meet the government's general expenses. Interest on the bonds, although only payable in notes, was guaranteed by a pledge of an additional export duty, while the coupons of the $500 million loan or coin could be used, after February 17, 1864, to pay import duties.[100] Thus, two years later, the Confederate Congress finally adopted the same program enacted by the federal Congress in the spring of 1862.

After a printing delay, the first auction of $5 million of the bonds was scheduled at noon on May 12, 1864 in Richmond.[101] But General Grant's offensive forced all the businessmen to repair to the trenches for local defense.[102] With conditions in Richmond so uncertain, the operation was entrusted to W. Y. Leitch, the assistant treasurer at Columbia, South Carolina. A new date, June 21, 1864 was set when $665,000 out of $2,900,000 of bonds were sold at prices ranging from $151 to $135.[103] Following this auction, the balance of the loan, priced at $135, was placed for sale with the Confederate depositories.[104]

In spite of substantial publicity, however, the Confederate government had limited success with the bonds. Although approximately $146 million worth of bonds were prepared (Appendix D),[105] the actual sales mentioned in the treasurer's report of January 28, 1865 discloses that a face value of only $44.5 million was sold. This, together with $14.5 million in premiums paid, represented $59 million of paper receipts.[106]

Another part of Memminger's program was to pay specie on the 6 percent nontaxable certificates (fourteenth section, Act of February 17, 1864). Accordingly, he wrote to the president asking him to seek congressional approval to sell $10 million of cotton for coin.[107] Although the president obliged, Congress took no action.[108] This uncooperative response reflected the view that the coin supply was too diffused to raise $10 million in specie by such means.

Although an economic historian can recognize the intrinsic merit of the concept of making bond coupons "equivalent" to specie, the problem was that the Confederate government did not have enough customs and export dues to sustain the value of such bonds, even had Congress raised the rates. It seems clear that the resort to such bonds was a confession that the government's specie policy in 1861–62 was inadequate, and that it would have been far better to maintain coin payments from the beginning. As it was, the neglect of those measures to keep the Confederacy's bonds and customs dues on a specie basis was, combined with the mismanagement of cotton, the failure to tax, and the failure to control the printers, the most serious blunder made by the Confederate Treasury Department.

The Need to Organize the Monetary Side of the Treasury

If the need to create a government currency should have induced the secretary to procure adequate printing facilities to produce the notes and to accumulate sufficient specie to pay the interest of the bonds into which they were fundable, then the need to dispose of those bonds should have stimulated the secretary to develop an adequate structure for their sale and distribution. But again the treasury failed in two key areas: the mode of issuing securities promoted delay, and an inadequate system of depositories limited sales.

Deficiencies in Securities Preparation and Distribution

Although it has been noted that the printers were slow to deliver adequate amounts of securities, that tardiness was only one of the reasons for delay. The Act of July 24, 1861 had relieved the register and the treasurer of the necessity of personally affixing their autographs to each and every note, yet even a corps of agents signing on their behalf could not maintain the necessary pace when millions of notes were involved.[109] In spite of repeated requests from the secretary that the technicality of signatures be dispensed with, the Congress never per-

mitted the government to print signatures, except in the case of the
50-cent notes.[110] Faced with such congressional obduracy, the secretary had to employ two hundred clerks to affix two signatures and
two numbers to each of more than eighty-one million notes.[111] Only
after this ridiculous misuse of scarce labor had became intolerable did
Memminger avail himself of a labor force unintentionally furnished
him by the Union; he hired several hundred widows and female
refugees to sign, number, and clip the notes.[112]

That is not to suggest that the production bottlenecks occurred only
in the treasury Note Bureau. There were also problems in the register's
office. As act succeeded act, the number of coupon bonds and stock
certificates which the register had to sign multiplied.[113] It is hardly
surprising that by 1863, the register, Robert Tyler, had fallen behind
in his work or that he should have replied to the secretary's criticisms
with justifiable asperity, pointing out that he had to supervise an
important bureau and sign a multitude of other documents. And, as
a parting shot, he noted that "You will allow me to observe that I do
not believe that it was ever intended by . . . the Congress, that a Chief
of Bureau should be a mere signer of Coupon Bonds."[114] That acerbic
comment led Congress to act speedily to correct the situation, and by
1864, two assistant registers took over most of Tyler's bond signing
duties.[115]

To augment the problems caused him by difficulties with printers
and note and bond signers, Secretary Memminger added yet another:
his mismanagement of the business of getting the notes speedily
distributed. This difficulty was accentuated in May 1862 when the
printers, in light of the threat to Richmond from the Union forces,
were required to remove their personnel and equipment to Columbia,
South Carolina. The move only intensified the bottleneck; the note
numberers, clippers, and signers remained in Richmond until April
of 1864.

Such a two-year bisection of the treasury Note Bureau necessitated
the shipment of securities from Columbia to Richmond. Meanwhile,
interruptions of train service and the shortage of security facilities and
couriers led to constant delays in getting notes to the capital. Thus, at
a time when government agents were months behind in their payments, as much as $40 million of securities were stacked up on the
floor of the treasury Note Bureau in Columbia. The time wasted in
shipping notes between the two parts of the bureau resulted in a two
months' delay in remitting funds to Alabama and Mississippi. Had
the whole bureau been moved to Columbia in the first place, and had
note distribution been made directly from that point by the assistant

treasurer at Charleston (as happened after April 1864), this source of damage to the Confederacy's credit could have been completely avoided.[116]

Nor was the secretary any more efficient in correcting other vexatious deficiencies in the treasury's operations. For example, military disbursements were supposed to be made by an officer cashing checks on his account at a depository, but in practice, the transfer of cash to cover deposited warrants was constantly behind, thus the depositories often had no funds to honor the drafts drawn on them. To guard against this and cut down the need to travel to the few pay depositories extant prior to 1864, agents deliberately cashed all warrants drawn to their order on receipt, so that by April 1, 1864, when government payments were weeks in arrears, more than $43 million of desperately needed cash lay idle in the hands of the disbursing officers, an abuse abated only in mid-1864.[117]

Confederate Depository Arrangements

Equally unsatisfactory was the secretary's management of the Treasury Department offices scattered about the country. As of May 17, 1861, the Treasury Department consisted of the secretary and his staff at the seat of government, the officers of the mints, and the collectors of customs at the various ports. In addition there were two assistant treasurers, one at Charleston and the other at New Orleans. Each Confederate collector wore two hats: one as collector and the other as the depository for the funds he collected.[118]

Additional government depositories existed at Wilmington, Savannah, Mobile, Nashville, Memphis, Galveston, and LaSalle, Texas. Because Memminger presumably believed that the value of the treasury notes was sustained by making them fundable into bonds, one might expect that he would have made funding as convenient as possible. But instead, the secretary required a would-be investor in Greenville, South Carolina, for example, to buy bonds in Charleston, more than two hundred miles away. And he contributed to dissension within Georgia's competitive banking community by making the bankers in Augusta and Macon tributary to those in Savannah, who charged the usual commissions for executing purchase orders. In addition, federal attacks on the ports made it advisable to disperse the government's funds among several locations.[119]

Yet no action to change the Confederate depository system of 1861 was taken until March 1862, when the Senate, responding to complaints, passed a resolution asking the secretary for information. In reply, Memminger told the Senate that depository placement was dictated by law, and he requested discretionary power to establish other depositories.[120] Although a law to expand the number of depositories was duly forthcoming, the secretary used his new authority sparingly until early 1863. Thus, during 1861–63, while the Confederate currency expanded from nothing to $410 million, the treasury still operated with a prewar establishment. Only the forced funding acts of 1862–63 compelled Memminger to change his dispositions. With a third forced funding act (February 17, 1864), the system was further expanded and refined to provide for "funding depositories" whose sole function was to fund notes.[121]

To deal with this vast increase in business, the secretary recruited banks to serve as depositories. The banks had trained staffs, business premises, and vaults to safeguard government funds. Thus banks, as Secretary Trenholm noted later to J. A. Seddon, the secretary of war, rendered signal services to the government.[122] Although the banks were reluctant to assume such a role from the beginning, by 1862, government securities were the only active part of their portfolios. Thus, by 1865, in North Carolina, $8 million out of total bank assets of $19 million were held in Confederate or state bonds.[123]

In addition to the banks, the treasury also employed factors— wealthy individuals and private bankers to be receivers of public funds under the title of depositories—chiefly in Texas, Arkansas, Florida, Mississippi, and northern Louisiana, where banking facilities were nonexistent.[124] Most of the locations opened in 1863–64 were only funding offices, the chief function of which was to receive notes and facilitate the exchange of funding certificates for taxes. Yet, despite Secretary Trenholm's efforts to close them and his feeling that they created unwarranted expectations of service, the offices had to be kept open until the end.[125]

The statistics of the 1864 funding act disclose that only 46.4 percent of all notes funded in 1864 were received at the pre-1863 depositories (table 11). Quite likely, had Secretary Memminger been more enterprising in establishing depositories at an earlier date, a considerably larger volume of currency might have been funded during 1861–63. But the secretary, concentrating on trifling savings, tried to carry out a funding program with a minimal staff. The economies, if any, were more than offset by the damage done to the currency and to the country.

Minor Errors of Confederate Debt Management

Even had the secretary controlled the recalcitrant printers, procured the requisite specie, and properly organized his department in every particular, he would still have had to decide how to manage the

Table 11. Funding (Act February 17, 1864) within the
Confederacy by Date of Depository Establishment

State	Depository Established	Amount Funded (000s of $)	% Funded
Total: Eastern Confederacy (includes eastern La.)	Pre 1863	$272,469	47.4
	1863	202,652	35.3
	1864	99,058	17.3
		$574,794	100.0
Total: Trans-Mississippi Department*	Pre 1863	$ 19,250	35.1
	1863	32,145	58.7
	1864	3,399	6.2
		$ 54,794	100.0
Total Confederacy	Pre 1863	$291,719	46.4
	1863	234,797	37.3
	1864	102,457	16.3
		$628,973	100.0

Source: Thian, ed., *Reports*, pp. 446–47; report from P. W. Gray (Trans-Mississippi agent to Secretary Trenholm), December 26, 1864, National Archives, Record Group 109, vol. 18, ch. 10, pp. 14–71.
* Louisiana, Arkansas, Texas, and Indian Territory.

funded debt and the types of securities that he should issue. That in turn would have required him to analyze the potential market for his securities and ascertain the demand for the monetary instruments at his disposal.

Failure to Segment the Market

As indicated in chapter 1, the Southern banking system and related financial intermediaries were in fairly liquid condition at the beginning of the war. But even allowing for a maximum effort on the part of the banks (a traditional source of government loans) and other "capitalists,"[126] the Confederacy could not hope to sell more than $100 million of long-term debt to the entire financial community. Short-term government borrowing had traditionally consisted of interest-bearing treasury notes and call certificates. Bankers preferred interest-bearing treasury notes because they could use them as income-earning cash reserves. Yet because the government was paying interest on these notes to prevent their circulation, it should have issued them in large denominations to limit their use to clearing-house settlements. As an alternative, the government could have safely sold call certificates in small denominations that, being transferable only by endorsement, could not be used as a substitute for money. But to market them, the treasury would have needed a widespread system of depositories so that the public could readily deposit their currency in exchange for the certificates.

In authorizing the April 17, 1862 interest-bearing treasury notes and the December 24, 1861 call certificates, Congress gave Memminger wide latitude in selecting their denominations, although Congress did set a $100 minimum denomination on the interest-bearing notes. Yet, in spite of the logic of the situation, Memminger made the 7.30 percent interest-bearing notes readily usable as currency by issuing them only in $100 denominations, whereas would-be purchasers of the 6 percent call certificates found themselves having to pay a minimum of $500.[127] Call certificates thus should have been issued for amounts as low as $50, while treasury notes should have been emitted in denominations $500 or higher. Instead, preference both in terms of denomination and interest rate was given to the more negotiable of the two securities, thereby augmenting the growing inflation both were designed to stop.

The selection of bond denominations was also important. In this regard, Congress catered to small investors by amending the Act of February 28, 1861 to require the issuance of $50 coupon bonds or stock certificates. A congressional amendment to the Act of August 19, 1861 also forced the issue of $50 bonds.[128]

These actions conflicted with the views of Denegre, who could not see the utility of issuing anything under $500.[129] Memminger shared Denegre's opinions, but the operation of the forced funding acts disclosed that substantial sums in small amounts were held outside the banking system. Examination of the stock subscription lists of 1861 shows a high correlation between sales and the denomination of the bonds, as well as the propinquity of the subscribers to the loan commissioners. Had more $50 certificates and bonds been employed, the government might have sold almost 10 percent more securities between 1861 and 1863 than it in fact did.[130]

Confederate Debt Maturity Scheduling

Confederate debt maturity scheduling discloses a further lack of foresight. In the expectation of a short war, Congress began with intermediate maturities for the bonds coupled with short-term call certificate and treasury note maturities. But as the war progressed, maturity dates on all issues were pushed back until, by the time of

Appomattox, non-callable thirty-year bonds were the standard. But early mistakes came back again and again to offset any advantages gained by experience. Appendix D discloses that the first loan (February 28, 1861), had ten years to run but could be called after five years. This call provision proved that the Confederates had absorbed at least one small lesson from the federal government's debt retirement problems during the 1850s.[131] In this emphasis on short-term loans, the Confederates were not unique; the North, motivated by similar considerations, also used bonds callable in five years.[132]

Probably the Confederacy's worst blunder in maturity management was the loan of May 16, 1861, which provided bonds into which the treasury notes of that act were fundable. Although the bonds were to run for ten years, they were convertible into treasury notes redeemable on demand in coin after July 25, 1863. On January 25, 1864 (six months after the notes came due) the notes would cease to be fundable unless, in the interlude, the treasury defaulted.[133]

Secretary Memminger, to be sure, had recommended a three-year term for the notes.[134] But the *Confederate Journal* discloses that he was on the floor when the bill was under debate and did nothing to defer their redemption date. Moreover, he personally moved the amendment that converted a funding loan into a species of call certificates.[135]

In view of the treasury's inability to adhere to these terms, the secretary of the treasury could have mitigated the default by any one of three devices. First, he could have tried to retire all the notes that were paid into the treasury and not reissue them. But as there were no tax collections and the treasury note printers were inefficient, the few notes that were received were promptly reissued and government officers instructed not to cancel them.[136] Second, the treasury might have procured an adequate stock of specie to pay off the notes when they fell due. Had bondholders been confident of the government's ability to pay in specie, they would have felt less compelled to exercise their option to convert the bonds into coin, particularly when they were payable on demand. Third, Secretary Memminger could have copied the U.S. program. In December 1861, Secretary of the Treasury Salmon P. Chase had found himself with $50 million of notes payable "on demand" in specie and "receivable in payment of public dues."[137] Unable to pay in coin, but anxious to avoid any imputation of default, Congress had decreed that the demand notes were receivable as if they were gold and, subsequently, made them legal tender.[138] From quotations appearing in *Hunt's Merchants' Magazine,* it would appear that the gold value of the demand notes fluctuated from a low of 90.8 cents on September 6, 1862 to a high of 99.1 cents on October 18, 1862.

Thereafter the discount on the notes never exceeded 4.8 percent.[139] Had the Confederates followed the federal example not only in making customs dues payable in specie, but also in making the May 16, 1861 issue uniquely receivable for customs dues after their maturity date, the same benefit might have accrued; that is, the notes would have been hoarded and thus effectively driven from circulation. But, instead of honorably attempting to compensate the note holders for the government's unintentional breach of faith, the Confederate Congress tried to legislate the problem away. The Act of March 23, 1863 required the holders to fund their notes while prohibiting the redemption of the certificates as provided by the original act. Yet the act proved ineffective, for such were the attractions of these 8 percent call certificates that of $11.5 million issued, only $247,000 were converted back into notes.[140] This was one occasion where the legalistically minded secretary should have stood by the letter of the bond contract rather than making himself a party to a damaging breach of faith.[141]

But the Congress persevered and by the Act of February 17, 1864 made a last effort to suppress the May 16, 1861 Act notes. When that failed to achieve the desired result, the Second Confederate Congress tried a more conciliatory approach; by the Act of June 13, 1864 it allowed further funding and the conversion of stock certificates into coupon bonds. When the end came, the government was still wrestling with this problem.[142] The notes authorized by the Act of August 19, 1861 were "payable six months after the Ratification of a Treaty of Peace between the Confederate States and the United States. . . ."[143] This provision, so far as can be ascertained, was a verbatim replica of the Bank of England suspension in 1797.[144] The rapid rise in the amount of notes issued ($210 million by April 1862) made it patently obvious that they would not be paid off as provided by law. As Kentucky Congressman Eli Bruce noted, the value of the notes fell because many Confederates saw the unrealistic payment terms and doubted the government's intention to pay its debts.[145]

The maturity scheduling of the August 19, 1861 bonds was more credible because the bonds were redeemable at various times between July 1864 and July 1881.[146] The genesis of this idea—without parallel in the history of the United States—casts light on the haphazard way in which Confederate policy was devised. The general concept was foreshadowed by a suggestion of Edward J. Forstall, the New Orleans banker and Baring Brothers agent, laying out in tabular form a system for progressively retiring $100 million of treasury notes within ten years by means of a $15 million war tax.[147] But the real source of the plan came from James G. Holmes, a Charleston stockbroker and bond agent, who had made some computations about how the loan of February 28, 1861 could be extinguished.[148] At the end of a series of conventions which he had attended on behalf of the Charleston bankers, he sent the secretary another letter requesting an interview. During their meeting, Holmes justified his proposal on the ground that a sinking fund was objectionable not the least because "it requires an annual legislative provision of ever-changing legislators, and may, therefore, be pretermitted."[149]

In reporting this arrangement for serial maturities to Congress, the secretary stated that the plan he had adopted was based "upon the plans suggested by Mr. Holmes of South Carolina, and adopted by the City of Charleston."[150] He adduced that a large number of maturity dates would have the widest appeal to the public, and he added that "In time of peace the distant bonds would be preferred, but I think that at this time the short bonds will be in greatest demand."

In the actual event the secretary proved mistaken; subscribers showed practically no interest in the bonds that would fall due from January 1864 to July 1865.[151] On the other hand, the sale of the long-term July 1881 bonds was brisk.[152] The intermediate bonds were sold primarily in early 1863, when purchasers undoubtedly preferred to avoid buying the callable five-to-thirty-year February 20, 1863 Act bonds.

Confederate maturity policies continued to be directed toward a medium-term policy. The Act of April 12, 1862 provided ten-year bonds callable in thirty years, which sold poorly. (An equal lack of success would have attended the February 20, 1863 issues, but for the forced funding law of October 13, 1862.) It was only in 1864 that maturities were put off for twenty and even thirty years; by that time, it was realized that the enormous debt could not possibly be discharged before 1894.

Short-term securities paralleled the development of the funded debt by a steady trend toward the most distant due dates. Ignoring Calhoun's suggestion of non-interest-bearing notes payable at no fixed time, the redemption of the interest-bearing treasury notes was set first at fourteen months, then six months after the ratification of a treaty of peace. The non-interest-bearing notes fell due first in two years, then six months after peace. Finally by the Act of February 17, 1864, payment was deferred to two years after peace, with the call certificates paralleling the notes into which they were convertible. By the Act of March 23, 1863, Congress reserved the right to defer payment on those call certificates for thirty years. However, by the Act of February 17, 1864, the Confederates reverted to their original custom, and the non-taxable certificates of indebtedness were redeemable two years after peace.[153]

In retrospect, it would appear that the Confederacy was not realistic in setting its debt maturities. By trying at the beginning to keep on the short side of the maturity scale, the government accumulated short-term debts it could not pay. A more prudent policy would have aimed at rigorous taxation to minimize the debt coupled with a balanced mix of security maturities that would appeal to the widest possible market. The failure to achieve this goal reduced funding and increased the inflation during 1861–62.

Confederate Term Structure of Interest Rates

Another debt management problem lay in the selection of a proper term-structure of interest rates for Confederate securities. Up until 1861, credit-worthy Southern states had floated bond issues, most of which bore 6 percent interest with a few 5 percents and 7 percents for variety. Because an incipient civil war does not inspire confidence, the prices of Southern state bonds plummeted by 20 percent to 33 percent in 1861. Nor was the credit of the federal government in Washington any better. Of the $10 million of treasury notes offered for sale on December 18, 1860, only $1,831,000 were taken at 12 percent, whereas another $465,000 were sold to yield 15 percent.[154] Subsequently, the New York banks lent money at 12 percent to the treasury, the low state of the government's credit being attributed to the general suspicion of Buchanan's pro-Southern advisors.[155]

In the South, uncertain political conditions led to a series of bank suspensions that started in Virginia on November 20, 1860 and spread rapidly to the rest of the South other than Louisiana and part of Alabama. Thus, when the Confederate Congress convened at Montgomery in February 1861, commercial conditions were by no means normal. However, at the outset, the Confederacy was debt-free and might in consequence expect to command a better credit rating than the Union or any single Southern state.

The historic interest rate for U.S. bonds was 6 percent; 8 percent bonds had last been issued during the undeclared war with France (1798–99). Yet, the Confederate Act of February 28, 1861 called for an 8 percent interest rate. Nor did anyone in the Provisional Congress challenge that abnormal rate; in fact, the only authoritative Southerner who discussed the question publicly was James D. B. DeBow, the respected editor of *DeBow's Review*, who noted that "The rate of interest—8 percent—is that which usually obtains among us, even in times which are not free of commercial embarrassments. It is the rate paid upon our bank stocks, which are usually at or above par, and *exceeds the rate which at this moment is realized upon our state and city bonds purchased in the market. It exceeds too, that accepted recently by the capitalists of New York upon a loan to the United States, with its empty Treasury, heavy debt and disrupted revolutionary condition"* (emphasis added).[156]

DeBow's statement implies that the 8 percent rate was too high. Confirmation of his appraisal came from Denegre, who wrote that if it were not for the five-year call provision "these bonds ought to be at a premium of 5 to 10 percent very soon. . . ."[157] Straight debt bonds do not go to a premium unless the interest paid is above the market. This is not to say, however, that a high rate of interest could never be justified. Had the Confederate government confined that rate exclusively to bonds sold for coin or foreign exchange, in order to accumulate a reserve, an 8 percent rate might have been appropriate. But to pay that rate in exchange for suspended bank paper seems, in retrospect, improvident; among other things, it would limit the capital amount of loans that the government could service. For example, had the Confederacy borrowed $100 million a year from 1861–64, the cost differential between a 6 percent and an 8 percent rate in gold coin would have been $16 million ($64 million versus $48 million), which represented the difference between the barely possible and an inevitable suspension of specie payments.

Yet having offered too high a rate, the Congress veered to the opposite extreme in the Act of March 9, 1861, which authorized $1 million worth of 3.65 percent treasury notes. The rate seemed so low in relation to the 6 percent paid on U.S. treasury notes that the Georgia bankers complained to Secretary Memminger that they charged themselves a minimum of 4 percent for interbank balances.[158] Despite this protest, the notes were sold at par because of their receivability at face plus interest for customs and for debts throughout the Confederacy. The interest rate question was therefore deferred until the Act of May 16, 1861. Eleven days after the Congress assembled on April 29, 1861, Secretary Memminger submitted his war finance recommendations. Yielding to the self-serving advice being offered by the New Orleans bankers, Memminger proposed that 8 percent interest-bearing treasury notes be issued in denominations of $20 and above, while the $5 and $10 denominations be non-interest-bearing.[159] This was a carbon copy of the policy already inaugurated by the Commonwealth of Virginia.[160]

When the currency and bond bill of May 16, 1861 reached the floor, its text, as drawn up by the Finance Committee, provided for the traditional 6 percent bonds. But on the motion of Secretary Memminger, the 6 percent rate was struck out and a rate "not exceeding 8%" substituted in its place.[161] This seemingly routine act had far-reaching implications.

Although the secretary's amendment gave him additional flexibility, he never used the authority to issue bonds at a rate of less than 8 percent. Nor is there any evidence that he even made inquiries as to the possibility of selling government debt at any rate other than 8 percent. Yet the arrangement upset the relation of the Confederate interest-rate structure to the term of the investments because with 8 percent paid for call loans and medium-term debt alike, longer-term bonds possessed no special advantage. Yet the secretary needed to sell long-term bonds to stretch out his debt maturities. Unwilling and unauthorized to raise long-term rates still higher, he retained the 8 percent coupon until April of 1863.

On December 24, 1861, to remedy a deficiency in the Act of August 19, 1861, Congress created a $30 million issue of 6 percent call certificates. That act marks the beginning of an attempt to initiate a rational system of interest differentials that encouraged long-term funding but still offered a liberal return for short-term securities. Unfortunately, on April 17, 1862, Congress passed an act calling for 7.30 percent interest (2 cents per day per $100) to be paid on treasury notes. Few Southerners needed to purchase bonds when for only 7/10 of 1 percent less they could possess a note that could be used as currency.

Yet Congress was learning. Tacitly conceding that the 8 percent rate was excessive, Congress on October 13, 1862 made the notes dated "December 2, 1862" fundable only in 7 percent bonds. The Act of March 23, 1863 went further by decreeing that new long-term bonds would bear 6 percent or 4 percent interest, depending on whether the notes to be exchanged for them were dated "April 6, 1863" or "December 2, 1862." Call certificates were to be issued in two forms: a 5 percent issue for the notes fundable in 6 percent bonds, and a 4 percent issue for notes fundable in 4 percent bonds. With equal interest paid on long- and short-term debt alike, it was not surprising that $1.85 million in 4 percent call certificates were sold, as against only $22,300 of 4 percent bonds. Thus, by 1863, the 6 percent rate once again became the norm.[162]

The Act of February 17, 1864 capped the government's program of interest rate reductions. The forced funding provisions of that act reduced rates to only 4 percent, and call certificates paid only 4 percent. Such 6 percent securities as were left were issued to compensate the states and defray the government's expenses during 1864. But even these last were purchasable only at a 35 percent premium for a nominal rate of 4.44 percent. This was in marked contrast to the prevailing specie discount rate of about 14 percent.

In retrospect, it would seem that the Confederacy's interest rate policies never recovered from a poor start. The Confederacy would have been well advised to have employed the traditional U.S. structure of 6 percent bonds with a special issue of 8 percent bonds subscribable only in specie funds. As in the War of 1812, treasury notes due in over three years could bear 5.4752 percent interest, with 3.65 percent paid for one-year notes. Call certificate rates should have been about 4 percent for deposits kept less than 180 days, with 5 percent paid thereafter. These lower interest rates would have allowed coin payments on the funded debt and would have marginally checked inflation by reducing government expense.

Conclusion

The failures described in this chapter created a vicious cycle. Secretary Memminger, in his mismanagement of Confederate security printers, inconsistently careened between spendthrift laissez-faire and penny-pinching. As a result, he provided the printers an inducement to be either inefficient or to seek more profitable outside work. He then erected a series of self-inflicted bottlenecks in his own department. Thus, the production and distribution of funds fell behind schedule, and the army, especially in the Trans-Mississippi Department, was left unpaid. This effectively undermined the morale of the soldiers and their families, which in turn crippled the army through desertions. These problems reached the crisis point in 1864, when the funding act overwhelmed the printers in a tidal wave of demand. Unable to respond, the printers fell behind, leaving every department and bureau of the government starved for funds in a year when it was vital that morale be maintained and a maximum effort made. The result was a collapse of the War Department and the nation's capacity to resist.

On the home front, the value of currency was diminished by the secretary's inability to secure the available stock of specie from the banks and the public for debt-service purposes. This resulted in a specie interest payments moratorium after July 1, 1862, which deprived the currency of the support derived from being fundable into a bond with interest payable in something of universally accepted value. Nor was the effort to curb the growth of the currency through monetary means assisted by the shortage of offices where the notes might be funded into bonds. That error, combined with misjudgments regarding interest rates and maturities, increased the burden placed on Confederate treasury notes and, in the absence of an effective fiscal system, the whole burden of sustaining the war fell on the Confederate printers. Yet the secretary, because of his inept management of the printers, assured that even in the middle of a hyperinflation the government could not produce the requisite funds. Thus, by relentlessly constricting pressures, the treasury lost all room to maneuver, while the undermined currency inevitably collapsed.

NOTES

1. Richard Cecil Todd, *Confederate Finance* (Athens: University of Georgia Press, 1954), pp. 25, 84; *Biennial Report of the Controller of Public Accounts . . . at its Eighth Biennial Session* (Montgomery, Ala.: Shorter and Reid, 1861), p. 1296; *Acts of the Called Season of the General Assembly of Alabama etc.* (Montgomery, Ala: Shorter and Reid, 1861), p. 16.

2. *Report of the Committee on Postal Affairs* (Montgomery: Barrett, Wimbish and Company, February 16, 1861); also John H. Reagan, *Memoires with Special Reference to Secession and the Civil War*, ed. Walter F. McCaleb (New York: Neal Publishing, 1906), p. 109. "An ordnance to transfer certain funds to the Government of the Confederate States of America," approved by the State Convention, March 7, 1861, Record Group 56, vol. 62b, National Archives; Frank Moore, comp., *The Rebellion Record*, 12 vols. (New York: G. P. Putnam's Sons, 1861–63, Van Nostrand, 1864–68).

3. Henry D. Capers, *The Life and Times of C. G. Memminger* (Richmond: Everett Waddey, 1893), pp. 309, 311. Among the carryovers with Washington experience were Philip Clayton (assistant secretary), Charles T. Jones (acting register), Lewis Cruger (comptroller), and Bolling Baker and W. H. S. Taylor (auditors).

4. Act of February 28, 1861, in *The Statutes at Large of the Provisional Government of the Confederate States of America . . .* , ed. James M. Mathews (Richmond: R. M. Smith, 1864), 1st sess., p. 42.

5. Act of March 9, 1861, 1st sess., in *The Statutes at Large*, ed. Mathews, Ch. 33, pp. 57–59.

6. Samuel Schmidt to Memminger, March 1, 1861 and James D. Denegre to C. G. Memminger, March 25, 1861 in *Correspondence with the Treasury Department of the Confederate States of America 1861–5, part 5: 1861–62*, ed. Raphael P. Thian (Washington, D.C.: Privately published, 1880), pp. 5–6, 18–19; also Memminger to Gazaway B. Lamar, March 13, 1861, March 16, 22, 23, April 2, 11, 19, 1861, in *Correspondence of the Treasury Department of the Confederate States of America 1861–1865, part 4*, ed. Raphael P. Thian (Washington, D.C.: Privately published, 1879), appendix, pp. 23–24, 30, 42, 58, 64.

7. Based upon a sample of two thousand different Southern bank notes in circulation in 1861 in the Charles J. Affleck collection and upon the printed portions of the Society of Paper Money currency publications.

8. Edson to Schmidt, May 1, 1861, in William H. Griffiths, *The Story of American Bank Note Company* (New York: American Bank Note, 1958), pp. 39–40.

9. Memminger to W. H. White (secretary of ABNCo), April 19, 1861, in *Correspondence of*, ed. Thian, p. 65.

10. Ball Collection, Museum of the Confederacy, Richmond, Virginia; also "Register of Treasury Notes," Record Group 109, ch. 10, vol. 99, pp. 3, 82, 161–62, National Archives. This book shows who signed which notes, what their denominations were, and the date of their issue from the treasury.

11. Denegre to Memminger, July 8, 1861, W. P. Reyburn to Memminger, July 20, 1861, and James D. Denegre to Memminger, October 5, 9, 1861, in *Correspondence with*, ed. Thian, pp. 197–98, 232–33, 272–73, 361, 372–73.

12. John Douglas to Memminger (not dated, but the internal evidence suggests December 1861), ibid., p. 454.

13. Thomas A. Ball to Memminger, November 25, 1861, December 18, 1861, ibid., pp. 442, 434; "Register of Miscellaneous Warrants," warrant 270, August 15, 1861, Record Group 365, vol. 103, National Archives.

14. Thompson Allen to C. G. Memminger, October 1861, in *Correspondence with*, ed. Thian, pp. 414–15.

15. Thompson Allen to C. G. Memminger, September 12, 1861; September 13, 1861 (memo), ibid., pp. 324–27.

16. "Register of Treasury Notes," Record Group 109, vol. 99, pp. 10–34, National Archives; see also J. D. Pope, Columbia Treasury Note Bureau, to Memminger, August 21, 1862, etc., in *Correspondence with*, ed. Thian, pp. 590–91.

17. W. H. Young (president of the Bank of Columbus, Georgia) to Memminger, August 31, 1861, ibid., pp. 304–5; see also Memminger to B. C. Pressley (assistant treasurer at Charleston), September 25, 1861; and Memminger to Robert Tyler, October 19, 1861, in *Correspondence of*, ed. Thian, pp. 193–94.

18. August Dietz, Sr., *The Postal Service of the Confederate States* (Richmond: Dietz Publishing, 1929), pp. 96, 177, provides interviews with surviving printers in Confederate security printing shops. See also Memminger to Colonel Blanton Duncan, October 7, 1861, in *Correspondence of*, ed. Thian, p. 198ff; Duncan to Memminger, January 9, 1862, in *Correspondence with*, ed. Thian, p. 466.

19. Memminger to General Winder (provost marshal at Richmond, Virginia), April 11, 1862, in *Correspondence of*, ed. Thian, p. 285. Ludwig and B. Duncan both ran up exorbitant bills by using lithograph stones for only 500–2,000 impressions, whereas such stones should have lasted for 5,000–7,000 impressions.

20. Under the Act of August 19, 1861 there were seven kinds of $5 notes, nine kinds of $10 notes, and five kinds of $20 notes. Grover C. Criswell, *Confederate and Southern States Currency* (Citrus, Fla.: Criswell Publications, 1976), pp. 13–33.

21. Blanton Duncan to C. G. Memminger, September 3, 8, 1861, October

10, 1861, in *Correspondence with,* ed. Thian, pp. 309, 322, 373–74; see also Memminger to J. D. Pope: "It is for the interest of the Government that rival establishments should be maintained," in Thian, *Correspondence of,* p. 306.

22. B. Duncan to Memminger, June 4, 1862, in *Correspondence with,* ed. Thian, p. 559. A government order to conscript the personnel of Douglas, Manouvrier, Simon, and Pessoux for service in Columbia, S.C., was abortive.

23. George Dunn to Memminger, August 19, 1862; Gemmell and J. McFarlane to Memminger, August 19, 1862, ibid., pp. 598–601.

24. Pope to Memminger, August 18, 1862, ibid., pp. 596–98.

25. Memminger to Blanton Duncan, April 7, 1862, ibid., p. 281. Memminger, of course, ultimately fired Duncan and James T. Paterson and broke, as can be seen, contracts freely, when he found it convenient.

26. Memminger to J. D. Pope, June 25, August 4, September 17, 1862, in *Correspondence of,* ed. Thian, pp. 314, 333, 354.

27. Memminger to Joseph D. Pope, May 17, 1861, ibid., pp. 295–96; see also *Correspondence with,* ed. Thian, pp. 560–61, 601–2, 640–41; Joseph D. Pope to Memminger, June 5, 1862, August 22, 1862, September 26, 1862 (two letters) and Keatinge to Memminger, October 28, 1862, ibid., pp. 656–57.

28. Joseph D. Pope and S. G. Jamison to Memminger, September 16, 1862, ibid., pp. 620–21.

29. Pope to Memminger, September 6, 1862, ibid., pp. 620–21.

30. Phillip Clayton (assistant secretary of the treasury) to Memminger, September 4, 10, 12, 1862, ibid., pp. 616–17, 619–20, 623–26. Clayton was sent to Charleston, Augusta, Atlanta, Montgomery, and Savannah to stem the panic and help identify the counterfeits.

31. Circular, *Correspondence of,* ed. Thian, p. 338; also Memminger to John Boston (depository at Savannah), September 26, 1862, ibid., pp. 357–58; Raphael P. Thian, *Register of the Confederate Debt,* ed. Douglas B. Ball (Boston: Boston Quarterman Publications, 1972), pp. 173–75; report of the register of the treasury, January 24, 1864, in Raphael P. Thian, *Reports of the Secretary of the Treasury of the Confederate States of America 1861–65,* part 3 (Washington, D.C.: Privately published, 1878), pp. 131–37; Memminger to Pope, September 26, 1862, *Correspondence of,* ed. Thian, p. 358.

32. Report of January 9, 1865, Thian, *Reports,* pp. 423–25.

33. J. E. Gaudey (cashier, Farmers' and Mechanics' Bank of Savannah) to Memminger, October 11, 1861, in *Correspondence with,* ed. Thian, p. 375; see also Pope to Memminger, December 8, 23, 1862, ibid., pp. 678, 696–97. Ludwig and Duncan printed $300,000 of $100 and $20 notes on the nonexistent Farmers' and Manufacturers' Bank of Savannah. Paterson was asked to print "facsimile" Confederate notes from his own plates. Pope to Memminger, December 10, 1862, ibid., pp. 678–79. Pope sent an Alabama agent away because "the Treasury Department requires all and much more force than we now have to supply the Department with Treasury Notes." Paterson, however, filled the Alabama order at his Augusta, Georgia, office.

34. Keatinge and Ball to George A. Trenholm (secretary of the treasury), February 3, 1865; S. G. Jamison to George A. Trenholm, February 21, 1865,

ibid., pp. 547–48, 556. Keatinge's pay was docked $25,000 for bad printing which he felt was the government's fault because it had failed to authorize the renewal of the plates.

35. Richard E. Beringer, Herman Hattaway, Archer Jones, and William N. Still, Jr., *Why the South Lost the Civil War* (Athens: University of Georgia Press, 1986), p. 11.

36. James L. Nichols, *The Confederate Quartermaster in the Trans-Mississippi* (Austin: University of Texas Press, 1964), pp. 20, 22, 24, 26–27, 33, 41, 96–101. Quartermaster personnel, lacking treasury notes, paid with receipts that fell to 50 cents on the dollar in treasury notes. See also Henry N. Scherber, "The Pay of the Troops in the Trans-Mississippi," *Arkansas Historical Quarterly* 18 (Winter 1959):352–53.

37. Thomas C. Hindman, *Report of Major General Hindman of His Operations in the Trans-Mississippi District,* published by order of Congress (Richmond: R. M. Smith, 1864), pp. 5–18; see also Stephen B. Oates, *Confederate Cavalry West of the River* (Austin: University of Texas Press, 1961), pp. 85–112. After this period, it was not until the spring of 1864 that General Smith was able to assemble a force in excess of fifteen thousand men.

38. Joseph H. Parks, *General Edmund Kirby-Smith CSA* (Baton Rouge: Louisiana State University Press, 1954), pp. 276–87, 448.

39. July 22, 1863, in *Correspondence of,* ed. Thian, p. 489.

40. Memminger to E. Kirby Smith, October 2, 1863, ibid., pp. 530–31; Trenholm to Congress, January 9, 1865, P. W. Gray to Trenholm, December 26, 1864, in Thian, *Reports,* pp. 423–25, 446–47. The Trans-Mississippi received $27 million out of $460 million issued in 1864 (4.3 percent) when that region had 16 percent of the Confederate population.

41. Edward Younger, ed., *Inside the Confederate Government: The Diary of Robert Garlich Hill Kean* (New York: Oxford University Press, 1957), p. 243.

42. Ella Lonn, *Desertion during the Civil War* (New York: Century, 1928), p. 7. Lonn lists the absence of pay for six to ten months, provisions for three or so months at a stretch as being the second most important cause of desertion after lack of loyalty to the cause. See also Frank E. Vandiver, *Rebel Brass: The Confederate Command System* (Baton Rouge: Louisiana State University Press, 1956), pp. 88–89. Vandiver reports that funds shortages were fatal to supply operations.

43. Frank E. Vandiver, *Ploughshares into Swords: Josiah Gorgas and Confederate Ordinance* (Austin: University of Texas Press, 1952), pp. 86–87, 114–15. Captain Caleb Huse's operations in Europe on Gorgas's behalf were crippled because of a failure to remit funds.

44. Seddon to Trenholm, December 29, 1864, in *War of the Rebellion: A Compilation of the Official Records of the Union and Confederate Armies,* 70 vols. (Washington, D.C.: Government Printing Office, 1880–1901), 4th ser., vol. 3, p. 975; see also James L. Nichols, *Confederate Engineers* (Tuscaloosa, Ala.: Confederate Publishing Company, 1957), pp. 35–37.

45. Mary Spencer Ringold, *The Role of the State Legislatures in the Confederacy* (Athens: University of Georgia Press, 1966), pp. 69–81. Ringold writes that

state aid was predicated upon "Confederate inability to care properly for the men. State aid outside Georgia and North Carolina was generally too little and too late. Confederate reimbursements of War expenses would have allowed the states to do more about the homefront."

46. George D. Green, *Finance and Economic Development in the Old South, Louisiana Banking 1804–1861* (Stanford: Stanford University Press, 1972), pp. 74–75. Foreign exchange transactions were based upon "horserace bills" (those that had to be covered by the shipment of specie) and "undoubted credits," those representing money already on deposit at a foreign bank.

47. Report of May 10, 1861, Thian, *Reports,* p. 7.

48. Thian, ed., *Correspondence of,* pp. 25–26. Initially, commissioners were located at Montgomery, Pensacola, Augusta, New Orleans, Jackson, Charleston, and Galveston. Additional offices were added at such points as Mobile and Savannah. Commissioners were appointed later at Fredericksburg, Norfolk, Petersburg, and Richmond. Douglas B. Ball, *Confederate Interim Depositary Receipts and Funding Certificates Issued in the Commonwealth of Virginia 1861–1865* (Hampton, Va.: Multiprint Press, 1972), pp. 22, 28, 32.

49. Paul Studenski and Herman E. Kross, *Financial History of the United States, Fiscal, Monetary, Banking and Tariff etc.* (New York: McGraw-Hill, 1952), pp. 76–80; see also C. G. Memminger to Messrs. Smith, Denegre, Noble, and Forstall, May 24, 1861, in *Correspondence of,* ed. Thian, pp. 90–91; Report of July 20, 1861, in *Reports,* ed. Thian, p. 15.

50. *Bankers' Magazine* 15 (June 1861):584; *New Bern* [N.C.] *Progress,* July 30, 1861; see also *Acts of the Called Session of the General Assembly of Alabama, Held in the City of Montgomery, Commencing on the Second Monday in January, 1861* (Montgomery: Shorter and Reid, 1861), pp. 9–11; "An Act to Legalize the Suspension of Specie Payments by Certain Banks of Alabama," sec. 1 and 2; and message of Governor Shorter to the Alabama Legislature, October 28, 1861, in *War of the Rebellion: Armies,* ser. 4, vol. 1, p. 699. Three Alabama banks lent $200,000 in coin. See *Acts of the General Assembly of Virginia, Passed in 1861 etc.* (Richmond: William F. Ritchie Public Printer, 1861), p. 124, sec. 5.

51. Memminger to R. R. Cuyler, March 27, 1861, in *Correspondence of,* ed. Thian, pp. 36–38. This letter was later issued as a circular.

52. E. Frost to Memminger, April 10, 1861, in *Correspondence with,* ed. Thian, pp. 60–61.

53. Memminger to Frost, April 8, 1861; Memminger to David Ravenel (president, South Carolina Bank), April 8, 1861; Alexander B. Clitherall (register, CSA.), to Thomas C. Daniel (cashier, Commercial Bank of Selma, Ala.), April 17, 1861, all in *Correspondence of,* ed. Thian, pp. 51–52, 53. The government was to deposit the funds it received with the bank of issue and then to draw on them. Banks had until April 17 to accede to these terms or have their notes rejected. Congress later approved these arrangements (Act of May 11, 1861). *Statutes at Large,* 2d sess., p. 108.

54. John Christopher Schwab, *The Confederate States of America 1861–65* (New York: Charles Scribner's Sons, 1901), p. 44. The available evidence suggests a smaller figure, particularly if one omits the purchase of foreign

exchange and foreign loans. In the 1960s when the gold cover for federal reserve notes was taken off, John Kenneth Galbraith testified before the Senate Finance Committee, chaired by Harry E. Byrd, Sr. (D-Va.), and pointed out that the South had fought the Civil War with only $20 million in specie. "Yes," replied Senator Byrd, who was opposing the bill, "and I think we all know what happened to the Confederacy."

55. Thian, *Register*, pp. 179–80.

56. Memminger to Denegre, December 4, 1861, in *Correspondence of*, ed. Thian, p. 235.

57. Denegre to Memminger, December 21, 1861, in *Correspondence with*, ed. Thian, pp. 446–47.

58. Hugh McCulloch, *Men and Measures over Half a Century: Sketches and Comments* (New York: Charles Scribner's Sons, 1888), p. 139. Such payments may have amounted to $4 million.

59. Alex M. Carr (of Charlesville, Habersham County, Georgia) to Memminger, November 1, 1862, in *Secretary's Office Collector's Correspondence, March 21, 1861–January 29, 1863*, vol. 164.

60. Denegre to Memminger, December 28, 1861; P. N. Wood and G. A. Freret to Duncan F. Kenner, January 7, 1862, in *Correspondence with*, ed. Thian, pp. 450–451, 458; Message of December 10, 1861, in Thian, *Reports*, p. 40; Act of December 24, 1861, *Public and Private Laws*, ed. Mathews, p. 231.

61. Memminger to Denegre, February 7, 1862, in *Correspondence of*, ed. Thian, pp. 262–63. Why Memminger should have been so optimistic in the absence of foreign recognition or good military news is beyond comprehension.

62. Moore to Davis, *War of the Rebellion: Armies*, ser. 1, vol. 53, p. 803. Moore had written to Davis in March but his letter miscarried and so was not available for action until April 5; ibid., p. 799.

63. Memminger to Governor Moore, April 8, 1862, in *Correspondence of*, ed. Thian, p. 282.

64. Davis to General Lovell, April 23, 1862, Davis to Governor Moore, April 24, 1862, in *War of the Rebellion: Armies*, ser. 1, vol. 6, p. 883. On April 23, Davis told Lovell to "leave all State institutions as far as possible undisturbed by military power" [Lovell had forced the banks to lend him money to keep his army together]. The next day Davis told Moore, "we will take the coin of the banks and be responsible for it. The Secretary of the Treasury will take action immediately." That action was quite belated; see Memminger to G. W. Randolph (secretary of war), October 9, 1862, in *Correspondence of*, ed. Thian, pp. 362–63.

65. *Report of U.S. Director of the Mint* (Washington, D.C.: Government Printing Office, 1862), p. 45 (report dated October 27, 1862). The production of a Confederate coinage was prevented by breaking the die collar, and $5 million in silver bullion on hand was concealed from Secretary Memminger.

66. Duncan Kenner resolution of July 29, 1861, *Journal of the Congress of the Confederate States of America 1861–65*, 7 vols. (Washington, D.C.: Government Printing Office, 1904–5), vol. 1, p. 290; August 3, 1861, p. 312. No action was

deemed necessary. See also the *Charleston Courier*, July 26, 1861; *Memphis Argus* (quoted in the *Courier* of the same date); and the *Savannah Republican*, July 4, August 5, 1861.

67. Act 4579 (December 21, 1861), *Acts of the General Assembly of the State of South Carolina, Passed in December 1861 etc.* (Columbia: Charles P. Pelham, State Printer, 1862), pp. 42–43; Act 106 (November 7, 1862), *Acts of the Called Session, 1862, and of the Second Regular Annual Session of the General Assembly of Alabama Held in the City of Montgomery etc.* (Montgomery: Montgomery Advertiser Book and Job Office, 1862), p. 103; Act no. 13, title 4 (November 22, 1861), *Acts of the General Assembly of the State of Georgia, Passed in Milledgeville, at an Annual Session in November and December, 1861* (Milledgeville: Boughton, Nisbet and Barnes, State Printers, 1862), p. 25.

68. Denegre to Memminger, May 4, 1861, in *Correspondence with*, ed. Thian, pp. 87–90. Denegre noted the danger to the city from federal attack. See also Richard Pritchard to Memminger, July 11, 1861, "Miscellaneous Correspondence," Record Group 56, National Archives: "Our Banks hold $16 million of Gold—it is a bait held out to the Lincoln forces to attack us to get possession of same. . . ."

69. Memminger to B. C. Pressley, December 9, 1861, in *Correspondence of*, ed. Thian, pp. 236–37; April 15, 1862, *War of the Rebellion: Armies*, ser. 1, vol. 6, pp. 876–77.

70. 240,000 troy ounces at $20.67 per ounce of gold equals about $4,960,000.

71. Stephen A. Caldwell, *A Banking History of Louisiana* (Baton Rouge: Louisiana State University Press, 1935), p. 90.

72. Thian, *Reports*, pp. 154–55.

73. Thian, ed., *Correspondence of*, pp. 377, 387; Thian, ed., *Correspondence with*, pp. 646–48; see also Memminger to Vice-President Stephens, January 16, 1863, in Thian, *Reports*, pp. 133–34.

74. Secretary of War to General Beauregard, October 14, 1862; F. H. Hatch (collector of New Orleans) to Beauregard, May 18, 1862; A. W. Rice to Beauregard, October 30, 1862, all in *War of the Rebellion: Armies*, ser. 4, vol. 1, pp. 11, 236, 1130–31, 1147–53.

75. Trenholm to President Davis, January 10, 1865, in Thian, *Reports*, p. 427.

76. Thian, ed., *Correspondence of*, p. 248; John M. Garth to Memminger, February 15, 1863, in *Correspondence with*, ed. Thian, pp. 21–22: Garth patriotically offered to sell $10,000 in coin at 100 percent premium when the rate was 200 percent; "Miscellaneous Documents," no. 5, House of Representatives, 45th Cong., 2d sess., pp. 1–94; Schwals, *Confederate States*, p. 127.

77. R. L. Garrison, "Administrative Problems of the Confederate Post Office Department," *South Western Historical Quarterly* 19 (1915–16):233–34; letter book, Post Office Department, p. 21 (Reagan to Davis, June 30, 1863); see also Davis to E. C. Elmore, October 5, 1863, in *Jefferson Davis Constitutionalist: His Letters, Papers, and Speeches*, ed. Dunbar Rowland, 10 vols. (Jackson: Mississippi Department of Archives and History, 1923), vol. 6, p. 56; Reagan, *Memoirs with Special Reference to Secession and the Civil War*, pp. 158–59.

78. C. G. Memminger to John Hardy, March 26, 1862, Record Group 365, vol. 165, National Archives; Thian, *Correspondence of,* pp. 340–42. This is another example of Memminger being penny-wise and pound-foolish. What kind of change, in the absence of Confederate change bills or fractional currency, was to be furnished, the secretary did not explain.

79. Memminger to John Fraser and Company, Charleston, October 12, 1862, and Memminger to Secretary Randolph, October 22, 1862, in *Correspondence of,* ed. Thian, pp. 366–67, 371–76; Memminger to T. S. Metcalf (depository, Augusta, Ga.), October 28, 1862, in *Correspondence with,* ed. Thian, pp. 411, 515–16. The secretary's inquiries in May 1864 were prompted by an anonymous letter from a soldier at Fort Fisher (Wilmington) reporting captured ships to W. A. Graham, May 3, 1864. Graham Papers, University of North Carolina, MSS Division.

80. Henry Savage (depository at Wilmington, N.C.) to Secretary Trenholm, October 4 and November 4, 1864, ibid., pp. 516–23. The purser was given $500 in gold for his heroism, by Trenholm's direction.

81. Schwab, *The Confederate States of America,* p. 8; Samuel B. Thompson, *Confederate Purchasing Operations Abroad* (Chapel Hill: University of North Carolina Press, 1935), p. 50; and Todd, *Confederate Finance,* p. 31. All of these authors confuse foreign exchange and coin. All say coin was "presumably" shipped without citing any references to support their conclusions except after 1863. Those coin shipments, of course, came from the Louisiana banks, not the February 28, 1861 loan. As discussed in chapter 3, only $1.7 million of foreign exchange was sent abroad in 1861.

82. Trenholm to W. G. Letch, assistant treasurer (formerly at Charleston), in *Correspondence of,* ed. Thian, p. 878; ibid., pp. 871, 876, 885, 890; Thian, ed., *Correspondence with,* 1863–85, pp. 557–61; *Record of Letters of Treasurer,* vol. 115F, pp. 325, 336–37, 353, 363.

83. Secretary Trenholm parted with $200,000 from his own purse. Memorandum, Judge Campbell to J. C. Breckenbridge (secretary of war), dated March 5, 1865, Campbell-Colston Papers, University of North Carolina, MSS Division; Act of March 17, 1865, in *Laws and Joint Resolutions of the Last Session of the Confederate Congress . . . ,* ed. Charles W. Ramsdell (Durham: Duke University Press, 1941), pp. 147–49, table 9. Claims that coin was sold primarily to lower the specie premium on Confederate notes cannot be sustained. See James F. Morgan, *Greybacks and Gold: Confederate Monetary Policy* (Pensacola, Fla.: Perdido Bay Press, 1985), p. 7.

84. Schwab, *The Confederate States of America,* p. 127. With 22 percent of the nation's bank capital, Southern banks held 39 percent ($34.8 million) of its specie—or, if Kentucky, Missouri, and Tennessee are excluded, 20 percent of the capital and 28 percent ($26 million) of the specie.

85. Resolution submitted April 4, 1863, *Proceedings of the First Confederate Congress—Third Session in Part March 20 to May 1, 1863,* Richmond 1943, Southern Historical Society Papers, n.s. 11, whole nos. 49, p. 89.

86. Elbridge G. Spalding, *History of the Legal Tender Paper Money Issued during the Great Rebellion* (Buffalo: Express Printing, 1869), pp. 138–48.

87. Sidney Homer, *A History of Interest Rates* (New Brunswick, N.J.: Rutgers University Press, 1963), p. 309.

88. Report of March 19, 1862, in *Reports,* ed. Thian, p. 60.

89. Reports of December 7, 1863, ibid., p. 180. As pointed out, the only "just expectations" anyone in the Confederacy was entitled to were that the secretary would do his duty and lay in a coin stock sufficient to pay the interest on the public debt.

90. Report of the Special Senate Committee on the Currency: January 1864. Richmond, 1864, Record Group 93, p. 2, National Archives.

91. John Watts, *The Facts of the Cotton Famine* (1866, repr. New York: Augustus M. Kelly, 1970), p. 364.

92. Thian, ed., *Correspondence of,* p. 474; editorial on the cotton bonds by John Strother (chief clerk) to the Lynchburg *Republic,* Jackson *Mississippian,* Knoxville *Register,* Montgomery *Advertiser,* Mobile *Tribune,* Atlanta *Confederacy,* Savannah *Republican,* Charleston *Courier,* Columbia *Carolinian,* Raleigh *Register,* Wilmington *Journal,* and the Augusta *Constitutionalist,* June 26, 1863.

93. *Charleston Mercury,* July 18, 1863.

94. The secretary's disappointment must have been considerable, as he had expected bids of up to 250–300 percent of par, P. V. Daniel (president, Richmond, Fredericksburg and Potomac Railroad) to Memminger, July 24, 1863, in *Correspondence with,* ed. Thian, pp. 120–21, 126.

95. Memminger to R. W. Barnwell (chairman, Finance Committee, C.S. Senate), December 15, 1863, in Thian, *Reports.*

96. George A. Trenholm to R. M. T. Hunter, president pro-tem of the Senate, November 10, 1864, ibid., pp. 385–86.

97. Thomas W. Dewey (president, Bank of North Carolina branch at Charlotte) to Secretary Trenholm, August 25, 1864, "Letters Received by the Secretary of the Treasury 1861–65," Record Group 365, National Archives. Many of the extant bonds have no clipped coupons.

98. *The Columbia Carolinian,* June 22, 1864, p. 1.

99. Thian, *Reports,* p. 181.

100. "An Act to reduce the currency and to authorize a new issue of notes and bonds," in *The Statutes at Large of the Confederate States,* ed. Mathews, pp. 205–8.

101. S. G. Jamison, chief clerk of the Treasury Note Bureau, to Memminger, May 21, 1864, in *Correspondence with,* ed. Thian, p. 409; John M. Strother to the editor of the *Floridian Journal,* Tallahassee, in *Correspondence of,* ed. Thian, p. 652. For a list of the newspapers to which this letter was sent, see the same letter.

102. Memminger to W. Y. Leitch, June 6, 1864, ibid., p. 668.

103. Memminger to the editor of the *Raleigh Confederate,* June 6, 1864, telegraphic messages to Treasury Department, p. 456; Leitch to Memminger, June 14, 1864, in *Correspondence with,* ed. Thian, pp. 419–20; see also Memminger to J. H. Reagan, June 6, 1864, in *Correspondence of,* p. 668.

104. Memminger to J. H. Fitts (depository at Tuscaloosa), May 13, 1864, (circular letter to Fitts and others), ibid., pp. 652–53.

105. Thian, *Register*, pp. 187–88.

106. Treasurer's statement showing the receipts into the treasury from the sales of 6 percent non-taxable bonds, in Thian, *Reports*, pp. 433–34.

107. Memminger to Davis, May 25, 1864, ibid., p. 349.

108. Message of May 30, 1864, in *A Compilation of the Messages and Papers of the Confederacy, Including the Diplomatic Correspondence 1861–1865*, 2 vols., ed. James D. Richardson (Nashville: United State Publishing, 1905), vol. 1, p. 455.

109. Mathews, ed., *Public and Private Laws*, 1st sess., sec. 3, p. 54; 3rd sess., sec. 1, ibid., p. 167; Capers, *Life*, p. 336.

110. Report of September 15, 1862 to Thomas S. Bocock, speaker of the House, in Thian, *Reports*, pp. 89–90; April 27, 1863, in *Public and Private Laws*, ed. Mathews, p. 128.

111. Thian, *Register*, pp. 3–5, 173–78. This was equal to approximately forty-one thousand days' work, or thirty-two men working from August 1861 to February 1865 without holidays. This makes no provision for cutting the sheets, packing the notes in bundles, or counting them.

112. Mary Boykin Chesnut, *Diary from Dixie*, ed. Ben Ames Williams (Boston: Houghton, Mifflin, 1949), p. 225.

113. Chesnut, *Diary*, pp. 129–90. There were eight hundred thousand stock certificates and coupon bonds to be signed, dated, numbered, and registered. Each coupon until 1864 was also signed and numbered.

114. Robert Tyler to Secretary Memminger, July 28, 1863, in "Miscellaneous Correspondence," Record Group 56, National Archives.

115. Act of February 14, 1863, in *Public and Private Laws*, ed. Mathews, 1st Cong., 3d sess., p. 97. Charles A. Rose, a Richmond notary public and chief clerk of the department; E. Apperson, a Richmond broker; and occasionally Charles T. Jones, acting register, based on an examination of the extant bonds, apparently took over 70 percent of the signing duties in 1863, while the coupon signatures were printed starting in 1864.

116. Pope to Memminger, September 26, 1862, in *Correspondence with*, ed. Thian, vol. 1, *1861–62*, pp. 620–41; Memminger to Pope, September 29, 1860; Memminger to E. C. Elmore (treasurer), Robert Tyler (register), and S. G. Jamison (chief of the treasury Note Bureau), April 18, 1864; Memminger to W. Y. Leitch, May 7, 1864, all in *Correspondence of*, ed. Thian, pp. 356–60, 627–29.

117. Memminger to Congressman W. H. N. Smith, May 18, 1864, ibid., p. 654; Trenholm to C. J. McRae, European treasury agent, December 10, 1864, in *Record Book of Copies of Letters of the Secretary of the Treasury from October 17, 1864 to March 31, 1865*, vol. 115F, National Archives, pp. 128–29. Government checks often bounced, which further encouraged this abuse. Report of May 2, 1864, in Thian, *Reports*, p. 257.

118. *Journal of the Congress of the Confederate States of America, 1861–1865*

(Washington, D.C.: Government Printing Office, 1904–5), vol. 1, p. 127. The New Orleans assistant treasurer was a Confederate-created post—the United States had no such officer.

119. Report of Memminger to Vice-President Stephens, March 17, 1862, in Thian, *Reports*, p. 67.

120. Ibid., p. 67; Act of April 15, 1862, in *Public and Private Laws*, ed. Mathews, p. 29.

121. Act of February 17, 1864, sec. 15.

122. Trenholm to Seddon (on behalf of the Banks of Charleston, concerning the inconvenience caused by General Order No. 77a and A.G.O.), dated October 20, 1864, in *Record Book of Copies of Letters of the Secretary of the Treasury*, p. 9.

123. North Carolina Convention, 1865, Doc. no. 1, *Treasurer's Report*, September 4, 1865 (Raleigh, N.C.: John Spelman, Printer to the State, 1865), pp. 18–73.

124. Carmelita S. Ryan, *Preliminary Inventory of the Treasury Department Collection of Confederate Records*, Publication 68–3 (Washington, D.C.: Government Printing Office, 1967), pp. 53–55; see also Ball, *Confederate Interim Depository Receipts*, pp. 1–46. I have checked the bankers' magazine list and found that most of the depositories were either bankers, private bankers, or prominent factors.

125. Trenholm to John McNab (depository, Eufaula, Ala.), August 17, 1864; circular, November 11, 1864; Trenholm to S. M. Hawkins (depository, Granada, Miss.), August 30, 1864; Trenholm to Ex-Governor Shorter (Ala.), September 12, 1864, all in *Correspondence of*, ed. Thian, pp. 737, 792, 748–49, 763–64; T. Sanford (Montgomery depository) to Trenholm, August 30, 1864, in *Correspondence with*, ed. Thian, pp. 480–81.

126. Memminger to Howell Cobb, July 24, 1861, in Thian, *Reports*, pp. 19–23.

127. Circular dated in January, 1862, in *Correspondence of*, ed. Thian, p. 245. Higher denominations up to $10,000 were suggested for treasury notes, but no action was taken.

128. Motion of Nisbet of Georgia, *Journal of the Congress*, February 26, 1861, p. 87, August 9, 1861, p. 329.

129. Denegre to Memminger, March 25, 1861, in *Correspondence with*, ed. Thian, p. 18. Memminger noted that the $50 denomination was required by Congress. March 29, 1861, in *Correspondence of*, ed. Thian, p. 38.

130. *Journals of Transferable Stock and Coupon Bonds*, Acts of February 28, May 16, August 19, 1861, February 20, 1863, vols. 125–54, Record Group 109, National Archives. $50 bonds made up 2.5 percent of value of February 28, 1861 loan.

131. Studenski and Kross, *Financial History*, p. 126.

132. James Gallatin, *Two Letters to the Hon. S. P. Chase, Secretary of the Treasury* (New York: Hosford and Ketcham, 1861), pp. 5–8.

133. Act of May 16, 1861, in *Public and Private Laws*, ed. Mathews, pp. 117–18.

134. Memminger to Howell Cobb, May 10, 1861, in Thian, *Reports*, p. 10.

135. *Journal of the Congress*, May 15, 1861, p. 228.

136. Secretary Memminger to B. C. Pressley, November 11, 1861, in "Miscellaneous Correspondence," Record Group 56, National Archives.

137. National Monetary Commission, *Laws of the United States Concerning Money, Banking and Loans, 1778–1901*, comp. A. T. Huntington and Robert J. Mawhinney, doc. no. 480, Sen., 61st Cong., 2d sess. (Washington, D.C.: Government Printing Office, 1910), pp. 164–65.

138. Ibid., pp. 16–58, 169–70.

139. *Hunt's Merchants' Magazine* 47 (1863):33, 338, 69.

140. Thian, *Reports*, pp. 181–89; Thian, *Register*, p. 181. People were much annoyed by the secretary's failure to keep his promises. J. D. Harward to Memminger, July 28, 1863, in "Miscellaneous Correspondence," Record Group 56, National Archives.

141. Noteholders were to fund by July 31, 1863; treasury circular dated May 11, 1863, Charleston *Courier*, May 20, 1863.

142. Act of December 29, 1864, no. 16, Ramsdell, *Laws*, pp. 12–13.

143. Mathews, ed., *Public and Private Laws*, sess. 3, sec. 1, p. 177.

144. "A British Merchant," *Currency, Self-Regulating and Explained in a Letter to His Grace the Duke of Argyll; etc.* (London: Longman, Brown, Green, 1855), p. 161.

145. Eli M. Bruce, *Speech of Hon. E. M. Bruce of Kentucky on the Financial Policy of the Government, Delivered in the House of Representatives, October 2, 1862* (Richmond, Va.: Published privately, 1862), pp. 1–4.

146. Thian, *Register*, p. 182; Act of August 19, 1861, in *Public and Private Laws*, ed. Mathews, sess. 3, sec. 2, p. 177.

147. Edward J. Forstall to Memminger, May 9, 1861, in *Correspondence with*, ed. Thian, pp. 91–95.

148. Holmes to Memminger, April 1, 1861, ibid., pp. 34–36.

149. Holmes to Memminger, May 13, May 14, 1861, ibid., pp. 91, 100–101, and 105; July 27, 1861, ibid., pp. 251–54.

150. Thian, *Register*, pp. 182–83. The actual bond issues followed Holmes's plan quite closely. Memminger to Howell Hobb, November 20, 1861, in Thian, *Reports*, p. 37.

151. Robert Tyler to Memminger, March 11, 1863, in Correspondence of the Register of the Treasury, vol. 118, Record Group 109, National Archives.

152. Thian, *Register*, pp. 182–84.

153. Acts of August 19, 1861 sec. 1; December 24, 1861 sec. 1; October 13, 1862 sec. 1; March 23, 1863 sec. 3; and February 17, 1864 sec. 5.

154. Act of December 17, 1860, *U.S. Laws*, pp. 156–57; *Bankers' Magazine*, February 1861, p. 621, May 1861, p. 917.

155. House of Representatives, *Miscellaneous Documents*, no. 20, 36th Cong., 2d sess. (Washington, D.C.: Government Printing Office, 1861), p. 3.

156. *DeBow's Review*, April 1861, p. 508.

157. Denegre to Memminger, April 3, 1861, in *Correspondence with*, ed. Thian, p. 37.

158. William M. D'Antignac (president, Augusta Insurance and Banking Company) to Memminger, June 20, 1861, ibid., pp. 146–47.

159. Denegre to Memminger, May 4, 1861, ibid., 1861–62, pp. 87–88.

160. Act of March 14, Acts of April 30 and June 28, 1861, *Acts of the General Assembly of the State of Virginia Passed 1861*, pp. 29–30.

161. May 15, 1861, *Journal of the Congress*, vol. 1, p. 227.

162. Thian, *Register*, pp. 179–90. The call certificates should have borne, say, 3 percent if only to make the bonds more attractive.

CHAPTER FOUR

Government Management
of the Confederate Currency

In view of the important role played by treasury notes in the financing of earlier wars, management of the currency was one of Secretary
Memminger's most pressing concerns. That task should have been
easy because a well-balanced program of blockade-running, domestic
produce purchases, foreign loans, bond sales, and taxes would have
limited the role of treasury notes to financing the residue of the war
expenditures not met from other sources.[1] Yet the success of even a
passive program required active measures.

Treasury notes traditionally fell into two groups: those bearing
interest and falling due on a particular day, and non-interest-bearing
notes intended for circulation. Yet against the strong advice of John
C. Calhoun, the Confederate Congress and Secretary Memminger
chose to employ interest-bearing notes ineptly, to the damage of the
government's credit and unnecessary expense to the Treasury.

Interest-Bearing Treasury Notes in Confederate Finance

By the Acts of March 9 and August 3, 1861, the Confederate Congress continued the tradition of financing the government's short-
term debt by issuing $2 million of 3.65 percent interest-bearing trea-
sury notes payable 425 days after date and receivable for all duties
except export dues. Moreover, it strictly adhered to the U.S. custom
of keeping the denomination at or above $50 (Appendix C). Although
the transfer by endorsement provision of the acts was more honored
in the breach than the observance, these notes remained closely held.
Undoubtedly, the only reason they did not enter more into circulation
was that half the notes were in denominations of $1,000 and $500.[2] As
such, they were often exchanged, or used as collateral for, more usable
bank notes.[3]

Improvidently, the Congress made no explicit provision about the
way in which the debt would be discharged, and in the hope of
ultimately getting specie, many holders retained their notes until the
end of the war. Thus, in his report of November 7, 1864, Secretary of

the Treasury George A. Trenholm reported that more than 25 percent ($516,050 with accrued interest) of the notes remained outstanding.[4]

The issue of March 9, 1861 proved ill conceived, both in regard to terms and to magnitude. While the act required notes to be in denominations of $50 and higher, the secretary ordered the notes in New York without specifying which denominations he wished. What he received were 607 sheets, each sheet consisting of a $50, $100, $500, and $1,000 note.[5] The secretary immediately realized his mistake and at once ordered an additional printing. Subsequently, 999 half-sheets of $50 and $100 notes reached Montgomery.[6]

Such a mistake in detail undoubtedly reflected the inexperience of the Treasury Department and its New York agent. What is most striking about this $1 million issue is its ludicrously inadequate size. Judgments after the fact should be restrained and qualified, and in 1861 few had the intuition to foresee exactly what the future might portend. Yet at a purely mechanical level, one might have expected some minimal precautions.[7] Cognizant of the Confederacy's shortage of security printers, Memminger should have used his prerogative to reissue the notes in order to accumulate a reserve stock. Thus, when he sent his first letter on about March 10, he might have ordered three plates with a face value of $2,300 and had printed fifteen thousand sheets each of the low denominations and ten thousand sheets of the high denominations. That would have given the Confederacy $26 million of notes for a mere $3,825.[8]

In addition, a prudent secretary might have availed himself of the opportunity to ask Congress to authorize the printing of $5 million of notes (5 cents up to $2 denomination), to make change for the customs houses and post offices in order to conserve coin. Such an order could have been completed and shipped South before hostilities got underway. The notes would have been useful both to discourage other parties from issuing fractional currency and change bills and also to facilitate the operations of the Post Office because treasury notes were not receivable for stamps.[9] Because this momentary opportunity, like so many others, was allowed to lapse, the treasury lost precious coin resources.

The Interest-Bearing Notes of the Acts of April 17, 1862

If the 3.65 percent treasury notes were a minor episode in Confederate finance, the next resort to interest-bearing notes in the spring of 1862 involved a number of serious blunders. Under section 3 of the authorizing legislation, the secretary was empowered to issue up to

$165 million of 7.30 percent treasury notes in denominations of not less than $100.[10] These notes were authorized in lieu of the 8 percent bonds provided in the Act of April 12, 1862, which the Congress, given the then market for long-term loans, evidently felt could not be sold. That proviso would now appear to have been a sloppily drafted afterthought; although the notes were payable to bearer and receivable for public dues at face value, no provision was made for paying the interest, although the redemption date was six months after peace. This deficiency was corrected by the Act of September 23, 1862, which required, at Memminger's own request, that the Treasury pay such interest every January first.[11]

In creating this issue, Congress clearly intended that it would be exchanged for the regular circulation, thereby curtailing the expansion of the currency, and had the public cooperated by holding the notes as an investment, the effect would have been deflationary. But bankers soon cornered the supply and simply substituted the notes as cash reserves for the non-interest-bearing notes they would have otherwise retained.[12]

Postwar bank balance sheets show that in North Carolina 40 percent of all Confederate notes held were 7.30 percent treasury notes.[13] With the inflation greatly exceeding the interest paid, only the banks, and those acquiring such notes just before January, had any incentive to hold them.[14] The denominations of the notes had much to do with this problem. While the law simply stated that nothing under $100 was to be emitted, the secretary, once more sticking to a narrowly legalistic approach, chose to interpret the law as authorizing only those of $100 denomination, and placed orders with the printers on that basis.

In September 1862, R. R. Cuyler, president of the Central Railroad Bank of Georgia, wrote urging that notes be issued in denominations of $1,000 to $10,000.[15] Although the secretary replied that he would act on the idea, much of the issue was already printed, and therefore no action was taken.[16] The use of $500 and higher denominations would have kept the notes out of circulation and prevented their use as currency substitutes while they at the same time facilitated interbank or clearing-house transactions.

Another deficiency of the issue, beyond the denominations employed and the interest rate used, involved the absence of any explicit provision for allowing the holders to exchange the notes for bonds. Those who tried to exchange their 7.3 percent notes for the 8 percent bonds authorized by the Act of April 12, 1862 were told by Memminger that such an exchange was prohibited. Yet an examination of the law's text in section 1 calls for the exchange of such bonds for treasury notes without distinction, provided the total 7.3 percent notes and 8 percent bonds did not exceed $165 million. Because only $3 million in bonds were issued, there was plenty of room to exchange notes for bonds at their face value.

By the Act of February 17, 1864, Congress, however, desirous of deleting such notes as a part of the currency, inaugurated a reversal of policy. Thus, such notes were declared to be bonds.[17] Because the holders paid no attention to the law and continued to use the notes as money, Congress then mandated the notes' exchange for thirty-year, 6 percent bonds.[18] The success of these programs was problematical; between April 30, 1864 and November 10, 1864, fewer than $27,000 of the notes out of the $99 million outstanding were retired from circulation, although some notes were retired under the new legislation.[19]

In retrospect, this issue of interest-bearing treasury notes clearly proved a nuisance to the Confederacy. While in theory the notes were supposed to be held as investment, in fact they were bearer instruments that actively circulated. Thus, contrary to their original purpose, they increased the volume of the currency, augmented the inflation by increasing the velocity of the regular currency, and added more than $18 million of unnecessary interest expense.[20]

The Disastrous Failure to Curtail Competing Currencies

Congress's inauguration of a bona fide treasury note currency by the Act of May 16, 1861, and Memminger's report of July 29, 1861, disclosed that he did not comprehend the full implications of a government currency. Although he was anything but an advocate of a fiat currency, he realized that if he were to pay his bills with treasury notes, they must be made generally acceptable. With this in mind, he commendably induced bankers to agree to make such notes the standard of value by receiving and paying them out.[21] Resolutions passed at the July 24, 1861 Bankers' Convention, which set the banks' seal of approval on this request, were crucial. If the banks, as Calhoun noted in chapter 1, received the notes, the public would follow suit.

The operation was not without its problems, for logic required that Memminger secure appropriate pledges from all the banks, including those in Mobile and New Orleans.[22] But because the Louisiana constitution prohibited bank specie payments moratoriums, the legislature was not empowered to legalize them, and the attorney general had to vacate his office if he did not bring quo warranto proceedings against any suspended bank, nothing was done. Yet these legal impediments were all dissolved when a suspension was ordered in September 1861. Why then the delay?

Secretary Memminger could scarcely have pleaded ignorance of the predicament. The New Orleans banks had failed to participate in any of the banking conventions, and the president of the Planters Bank of Tennessee at Memphis had suggested that the best way to raise the Confederate currency to par was to induce the New Orleans banks to receive and pay out such notes as soon as possible. Memminger had applauded the plan and had written to the presidents of the Mobile banks imploring their aid.[23] He had expatiated at length on his problems with the printers, on his need for loans, and his desire that the Mobile banks should receive and pay out treasury notes. But nowhere did the secretary request the requisite suspension of specie payments.[24]

Although legally permitted to suspend, the Mobile bankers' amour-propre would not allow them to break their agreement with the New Orleans bankers to maintain coin payments.[25] They did intimate, however, that they would be only too happy to follow New Orleans' lead. Thus, the key to a bank suspension in Mobile lay in New Orleans.[26]

In the meantime, storm signals were coming from Secretary of the Navy Stephen Mallory. In the spring of 1861, some of the more foresighted Louisiana secessionists inaugurated an ironclad shipbuilding program in New Orleans. But the contractors objected to payment at par with large-denomination treasury notes, yet although Secretary Mallory relayed that fact to Memminger, the treasury took no direct action.[27] For a while, the contractors made up the difference between the value of the notes and coin out of their own pockets. But as the premium grew, this proved impracticable. Nor could the contractors pass the loss onto the workers, who demanded specie for their labors. Although pay disputes led to wildcat strikes and slowdowns, the Navy declined to pay the workers a specie premium, and early in September they walked out.

That strike at last goaded President Davis and Secretary Memminger into action. Writing to the bankers, Memminger explained the government's currency policy: "At New Orleans (the largest and most important city in the Confederacy) the necessity is most urgent that our Treasury notes be made available. Impressed with the necessity, the President, with the concurrence of his entire cabinet have directed me to ask your immediate adoption of the only measure which can secure the credit of the Government, namely, the temporary suspension of specie payments by the banks and the reception of treasury notes as currency."[28]

Why had this letter not been written four months earlier, in May when it was no less imperative that Louisiana should join her sister states economically as well as politically? The answer, apparently, is that Memminger was determined to conduct his office with "the least possible disturbance of private right and commercial integrity." His September letter marks one of the few occasions when he exhibited a deeply felt zeal, and his success demonstrates that he might have profitably displayed his sense of urgency more frequently.

That point is important, for the weeks lost in solving the problem helped to scuttle the already troubled ironclad program. Only one ship, the *Louisiana*, was partially finished, while its sister ships were still a month or so away from completion when federal forces attacked New Orleans. Had the secretary acted more incisively in May 1861, those ships would have been finished and ready to defend the city; because they were not, Admiral David Farragut won an easy victory. It was not to be the last time that inept treasury policies featured in a serious Confederate military reverse.[29]

The antecedents of the disaster can be traced directly to Secretary Memminger's feeling that "It would be neither judicious nor just to attempt to occupy the whole field of circulation by driving in the currency of the banks."[30] Yet some portions of the banking community were flooding him with patriotic, disinterested, and quite contrary advice. For example, President Ewing of the Planters Bank of Tennessee in July 1861 wrote that "We are willing to aid the Confederacy all we can, and can do so materially by giving place to your circulation of Confederate issues, if they were put out in denominations to suit the popular wants, say . . . mainly of the 5's, 10's and 20's."[31]

Thomas Layton, cashier of the Southern Bank of New Orleans, observed in September 1861 that "In the present crisis . . . it strikes me that no currency other than that of our Confederate Government can be legitimately issued. . . ."[32] He urged the banks to receive and pay out treasury notes immediately. The next day, in an article published in the New Orleans *Crescent*, Layton declared that "Our leading banks may as well take the bull by the horns first as last, and not wait until they have lost all their coin. . . . Let our banks stop issuing their own notes, and instead base their movements [short-term paper] on Confederate Treasury notes. If these Treasury notes . . . are not creditable, then there will be nothing creditable throughout the great South. . . . The war may be ended in six months and it may not be ended in three years. . . . We urge, take steps for making the Government issue currency of the country."[33]

When the President of the Planters Bank of Savannah proposed that the banks help the government take exclusive possession of the currency, the secretary replied: "Of course it will be the duty of this Department, so to shape its course as to produce the least possible injury to those who are influenced by motives so pure and elevated, and it is not expected to require any such sacrifice as that which is tendered."[34]

Most men, given the opportunity to explore the possibility of increasing the treasury's circulation by $85 million through noninflationary means, would have leaped at the chance. Yet Memminger not only failed to urge concrete steps to curtail forcibly the banks' circulation (which was politically understandable), but he also failed even to inquire about the execution of a voluntary program. And this despite the fact that providentially the bankers were gathering at Richmond (July 24, 1861) to deliberate on the secretary's program at a time when he might hope to cash in on their mood of euphoric patriotism.

Nor was the secretary's disinclination to control the currency confined to bank notes. The Provisional Constitution expressly forbade state governments to emit bills of credit. Yet by January 1862, every state in the Confederacy, excepting only Kentucky, Tennessee, and South Carolina, had issued or authorized notes. The inflationary effects of these issues can be seen in table 12. Memminger could have slowed the outflow of these issues by reimbursing the states promptly for their military expenditures and asking their assistance in suppressing illegal change bills. But that would have required the secretary to secure the enactment of a productive tax law, force the security printers to do their work in an efficient manner, and emit enough fractional currency and notes under $5 denomination to obviate the necessity of alternative currencies. He was either unable or unwilling to undertake these actions.[35]

The problem posed by irresponsible note-issuers had been brought forcibly to Memminger's attention on June 10, 1861, when he had received Samuel Younger, a Virginia Fire and Marine Insurance Company agent. Younger had pointed out the plethora of small private bills circulating in Richmond and had urged the Confederate government to take appropriate remedial action. Younger had also observed that even the notes of chartered banks were only at par in their home states.[36] Even more important, Younger had asked Memminger the key question, Who was to control the currency under the denomina-

Table 12. State Treasury Note Issues Outstanding in 1865*

State	Amount
Alabama	$ 4.6
Arkansas	2.5[†]
Florida	2.2
Georgia	17.8
Louisiana	8.5
Mississippi	8.0
Missouri	4.0
North Carolina	5.2
Texas	8.0
Virginia	4.2
Total	$65.0

Sources: Figures based on acts of the legislatures; reports of the treasurers, auditors, or comptrollers; and state notes in the hands of collectors. (Kentucky, South Carolina, and Tennessee issued no notes. However, banks owned by the last two states issued large sums of bank notes, which were lent to state governments.
* All figures in millions
† Estimated.

tion of $5? He felt that the Confederacy could best do this job and that Congress should enact legislation filling the gap in the currency, making such notes a legal tender and forcing the quiet withdrawal of all notes under $5 put out by other parties.[37]

The secretary's reluctance to take that sensible advice no doubt stemmed in part from his former position as a bank director. But his neglect to request authorization for bills from 5 cents up to $2 to replace the hoarded specie is inexplicable, except on the grounds of his printing troubles. Left to their own devices, state legislatures tried to meet the public's needs and shut out undesirable issuers by forcing banks to expand their issues of fractional currency and change bills. Yet it was such issues, equal to from 3 to 10 percent of the issuing banks' capital, that helped fuel the inflation.[38]

Because banks in 1861 were providing the money to mobilize the Confederate army, the secretary no doubt felt under some constraints in dealing with them. But his failure to secure the withdrawal of such notes from circulation after February 1862 had serious repercussions. Because they could be used to purchase goods outside the Confederacy, bank notes were, beginning in 1862, at a premium over the treasury notes.[39] Schwab claims that the average bank note never fell below 30 cents on the dollar. Because price quotations varied from bank to bank, however, an average is relatively meaningless.

As far as the quantities in circulation are concerned, Schwab correctly postulates an increase in the bank-note circulation, especially because of the pressure to issue change bills.[40] Moreover, because of the printing firms' deficiencies, banks had to advance $10 million of their notes to the Confederacy in October 1861. From the surviving scattered statistics it would appear that the circulation of the North Carolina banks advanced from $5.2 million to $7.1 million between 1860 and 1865, while the circulation of Georgian banks jumped from $8.8 million to approximately $15.2 million by the end of 1864.[41] Total issues probably reached $125 million, for a net increase of $40 million.

Private and Local Government Issues

Under normal circumstances, the secretary could have counted on state support for the suppression of illicit issues of currency by cities, counties, corporations, or individuals. But the situation in 1861 was anything but normal. Because of a fire, the city of Charleston was authorized to issue $300,000 of small bills, while the state of Georgia gave permission to Augusta to issue $100,000 of fractional currency.[42] The treasury compounded the evil by accepting a loan from the city of Richmond for $50,000 in illegal city notes—a note issue that resulted in the indictment of the mayor and his council.[43] Yet instead of supporting this effort to enforce its own laws, the Virginia Legislature pardoned the offenders and permitted every independent city and county with a population of more than two thousand to issue notes equal to the average state tax paid for the years 1858–60.[44]

As Virginia taxes averaged $2.5 million, and as most local governments issued notes (table 13), the aggregate issues were approximately $2 million. This unsatisfactory situation was made worse in 1862, when the legislature deferred the redemption period from three to six years. By the fall of 1863, shocked by the auditor's report showing massive issue overruns, the legislature repealed the note issue authorization on September 22.[45]

Other state legislatures also opened the doors to such issues. For example, Mississippi granted various railroads permission to issue up to $380,000 of notes.[46] Another act granted the Columbus Life and General Insurance Company and the Mississippi Mutual Life Insurance Company issue privileges.[47] Similar indulgence was accorded by Georgia to the state-owned Western and Atlantic Railroad, which was given permission to issue $200,000 of fractional currency.[48] Likewise, the Palace Mills Company of Columbus, Georgia, was excused from the penalties which it had incurred by illegally issuing notes.[49] No one

Table 13. Local Confederacy Currency Issues

State	State Issues	County/Parish Issues	City and Town Issues
Alabama	yes	3	2
Arkansas	yes	4	5
Florida	yes	2	1
Georgia	yes	11	4
Louisiana	yes	30	19
Mississippi	yes	9	1
Missouri	yes	no	no
N. Carolina	yes	8	4
S. Carolina	*	0	0
Tennessee	*	3	1
Texas	yes	84	3
Virginia	yes	56	16

* Wholly owned state banks issued currency to pay state expenses.

cay say for certain how much of this paper was issued, but an estimate of $25 million of local government and private script would seem conservative.[50]

The secretary could thwart such issues only by changing his evident conviction that a national currency was an inherent evil. Yet, in his report of May 10, 1861, he accepted the bankers' contention that he should issue only a few $5 and $10 circulating notes. Then, backed by public opinion and opposed by Memminger, Congress provided a bank-note-type circulation of $5 denomination and up (Act of May 16, 1861), and—again without the secretary's blessing—it created an issue of $1 and $2 change bills (Act of April 17, 1862). Finally, by the Acts of March 23 and April 27, 1863, Congress provided an issue of 50 cent fractional notes. Yet this slow response opened the way for rival issuers.[51]

State Treasury Notes

While banks, local governments, corporations, and individuals were adding at least $65 million to the circulation of the country, state governments were pursuing the same goal with equal success. As can be seen from table 12, some $65 million worth of treasury notes and warrants were outstanding at the end of the war, with Georgia far and away the worst offender. It is true that Virginia and North Carolina issued 6 percent treasury notes before 1862, but they were in such large denominations and small quantities that they were clearly intended for investment, not circulation.[52] Had the permanent Confederate Constitution, like the Provisional Constitution, banned the issue of bills of credit, the states probably would have obeyed the prohibition, for North Carolina and Louisiana specifically deferred their currency issues until after February 18, 1862.

Experiences with the states' non-interest-bearing notes vary. Because state credit was better than Confederate credit, there was a tendency to hoard state notes. Thus, on October 21, 1862, the comptroller general of Georgia reported that while the state's non-interest-bearing notes were not even fundable, they were so eagerly sought after and hoarded that practically no one, outside the banks, had seen the $50 or $100 bills. Therefore, instead of paying interest to the banks, he argued that Georgia should pay its way with still more notes.[53] A similar disparity in creditworthiness was reflected in bond prices. For example, in Richmond on December 11, 1862, the Confederate $15 million loan was at $110 in currency, while North Carolina's 6 percent bonds were at $135 and Virginia's 6 percent bonds (with interest in default) at $125.[54]

This preference for state securities and state treasury notes would not have been particularly damaging had bankers not hoarded such notes and paid out Confederate treasury notes instead. With state, local, private, and bank-note issues alone 150 percent above the antebellum circulation, and with the public validating Gresham's law by hoarding these notes along with Confederate interest-bearing treasury notes, the Confederate circulating treasury notes comprised the most active and certainly most inflationary portion of the currency. Secretary Memminger may well have wished, by the fall of 1863, that he had heeded the advice offered by Andrew Miller, a North Carolina businessman, in 1861. In an unsigned pamphlet, Miller noted that the bank-note currency of the Confederacy was beyond the control of any government, the central authorities having heretofore renounced any power to regulate it and the state authorities being incapable of doing so. Miller recommended that the Confederate Congress prohibit state bills of credit or the emission of currency by anyone acting under state authority. In the manner of Calhoun, Miller advocated an irredeemable, tax-receivable, government currency put out in such denominations as the public's needs might require.[55]

An Alternate Solution: National Bank Notes

Throughout the war there were proposals for the creation of a Confederate National Bank. The schemes fell into two categories: former Whigs favored something like the Second Bank of the United

States, with "branches in every considerable trading town and city within the Confederacy."[56] But even men with Whig propensities were doubtful about the political practicability of such a proposal and feared a revival of the abuses of the Second Bank of the United States.[57]

A more substantial stream of thought was represented by those who supported a Southern equivalent of Chase's national banking system. Secretary Memminger had backed the creation of free banks in South Carolina in 1858, in the hope that bank notes backed by government bonds would strengthen both the currency and state credit.[58] Given the need to sell Confederate bonds in 1861, the idea had its attractions.[59] But national bank notes would be no better than the bonds that backed them, and without interest payments in specie, that value would be minimal. Moreover, any such scheme was bound to founder in the face of anti-bank sentiments such as those in Berley's letter to Davis.[60]

Another recurring idea was to establish a Confederate institution modeled on the Bank of England. Each state would subscribe $1 million while private citizens would take the balance of the shares. The bank would issue notes in the denomination of $25 and higher to the aggregate amount of $40 million, and the government would keep its accounts there.[61] Other schemes contemplated a Confederate bank with a capital of $50 million and note issues of $150 million or a "bank" owned by a foreign government, which in exchange for lending the Confederacy $75 million in gold would receive the exclusive privilege to issue $300 million in treasury notes.[62]

Another grandiose scheme was that presented in mid-1864 through L. J. Bowers, agent of Emile D. L. Erlanger and Company. Erlanger together with J. H. Schroder and Company proposed to establish a Confederate bank in London with a capital of $10 million. That bank would supposedly help the Confederacy float foreign loans and improve its direct trade with Europe after the war. However, Erlanger's unpopularity guaranteed rejection of any proposal emanating from that quarter.[63]

All these schemes came to naught not only because they might seem self-interested or visionary, but also because of fear that the Confederacy would not survive. Thus efforts to create an effective currency had to be focused on the government's treasury notes.

Confederate Currency as a Legal Tender

One of the hottest controversies in the South during the war was whether or not Confederate treasury notes should be made a legal tender. The most sensible advocates of a legal-tender law felt that legislation to that effect should be passed at once to avoid any imputation of insolvency. William C. Smedes, president of the Southern Railroad Company of Vicksburg, argued that the "forced obligations of the Government" were required to thwart "these Banks . . . who prefer their Charters to the Constitution, and the millions of idle gold in their bank vaults to the salvation and security of the whole land. . . ." Smedes casually dismissed the controversial character of his proposal, claiming that it was perfectly constitutional and the central question was only one of expediency.[64] Another correspondent justified a legal-tender law because it was an appropriate means for repelling invasion.[65]

During the Provisional Congress, two attempts were made to give Confederate notes legal-tender status. On July 26, 1861, on the motion of A. H. Garland of Arkansas, the Committee on Finance was instructed to inquire into the expediency and necessity of making the two-year notes authorized by the Act of May 16, 1861 legal tender for the duration of the war. Evidently the Finance Committee pigeonholed the proposal, because on August 9, James A. Seddon of Virginia, the future secretary of war, moved to make the $100 million of notes (under the Act of August 19, 1861) legal tender with the proviso that in the event of a refusal debtors could defer payment on a non-interest-bearing basis. That motion was voted down.[67]

When the First Congress assembled in Richmond, Joseph B. Heiskell of Tennessee secured the adoption of a resolution requiring the House Judiciary Committee to report on the constitutionality of making treasury notes legal tender.[68] The chairman of the committee, L. J. Gartrell of Georgia, requested Secretary Memminger's thoughts, and the secretary, like Secretary Chase before him, was compelled to render a comprehensive opinion on this pressing issue. In his response, the secretary atypically confined himself to considerations of finance rather than law. As he cogently observed:

> Treasury notes are now the accepted currency of our whole country. . . . They therefore need no assistance at present to enable them to perform the function of legal tender. A law of Congress making their acceptance compulsory will immediately induce the inquiry into the reasons for such a law. It will be asked, why enforce by penalty that which is freely done by everyone? And it will be difficult to escape the conclusion . . . that lawmakers anticipate an expected refusal. . . .
> There are two classes of persons to whom the notes will be tendered; creditors and sellers. The first are required to accept in payment less than they contracted to receive. . . . As to sellers, they are at liberty to decline accepting the notes unless an additional price is added to cover the depreciation. The law therefore cannot reach them. . . .

> If the Government should attempt to constrain the receipt of the notes
> by penalties, they have before them the experience of all nations as to
> its utter failure. . . . My judgment is against the passage of the law at
> the present time.[69]

With his ardor cooled by this message, on March 29, 1862, Gartrell filed a noncommittal report.[70] A similar effort in the Senate had no better success; the Committee on Finance headed by Robert Barnwell filed a negative report on March 13. Senator Thomas Semmes of Louisiana tried to bypass the committee by a resolution on March 14, and the matter was debated in a desultory fashion from March 21 to March 25 without any action being taken.[71]

During the second session of the First Congress, further motions were made to vote a legal-tender law, but the Judiciary Committee reported adversely for the third time on September 20, 1862. Although efforts by Henry S. Foote of Tennessee failed on October 6–8 to attach legal-tender riders to other legislation, in September and October 1862, no less a personage than General Lee proposed that the currency be made a legal tender.[72]

In December 1863, Senator James Phelan of Missouri and Senators Albert G. Brown and James L. Orr of Mississippi made a last attempt at endowing treasury notes, or even bond coupons, with legal-tender status. In vain they argued that the question was one merely of expediency; that there was no direct constitutional prohibition of a legal-tender law; that the government had already made its notes legal tender for soldiers and other creditors; and that the rest of the population deserved to be treated in the same way. Moreover, the senators contended that a legal-tender law would increase the value of the notes.[73]

These arguments are of interest because although neither side was paying much attention to the other, they uncannily echoed the parallel debate in the federal Congress. Indeed, on the federal side there was a good deal of ignorance about what the Confederacy's policies were. During the legal-tender debates, Roscoe Conkling (an anti-legal-tender New York Republican) chided legal-tender advocates for copying the rebels by making notes a legal tender and executing those who disagreed with the proposition.[74]

Frances W. Kellogg, an Illinois Republican who supported a legal-tender law, claimed that Confederate currency had depreciated because the South was less wealthy than the North, its production was declining, and the public lacked confidence in its government. Such considerations, he felt, did not apply to the North.[75] Apparently no opponent of legal-tender legislation had the temerity or information needed to ask why the Union, with all its resources, required a stringent legal-tender law while its less well endowed opponent did not.

In part, the answers to this anomaly may lie in the initially better credit of the Confederacy, the greater patriotism of most of its financial community, and the fact that most Southern banks had suspended specie payments in late 1860. The people of the South were therefore getting used to dealing in paper. Many Northern bankers, on the other hand, saw in a universally receivable government currency a superior rival to their own bills and had done everything possible to prevent the circulation of the demand notes of 1861.[76]

Nor in practice did it make much difference whether or not such notes were legal tender. Both lost value for the same reasons: a lack of faith in the government and excessive issues. Thus an attempt of Secretary Chase and the federal Congress to abolish the specie premium by legislative fiat through the prohibition of gold futures sales (the Act of June 17, 1864) misfired. Far from sustaining the value of the greenbacks, the act caused a precipitous rise in the premium from $1.95 to $1 to $2.88 to $1. Congress panicked and repealed the act on July 2. Secretary Chase's resignation, although based upon other considerations, was a natural sequel to this fiasco.[77]

With its defeat in early 1862, the legal-tender question passed from the Confederate Congress to the state legislatures. Various state governments made treasury notes receivable for all local dues.[78] Other legislatures used devious methods to evade the constitutional provision prohibiting states from making anything other than gold and silver a legal tender. Thus they sought by various means to compel creditors to receive treasury notes at face value. For example, Alabama permitted any defendant against whom a judgment was given to force his creditor to accept bank notes or Confederate and state treasury notes at par—a strong inducement to creditors to defer their claims until after the war. Georgia required each taxpayer to swear that he or she had not refused such notes in payment of any claims due.[79] Virginia provided that if any bank refused such notes, its notes would cease to be tax receivable. Going one step further, the commonwealth's Secession Convention provided that after October 20, 1863 all debts were payable in notes unless it was otherwise stipulated.[80] Such legislation was effectively backed by public opinion. Thus, although many writers complained about alleged refusals of Confederate money, such refusals were probably a tiny percentage of the overall volume of transactions within the Confederacy.[81]

In retrospect, it seems that a legal-tender law was irrelevant without the support of price and wage controls. Like the threats of dire punishment that appeared on so many eighteenth-century notes ("'tis death to counterfeit"), the ritualistic proclamation that "this note is a legal tender for all debts public and private" was without practical effect. Governments assure the acceptance of their notes far more effectively by suppressing rival currencies and taking appropriate monetary and fiscal measures than by threats of punishment.

A State Guarantee of the Confederate Debt

At the end of August 1862, the gold value of the Confederate dollar was still approximately 67 cents. It had lost 24 cents of its value in the preceding year, which, under the circumstances, was not surprising. But by early October, the gold value of the dollar plummeted to only 40 cents. This drop of 27 cents in one month, a loss in excess of that suffered during the entire year, undoubtedly reflected uncertainty regarding the military situation, the knowledge that Confederate notes were not good beyond the lines, and the rapid expansion of the currency. But another factor may well have been the public's recognition that inflation and shortages were becoming a way of life.

As John Maynard Keynes observed, at the beginning of any currency inflation, there is a tendency to hoard cash and to defer purchases in the hope that prices will fall. This practice sterilizes a large amount of money and checks inflation. Sooner or later, however, consumers realize that prices can only go up and rush to convert cash into merchandise, as well as to economize on cash balances. This in turn drastically increases the velocity of money and, with it, price inflation (table 14).[82] If Secretary Memminger's reports of March 14, 1862 and January 10, 1863 were correct, the hoarding process was well underway in early 1862.[83] Lerner has noted gains in bank deposits as a percentage of the preceding period's deposits, chiefly created during the winter of 1861–62. From these facts it is possible to conclude that September 1862 marked the point where the shift from cash to commodities began.[84]

Alarmed at the resulting inflationary symptoms, Secretary Memminger devoted a considerable amount of time and effort to promote the enactment of another device, old as the American Republic itself, to sustain the Confederate government's credit. The secretary proposed that the states guarantee $500 million of Confederate bonds, evidently assuming that the states' superior credit would permit a reduction in interest rate from 8 percent to 6 percent and that such bonds would

Table 14. Confederate Currency Depreciation*

	1861	1862	1863	1864	1865
	\multicolumn{5}{c}{Cents per Dollar}				
March	—	77	24	4.5	1.9[†]
June	97	67	14	5.9[‡]	—
September	90	50	8.3	4.3	—
December	83	33	5.0	2.6	—

Sources: Schwab *CSA*, Appendix I. Schwab is to be preferred to other tables because Schwab uses an average of depreciation in several cities.
* The average value of treasury votes in terms of gold.
[†] The rate rose to 1.9 cents per dollar from 1.7 cents because of government specie sales on the Richmond market.
[‡] Rise due to currency reform.

be sold at a premium.[85] This idea had characterized the finances of the Confederation period and had been revived during 1861 in the North by Buchanan's lame duck secretary of the treasury, John Dix.[86] But it was a futile retrogression to the failed policies of the past.

Even in the conservative Confederacy, the prospects of success were not promising. In Virginia, a guarantee resolution was introduced in its legislature in May 1862. Although Schwab contends that this resolution was adopted, that seems quite doubtful because otherwise there would have been no need to reintroduce another resolution in January of 1863, which was rejected.[87] Alabama was in a more cooperative mood, and its legislature on December 1, 1862 passed a resolution guaranteeing the entire Confederate debt proportionate to its representation in Congress. But that guarantee was ominously conditional on all other states taking their share.[88] South Carolina only guaranteed her share of two hundred millions as did Mississippi, while Florida, copying Alabama, assumed her share providing all the other states did likewise. Texas, with her secessionist proclivities ill-concealed, merely provided that if she withdrew from the Confederacy, she would pay her quota.[89]

The fatuity of the whole plan was quickly exposed when Georgia and North Carolina dug in to oppose it. North Carolina declared that because the Confederacy was merely a creature of the states, a specific guarantee was superfluous.[90] In Georgia, Governor Joseph Brown objected that such a guarantee would commingle Confederate and state finances with adverse effects on both.[91]

Former Secretary of State Robert Toombs was on sounder ground when he wrote to Vice-President Alexander H. Stephens: "You are right in opposing the assumption of Confederate debt by the States. I would not endorse a dime of it. It is puerile and disastrous. The C[onfederate] States have unlimited power of taxation over everything within its limits and also over imports and exports. What more do they want but sense and nerve?"[92]

The months devoted to the scheme must, in retrospect, be viewed as so much lost time. With the states saddled with their own rapidly mounting debts, the Confederacy should have looked to its own unexploited fiscal resources. What was wanting, as Toombs suggested, was a secretary of the treasury with the nerve to ask for taxes and a Congress with the sense to provide them. Because timely and effective taxation was the last thing the Congress intended to provide, the Confederates drifted into a series of radical monetary measures that destroyed the currency.

Forced Funding, the Last Step

Even the best program of taxation, coupled with skillful debt and currency management, could not keep four hundred thousand men in the field at a cost of $400 million a year without the currency ultimately becoming redundant and the printers no longer able to keep pace with the demands being made on them. At such a time, urgent measures would be required to shrink the bloated currency, such as limiting the funding privilege or compelling note-holders to purchase bonds.

Well aware of the importance of note funding, Secretary Memminger and Congress provided for issues of bonds for each currency act from May 16, 1861 to March 23, 1863. Moreover, every non-interest-bearing note emitted, except for the March 23, 1863 50 cent $1 and $2 bills, was fundable (Appendix C). That this program was only moderately successful can be seen from the secretary's report of January 10, 1863, wherein only $89 million of $385 million of bonds authorized (28 percent) had been taken, whereas nearly $59 million of $100 million (59 percent) of call certificates authorized by the Acts of December 24, 1861, April 12, 1862, and September 23, 1862 were disposed of. The secretary also reported that between August 1, 1862, and December 31, 1862, the treasury had sold $17,422,150 worth of bonds. With an average of $3.5 million being funded each month, bond sales were at a $42 million annual rate.[93] And this miserable result took no account of the fact that bonds had been forced onto many public creditors.

The First Step: Interest Rate Reductions

Three months before his January 1863 report, with Congress procrastinating about taxation and with the government's payments in arrears, Secretary Memminger advised President Davis that, although bond and call certificate sales were working well, other measures were needed to check the growth of the currency.[94] Paradoxically, the secretary proposed to improve bond sales by reducing the rate of interest paid upon them. In defending this position he asserted that although current bond rates were all 8 percent, if future note issues were fundable at a lower rate, people would prefer the old issues. In proof of this contention, he noted that because the May 16, 1861 act notes were fundable in what amounted to 8 percent call certificates, they were all closely held. Memminger therefore recommended that a time limitation be placed on funding notes into 8 percent bonds.[95]

Congress promptly responded to this suggestion and by the Act of October 13, 1862 provided that all notes issued after December 1, 1862 should be fundable only into 7 percent bonds. Furthermore, the secretary was empowered to notify holders of notes already outstanding that if they wished to purchase 8 percent bonds at par, they must do so within six months.[96] The secretary responded swiftly and, on October 22, issued a circular announcing a reduced rate for the notes to be issued after December 1, 1862 and fixed the last day for funding notes at 8 percent on April 22, 1863.[97] In addition, the secretary urged Congress to abrogate the privilege of funding any note in 7 percent bonds after July 1, 1863. These proposals were based on the apparent assumption that all in position to do so would fund their notes into 8 percent or 7 percent bonds, and that the small residual currency would cease to circulate (except by special contract) or have any purchasing value other than that derived from tax-receivable status. Because he asserted that three-quarters of the outstanding notes would be funded into bonds, he was confident that an effective tax could absorb the remainder.

But Memminger candidly conceded that there were serious objections to his program, the most obvious being that it was an infringement of the contract printed on each and every note. Still he felt that "A limitation of time for the performance of contracts has never been considered an infringement where sufficient opportunity is given to claim performance . . .,"[98] and went on to cite various legal precedents to support his contention. As his chief justification, however, he relied on a crude concept of the quantity theory of money, which suggested that if everyone funded an equal proportion of the notes they held, any currency they had left over would have the same purchasing power as the original amount.

Another objection Memminger felt required to answer was that a limitation on the funding privilege would impair the value of the notes as money. Although concerned that the notes might lose their monetary status, he argued that their value would remain unimpaired because they were receivable for taxes and their payment was guaranteed by the Confederacy.

Finally, the secretary denied that the price of bonds was bound to be greatly depressed even though more bonds would be sold under this forced funding scheme than the public was interested in acquiring voluntarily. While admitting that bond prices might decline, he offered the cold comfort that the profits or losses of speculators were their own problem. They should, he felt, join honest investors in holding onto such securities for the long term. In any event, he insisted, the depreciation of the bonds could never exceed the depreciation of the currency, nor would bond depreciation affect commodity prices.[99]

Once again, Memminger's basic assumptions require examination. Was he not inconsistent in contending that Confederate treasury notes derived their value not from their general acceptability (why then had he worked so hard to get the banks to receive them?) or from their tax receivability, but from their fundability? Had specie payments been maintained on the bonds, that hypothesis might at least have been arguable. But the notes were generally receivable and the Congress, however belatedly, was in the process of voting internal revenues payable in such notes. Under Gresham's law, people would use such notes to pay their Confederate taxes and retain those treasury notes that were still fundable. Nor was there any guarantee that most of the notes would be funded into fixed-interest securities in a period of rampant inflation when the interest was payable only in depreciating notes.

The secretary might also be faulted for his original proposal not to reduce the interest rate to 5 percent or 6 percent rather than 7 percent, since in the middle of a hyperinflation, such a small differential would not provide an adequate incentive to surrender the notes. On the other hand, if he caused their tax-receivable status to disappear together with their fundability, holders would have a real incentive to fund the notes before they should become mere certificates of indebtedness due at some vague future day. Yet no such proposal was made.

Nor was his prediction of a rise in the value of the currency valid unless the volume of notes outstanding was reduced to an amount consistent with the needs of trade. Obviously, he could not afford to keep several different currencies in circulation simultaneously, some current, some discredited, and all subject to confusion and under suspicion in the minds of an uninformed and unsophisticated public. As events transpired (tables 15, 16), there was no reduction in the currency because a large portion of the notes received were promptly reissued while those destroyed were more than replaced by new issues. Yet the secretary proved to be right in one particular—the price of the 8 percent bonds did go to a premium against the currency.

Confederate Funding Operations to February 17, 1864

The secretary's recommendations were substantially embodied in the Act of March 23, 1863, which, in its funding provisions, looked both to the past and to the future. Codifying the secretary's circular, Congress provided that all notes fundable in 7 percent bonds must be

Table 15. Results of the Funding Act of October 13, 1862

Act	Notes Issued	Notes Outstanding
Currency on October 13, 1862		
May 16, 1861	$ 17,347,955	$ 11,289,025
August 19, 1861	211,361,835	211,360,045
April 17, 1862 ($1 and $2)	3,189,000	3,189,000
October 13, 1862 ($1 and $2)	0	0
October 13, 1862 ($5 plus)	0	0
Total	$231,898,790	$225,938,070
Currency on January 1, 1864 at End of Funding Operation		
May 16, 1861	$ 17,347,955	$ 8,320,875
August 19, 1861	291,961,830	189,719,151
April 17, 1861 ($1 and $2)	5,601,400	4,660,278
October 13,1862 ($1 and $2)	2,347,200	2,344,800
October 13,1862 ($5 plus)	138,053,600	131,028,366
Total	$455,311,985	$336,073,470
		− 37,000,000*
		$299,073,470
Net Increase:	$223,413,195*	$ 73,135,400[†]

* Notes on hand awaiting cancellation.
[†] To this must be added $450 million of notes dated April through December 1863 (March 23, 1863 Act) emitted during this period.

Table 16. Funded Debt, October 13, 1862

Act	Amount Outstanding
May 16, 1861	$ 5,944,300
August 19, 1861	41,273,500
April 12, 1862	0
February 20, 1863 (8 percent)	0
February 20, 1863 (7 percent)	0
Total	$ 47,217,800

Funded Debt as of January 1, 1864 at End of Funding Operation.

May 16, 1861	$ 8,774,900
August 19, 1861	100,000,000
April 12, 1862	3,612,300
February 20, 1863 (8 percent)	95,785,000
February 20, 1863 (7 percent)	63,615,750
Total	$271,785,950
Net increase in the debt (notes received)	$224,468,150
Net notes issued	$223,413,195
Net nominal note issue decrease	($ 1,054,955)
Actual increase	$ 73,135,400
Net reissue of notes	$ 72,080,545*

Source: Thian, *Reports*, pp. 136–38, 243–45.

* This figure makes no provision for the sale of over $72 million of call certificates under the Act of March 23, 1863 which could be converted back into 1863 treasury notes. Since no reserve was kept, expenditures for the last quarter of 1863 averaged $100 million a month, almost twice the printers' production capacity.

turned in by August 1, 1863. After that, the "December 1, 1862" notes were fundable in 4 percent bonds. Finally, all the call certificates were converted into funded debt.[100]

For the future, Congress repealed the secretary's unlimited note-issuing authority under the Act of September 23, 1862, but provided instead the right to issue $50 million per month of notes $5 and higher, to which was added, by way of contingency funds, the power to increase the issue of $1 and $2 bills by $5 million. To provide an absorbent for this mass of currency, an issue of 6 percent bonds was voted and two issues of call certificates authorized. The "April 6, 1863" notes were made exchangeable for 5 percent certificates which, unless redeemed, would become bonds after six months. The holders of "December 2, 1862" notes could buy 4 percent call certificates.[101]

As measures for reducing the currency, the Acts of October 13, 1862, and March 23, 1863, were a failure. It was not that people did not buy bonds—on the contrary, more than $224 million worth of 8 percent and 7 percent bonds were sold by August 1, 1863, which amounted to four and a half times the amount of bonds sold between July 1, 1861 and October 13, 1862. Yet, even leaving aside the fact that the treasury issued $50 million of notes a month from April 1863 onward,[102] the amount of pre-1863 notes outstanding showed a net increase between October 13, 1862 and January 1, 1864. As can be seen from Table 16, almost a third of the notes received ($72 million) were reissued. Indeed, even before the Act of March 23, 1863, the secretary had been issuing $52 million a month just to meet current expenses. These funding notes providentially allowed him to spend $58–$60 million a month. When that source of extra funds dried up, as occurred after February 17, 1864, treasury payments would fall even further into arrears.

It is interesting to note that Secretary Memminger's scheme was far more successful than Secretary Chase's funding and bond interest reduction program, which also took place in July 1863. The reason for this is not hard to discover. Those desiring to buy twenty-year, 6 percent bonds in the North only had to pay a 4–10 percent premium after July 1863, while the reduction of interest was only from 6 percent to 5 percent. Those who tried to buy an 8 percent Confederate bond after April 22, 1863, had to pay a 35 percent premium, around which figure the price fluctuated until the Confederate defeats in the fall of 1864.[103]

Forced Funding

By the time the Congress had reassembled on December 7, 1863, the failure of nominally voluntary funding had become amply apparent. Exclusive of the interest-bearing notes, the aggregate currency in circulation was $579 million on September 30, on top of which another $100 million was issued during October and November. Thus, within scarcely a year, the "general circulation" had risen 200 percent, with further increases readily in sight. No wonder the secretary urgently declared that "the currency must be reduced."[104] To achieve that goal he proposed: 1) to exchange the outstanding currency for a new issue of 6 percent, twenty-year bonds; 2) to require every note-holder to present all treasury notes for funding by April 1, 1864; 3) to abrogate the tax receivability of such notes; and 4) to give a certificate of indebtedness to any holder who presented notes by October 1, 1864; any note not funded or registered would be repudiated.

In addition, his plan called for a three months' postponement of the effective dates for these actions in the Trans-Mississippi (because of the time delay in getting the act's provisions carried out there), the exemption of the $2 and lower notes from the terms of the act, and a new issue of $200 million to be exchanged for the old issues, with a firm government pledge not to issue any more notes.

Although sound enough in its general principles, there were key weaknesses in the secretary's proposals. Urging a contraction of the currency, he nevertheless felt that "it would not be expedient to reduce the circulation to its proper normal standard"; that would have to be deferred until after the war. Moreover, by suggesting a $200 million figure (2.5 times the prewar circulation), the secretary, as one cognizant of the quantity theory of money, should have recognized that goods and velocity remaining the same, the new currency could not have a greater purchasing power than 40 cents on the dollar. Finally, he failed to suggest the basis on which the $200 million worth of new notes were to be exchanged for the old issues,[105] and worse still, he made no provision for further issues to cover his budget.

President Davis, in his message to Congress, emphatically backed Secretary Memminger. But he too based his optimistic conclusions on the assumption that the value of the currency would increase in proportion to the amount recalled.[106]

Other Proposals

In time of crisis plenty of people are prepared to offer unsolicited opinions. The bankers, on whom Secretary Memminger had leaned so heavily in better days, proposed that the government levy a new $60 million government tax and accept in payment either specie or the coupons of a new issue of $1 billion worth of 6 percent bonds. Because that would have compelled most taxpayers to buy large quantities of the new bonds, it was, in effect, a system of forced funding, although that term was scrupulously scouted.[107]

Nor were the bankers the only source of free advice. One Georgian, Cary Cox, proposed that the government levy a 20 percent tax on the face value of all Confederate notes in circulation, thereby compelling note-holders to fund their notes. Another individual, W. Goodman, proposed a scheme comparable to that of the bankers except that the coupon bonds were to bear 5 percent interest.[108] One of the most eccentric schemes called for compelling every citizen to give the government a mortgage note equal to 25 percent of the assessed value of his or her real estate within the Confederacy. The author of the scheme, C. P. Culver, estimated the nominal value of the loan at $625 million. For a period of ninety days the individual giving the note would have the option of buying it back at a 50 percent premium. By exercising this option, he or she would receive a Confederate bond bearing interest at 8 percent and payable thirty years after date.

If one ignores currency depreciation and other variables, the net effect of the scheme would have been to require that each landed taxpayer lend the government money at something like 5 percent. On the other hand, if the taxpayer did not buy back the note, he or she could sell it and its attached bond to other parties (hypothetically at 100 percent premium), so all the government indebtedness could be retired and even a surplus realized to pay future needs.[109]

Another curious scheme was that of C. H. Minge, who, observing the higher degree of public confidence in the state currencies, proposed that the Confederate government should stop issuing its own notes and fund them in 6 percent or 4 percent bonds. The states would then lend the Confederate government $150 million of their own notes, for which the government would reimburse them.[110]

Congressional Action on the Act of February 17, 1864

Like everyone else, the congressmen had their own pet schemes and filed a large number of them as bills. Not surprisingly, they saw a much wider range of options than did the secretary. Yet although they agreed with Memminger's proposition that the currency must be reduced and a more acceptable means found for financing the country's needs, they differed widely over how to translate those sentiments into legislation.

The secretary had advocated that treasury notes be funded at par in bonds. But Congressmen Frances S. Lyon and H. W. Bruce proposed to levy a 50 percent tax on the entire currency and fund the untaxed remainder in 5 percent or 6 percent bonds, while Congressman Charles Russell of Virginia proposed a 60 percent tax on the face value of the notes.[111] These "taxes" were actually disguised forms of debt scaling or repudiation and, to judge by their number, the proposals were extremely popular. Diverse individuals, such as Congressmen Muscoe Garnett and Walter Preston of Virginia, William Smith of Alabama, and William M. Boyce of South Carolina all advocated such an approach. Had their bills been enacted, the currency would have been exchanged for new notes or bonds at ratios ranging from five to one up to twenty to one. The median for such proposals, about ten to one, would have been a fair average between what the noteholders had given and what they had received.[112]

Not only were there a variety of proposals, but there was also a considerable disparity of view regarding technical details. Almost every congressional speech betrayed a strong revulsion against the further issue of treasury notes. Only a few members, like Lyon of Alabama, recognized the need for treasury notes and provided for them. Even so, the maximum that anyone was prepared to allow was $250 million.

Faced by an intractable problem, the House appointed a Special Committee on the Currency, which filed its report on December 30, 1863. Despite a vigorous dissent from Chairman Boyce, the House adopted the majority report submitted by Baldwin of Virginia that proposed to give note-holders until April 1 to fund in 6 percent bonds; thereafter they might fund only in 4 percent bonds. Any notes not funded by June 1, 1864 would be taxed at 25 percent per month on face value until they became worthless in October. Those improvident enough to fund their notes after August could do so only at 10 percent of face value.

In view of the impossibility of preparing such an immense quantity of bonds by April, Secretary Memminger was authorized to issue certificates receivable for taxes. All treasury notes of $5 denomination and under were made part of the new issue, while call certificates were to be accorded the same treatment as the notes into which they were convertible. Finally, as a concession to the army, soldiers were permitted to exchange one month's pay into new notes.

The House prohibited the secretary from issuing more than $200 million worth of new currency with the further restriction that the new notes, coupled with old notes with denominations of $5 and under, were not to exceed $250 million. Such notes were expressly not receivable for export duties or any other specie levy. To help the secretary pay current expenses of the government, the House provided $500 million of 6 percent, thirty-year, tax-free bonds.[113]

H.R. 192, "An Act to Tax, Fund and Limit the Currency," reached the Senate on January 18, 1864 and was referred to the Senate Finance Committee. On January 25, R. M. T. Hunter and Semmes submitted the majority report.[114] Although they disagreed over the competence of President Davis, they concurred on the ills facing the country and the need to oppose the House bill. They felt very strongly that any scheme to tax away the currency would fail and that the Congress would be compelled, by the weight of public opinion, to retrace its steps. In view of the fact that the Congress reversed itself in December 1864, it was not a bad prognostication.[115]

But when it came to proposing alternatives, the two senators were on shakier ground. Instead of funding and taxing the old currency, they proposed to scale it down to the $200 million suggested by Secretary Memminger. That would permit the government to concentrate its taxing powers on more legitimate subjects. Like the secretary, they failed to see that debt-scaling would constitute a form of repudiation even if $200 million would have the same purchasing power as $800 million. And, like the House, the two senators placed an unfounded reliance on the capacity of the secretary to sell his $500 million worth of tax-free bonds.

All these proposals had substantial deficiencies. The House had adopted a realistic attitude toward the currency inasmuch as the old notes were to be retired and the government given a new authorization of $200 million. Unfortunately, by making the 4 percent bonds and certificates tax receivable in 1864, the government's fiscal power was emasculated. While the Senate would keep the government's taxing power unimpaired, it would leave an excessive residual currency while making no provision for new treasury notes. If the best ideas of both houses and the secretary had been combined, the final plan would probably have involved forced funding of the entire currency into interim certificates exchangeable for registered 4 percent bonds, transferable by endorsement only. Only soldiers would be entitled to exchange a month's pay in old notes for the new. No old notes, except those under the denomination of $5, would be retained or made tax receivable, and such issues would be extended to $20 million. That would allow the printers to concentrate on getting out $200 million in new currency in higher denominations.

Such a plan would have given the treasury an issuing power of $210 million and a tax-gathering capability of roughly $150 million. It should then have been within the realm of possibility to meet the $100 million balance of the secretary's $460 million budget by selling some of the 6 percent bonds and a larger quantity of new 4 percent call certificates.

The Act of February 17, 1864

Unhappily, the bill reported out of the Senate-House Conference Committee on the evening of February 16, 1864 was a crude amalgam of two opposing plans. No wonder that Henry D. Capers, Memminger's biographer, indignantly wrote that "Well would it have been for the Confederate cause if the Congress had simply followed the sound and carefully digested financial plans of the Secretary, instead of forcing on the country a policy . . . which was a jumble, resulting from a confusion of ideas, that at best, was a compromise between opposing factions."[116]

Under the terms of the act, all notes would be made fundable at par in 4 percent, twenty-year bonds on or by April 1, 1864. Any notes not funded by that time would be subject either to repudiation or to an exchange tax that would completely extinguish their value by January 1, 1865. Notes of $100 denomination, if not funded, were proscribed by Congress; other notes might be exchanged for new notes at a rate of three for two. In addition, the 4 percent interim certificates, which were exchangeable for the stock certificates, would also be tax-receivable for the year 1864. Under section 18, the secretary might, at his pleasure, issue a 6 percent non-taxable certificate of indebtedness transferable only by endorsement. By a rather liberal interpretation of section 7, Secretary Trenholm did issue 4 percent receipts payable "on demand," which were in effect call certificates. The certificates were secured by a pledge of the 6 percent coupon bonds that many people were unwilling to buy.[117]

But any benefit that the Confederacy might have derived from this legislation was canceled by the damage done to all the government's main financial resources. It is true that the Confederate government sold a substantial number of bonds during the last year of its life (Appendix B). But the sales were due to the continued expanded state of the currency and the lack of alternative investments for the banks. The closely similar quantity of bonds and call certificates sold ($70–$80 million) shows that there was little interest in long-term investments.

In its management of the currency the government swiftly found itself in the worst of all possible worlds. The old currency, although nominally repudiated, remained outstanding in such large quantities that by the Act of December 30, 1864, the government was forced to defer the penalty date.[118] That made the old notes current for taxing and funding purposes until July 1, 1865, while the tax-receivable 4 percent certificates swelled the currency further. As P. W. Gray put it, "The object of the people in funding seems to have been merely for the purpose of paying their taxes with the certificates. . . . The process has caused great labor, expense, and complications, and produced inconvenience and dissatisfaction without corresponding benefit to the Government."[119]

As had been foreseen, the government needed the new treasury notes to meet current expenses. Thus, by September 30, 1864, some $278.5 million had been issued, of which only $29 million had been exchanged for $43.5 million worth of old notes. That left $286.5 million worth of old notes to be exchanged for $191 million of the new, thereby raising the minimum total of new notes to approximately $480 million.[120]

Moreover, even the format of the new notes told against them. To save time, the old designs had been used, except a red lace overprint that was placed on the faces while crude new backs were substituted for the old. Thus, at a time when it was desirable to emphasize the break with bad past practices, the public found itself using notes only marginally different from the old.[121] This lack of differentiation contributed to the public's failure to accord the new issues with the premium that President Davis, Secretary Memminger, and others had expected. In fact (table 14), the value in gold of Confederate money rose from 4 cents in February 1864 to only 5.9 cents in July 1864, an almost perfect correlation of the three to two ratio for exchange purposes. With the rapid increase in the currency and with military defeats multiplying at the end of 1864, the benefits of the act were dissipated by November.

The combination of these misfortunes seems to have instilled into both the administration and Congress a sense of hopelessness. Although the Congress continued to tinker with the Act of February 17, 1864, both in the first session of the Second Congress (May 2–June 14, 1864) and the second session (November 7, 1864–March 18, 1865), it was aimless tinkering.[122]

Finally, in March 1865, Congress clashed with the president by voting $80 million worth of treasury notes to pay the troops. In spite of the president's protest that no printing establishment was available for the purpose, the House passed the bill over his veto, and two-thirds of the senators in attendance did the same. Yet, because the Senate was one member short of a quorum, the bill did not, as Todd suggests, become law.[123]

Why Did the Confederacy's Currency Policies Fail?

In looking back at the Confederacy's currency management program, one is struck by the absence of any conscious planning outside the inchoate desire of Congress for a government currency. The result was a series of failures: the failure to preempt the issuance of currency for the Confederacy and thus provide a uniform circulation for the country; the failure to confine the currency within proper limits; and the failure to reduce it to proper size when it became redundant.

The first failure was within the treasury's capacity to solve, yet Secretary Memminger viewed the task with mixed feelings. He realized the importance of Confederate treasury notes as a borrowing device and deserved commendation for inducing the banks to receive and pay them out. On the other hand, he opposed a paper currency until it was forced on him by the Congress. And although it was important to increase his borrowing capacity by retiring bank notes from circulation and getting Gulf Coast banks to suspend, the secretary, although urged to do this by some of the bankers, was not prepared to force the issue. Had New Orleans' banks suspended in May 1861, as opposed to September 1861, the shipbuilders' strike would have been averted and New Orleans' capture possibly deferred. But the secretary was content to pursue cautious peace time methods even in the middle of a war.

Nor did he even try to limit alternative currencies by prohibiting Confederate printers from filling such orders. To judge by the treasurers' reports, state issues were largely occasioned by war expenditures. Yet the secretary did not make any effort to reimburse the states or even make conciliatory gestures in that direction.[124] In sum, his failure to get the Southern printers under control or to secure the adoption of an adequate tax system told heavily against him. So did his reluctance to undertake the circulation of $1 and $2 bills and fractional currency. With specie withdrawn from circulation, the government had a duty to regulate the currency either by controlling the shin plasters or by providing a substitute currency. While the Congress was clearly responsible for many of the Confederacy's problems, when it took the initiative in issuing low-denomination notes, it was clearly more in accord with reality and public opinion than the secretary.

Even when Memminger, despite his wishes, found himself in charge of a national currency, he did not comprehend the basis of its acceptability or the means of maintaining its value. Although he was probably right to scout the idea of a legal-tender law, he never seems to have decided whether treasury notes derived their value from their public acceptance, their fundability, or their tax receivability. In retrospect, his abortive maneuvering for an indirect state guarantee of the currency merely delayed other, more effective, solutions for the rampant inflation. Even his interest rate reduction program came too late and was not coupled with an attack on the notes' tax-receivability status. And the inevitable forced-funding operation came to grief when the secretary failed to provide a comprehensive program for congressional consideration that would clear off the old currency while furnishing him with enough notes, bonds, call certificates, and taxes to do his job.

An adequate currency program would have curtailed the circulation of prewar paper, crimped new issues, and substituted in its stead a

Table 17. Price Indices of Gold, Domestic, Mixed, and Foreign
Merchandise in Confederate Treasury Notes 1861–65,
at Three-month Intervals

Date	Gold	Domestic Goods	Domestic Goods Using Foreign Components	Foreign Goods
April 1861	100	104	101	100
October 1861	110	119	161	226
January 1862	120	145	230	350
July 1862	150	252	377	860
October 1862	200	329	632	1,215
April 1863	450	627	1,646	1,642
July 1863	900	807	1,917	1,823
October 1863	1,300	1,128	2,587	2,760
January 1864	2,100	1,684	4,077	3,228
April 1864	1,900	2,931	5,396	5,596
October 1864	2,600	2,767	5,056	5,124
January 1865	5,300	3,850	7,151	8,816

Source: Lerner, *Money*, p. 165, Appendix viii.
* January 1861 = 100.

Confederate currency. That would have served the double purpose of providing the government with a free loan while stimulating the economy; it would also have headed off most of the $130 million of bank, state, local government, and private issues. In short, in early 1864 (all things being equal) the secretary could have effected a reduction of the currency from $1,070 million to $865 million—or $205 million, a sum equal to 2½ times the entire prewar money stock (table 2). This would have reduced the domestic price index from 1,684 in January 1864 to 1,403 (table 17). Proper taxation would have prevented the currency from reaching more than $450 million without taking account of funding or savings from reduced price inflation. In addition, a proper commodity and foreign loan program would have contributed to the same effect. The currency was simply part of a complex combination of interrelated problems for which neither the secretary nor Congress had timely answers.

NOTES

1. Report of December 7, 1863, in Raphael P. Thian, *Reports of the Secretary of the Treasury of the Confederate States of America, 1861–1865* (Washington, D.C.: Privately published, 1878), p. 180.

2. James M. Mathews, ed., *The Statutes at Large of the Provisional Government of the Confederate States of America etc.* (Richmond: R. M. Smith, 1864), 1st sess., pp. 54–56; see also 3d sess., p. 171.

3. W. B. Tinsley to Memminger, June 11, 1861, in *Correspondence with the Treasury of the Confederate States of America, 1861–2*, Raphael P. Thian (Washington, D.C.: Privately published, 1880), p. 131.

4. Trenholm to R. M. T. Hunter, November 7, 1864, in Thian, *Reports*, p. 354.

5. Raphael P. Thian, *Register of the Confederate Debt*, ed. Douglas B. Ball (Boston: Boston Quarterman Publications, 1972), pp. 5–6.

6. Memminger to Gazaway B. Lamar (vice president, Bank of the Republic, N.Y.), April 2, 1861, in Raphael P. Thian, ed., *Correspondence of the Treasury of the Confederate States of America, 1861–65* (Washington, D.C.: Privately published, 1879), p. 41.

7. Memminger to Denegre, September 19, 1861, in *Correspondence of*, ed. Thian, p. 190; Denegre to Memminger, September 9, 1861, in *Correspondence with*, ed. Thian, pp. 322–23. Denegre suggested that Memminger should keep an extra stock on hand, which the secretary thought a good idea.

8. "Register of Civil Warrants March 28, 1861–June 20, 1864," Record Group 36, National Archives. Estimate based on the National Banknote Company statement. The notes would have been arrayed by four 50s, four 100s, and two 100s, one 500, and one 1,000, for a total of $3 million of $50s, $8 million in $100s, $5 million in $500s, and $10 million in $1,000s.

9. The Act of August 30, 1861 was the first providing that $5 treasury notes be expressly receivable at the post office. Mathews, ed., *Statutes*, 3d sess., p. 200; James M. Mathews, ed., *Public and Private Laws of the Confederate States of America, Passed at the First and Second Congress, 1862–64* (Richmond: R. M. Smith, 1864), 1st sess, p. 34. The Act of April 17, 1862 made the $1 and $2 notes of the act receivable at post offices.

10. Mathews, ed., *Public and Private Laws*, 1st sess., pp. 28–29. Because the rate was 2 cents per day per $100, the rate in 1864 (a leap year) was 7.32 percent.

11. Act of September 23, 1862, 2d sess., ibid., p. 59.

12. Charles F. Pollard (president, Montgomery and West Point Railroad) to Major J. S. Calhoun, June 16, 1862, in *Correspondence with*, ed. Thian, pp. 570–71.

13. Jonathan Worth, *N.C. Treasury Report, September 4, 1865* (Raleigh, N.C.: Spelman, 1865), North Carolina Convention (Jonathan Worth) Treasurer's Report, doc. no. 1, pp. 16–70.

14. Thian, ed., *Correspondence of*, p. 356. A Treasury Department advertisement dated September 26, 1862 announced that interest would be paid on the said notes each January 1. Eugene Lerner, *Money, Prices and Wages in the Confederacy 1861–5* (Chicago: Privately mimeographed, 1954), pp. 39a–40. Bank liquidity rose during the war, with cash reserves rising from 25 percent of liabilities to 70 percent in Georgia in June 1863. The rate of growth of these deposits declined after late 1862.

15. Cuyler to Memminger, September 20, 1862, in *Correspondence with,* ed. Thian, pp. 632–33.

16. Memminger to Cuyler, September 23, 1862, in *Correspondence of,* ed. Thian, p. 357.

17. Mathews, ed., *Public and Private Laws,* p. 197; J. K. Sass (president, Bank of Charleston) to Memminger, January 22, 1863, in *Correspondence with,* ed. Thian, p. 12. The banks compelled customers to receive such notes at face plus accumulated interest while taking such notes only at face. John D. Butt to Memminger, April 20, 1863, ibid., p. 80.

18. Act of November 28, 1864, in *Laws and Joint Resolutions of the Last Session of the Confederate Congress (November 6, 1864–March 18, 1865). Together with the Secret Acts of the Preceding Congresses,* ed. Charles W. Ramsdell (Durham, N.C.: Duke University Press, 1941), p. 5.

19. Tyler to Memminger, April 3, 1864, in Thian, *Reports,* p. 288; see also Report of November 7, 1864, Trenholm to Hunter, p. 354; "Register of Call Certificates and Bonds Issued," Record Group 365, vols. 175, 179, National Archives. Six pages record about $320,000 of bonds being issued, but no such bonds were printed or issued. Receipts were issued under the Act of November 28, 1864 to fund the notes into 6 percent bonds.

20. Thian, *Register,* p. 175. The total issued came to $122,916,000.

21. July 29, 1861, in Thian, *Reports,* p. 30; see also Daniel Ravenal, president Planters and Mechanics Bank, Charleston, to Memminger, in *Correspondence with,* ed. Thian, p. 132; *Proceedings of the Bank Convention of the Confederate States Held at Richmond, Va. July 24th, 25th and 26th, 1861* (Charleston: Evans and Cogswell, 1861), pp. 1–14. Claims made by James P. Morgan that Memminger was an ardent advocate of fiat money and an enemy of a metallic currency do not tally with Memminger's record before the war or his correspondence during it. The fact that the mints were closed was due entirely to an absence of dies and essential supplies and an inability to procure replacements. James F. Morgan, *Graybacks and Gold: Confederate Monetary Policy* (Pensacola, Fla.: Perdido Bay Press, 1985), pp. 5, 133.

22. This voluntary compliance was never secured in the North, hence the use of the legal-tender law. Bray Hammond, *Sovereignty and an Empty Purse: Banks and Politics in the Civil War* (Princeton, N.J.: Princeton University Press, 1970), pp. 94–97.

23. D. Ewing to Memminger, June 11, 1861 in *Correspondence with,* ed. Thian, p. 131; Thian, ed., *Correspondence of,* p. 104.

24. Memminger to Walsh, June 26, 1861, ibid., p. 130.

25. J. J. Donegan to Memminger, July 3, 1861, in *Correspondence with,* ed. Thian, pp. 189–90.

26. Walsh to Memminger, July 3, 1861, ibid., p. 186; Schroeder to Memminger, July 4, 1861, ibid., p. 191.

27. Memminger to Mallory, June 21, 1861 in *Correspondence of,* ed. Thian, p. 121. Similar problems existed at Mobile. See also Thian, ed., *Correspondence with,* pp. 132–33; and Brown to Davis, June 28, 1861, in *Correspondence of,* ed. Thian, pp. 171–73. Brown enclosed an article by J. O. Harrison, a former

neighbor of Davis's near Vicksburg, Mississippi. Fletcher Pratt, *Civil War on Western Waters* (New York: Henry Holt, 1956), pp. 38–40.

28. Memminger to Thomas O. Moore (governor of Louisiana) and to the presidents and directors of the Banks of New Orleans, September 11, 1861, in Thian, *Reports*, pp. 45–46a; Memminger to Thomas J. Semmes, attorney general of Louisiana, September 17, 1861.

29. Fletcher Pratt, *A Short History of the Civil War* (New York: Bantam, 1954), p. 39; see also James M. Merrill, "Confederate Shipbuilding at New Orleans," *Journal of Southern History* 28 (February 1962): 87–93. Merrill mentions naval incompetence, lack of supervision, and uncooperative workers as the causes of the debacle.

30. Report of July 29, 1861, in Thian, *Reports*, p. 30.

31. July 22, 1861, in *Correspondence with*, ed. Thian, pp. 239–40.

32. September 12, 1861, ibid., pp. 325–26.

33. New Orleans *Crescent*, September 13, 1861, p. 1.

34. Memminger to President Davis, June 28, 1861, in *Correspondence of*, ed. Thian, p. 134. For public opposition to bank issues, see Richmond *Examiner*, November 9, 1861; Charleston *Courier*, April 7, 1862; (Correspondence) Richmond *Dispatch*, September 9, 1863; Langdon Cheves Correspondence. For an opposite view against government money, see the Richmond *Whig*, December 20, 1861, "banknotes are a better currency than Treasury Notes and bankers better financiers than legislatures" (p. 2).

35. Confederate printers could have produced these notes for the Confederacy, rather than for the states. Grover C. Criswell, *Confederate and Southern States Currency* (St. Petersburg Beach, Fla.: Criswell Publications, 1964), pp. 105–286.

36. Memminger to George Frederick Holmes et al., May 17, 1861 in *Correspondence of*, ed. Thian, pp. 82–83. Holmes was wrong, inasmuch as bank notes could be received voluntarily anywhere but were subject to a discount.

37. Samuel Younger to Memminger, June 25, 1861, in *Correspondence with*, ed. Thian, pp. 156–60.

38. *Acts of the General Assembly of the State of Georgia etc.* (Milledgeville: Boughton, Nesbit and Barnes, State Printers, 1862), sess. of November–December 1861, pp. 18–19; "An Act to re-enact and continue in force . . . an Act to grant relief to the Banks and people of the State etc," pp. 18–19. *Acts of the General Assembly of the State of Georgia, Passed in Milledgeville, at an Annual Session in November and December 1862; also Extra Session 1863*, "An Act to grant relief to the Banks and People of this State," (Milledgeville: Boughton, Nesbit and Barnes, State Printers, 1863), pp. 18–19, act approved November 29, 1862.

39. John C. Schwab, *The Confederate States of America 1861–5: A Financial and Industrial History of the South during the Civil War* (New York: Charles Scribner's Sons, 1901), p. 133. Some states tried to stop this premium. See South Carolina Senate Committee on Finance and Banks, *A Bill to Punish Persons or Corporations for Sale or Purchase of Bills of Any of the Local Banks of Any State in the Confederacy at a Premium* (Columbia: Charles P. Pelham, 1862); see

also George F. Gerding to Memminger, March 22, 1863, in *Correspondence with,* ed. Thian, p. 61.

40. Ibid., pp. 132–34; Lerner, *Money,* pp. 39a–39c (tables 4–7); *Laws of the State of Mississippi, Passed at a Regular Session of the Mississippi Legislature, Held in the City of Jackson, November and December 1861, and January 1862* (Jackson: Cooper and Kimball, State Printers, 1862), pp. 78–81, 147–63; *Ordnances and Resolutions Passed by the State Convention of North Carolina, at Its Several Sessions in 1861–62* (Raleigh: John W. Syme, Printer to the Convention, 1862), pp. 11–13; *Reports and Resolutions of the General Assembly of the State of South Carolina, Passed at the Annual Session of 1862* (Columbia: Charles P. Pelham, State Printer, 1862), pp. 21–22; *Reports and Resolutions of the State of South Carolina, Passed at the Annual Session of 1863* (Columbia: Charles P. Pelham, State Printer, 1863), p. 150; *Journal of the Acts and Proceedings of a General Convention of the State of Virginia, Assembled at Richmond, on Wednesday, the Thirteenth Day of February, Eighteen Hundred and Sixty-one* (Richmond: Wyatt M. Elliott, Printer, 1861), pp. 29–30.

41. Bureau of the Census, *Statistics of the United States (Including Mortality, Property etc.) in 1860,* 8th Census (Washington, D.C.: Government Printing Office, 1866), P. 296; *Annual Report of the Comptroller General's Office, October 17, 1864* (Milledgeville: Broughton, Nisbet, Barnes and Moore, State Printers, 1864), p. 22; *North Carolina Convention 1865,* document no. 1: (Jonathan Worth) *Treasurer's Report* (Raleigh: Spelman, 1865), pp. 17–73.

42. Act of December 21, 1861, Act no. 4573, *Acts of the General Assembly of the State of South Carolina passed in December 1861 etc.* (Columbia: Charles P. Pelham State Printer, 1862), pp. 21–22; Act of November 26, 1861, Act no. 16, *Acts of the General Assembly of the State of Georgia,* pp. 25–26.

43. Memminger to David Saunders (council president), August 26, 1861 in *Correspondence of,* ed. Thian, p. 179; minutes of August 12, 1861 meeting, in *Richmond at War: Minutes of the City Council 1861–5,* ed. Louis A. Manarin (Chapel Hill: University of North Carolina Press, 1965), p. 65.

44. Virginia Acts of March 19 and 29, May 15 and 19, 1862, Manarin, *Richmond,* pp. 78–85 (November 1–11, 1861).

45. Virginia Legislature, *Called Session 1862 and Adjourned Session 1863,* Richmond, 1862–63, doc. no. 3 (adjourned session), table 14, p. 39.

46. *Laws of the State of Mississippi; Passed at a Regular Session of the Legislature etc.,* pp. 78–81, act approved December 20, 1861.

47. Act of January 25, 1862, ibid., pp. 288–96.

48. *Statutes of Georgia* (Milledgeville: Boughton, Nesbit and Barnes, 1861), pp. 26–28, approved December 17, 1861.

49. Ibid., p. 25, approved December 17, 1861.

50. Notes in the Affleck Collection (see table 11B). There were hundreds of private issuers.

51. Thian, *Reports,* p. 10 (May 10, 1861); Denegre to Memminger, May 21, 26, 1861, in *Correspondence with,* ed. Thian, pp. 87, 117.

52. Ordnance no. 34, ratified June 28, 1861, *Ordnances and Resolutions Passed*

by the State Convention of North Carolina 1861–62, p. 45; Act of January 23, 1862, *Acts Passed by the Sixth Legislature of the State of Louisiana, at Its First Session Held and Begun in the City of Baton Rouge, on the 25th of November, 1861. Published by Authority* (Baton Rouge: Tom Bynum, State Printer, 1861), p. 85; see also Virginia Acts of March 19, 1861 and North Carolina, December 1, 1861.

53. *Annual Report of the Comptroller General of the State of Georgia Made to the Governor, October 31, 1862* (Milledgeville: Boughton, Nesbit and Barnes, 1862), pp. 15–16. The larger-denominated Georgia notes today seldom show much sign of circulation.

54. Ashville, N.C., *News*, December 11, 1862, p. 3. Quotations furnished by John Lancaster and Company of Richmond, Va.

55. Andrew Miller, *Our Currency: Some of Its Evils and Remedies for Them by a Citizen of North Carolina* (Raleigh: John W. Syme, Printer to the State Convention, 1861), pp. 14–15, 30–31, 35–36; see also *The Papers of John C. Calhoun 1801–1817*, 6 vols., ed. Robert L. Merriwether (Columbia: University of South Carolina Press, 1959–72), vol. 4, p. 334.

56. W. Berley (a minister) to Jefferson Davis, September 4, 1861, in *Correspondence with*, ed. Thian, pp. 316–17.

57. Mansell White to J. D. B. DeBow, December 12, 1861, J. D. DeBow Papers, MSS Division, Duke University.

58. William H. Spiegel, *The Rise of American Economic Thought* (Philadelphia: Chilton, 1960), p. 141.

59. Richmond *Whig*, February 19, 1862, p. 2. For similar ideas see also the Richmond *Examiner*, October 10, 1862, p. 1; Charleston *Courier*, October 15, 1862, p. 2; Richmond *Enquirer*, January 16, 1864, p. 2.

60. W. Berley to Davis, September 2, 1861, in *Correspondence with*, ed. Thian, pp. 316–17. (Thian lists the letter in error as written on September 4.)

61. William Murdock to Davis, April 18, 1861, ibid., p. 66.

62. W. Yerger to W. P. Harris, July 14, 1861, "Miscellaneous Correspondence of the Confederate Treasury," Record Group 56, National Archives; B. Melchier to T. W. Lee, September 22, 1862, ibid.

63. Bowers to Memminger, June 13, 1864, in *Correspondence with*, ed. Thian, p. 419.

64. William C. Smedes to Jefferson Davis, July 10, 1861, ibid., pp. 203–5. Smedes was right about one thing—the bankers, particularly Denegre, were vigorously opposed to any such scheme. See also Denegre to Memminger, May 11, 1861, ibid., p. 95.

65. P. H. Skipwith to Memminger, July 19, 1861, ibid., pp. 230–32.

66. *Journal of the Congress of the Confederate States of America 1861–65*, 7 vols. (Washington, D.C.: Government Printing Office, 1904–5), vol. 1, p. 285.

67. Ibid., p. 331.

68. *Journal of the Confederate States*, House, vol. 5, p. 26, February 25, 1862.

69. Memminger to L. J. Gartrell, March 13, 1862, in *Correspondence of*, ed. Thian, pp. 270–71. Memminger was referring to the French Assignments of 1789–95.

70. *Journal of the Confederate States*, House, vol. 5, p. 161.

71. Ibid., Senate, vol. 3, pp. 58–59, 62, 84–89.

72. Ibid., House, vol. 5, pp. 410–11, 498, 508; see also Lee to President Davis, *War of the Rebellion: Armies*, ser. 4, vol. 2, p. 116.

73. Frank E. Vandiver, ed., *Proceedings of the First Confederate Congress, Fourth Session December 7, 1863–February 18, 1864*, Southern Historical Society Papers, n.s. no. 12, whole number L.; Richmond, Virginia Historical Society, 1953, pp. 122–24; see also *State of the Country, Speech of Hon. A. C. Brown of Mississippi*, December 24, 1863 (n.p., n.d.), pp. 12–13; "Miscellaneous Documents," a congressional report of a speech, Record Group 94, National Archives.

74. *Congressional Globe*, 37th Cong., 2d sess., House, February 8, 1862, p. 691.

75. *Congressional Globe*, 37th Cong., 2d sess., part 1, pp. 680–81, House, February 6, 1862.

76. Hammond, *Sovereignty*, pp. 168–70.

77. A. T. Huntington and Robert J. Mawhinney, comps., *Laws of the United States Concerning Money, Banking and Loans, 1778–1909*, doc. no. 480, Senate 61st Cong., 2d sess. (Washington, D.C.: Government Printing Office, 1910), pp. 182–83. The act was repealed on July 2, 1864 (see Stat. L. 344). See also Henrietta Malin Larson, *J. Cook, Private Banker* (Cambridge: Harvard University Press, 1936), pp. 126–32; and Albert Sidney Bolles, *The Financial History of the United States from 1861–1885* (New York: D. Appleton, 1886), pp. 114–47.

78. Mississippi Act of August 2, 1861, Resolution of Legislature December 9, 1863; see also North Carolina Ordnance of the Convention, February 25, 1862, no. 35 and Louisiana, Act of January 23, 1862.

79. Alabama *Acts*, December 9, 1861, pp. 21–22; December 10, 1861, pp. 37–38; Act of December 14, 1863.

80. Ordnance no. 85, Virginia State Convention, July 1, 1861.

81. C. A. Dubuissen to Memminger in *Correspondence with*, ed. Thian, pp. 26–27, complains that sheriffs and merchants would not take C.S.A. notes. See also W. A. James to Memminger, February 9, 1863, Greenboro, Ala., Record Group 356, National Archives; James A. Higgs to Memminger, February 25, 1863, Halifax Court House, N.C.; and John H. Dent to Memminger, January 24, 1863, in *Correspondence with,,* p. 13, for the reaction of a creditor stuck with C.S.A. notes.

82. John M. Keynes, *A Tract on Monetary Reform* (London: Macmillan, 1923), pp. 50–51.

83. Thian, *Reports*, pp. 66, 102–3.

84. Lerner, *Money*, pp. 39a–40. This process was helped along by the suspension of specie payments on the Confederate debt noted in chapter 3.

85. Report of January 10, 1863, Memminger to T. S. Bocock, in Thian, *Reports*, pp. 111–12.

86. *Congressional Globe*, 36th Cong., 2d sess., Part 1, pp. 871–72.

87. Schwab, *Confederate States*, p. 50; Richmond *Dispatch*, January 9, 1863, p. 1.

88. John Gill Shorter (governor of Alabama) to Memminger, December 4, 1862, in *Correspondence with*, ed. Thian, pp. 677–78.
89. South Carolina Acts of December 18, 1862, January 28, and February 6, 1863; Florida Resolution of December 15, 1862 and January 3, 1863; Texas Resolution of February 27, 1863.
90. Raleigh *Progress*, March 27 and April 14 and 17, 1863.
91. Charleston *Courier*, January 15, 1863, p. 1 (quoting the Augusta *Constitutionalist*); see also the Memphis *Appeal* published at Atlanta, November 9, 1863. The *Appeal* moved from Memphis in 1862 and changed its place of business so often as to be known as the "Moving Appeal." See also the Richmond *Examiner*, December 5, 1863, p. 1.
92. Letter of March 2, 1863 in "The Correspondence of Robert Toombs, Alexander H. Stephens and Howell Cobb," in *Annual Report of the American Historical Association 1911*, ed. Ulrich B. Phillips (Washington, D.C.: Government Printing Office, 1913), vol. 2, p. 611.
93. Report dated August 18, 1862 and Report of January 10, 1863, in *Reports*, ed. Thian, pp. 73–77, 99–101.
94. Reports of September 15, 1862 and October 3, 1862; Memminger to Bocock, ibid., pp. 89–92.
95. Memminger to President Davis, October 6, 1862, ibid., pp. 93–94.
96. Mathews, ed., *Public and Private Laws*, 1st Cong., 2d sess., p. 81, approved October 13, 1862.
97. "Treasury Notice as to Funding Treasury Notes," October 22, 1862, in *Correspondence of*, ed. Thian, p. 370.
98. Report of January 10, 1863, in Thian, *Reports*, p. 106.
99. Ibid., pp. 106–7.
100. Act of March 23, 1863, in *Public and Private Laws*, ed. Mathews, 1st Cong., 3d sess., pp. 99–100.
101. Ibid., secs. 3, 6, 7, pp. 100–101. "April 6, 1863" notes were of the Act of March 23, 1863, whereas the "December 2, 1862" notes pertained to the Acts of September 23 and October 13, 1862.
102. Thian, *Register*, pp. 176–77.
103. Richmond *Examiner*, May 1, 1863, Richmond *Enquirer*, September 2, 1864.
104. Thian, *Reports*, December 7, 1863, pp. 177–79.
105. Ibid., pp. 183–87; William Gregg to Memminger, September 11, 1863, in *Correspondence with*, ed. Thian, p. 137. Gregg was fully persuaded that $75 million would be ample for a circulating medium for the Confederate states.
106. James D. Richardson, ed., *A Compilation of the Messages and Papers of the Confederacy: Including the Diplomatic Correspondence, 1861–1865*, 2 vols. (Nashville: United States Publishing, 1906), vol. 1, pp. 367–69.
107. Report of the Bank Convention at Augusta, Georgia (November 16–17, 1863) and G. C. Mordecai to Memminger, November 19, 1863, in *Correspondence with*, ed. Thian, pp. 214–21.
108. Cary Cox to Memminger, November 8, 1863, and W. Goodman to Memminger, November 13, 1863, ibid., pp. 199–200, 204–6.

109. C. P. Culver to Herschel V. Johnson (Confederate senator from Georgia), October 27, 1863, ibid., pp. 206–11.

110. C. H. Minge to Memminger, November 19, 1863, quoting proposals of one Morris published in the Mobile *Tribune* (date not specified), ibid., pp. 221–22.

111. "House of Representatives Secret Session Resolutions of Instructions by Mr. Lyon," January 9, 1864, Record Group 94, p. 1, National Archives; see also "House of Representatives No. 3 Suggestions for Financial Relief by Mr. H. W. Bruce," December 21, 1863, and "House Bill No. 23½ a Bill to Be Entitled an Act Imposing a Tax on Treasury Notes by Mr. Russell," December 14, 1863, ibid.

112. House of Representatives, "Secret Session by Mr. Garnett Proposition of Finance," January 11, 1864, Record Group 94, National Archives; see also "House of Representatives Secret Session by Mr. Boyce Minority Report on the Currency," December 30, 1863, Record Group 94, pp. 1–2, National Archives.

113. "House of Representatives Secret Session by Mr. Baldwin from the Special Committee on Currency 'A Bill to Be Entitled an Act to Tax, Fund and Limit the Currency,' " Record Group 94, p. 105, National Archives; see also House Bill. No. 192, "Secret Bill to Tax, Fund and Limit the Currency," pp. 1–6, presented to the Senate on January 18, 1864.

114. "Senate Document 18 Secret Report of the Committee on Finance on the Bill H.R. 192 to Tax, Fund and Limit the Currency," ibid., pp. 1–12.

115. Act of December 30, 1864, in *Laws*, ed. Ramsdell, pp. 12–13; Secretary Trenholm to R. M. T. Hunter, November 7, 1864, in Thian, *Reports*, pp. 358–59.

116. Henry D. Capers, *The Life and Times of C. G. Memminger* (Richmond: Everett Waddey, 1893), pp. 347–48.

117. Mathews, ed., *Public and Private Laws*, 1st Cong., 4th sess., pp. 205–8.

118. Act of December 30, 1864, in *Laws*, ed. Ramsdell, pp. 12–13.

119. P. W. Gray to Secretary Trenholm, December 26, 1864, in Thian, *Reports*, p. 448.

120. November 7, 1864, ibid., p. 353.

121. Wytheville (Va.) *Dispatch*, April 22, 1864, p. 2.

122. Mathews, ed., *Public and Private Laws*, pp. 272–77, 2nd Cong., 1st sess., approved June 14, 1864; Acts of November 28, 1864, March 13, 1865, March 17, 1865, in Ramsdell, *Laws*, pp. 5, 73–74, 121–22, 147–49.

123. *Journal of the Congress*, vol. 7, House, March 16, 1865, pp. 789–90; also vol. 4, Senate, March 18, 1864, p. 472. Only twelve senators were present, the vote being 11–1. Richardson, comp., *A Compilation*, pp. 561–63; Schwab, *Confederate States*, p. 80; Richard C. Todd, *Confederate Finance* (Athens: University of Georgia Press, 1954), p. 115. Todd repeats Schwab without independent investigation. See also Rembert W. Patrick, *Jefferson Davis and His Cabinet* (Baton Rouge: Louisiana State University Press, 1944), p. 241. It was Patrick who discovered the absence of a quorum.

124. Edward Frost (treasurer, South Carolina) to Memminger, April 9, 24, 1861, in *Correspondence with*, ed. Thian, pp. 55, 79.

CHAPTER FIVE

Confederate Fiscal Policy

Taxation and the Confederate Constitution

The Provisional Confederate Congress, which met on February 4, 1861, was both a constitutional convention and a legislative body. Within twenty-four hours after convening, a committee of twelve (two from each state) was ordered to prepare a provisional constitution for the Confederacy. The chairman, Christopher, G. Memminger, had already published his constitutional proposals in an anonymous pamphlet, and evidently his blueprint commanded majority support.[1] The provisions he had suggested were submitted for Congress's consideration and were adopted by Congress as the Provisional Constitution, with one amendment that is of particular interest to this discussion.

Memminger had included in his draft two new provisos: one that Congress might not levy protective duties and the other that no duty should exceed 15 percent ad valorem. When these provisos came up for debate, Duncan F. Kenner, a protectionist Louisiana sugar planter and chairman of the House Ways and Means Committee in the first Congress (1862–64), moved successfully for their deletion on the ground that the definitive disposition of the tariff should await the permanent constitution.[2]

On the day following the adoption of the Provisional Constitution, February 8, 1861, arrangements for the formulation of a permanent constitution were made the first order of business. On a motion by Robert Barnwell Rhett, Congress promptly appointed a second committee to prepare a draft of such a document. That committee consisted of Rhett (as chairman) and such luminaries as Robert Toombs and T. R. R. Cobb of Georgia (brother of Howell Cobb, president of the Congress). Unlike Memminger's preparation for the Provisional Constitution, Rhett had not come to Montgomery with a ready draft; he merely had firm ideas. As a grimly dedicated states' rights advocate, he was determined to curb the economic powers of the Confederacy in such diverse matters as the tariff and internal improvements. Because the authorizing resolution gave the committee only one month to prepare a draft, there was no time for a fresh look at the allocation of powers, a move that past problems with the federal Constitution might have suggested.[3]

The Provisional Congress's urgency to adopt a permanent constitution is evidence, as has been noted, of Southern conservatism—compounded by too many lawyers and an obsessive preoccupation with foreign recognition. Forty-two of the fifty delegates then seated in the Provisional Congress were members of the bar, and almost all the Confederate leaders, lawyers and laymen alike, showed a passionate interest in the metaphysics of legitimacy.[4] The Confederacy was painfully anxious to secure the approbation of foreign governments, and it feared that recognition would be accorded only after its government had tidied up its juridical situation. Still, as evolving events demonstrated, the Southerners should have worried less about what others thought of them and used the breathing space afforded by the Provisional Constitution to arrange their affairs to suit themselves.

To rationalize their haste the Confederate leaders claimed that they had no serious quarrel with the federal Constitution. What was needed, they said, was a return to proper principles of strict construction and the application of these principles by the courts and Congress.[5] Yet Southerners held divergent convictions on states' rights and the central government's role. As a legislative body with the duties of a constitutional convention, the Provisional Congress, if the new regime were effectively to fulfill its people's desires, had the duty of sorting these problems out.

Among the matters requiring careful examination were the government's fiscal powers. The question of tariff policy arose on March 4, 1861, when the drafting committee recommended that "excises" were to be limited to those that were "necessary." The committee also recommended that the federal general welfare clause be deleted. Clearly these amendments were intended to prevent protectionism and internal improvements. It was a blow struck for laissez-faire and limited government, which fully reflected the mood of the convention.

If anything, the Provisional Congress sitting as a constitutional convention wished to go further in its genuflections to the "true doctrines of political economy"; indeed Rhett proposed that "no bounties shall be paid from the Treasury, nor shall any duties or taxes on importation from foreign nations be laid to promote or foster any branch of industry."[6] That amendment was speedily adopted.

In shaping the permanent constitution in the Provisional Congress, Secretary Memminger offered an amendment incorporating a slight revision of Rhett's language that forbade any appropriation to foster or promote any branch of industry. Because it was realized that such language would have fatally hobbled the Confederacy's war powers and aborted railroad-building and the production of armaments, the convention voted it down. Yet it was ominous that such a constricting amendment should have been offered by the future secretary of the treasury, because it foreshadowed the narrow concept of government responsibility that Memminger was to exhibit throughout his tenure of office.

Unable to leave the subject alone, Memminger proposed another proviso to section 8 of clause 4, stating "but neither this, nor any other clause pertaining to the Constitution shall ever be construed to delegate the power to Congress to appropriate money for any internal improvement intended to facilitate commerce."[7] Memminger later cited this and the abolished general welfare clause as justification for his refusal to lend money to buy or borrow the cotton crop.

Toombs, in keeping with Vice-President Alexander H. Stephens's views, inserted an amendment allowing navigation improvements provided they were paid for by levies on shipping. As Stephens had put it, "the true principle is to subject the commerce to every locality to whatever burdens may be necessary to facilitate it. If Charleston Harbor needs improvement, let the commerce of Charleston bear the burden."[8]

Not every constitutional action in the economic sphere was of a purely negative character. For example, the Provisional Constitution had granted the government power to levy a direct tax without apportionment and also, as will be seen, authorized export duties. Unfortunately this language was not carried over to the permanent Constitution, and the 1789 federal clause apportioning taxes based on the House membership pending a canvas was left out. These omissions greatly impeded efforts to levy direct taxes.

Even more curious was what the debaters failed to discuss. In a body where the hope of foreign intervention and recognition was on everyone's mind, there was no mention of free trade. Many had been convinced that the best way to deal a heavy blow to the North while appealing to the cupidity of Europe was to abolish tariffs and adopt a policy of internal taxes. Eager to gain markets from which they had been debarred by Northern imposed tariffs, the Europeans, they hoped, would soon see the advantages of an independent South.

Moreover, it was realized that if the South erected customs barriers on the Mississippi, it would reduce the traffic on that river, encourage shipments by rail to New York, and anger the old Northwest and those states bordering the Mississippi which, as former political allies, the South wished to conciliate. But if there were free trade on the Mississippi, it would be difficult to avoid free trade with the North. Given that, there was no purpose in having customs houses on the coast. Thus free trade with Europe meant free trade with the Union and inevitably a system of direct taxes on property, income, and the like.

These conflicting positions and the division of views among experienced men over their propriety all required earnest debate. But, without deliberation, the Provisional Congress reflexively rushed toward a tariff system without any consideration of the alternatives.[9]

The Search for a Customs Revenue

When the legislators first forgathered on February 4, 1861, all revenue-raising machinery in the South was in the hands of the state governments. Thus, one of the first acts (February 9, 1861) of the convention assembled at Montgomery was to continue the customs officials in office and to order that the tariff of 1857 be enforced until a new one could be devised.[10]

With this legislative authority in hand, Secretary Memminger arranged to transfer the customs houses to Confederate control. The potential volume of revenue was limited by the fact that only $4 million of U.S. customs receipts were collected at Southern ports,[11] and it would clearly take time for direct trade with Europe to burgeon into substantial volume. In the meantime, Memminger needed to reduce expenditures while establishing new customs posts on the land frontier with the United States. In February 1861, he found himself operating 27 customs houses employing 426 men at an annual cost of $444,000; five months later, while adding six new posts, he had eliminated 12 offices and 106 men at a net saving of $113,000.[12]

While Secretary Memminger was preoccupied with these unimportant housekeeping details, Congress undertook certain provisional adjustments in the tariff. For instance, on February 18, it placed living animals, meats, and war materiel on the free list. On March 4, it reduced duties on such items as iron and paper, while charging a harbor fee of 5 cents per ton on all vessels entering Confederate ports after May 1.[13] These actions were stop-gap measures designed to eliminate the more objectionable protectionist features of the Tariff of 1857. Any comprehensive effort to design a Confederate tariff had to await the outcome of ongoing negotiations among those who advocated free trade, those who believed that a protective tariff would make the South industrially as well as politically independent, and those (certainly a majority) who advocated a tariff for revenue only.[14]

A comparison of the final Confederate tariff of May 21, 1861 with the federal Morrill tariff of March 2, 1861 shows the contrast in attitudes between a Confederate Congress, purged of Northern protectionists, and a federal Congress no longer influenced by Southern free-traders. The contrast was manifest not only in rate levels, but also in the techniques employed. In the Morrill tariff, the United States moved away from ad valorem duties—a progressive innovation in 1857—toward heavier reliance on specific duties. The Confederate Congress, on the other hand, limited specific duties to coffee, tea, and salt. The proponents of a revenue tariff had triumphed; of the 788 items enumerated, 44 were placed on the free list, 207 had the same rates as formerly, and rates on 311 items fell. Cloth and iron rates were reduced from 24 percent to 15 percent ad valorem while sugar duties fell only slightly (24–20 percent), reflecting the opposition of the Louisiana cane-growers. Yet the trend was not all one way, for the need to augment the revenue required the South to remove coffee and tea from the free list. Economically productive items, however, such as guano, ships, dredging vessels, and equipment used in the construction of harbors, were given a duty-free status.[15]

In his May 10 report, Secretary Memminger provided estimates of the revenue to be derived from the tariff. He recognized that receipts were keyed to the annual autumnal export of the South's staple products and were thus seasonal in their character; without credits from New York, Southern trade would be disrupted until credits were established abroad. Thus import duties would not yield much revenue until November 1861. To arrive at an estimate of customs revenues, Memminger guessed that Southern exports would be worth approximately $235 million. Allowing a 10 percent margin for price fluctuations, he calculated dutiable imports as slightly more than $200 million, from which the treasury might expect to derive a revenue of $25 million. It is apparent that these estimates were based on several hypotheses of dubious certitude.

First, Memminger assumed that all the goods imported would come through Southern ports, thus making no allowance for contraband from the North. Yet, even while he was establishing customs houses on the land frontier, there were reports of smuggling.[16] Second, his assumption of $200 million worth of imports bore little relation to reality. With total United States imports valued at $354 million (table 18) in 1860, the secretary evidently assumed that 56 percent of all imports would be sold in the South, where only 20 percent of the white population of the United States lived. As it turned out, however, even after he had made liberal allowances for pre-1861 trade with the North at $75 million, imports from Europe would amount to only $75 million, for total imports of $150 million rather than $200 million.

Table 18. Trade Figures by Port in 1860*

Port	Exports	Imports
New York	$ 80.0	$231.3
Other Northern ports	71.5	$ 95.3
Total North	$151.5	$327.0
Charleston	$ 16.0	$ 2.0
Savannah	2.4	.8
Mobile	27.0	.6
New Orleans	108.2	20.6
Other Southern ports	28.9	$ 3.0
Total South	$182.5	$ 27.0
Total U.S.A.	$337.0	$354.0

Customs Collections by Major Port† (1860)	
New York	$ 34.9
New Orleans	3.1
Total South	4.0
Total North	48.3
Total U.S.A.	$ 52.3

Sources: Census Bureau *Abstract 1951*, pp. 153–213; U.S. Bureau of the Census, *Historical Statistics of the United States Colonial Times to 1957* (Washington, D.C.: Government Printing Office, 1957), pp. 543, 712.
* All figures in millions.
† Average rate about 17.7 percent because 15 percent of goods were not dutiable.

Third, the $25 million of estimated revenue would have proved inadequate to meet the normal civil expenses of the government, never mind the war establishment that the outbreak of hostilities clearly indicated. Fourth, even more fundamentally, Memminger ignored the adverse effect on customs receipts of Lincoln's blockade proclamation.

Because Memminger conceded that only half of his estimated revenues would be in hand by February 18, 1862, which meant a yield of only $12.5 million in nine months, it is hard to see why he expected a $25 million annual yield.[17] Moreover, his proposals ignored the revenue implications of proposals to offer free trade to any European nation extending recognition or the states abutting the Mississippi River.[18]

As early as May 21, 1861, blockade reports were already showing that Memminger's revenue estimates would be wide of the mark.[19] On October 9, the beleaguered secretary belatedly dispatched a circular letter to all collectors, asking whether ships had been allowed in or out, whether the blockade had been interrupted by weather, and if the blockaders had been ordered away or had been diverted to pursue blockade-runners. Finally, was the posting of the ships sufficient to be a danger to the blockade-runners? Replies indicated that federal forces were blockading the ports although frequent intermissions had been occasioned by bad weather or causes unknown to the collectors.[20] Moreover, the Union warships were inadequate both in number and fire power to maintain an effective blockade. Yet, because very few ships had actually entered Southern harbors, it was obvious that the blockade was achieving the effect Lincoln intended.[21]

Whatever further illusions the secretary may have had about the revenue potential of the tariff should have been dispelled by January 13, 1862, when he reported that only $63,000 of customs dues had been received since July 1, 1861 on goods imported after that date. On the basis of his own reports, Secretary Memminger knew that by the end of the Provisional Government, on February 18, 1862, he had collected only $1,270,000.[22] Manifestly, the treasury urgently needed other fiscal revenues. As a measure for raising revenue for the Confederacy, the tariff had provided a failure. Instead of the substantial revenues Memminger had predicted, the Confederacy eventually grossed no more than $3.5 million. Income was concentrated in the first year, but as the blockade was tightened during 1862, collections fell to only $668,000. The $930,000 collected during the first five months of 1863 probably reflected price inflation rather than an increased flow of goods.[23]

Thus, in retrospect, the Confederate tariff appears more as an exercise in abstract philosophy than a serious effort to raise revenue under war conditions. Certainly Confederate leaders can be legitimately faulted for ignoring the lessons John C. Calhoun and Albert Gallatin had derived from the War of 1812. That unsatisfactory experience should have been familiar to the legislators in Richmond, but apathy and wishful thinking proved stronger than the wisdom derived from history.

The Export Tax under the Confederacy

Since the federal Constitution had explicitly prohibited export duties at the insistence of the Southern delegates to the Philadelphia Convention, one might have expected the Confederates to write a parallel prohibition into their own Constitution. But that overlooks the fact that, unlike the delegates at Philadelphia, the Montgomery Convention did not have to reconcile sectional interests. Freed from the fear that antislavery advocates might put a punitive tax on the products of slave labor, Memminger, who had drafted the tax and tariff articles of the Provisional Constitution, felt it safe to omit the language that had prohibited export duties.[24] The action was a revealing sign that Memminger, unlike some of his colleagues, had at least given some thought to the special needs of a Southern nation and was not content with a slavish copy of the federal Constitution.

The first practical application of the power to levy export duties came about in an unexpected way. On February 28, 1861, the Provisional Congress had floated a loan of $15 million "to provide for the Defense of the Confederate States of America." To secure both principal and interest of the loan, Congress needed another source of revenue in addition to the customs dues already committed to defray the regular expenses of the government. The proposed solution was an export duty of one-eighth cent per pound on all cotton shipped from the Confederacy after August 1, 1861. As a sweetener, Congress provided that the coupons—and later, the interest certificates of the February 28 loan—would be receivable for the export dues.

Legislative History and Use of Confederate Export Dues

Although the export tariff was intended to shore up the government's credit, the Confederate *Journal* records vigorous congressional opposition to the principle of export duties and the proposed rate and the mode of applying them. In large part, the difference in view reflected divergent assessments of the South's bargaining position in the international cotton market. Calhoun had noted earlier that "Our market is the World. . . . We have no monopoly in the supply of our products, one half of the globe may produce them. Should we reduce our productions, others stand ready . . . to take our place; and, instead of raising prices, we would only diminish our share of the supply. We are thus compelled to produce, on the penalty of losing our hold on the general market."[25]

Those who agreed with Calhoun were firmly opposed to an export duty. Others, like J. W. Wilkinson of Charleston, saw the matter differently. Wilkinson believed that a moderate export duty would fall primarily on foreigners, only a tenth being paid by the Southerners. That Wilkinson differed with Calhoun is not surprising; Calhoun's remarks were made in the middle of a depression, and Wilkinson's at the end of an extended period of prosperity. Wilkinson based his contention on the assumption (which Jacob Cardozo, the South Carolinian economist, had disproved) that the demand for cotton outran the supply—and thus, an export duty would not materially affect the market because it would increase prices less than 3 percent.[26]

The export tax was added to the bill on February 21 on the initiative of Howell Cobb. In opening the debate, Edward Sparrow of Louisiana moved that a 2 percent ad valorem export duty be substituted for the specific duty of one-eighth cent per pound. Memminger opposed that motion, which was promptly defeated, as was a motion by Stephens that sought to eliminate the entire section.

When Congress resumed debate on February 22, the Louisiana, Mississippi, and South Carolina delegations, which backed the measure, had to ward off a variety of amendments, which included a 1 percent ad valorem duty "upon all cotton, rice, sugar, molasses, syrup, tobacco, lumber, tar, pitch, turpentine and resin exported from this Confederacy." Finally, on February 27, the amendment was adopted over Stephens's objections, and the bill was signed by President Davis the next day.[27]

Significantly, the legislation, even at this early date, disclosed an endemic failing of the Congress—an inability to levy taxes sufficient for their stated purposes. If one assumes a cotton crop of about three million bales in 1861 weighing roughly five hundred pounds each, an export duty of one-eighth cent per pound would produce about $1,750,000. Although that revenue would be sufficient to pay the $1.2 million annual interest on the $15 million, 8 percent loan, it would leave $9.5 million of the principal unpaid at the end of ten years. In order to call in this debt after five years, as Congress had provided, a rate of eight-tenths cent per pound—or nearly seven times that levied—was required. Thus, the 2 percent proposal, which Congress rejected, had been clearly more realistic inasmuch as its $4 million a year of nominal revenue would have discharged the bonds in six years, while the rise in cotton prices would have increased the government's revenue.

Subsequent Abortive Export Duty Proposals

Although similar proposals were put before Congress, the Act of February 28, 1861 was the only export duty the Confederacy ever attempted. On May 1, 1861, Memminger recommended a further resort to export duties. Such duties, he argued, could be collected with so much more facility than direct taxes, were more consistent with the habits of the people, and were rendered necessary by the uncertainty of imports. Furthermore, Memminger thought that such a tax would not be affected by war. In trying (unsuccessfully) to induce Congress to support the measure, Memminger reversed his February position, when he had not joined the opposition to a 2 percent ad valorem export duty. Instead, he now recommended a comprehensive 12.5 percent export duty, which he estimated would yield $30 million. Memminger's justification for this extraordinary reliance on export taxes was that a system of rebates to the exporters, which would accompany it, would encourage exporters to insist on direct trade with Southern ports and merchants.[28]

The secretary's proposals were based on a practical consideration; because planters would have to pay the export duty, the fair thing to do was to redistribute the burden onto consumers of foreign goods— hence the rebate given the planters in the form of certificates that they could sell to others to pay customs dues. Thus the secretary's export duty plan was, in effect, a cumbersome method of anticipating the customs receipts. As such, it did not meet the South's need for a fiscal revenue independent of foreign trade. When the blockade, the vigilante-imposed cotton embargo, the shortage of shipping, and the admitted customs revenue shortfall are taken into account, the secretary's view that those factors were irrelevant to the collection of export duties defies logic.

His proposals demonstrate two of Memminger's weaker points (shared with the Confederate Congress): a refusal to face reality coupled with a fondness for permitting payments on one tax to offset those due on another. In pursuing such a course, Congress and the secretary ignored Calhoun's advice about the need to take the public into their confidence. Worse still, their timidity demonstrates beyond a doubt that they were highly dubious about whether Southerners were sufficiently committed to the Confederacy to pay the heavy taxes that the war required. This fundamental failure in leadership and patriotism goes far, as shall be seen, to explain the Southern inability to produce an effective fiscal program.

After Congress had ignored Memminger's appeal for an export tax, the secretary waited until April 7, 1863, to propose that a funding loan of March 23, 1863 be secured by a 2 cent per pound tax on exported agricultural products. This increase in the export tax rate from one-eighth cent per pound of cotton would, he predicted, yield an additional $48 million. The funds would do much to bolster market support for the new issue.

One would have thought that after two years' experience in office Memminger would turn toward a more realistic approach to the treasury's problems. Yet his report still ignored the blockade in contending that export taxes would materially augment receipts. But even fantasy may have some basis in fact, and it was true that the loan of February 28, 1861, secured by an export tax, consistently commanded a pre-

mium in the bond market. Whether, as Memminger thought, an en-
larged export duty would have a similar impact on the great mass of
Confederate indebtedness is questionable.[29]

Congress, for one, took a different view; an export tax might secure
a $15 million loan, but its proceeds were too small for any other
purpose. Moreover, an inadequate tax pledged for one loan could
scarcely in good faith be diverted for the benefit of another. Nevertheless, in the Act of February 17, 1864, Congress pledged that coupons
of the $500 million tax-free loan would be receivable for "the entire
net receipts of any export duty hereafter laid on the value of all
cotton, tobacco, and naval stores, which shall be exported from the
Confederate States. . . ." But that pledge was a meaningless gesture
because Congress never passed a law to provide a new export duty,
and the war ended with no further legislation on that subject.

In retrospect, it seems that any export taxes Congress might have
voted would have added only a small increment to the treasury's
revenues because from August 1, 1861 until the end of the Confederacy, the one-eighth cent per pound duty yielded only about $45,000,
which would indicate that the levy was paid on eighty thousand bales
at most.[30] Yet Owsley estimates that at least one million bales were
exported in the years of 1862–64, and this takes no account of dutiable
shipments in 1861 as well as 1865. More recent scholarship suggests
total exports directly to Europe aggregated fewer than 464,000 bales,
while 830,000 reached the North via the land blockade. Even given this
modest total, $290,000 should have been derived from the maritime
exports alone, a sum six times that actually collected.[31]

The disparity between actual and theoretical collections, leaving
aside surreptitious trading between the citizens of the Confederacy
and the Unionists, was undoubtedly due in part to the cotton exported
tax-free on the Confederacy's or the states' account. There must also
have been hasty landings and hurried departures from places that had
rarely, if ever, seen a customs officer. Thus Gallatin's and Calhoun's
solemn warnings that taxes based on foreign trade would prove a
broken reed in wartime were once again validated.[32] The fatal consequence of ignoring the principle was that Congress deferred levying
internal taxes, which were needed because they were less vulnerable
to the vicissitudes of war.

The Search for an Internal Revenue

Immediately after Fort Sumter, Secretary Memminger and the more
thoughtful members of Congress might well have recognized that
revenues from customs or export dues were uncertain at best. Because

the currency was, by its terms, "receivable for all dues except export dues," Congress had an implied duty to provide alternative tax revenues for their support. Moreover, vigorous action was urgently needed. The War of 1812 had demonstrated that it took time to assess and collect taxes and that the government's credit would be damaged if such revenues were not promptly forthcoming. Lacking alternate revenues, it was Memminger's job to formulate a program of internal taxes no responsible statesman could oppose, and, had he done so, the debate could have been profitably focused on the rates and distribution.

But, in view of the instinctive opposition to internal taxes, that task would have required a high degree of preparation and candor. As Gallatin put it in 1831 (echoing Calhoun's sentiments fifteen years earlier):

> When our Government relies on the people . . . in making war, its confidence must be entire. They must be told the whole truth, and if they are really in favor of war, they will cheerfully sustain the government. . . . If, instead of telling the people the whole truth, they [the Government] attempt to conceal from them the necessity of the measures required for carrying on the war . . . a reaction of public sentiment will almost certainly take place whenever it will have become impossible to delay any longer the heavy burden of taxation for which the nation has not been prepared.[33]

These sentiments were echoed in 1861 by Gazaway B. Lamar, a banker friend of the South, who strongly believed in free trade and direct taxes. As he put it in a letter to Howell Cobb, "Don't be afraid to tax the people; the people will pay taxes to get rid of [the] Abolitionists, and if they will not, let them give up their negroes at once. But they are more intelligent than most people give them credit for. Deal frankly and honestly with them, and they will pay taxes and lend money too."[34]

Confederate Tax Goals

Memminger's first task was to decide when to levy taxes and how much revenue was needed. So far as timing was concerned, the sooner taxes were levied and collected, the better; economic decay and a subsiding of popular enthusiasm might both be anticipated as the war progressed. Memminger at least theoretically understood the need for adequate taxes, and he publicly recognized that a modern war could not be conducted on a pay-as-you-go basis, pointing out that the taxes laid must establish "a solid basis for loans" and sufficient revenues created to discharge the maturing principal and interest of the war debt.[35]

In so saying, Secretary Memminger paraphrased Adam Smith and Secretary Gallatin. But, whereas both Smith and Gallatin had strongly emphasized the need to develop tax revenues to cover not only the regular expenses of government but also as much war expense as possible, the Confederate secretary was willing to settle for much less.[36] Although he asserted the need to levy sufficient funds to pay the interest and the maturing principal of the public debt, he seemed unwilling to do anything more than merely pledge future taxes for their payment. Nor did he make provision for the regular peacetime establishment, even though Memminger's budget should have taken into consideration that a new nation had a host of responsibilities. For example, the expenses of the U.S. government in 1860 totaled approximately $70 million. Even had Horace Greeley's advice to let the "Erring Sisters" depart in peace been followed, the new Confederate government would probably have needed an army of more than ten thousand men, a coast guard and navy, and a civil administration. Although the Post Office deficit might be reduced by raising rates and terminating superfluous routes, no similar economies could be effected at the treasury. Direct trade with Southern ports would necessitate more officers at all the major harbors, and there would be the added expense of policing a thousand-mile border with the United States. Alternatively, if the South abolished customs dues and relied on internal taxes, a bureau of internal revenue with a force of collectors would be required. Finally, the Confederacy would have to assume the U.S. pensions in the South, the costs of foreign representation, and the usual payoffs to purchase immunity from Indian depredations. Given all these sources of expense, the Confederacy would require, at a minimum, a budget of $30 million (table 19).

To these expenses, Memminger should have provided for these extraordinary expenditures connected with the war. Using Gallatin's formulation, Memminger would be required to raise revenues to pay the interest on the public debt and amortize the principal of the loans then outstanding. Table 19 also discloses that $65 million would be due on the debt by July 1, 1863, not including another $10 million the secretary wanted available to redeem the 6 percent call certificates. By July 1, 1863, these sums and the $75 million needed to meet regular government expenses would have amounted to approximately $150 million, which would require at least $60 million a year in internal taxes.

With the Gross National Product of the thirteen Confederate states

Table 19. U.S. Expenditures, 1860, and Estimated Regular
and Extraordinary Budgets for the Confederacy, 1861–63*

	U.S. (1860)	Projected Estimated CSA (1861)
1. U.S. army (16,215 men)	$ 16.5	$ 12.5
2. U.S. navy (9,900 + 1,800 marines)	11.5	4.0
3. Interest in the public debt	9.2	—
4. Post Office	19.2	3.5
5. Foreign representation	1.1	1.1
6. Indian payments	3.0	1.5
7. Civil list (executive, Congress, and judiciary)	6.1	4.0
8. Pensions	1.1	.2
9. Miscellaneous	1.5	—
	$ 63.2	$ 30.0

Total Regular Confederate Expenses to July 1, 1863:	$ 75.0
Extraordinary expenses to July 1, 1863 (to be retired by taxation):	
1. Treasury notes of March 9, 1861 principal due (July 4, 1862–December 22, 1862)	$ 2.1
2. Treasury notes of July 25, 1861 (due July 25, 1863)	20.0
3. Interest on bonds, February 28, 1861 (8 percent)	2.0
August 19, 1861 (8 percent)	8.0
December 24, 1861 (6 percent)	5.4
4. Interest on 7.30 percent treasury notes, April 17, 1862	6.2
5. Principal of loan of February 28, 1861	6.0
December 24, 1861	15.0
Total extraordinary expenses:	$ 64.7
Total expenses to be raised by taxation:	$139.7

Source: Davis R. Dewey, *Financial History of the United States* (New York: Touzonaus, Green, 1912), p. 267.
* All figures in millions.

in 1860 estimated at something over $800 million, a tax levy of 7.5 percent of the GNP, or $80 per family, does not seem particularly ambitious (table 20).[37] Yet, in fact, by mid-1863 the Confederacy had actually collected only $5 million of bona fide taxes.

Unhappily, the secretary's estimation of future expenditures was quite as imperfect as his revenue projections. Like so many treasury officials, Memminger tended to underestimate expenses. For example, on July 29, 1861, he projected expenditures at $124 million by February 1862; the actual figure was $139 million.[38] His budget for February 18, 1862–December 31, 1862, called for expenditures totaling $214 million;

Financial Failure and Confederate Defeat

Table 20. Hypothetical Tax Revenues for the Thirteen Nominal States of the Confederacy*

Total slave values	$2,400
2 percent tax less 20 percent for losses	$ 38.4
Total corporate values	
1. Banks and others	$ 300
2. Railways	$ 280
1 percent tax less 20 percent for losses	$ 46.4
Total other property values	
1. Real estate	$3,438.1
2. Personality	$2,347.7
Total tax less 20 percent for losses	$ 46.3
Total taxes	$ 89.3
Double tax 1861–62	$ 89.3
	$ 178.6
Number of families less 20 percent	1,109,081
(Average 5.5 persons per family)	
Average tax per family	$ 161.03

* All figures in millions.

the actual sum expended was about $443 million.[39] Much of this growing spread between estimates and expenditures can be attributed to inflation, for which no provision had been made. To take account of inflation, Congress habitually appropriated money for only six months at a time.

Careful calculations should have assumed a need to budget for a four-hundred-thousand man force from January 1862 onward until either the Republicans in Congress were defeated in 1862 or Lincoln driven out of office in March 1865. At a minimum of $400 million a year, including civil and debt service expense, total public expenditures for the Confederacy would aggregate at the worst roughly $1.5 billion.

With an estimated public debt in funded form of $550 million, call certificates and interest-bearing treasury notes totaling $150 million, and a treasury note currency at a maximum of $250 million in 1865, $600 million—or $150 million a year (20 percent of prewar GNP)—would be needed in tax collections to prevent runaway inflation and service the massive, accumulating public debt.

What Was to be Taxed?

It was Memminger's task to tell the Congress not only how much money was needed but also what should be taxed, and, unlike Secretary Chase in the North, Memminger, to his credit, had a plan. Congress had directed him to provide a detailed report on internal taxes after he had tried to insert a vague $10 million tax section into the Act of May 16, 1861 without notifying the Finance Committee, discussing it in the Cabinet, or securing a covering a message from Davis.[40] To prepare that report, the secretary had solicited information from each of the Confederate states. Thus on July 20, 1861, when the Provisional Congress reassembled in Richmond, he was still hastily compiling the states' replies to his inquiries.[41] Consequently, it was not until July 24 (and with a strong message from Davis favoring taxes) that he responded to the congressional mandate.

His report contained what any informed person might well have guessed. Because each state had its own revenue system, only the major items of taxation could be used for comparison. Even in those cases, however, comparisons were difficult; South Carolina, for example had not appraised its lands since 1840, while no state, as yet, had levied slave taxes on an ad valorem basis. Congress would therefore have to adopt a system of its own.

By what formula could Congress distribute this tax? The tradition embodied in the federal Constitution called for the selection of a fixed sum and its apportionment among the states in accordance with the allotment of seats in the House of Representatives. Secretary Memminger dismissed this procedure as impracticable because, he said, he didn't have the 1860 census returns. But that was a strange excuse because the returns were officially available from a federal circular to the governors of each state reporting the allocation of House seats under the 1860 census, and reports were also available in Northern newspapers.[42] Memminger might also have secured the assistance of Thompson Allan (later the commissioner of internal revenue), who had worked in the Census Bureau, or obtained advice and assistance from the erstwhile federal census-takers in the South. But since the Confederate Congress refused to consider paying them off until after the war (possibly with a view to heading off direct taxes), Memminger could not expect much cooperation in that quarter.[43] But he still might have ascertained the 1860 census statistics by reading the text of the United States direct tax of August 5, 1861 or the *Congressional Globe* of January 28, 1862.[44] There seems little doubt that the census statistics were available, and there was no reason why the 1860 census should not have been declared by Congress to be a valid census. What was wanting was the disposition to procure and use the figures.

In any event, the absence of census figures was not an immediate problem because the Provisional Constitution permitted Congress to levy direct taxes on an ad valorem basis without the need for any apportionment. No doubt such a system was theoretically fairer in its distributive aspects because taxes were laid on the basis of wealth, not population, and all slaves and not merely the three-fifths figure mandated by the federal Constitution were taxable. On the other hand, an apportioned tax involved a fixed sum of money, whereas under an ad valorem system, revenue yields were uncertain and the Confederate government might lose revenue from a faulty appraisal system.

In adopting an ad valorem tax in his July 29 report, Memminger urged that any commonly held assets such as real estate, merchandise, slaves, and securities were suitable objects of taxation. He estimated the total value of these items in the Confederacy at $4,632 million. He then calculated that, at a rate of 54 cents per $100, he could collect $25 million, provided he was helped by the states. He recognized that state law might prohibit the use of state officers by the Confederacy, but no matter how the tax was collected, the total revenue must be $25 million.

While passing this major task to the Congress, Memminger did not neglect to suggest the elements of equity that ought to govern the tax's incidence. Because the prime purpose of the war was to protect the slaveholders and their property from the clutches of the abolitionists, he might even have recommended a double tax on slaves not only because it would fall on those who stood to gain the most, but also because, as he had correctly noted, slave ownership was generally a sign of wealth and an ability to pay. Because the secretary's inquiries had disclosed that no state had effected a real ad valorem appraisal of slaves, he should have furnished the Congress with a proposed tax scale of values with specific tax rates levied on slaves based on their age and gender. Only crippled, mentally incompetent, or aged slaves would have been exempted. This would have reduced the appraisal problem to a bare minimum and thus saved time and expense.

To Memminger, the owner of fifteen slaves, the logic of taxing slave ownership seemed unanswerable.[45] Yet, it is clear that his viewpoint was far from universally shared. The Confederacy may have been founded to protect planters' property rights in slaves, but many planters were unprepared to pay for the right to possess this property. Not only did they oppose taxing slave ownership, but they also obstructed every effort of the Confederacy to lease slaves to build the Danville-Greensboro rail link, thus forcing the government to buy outright such few workers as were available.[46]

Even the states faced resistance in requisitioning slaves for public purposes. For example, the Governor's Council in South Carolina was openly defied when it tried to impose a slave corvée for coastal defense. Indeed, the indignant planters, who controlled the legislature, sealed their triumph by abolishing the council in the fall of 1862. Lawrence M. Keitt was nearer the truth than he knew when he observed that the planters would rather "give ten dollars which they have never seen than one they have in their pockets."[47]

This selfish and short-sighted attitude was amply reflected in the discussions that led to the War Tax of August 19, 1861. Of the members of the Provisional Congress who owned no slaves or fewer than nineteen slaves, 65 percent favored taxation. But of the planters who owned twenty or more slaves, only 46 percent favored taxes. Similarly, 65 percent of those having estates valued at less than $50,000 favored direct taxes, whereas only 43 percent of those worth more than $50,000 were on the affirmative side. Thus an ancient paradox was once more illustrated: those with the most to lose were least inclined to pay their share, while those with the least to lose were willing to make the essential sacrifices.[48]

In addition to slaves, Memminger regarded city lots as another subject for heavy taxation: "The ownership of a town lot is a better indication of ability to pay than the ownership of mere land . . . and when we consider the inducement that [towns] offer to the invading army, it seems proper that they should bear a heavier burden than the country at large." In making these remarks the secretary was doubtless thinking of Charleston, where the planters maintained town houses for the social season, overlooking the fact that most townspeople were persons of modest means for whom home ownership was not a luxurious indulgence but merely evidence of middle-class achievement.

Property taxes on merchandise, Memminger felt, should be heavy because the merchant could pass the burden onto the consumer. On the other hand, because many merchants had been compelled to reduce their inventories for lack of Northern credits, the secretary admitted that the merchandise tax yield would be trifling.[49]

There were also special problems posed by the mixed nature of securities. Memminger thought that special consideration should be given to the railroads' securities because those companies were handling freight for the government at half price in exchange for Confederate bonds.[50] Banks also should be leniently treated because of their services to the government. Thus railroad and bank shares should, he suggested, bear no more than the average rate applied to other property.[51] The cynic might detect in these comments the conditioned reflexes of a lawyer who had been a bank director.

Two things were outstandingly disappointing in Memminger's report: the absence of recommendations regarding the specific rates to be levied on each kind of property, and the unduly modest size of the tax requested. In determining tax rates, Memminger should have realized from his inquiries that every state had granted its taxpayers a minimal exemption and that if he desired to avoid an amendment calling for an excessive exclusionary level, he must propose a modest one himself. Moreover, in light of the low pay offered to Confederate soldiers, he should have advocated an exemption to those actually on active duty with the armed forces. Thus a $200 base valuation exemption with an additional $300 military exemption would have conformed with state practice and public opinion.

Finally, one wonders at the modest rate proposed by the secretary. In view of the certainty of exemptions and the loss of peripheral territories to the enemy, a higher rate was clearly needed. Thus a minimum rate of 1.25 percent was needed to raise around $40 million on real estate and personal property, while the double rate on the $2.5 billion worth of slaves would yield another $60 million.

On this subject, at any rate, the bankers gave Memminger sound advice; indeed, his remarkable conversion to direct taxes in May 1861 can be attributed to James D. Denegre, the president of the Citizens Bank at New Orleans. Denegre told Memminger that, if New Orleans were typical, customs revenues would prove minuscule and a substantial internal revenue would be needed. What Denegre proposed was a 1 percent tax on all property, from which the Confederate government might secure $40 million. Alarmed at the prospect of excessive note issues, Denegre urged that taxes be increased to $80 million.[52] It was sound advice as events would prove—sounder and far less tinged with self-interest than the opinions Denegre had earlier rendered in monetary affairs.

Similar counsel and even a draft bill were forwarded by Edward J. Forstall on May 9. Forstall strongly favored direct taxation and was still talking about the need for internal revenues at ex-Governor Roman's house during William H. Russell's visit to Louisiana.[53]

On July 25, 1861, the day after Secretary Memminger's report reached Congress, Duncan Kenner of Louisiana, at the instigation of the secretary, introduced "a Bill to . . . provide a war tax . . . of ½ to 1% on all taxable property in the several states in the Confederate States of America, as described in their last representative assessment rolls, and other purposes."[54] The bill was referred to the Finance Committee and was taken up as the "special order of the day" on Thursday, August 8. Kenner led off the debate by offering an amendment that exempted from tax all heads of families having less than $500 in property. Because the amendment would have exempted about a third of all taxable property, the secretary opposed it, but his opposition was defeated seven states to three. On the other hand, he was successful in thwarting an amendment offered by Hugh Thomason of Arkansas that would have granted a further $1,000 exemption to Confederate servicemen.[55]

In further skirmishes the treasury fared well enough. Congress defeated an effort to reduce the tax rate by 75 percent, as well as an amendment that would have made state bonds tax-exempt.[56] Also discarded was an effort to impose an 8 percent income tax on corporate stocks. Finally, after administration supporters turned back an attempt to adjourn Congress (five states to five), the bill was passed unanimously on August 16, 1861, and signed by Davis on August 19. It had encountered opposition from some of the most powerful vested interests, but the main provisions, as Memminger had conceived them, came through intact.[57]

The Congressional Distribution
of Tax Liability under the War Tax

It is apparent from the bill's legislative history that the Provisional Congress of the Confederacy was reluctant to embark upon, and President Davis to recommend, a policy of internal taxation. Quite likely many congressmen were influenced by the widely held view that import duties were the only effective fiscal resource. That Congress, without effective executive prodding, should have been willing to undertake such an unpopular experiment in public finance goes far to support Wilkinson's belief that the South was peculiarly fortunate in the men selected by the state secession conventions to sit in the Provisional Congress.[58] If such a body, which was in effect a convention of notables containing many men not beholden to anyone, was thus only barely able to depart from past practice, it is doubtful whether a regularly elected body would have done better, particularly without effective presidential guidance.

In distributing the burden of the tax, Congress accepted some, but by no means all, of the secretary's basic premises. City real estate, slaves, and merchandise were not subjected, as they might have been, to surtaxes, while an excessive exemption was granted to the lower middle class. At the same time, Congress resisted political temptations, such as the soldiers' exemption or the proposals to reduce rates. Nevertheless, several distributive aspects of the legislation were unsatisfactory. For instance, people were taxed on their gross rather than their net assets. Thus, an individual who owned $100,000 of property, $90,000 of which was mortgaged, paid the same tax as a person holding $100,000 free and clear. As was later to characterize the federal income tax, corporations and their stockholders were both subjected to taxation on the same assets. Not only did companies have to pay tax on all of their gross assets, good or bad, but their stockholders had to pay on their shares (which derived their value from those assets) as well. A tax on the corporate assets net of the capital coupled with a tax on the stock would have been fairer. Another objection could have been raised in the handling of the $500 exemption. A person possessing less than $500 in property was tax-exempt, yet a neighbor with $600 had to pay tax on the entire amount and not just the excess over $500. The $500 exemption cost the treasury more than $5 million.[59]

Undoubtedly, the key deficiency of the act was the failure to levy a fixed tax on slaves. Local variations in appraisal methods assured that an ad valorem system would lead to arbitrary and discriminatory results. To avoid this, a variable poll tax might have been levied, the exact amount being based on age. Had the Confederacy adopted the Alabama system current in 1860 of taxing slaves as property, the result would have been as shown in table 21.[60] If the Confederacy had adopted a tax rate of 2.5 percent, the Confederate revenue in Alabama from that one tax alone would have been about $5.8 million, or twice

Table 21. Slave Taxes in Alabama (2.5% Ad Valorem Rate)

Age and Number of Slaves	State Tax Rate	Estimated Average Value	Confederate Tax Yield*
Under 5 years (58,400)	50 cents	$ 250	$ 365,000
5–9 years (50,133)	70 cents	$ 375	470,000
10–14 years (47,467)	$1.50	$ 750	890,000
15–29 years (103,920)	$2.00	$1,000	2,598,000
30–39 years (51,429)	$1.50	$ 875	1,125,000
40–49 years (16,693)	$1.00	$ 750	313,000
50–60 years (12,600)	40 cents	$ 200	63,000
340,642 Total Number Slaves			$5,824,000

Source: Bureau of the Census, *Population of the United States* (Washington, D.C.: Government Printing Office, 1864), pp. 6–7.
* At 2.5 percent of estimated average value.
Slaves over sixty were tax-exempt, as were the physically and mentally incompetent.

the amount raised under the actual war tax.[61] This system would have produced the revenues indicated in table 22.

Public Opinion and the War Tax

Public reaction to the law displayed the same confusion and divergence of view that had been manifest in the Provisional Congress. Sentiment in North Carolina throughout the war was hostile to taxes of any kind. As W. N. Evands, commenting on the North Carolina delegation's opposition to the Tax Act of April 24, 1863, observed: "*It is a strange opinion that a war can be prosecuted without taxes.*"[62] More typical was the Asheville *News* editorial that thundered indignantly "THAT DIRECT TAXATION WAS TYRANNY."[63] It would, so the *News* declared, destroy the South by dividing its people; the only consolation was that as the North had voted a similar tax, it would collapse first and thereby render tax collections unnecessary.

The Richmond *Examiner*, generally a detractor of Davis's, asserted that the government of a confederacy was not an appropriate vehicle for direct taxes. The government, the editor argued, should finance its war expenses with loans not taxes, so that the people would not be subjected to both state and Confederate tax-gatherers.[64] Vice-President Stephens believed that those who did the fighting should not also defray the expenses of the war, an attitude that prevailed as late as 1863 in some parts of the press.[65]

Any inference that such views were limited to the South is dispelled by the columns of the London *Times*, which, in commenting on the taxes levied by the Union during 1862–63, declared that "one tenth of these taxes would bring any American community to the resistance point in a month" and "the scheme can never be intended to be carried out."[66] A more responsible view of the tax problem was voiced by the editor of the Salisbury, North Carolina, *Watchman*, who urged people not to panic and properly reminded his readers that the one thing

Table 22. Hypothetical War Tax Revenues*

1. Tax on slaves	$ 38.4
2. Tax on real estate and personal items	46.3
3. Tax on corporations	4.6
	$ 89.3
Double tax 1861, 1862	$178.6

Source: July 24, 1861, in Thian, *Reports*, p. 23.
* All figures in millions.

they could not afford was defeat. Warming to his theme the following day, August 26, 1861, the editor exhorted that if people were not willing to pay a large part of their substance to prosecute the war, they would expose themselves to murder, outrage, and robbery at the hands of the Yankees. Therefore, they should not grumble about taxes.[67]

The next day, the Richmond *Dispatch*, a pro-Davis paper, delivered a stinging rebuke to the pessimistic *Examiner*, censuring its editor for baseless fears regarding public resistance to taxes and encouraging whining murmurs and complaints: "the man who can be guilty of attempting to breed discontent in the land by complaining against the tax law, will convict himself at one and the same time of a want of patriotism and a want of sense."[68]

The editor of the Richmond *Enquirer* echoed Gallatin's views that people who intend to pay their debts demonstrate it by their tax legislation. If congressmen were afraid to ask for taxes, then no would-be lender would give the nation credit. Above all, people must remember that the American Revolution nearly came to disaster because of the failure to support the Continental currency with taxes. "Our Congress, as we have seen, have *commenced* right. History is philosophy teaching by example and they [the Congressmen] are profiting by teaching. . . ."[69]

While newspaper opinion was divided, the government, for the moment, enjoyed substantial popular support. Public sentiment, as reflected in the treasury's correspondence, was enthusiastic, although in light of the blockade, many wondered how the planters were to pay their taxes.[70]

Certainly the most perceptive commentator was James Dunwoody Brownson DeBow. In the September edition of his *Review*, DeBow devoted a good deal of insightful analysis to the new measure. His views mirrored those of the New Orleans bankers and were at sharp variance with most Southern opinion. In the months preceding the adoption of the war tax, DeBow had advocated a direct tax but felt that the Confederacy ought to retain a tariff in order to avoid too sharp a break with the past.[71] DeBow justified the war tax on both theoretical and practical grounds. Unlike other writers, he censured Congress for being slow in passing a direct tax, particularly since the blockade had destroyed any hope of substantial customs revenues. He also saw the war tax as an indispensable instrument for sustaining the value of the authorized treasury notes. In short, the Confederate monetary and fiscal program embodied essentially "the suggestion of Mr. Calhoun

. . . adopted without acknowledgment, under the guise of another name and a different form."[72]

How the War Tax Was Intended to Operate

As finally adopted, the war tax of August 19, 1861, imposed a ½ percent tax on the major categories of real and personal property in the South. The only groups exempted were state and local governments, churches and other eleemosynary institutions, and those having property worth less than $500.

By the terms of the act, the secretary of the treasury was to appoint a chief collector for each state. Each chief collector was to divide his state into collection districts headed by collectors; and each collector, in turn, was to recruit a number of assessors, each of whom would have the duty of appraising all taxable property in the district by November 1, 1861. Assessors were required to announce their intention to levy the tax, and to speed up the process, all propertyholders had to submit a list of taxable property. In addition to the usual stiff penalties for tax evasion, the law laid a double tax on those who failed to submit the list on time and empowered assessors to visit a taxpayer's property to ascertain the veracity of his or her declaration.

Property declarations were supposed to be submitted by October 1, but through a legislative oversight were not required to be in the hands of the collectors until December 1. For twenty-one days thereafter, taxpayers might appeal their assessments, but each district collector had the power of final decision. The district collectors were then to forward their lists to the chief collector by February 1, 1862, and he in turn was to collate their reports and forward them to the secretary of the treasury. Finally, on May 1, 1862, the tax became payable. Any state might avoid this vexatious rigmarole by paying the estimated tax in either treasury notes or specie. If paid before April 1, 1862, the state would be entitled to a 10 percent rebate.[73]

Government Action under the War Tax

Although the secretary assumed that the states would collect the tax, he still had to hire a collection staff to ascertain the amount due. But here Memminger proved unaccountably dilatory for he did not present a list of nominees to President Davis until September 17, 1861. A month later, the secretary was still getting his chief collectors qualified, and the final list was not ready until December 13, 1861.

Even after this delay, some of the appointments proved less than ideal.[74]

In his report of January 6, 1863, Thompson Allan, chief clerk of the War Tax Bureau, alluded to the specific difficulties he had encountered in each state while trying to carry out the act. For example, Alabama had proved unaccountably troublesome. Joseph C. Bradley, a wealthy Huntsville businessman, although appointed chief collector in September, had not yet selected his staff by April 11, 1862, when, panic-stricken because federal forces occupied Huntsville, Bradley decamped, leaving his papers behind. He then distractedly frittered away two more months before the governor of Alabama (not Memminger) forced him to resign.[75]

In time, other problems also developed. Due to inept drafting, the war tax law made no provision for paying assessors and collectors in Alabama because the state had assumed the tax. Nor did the Confederate government accept the legislature's offer of Alabama's officers as collectors and assessors.[76] Thus, the work that should have been finished in December 1861 was still incomplete in 1863.

In Arkansas the legislature had assumed the tax, but, owing to the absence of any incorporated banks, the state had to borrow money by issuing its own warrants bearing 8 percent interest. The treasurer then illegally paid $400,000 of these warrants directly to a Confederate general, and as late as January 1863, Arkansas was still haggling over the payment of the $252,000 balance.

In Florida, Georgia, Louisiana, and North Carolina, state bonds or treasury notes were exchanged for Confederate notes, and the tax assumed by the state.[77] South Carolina, on the other hand, assumed the tax and promptly reimbursed itself by employing the Confederate appraisal lists to collect the money from the taxpayers. In April 1862, Joseph Daniel Pope, the former chief clerk of the Treasury Note Bureau in Columbia (1862–63) was the chief collector in South Carolina (1863–65). In April 1862 Pope recounted his problems in a report to the secretary. South Carolina did not know the value of its land because taxes were charged at a fixed sum per acre. Nor was the effort to collect an equitable real estate tax made easier when town lots and rural fields were jumbled together on the taxpayers' returns. Pope's biggest problem lay in appraising the value of slaves. Although South Carolina had avoided the issue by levying a poll tax, Congress had rejected that solution. Instead, slave values were left to the independent judgment of the assessors, whose valuations for slaves of comparable age and sex ranged from $340 to $506. The average appraisal came to only about $400 a slave, although Pope thought it should be $500.

Difficulties were also encountered in securing a proper valuation for livestock. Indeed, the collectors' reports were wildly at variance with the 1860 census, which showed the total value of cattle, horses, and mules to be about $24 million. Yet the tax returns showed only 4,032 animals valued at $116,755. Either the collectors were derelict or else almost all domestic animals in the state belonged to citizens owning less than $500 worth of property. The first hypothesis is clearly the more probable, for it is inconceivable that those who owned $28 million in land held $24 million of livestock, while those who owned $112 million in land had virtually no animals at all. The obvious explanation is that taxpayers found animals easier to conceal than cotton fields, and slave values more subject to manipulation than town houses.[78]

The chief collector in Virginia, Colonel Henry T. Garnett, also inveighed against disparities in slave values. He proposed that Congress should either establish a nationwide uniform value for slaves or that there should be a statewide value as a guide for the assessors. His report also estimated the losses imposed by the $500 exemption. Individuals with less than $500 of property held $280 million of the $934 million of real and personal property in the Commonwealth. After also taking account of another $115 million of property captured by the enemy, Virginia's share of the tax was reduced from $4.7 million to $2.7 million.

Although results were generally disappointing, an unintended success was achieved in Mississippi and Texas. In Mississippi, the legislature and the governor fell out over the mode of paying the tax; the Texans did nothing, on the assumption that without state aid the tax was uncollectible. Efforts to pay the tax directly with state warrants failed because Memminger insisted that, because one purpose of the tax was to create a demand for treasury notes, accepting alternative monies (other than coin) would defeat that object.[79]

Ultimately, because Texas and Mississippi passively resisted the tax, the Confederacy had no option but to collect it directly. Of the $2.2 million due in Mississippi, more than $2 million was collected by early 1863. The failure to collect the remaining balance reflected the occupation of the northern counties by the enemy. In Texas, Confederate agents reported receiving $1.2 million of the $1.6 million assessed. No explanation for this 25 percent delinquency rate was forthcoming.

From the wider perspective of the Richmond government, Commissioner Allan saw these cumulative problems as disclosing basic deficiencies in the war tax system. That system failed to pay officers in those states that assumed the tax and made no provision for travel expenses or postage. The most notable mistake in the drafting of the act was the 10 percent rebate granted to each state that assumed payment. That rebate, Allan insisted, was excessive. He had expended only $40,000 (2 percent) to collect more than $2 million in Mississippi, and he saw no purpose in paying the states 10 percent to flood the country with their own debt instruments. It would, he concluded, be better for the Confederate government to save $2 million and collect its own taxes directly from the people.[80]

Tested under the conditions of the day, the Tax Act of August 19, 1861 proved inadequate. Even its principal virtue—that it applied uniformly throughout the new nation—proved in application to be a substantial disability. To mobilize a staff of collectors and assessors capable of appraising and levying direct taxes, to train them in their arduous duties, and to devise the appropriate instructions and regulations required far more will and, to a lesser degree, more skill than the Confederacy possessed. One can understand, therefore, why Confederate leaders tried to finesse the problem by turning the task of collection over to the states. But the states were by no means eager to assume the burden. Governor A. B. Moore of Alabama, although otherwise well-disposed to the Confederacy, declared that the states should not put themselves in the onerous and unpleasant situation of enforcing Confederate laws against its citizens except when absolutely necessary.[81] The ostensible justification for such an obstructionist position was that local sheriffs would be too busy collecting state taxes to take on an additional burden for the Confederate authorities. But an examination of state legislation of the period discloses that sheriffs had already begun to defer state tax collections.[82] That should have encouraged the Confederate government to take up the slack with increased taxation of its own.

There was a reasonable argument for purchasing state cooperation, but only if it were in the form of a punitive surcharge for a state's failure to collect the tax promptly. On the basis of experience gained during the War of 1812, and assuming a tax of 2.5 percent on slaves and 1.25 percent on all other property (tables 20, 21, 22) the Confederacy might have levied a double tax; one for 1861 payable, say, on November 1, 1861, and another for 1862 payable February 1, 1862. Because the states would have found it impossible to borrow $178 million, they would have had no choice but to collect the tax themselves. To thwart any effort at passive resistance, a 25 percent penalty would then be laid on funds collected after February 1, 1862. The legislators would not have dared to face their constituents after having saddled them with an unnecessary surtax, far larger than the state levies they were accustomed to paying.

But the worse misconception implicit in the tax came not merely from the deficiencies noted (serious as they were), but from the fact that the law was a one-event affair. Although the tax was supposed to provide a foundation for a $100 million treasury note and bond issue, no provision was made for a repetition of this tax for the years 1862 or 1863. As a result, by May 1862, the Confederacy had no productive tax system and had let lapse the machinery that had been set up with so much effort and expense.

Drift and Self-Delusion: August 19, 1861–April 24, 1863

The twenty months that followed passage of the Act of August 19, 1861 were, in terms of Confederate fiscal policy, a time of disastrous inertia. This indolence sharply contrasted with the energy then being displayed by the federal government. Having secured a modest $20 million war tax in 1861,[83] Secretary Chase in December 1861 cautiously proposed doubling the war tax to raise another $20 million; the laying of excise duties on liquor and other items for a further $20 million; and the imposition of an income tax to yield $10 million more.[84]

In contrast to the timidity displayed by the Confederate Congress or even the North's own Secretary Chase, the federal Congress rejected the notion that heavy taxation might dampen the public ardor for the war. No doubt the Northern bankers, the strong leadership of Thaddeus Stevens in the Ways and Means Committee, and even the newspapers all had a hand in this.[85] Thus, the federal Congress pressed for heavier taxes than a cautious treasury secretary was prepared to request. It did not settle for the $50 million Chase proposed, but instead insisted upon taxes amounting to $150 million above and beyond the $60 million of customs dues. The resulting tax law of July 25, 1862 strikingly anticipated the Confederate tax act of April 24, 1863, which was not adopted for another nine months. The federal law levied a variety of excises on liquors, wines, tobacco, and other commodities; it imposed license fees for the practice of various occupations and required government officers to pay income taxes; it also provided for inheritance taxes and stamp taxes on real estate transfers. Yet it was adopted without opposition in the Senate and by a vote of 106–11 in the House.[86] The result was a remarkable reflection of the principle later expressed by the special commissioner for internal revenue, David A. Wells: "Whenever you find an article, a product, a trade, a profession, or source of income, tax it."[87]

Tax Proposals 1861–63

Meanwhile, the embattled citizenry south of the border—although ready to die for the Confederate cause—were not asked to pay for it. The president deftly avoided the subject of new taxes, while his secretary of the treasury mentioned them in passing only twice.

By the time that the fifth session of the Confederate Provisional Congress convened on November 18, 1861, it was already apparent that the customs dues would produce little or no revenue; that the government needed some source of revenue other than treasury notes, if only to relieve the pressure on the printers; and that the escalating level of public expenditure and indebtedness needed to be checked before the nation's credit was exhausted. That should have suggested the urgent need to double or even triple the tax already laid.

Yet in his message to Congress, President Davis, while declaring that the value of treasury notes depended upon their exchange value and the amount of currency they were replacing, made no allusion to the fact that the issue of treasury notes by April 1, 1862 would reach $120 million, or nearly 50 percent higher than the prewar bank circulation. Instead of suggesting increases in the old taxes or the adoption of new taxes, the president merely mentioned that the war tax would be adequate to pay the interest on the public debt, as if that were the only expenditure for which taxes were needed.[88] Nor did Secretary Memminger's report, although it touched on various tax collecting technicalities, suggest that more revenue was urgently needed. And no one seems to have mentioned the need to extend the war tax for 1862.[89]

In February 1862, when the First Congress of the Confederate States convened, President Davis scarcely touched on financial matters. Taxation—apparently regarded as an obscene word—he did not mention at all. Nor was Secretary Memminger's report any more satisfactory. After reviewing the affairs of the provisional government, the secretary observed that one method of meeting future expenses was through taxation, yet he had already ruled out the idea of securing a fiscal revenue that would cover normal governmental costs—let alone extraordinary war expenses.

But Memminger seemed quite oblivious of taxation's full implications. His report ended with nothing more than a request, in general terms, that "Congress impose an additional war tax for such amount as will sustain the additional loans which they may authorize; and that the said tax be collected as at early a day in the present year as may be practicable."[90] Nor did he express a need for taxation in more urgent tones even in August 1862, when the second session of the Congress convened. On that occasion President Davis dismissed the affairs of the treasury with a brief paragraph of banalities, while Secretary Memminger failed to make any recommendation regarding new and heavier taxation.[91] It was only on October 6, 1862, in a private letter to President Davis, that he invoked his close relationship with his chief to press for new taxes.

In that letter, Memminger pointed out that the war tax furnished the basis for the treasury's credit and should, therefore, be imposed annually. He also noted that the small size of the tax would allow it to be easily doubled. As for additional revenues, he suggested a forced loan equal to 20 percent of the gross national income of $400 million, or $80 million.[92]

The secretary's letter is a remarkable document. His lack of vigorous advocacy of taxes for a whole year, and his equally glaring fault in not getting Davis's backing for such a program at an earlier day, displays serious deficiencies of vision and energy. For a lawyer with ingrained legalistic tendencies, he displayed an extraordinary disregard of the constitutional impediment to the war tax as originally levied. At the same time, his advocacy of a forced loan from taxpayers raises a number of questions. Why push such an easily evaded tax? Still worse, why levy a so-called tax that practically involved robbing citizens at gunpoint when he had declared it immoral to seize the cotton crop, the banks' specie, or the printers' establishments?

In fairness to the secretary, the forced loan scheme was the brainchild of Duncan F. Kenner, who reported out a bill to that end on September 23, 1862. Under Kenner's proposal, everyone was to pay 20 percent of their gross 1862 income on January 1, 1863. Only the interest paid on government securities was exempt, as were persons having incomes under $500. In exchange, the taxpayer would receive "income tax bonds" bearing 6 percent interest and payable anywhere from ten to thirty years later. In rising to support his own motion, Kenner pointed out that the time had arrived for vigorous action. Treasury notes could not be used any further without ruinous inflation. What was needed were revenues based on taxation; the duty of Congress was not, he asserted, to lighten the financial burdens of the people, but to devise measures that would meet the growing expenses of the war.[93]

Although his analysis was on target, Kenner's appeal stirred few congressional hearts. Their general reaction, understandably enough, was that "taxation" in such a form was "monstrous" and "insane," particularly when the government was paying exorbitant interest on its bonds. Congress, therefore, tabled the bill.[94] At the same time, the House of Representatives showed that it was not opposed to all taxes by instructing the Ways and Means Committee to report a comprehensive tax bill which would yield at least $50 million of revenue.[95]

President Davis's persistent refusal to face the facts of financial life came to a belated end three months later with the convening of the third session of the First Confederate Congress. Exhorting Congress, he asserted: "The increasing public debt, the great augmentation in the volume of the currency . . . the want of revenue from a taxation adequate to support the public credit, are united in admonishing us that energetic and wise legislation alone can prevent a serious embarrassment in our monetary affairs. It is my conviction that the people of the Confederacy will freely meet taxation on a scale adequate to the maintenance of the public credit and the support of their government. . . ." Davis ended by urging that Congress devise a proper tax law without delay, without, however, making any precise request.[96]

Why had the president not expressed similar views in November 1861, when the need for fiscal legislation was equally apparent? There is no evidence that he refrained from asking for the taxes out of any deference for Congress. Indeed, Representative J. L. M. Curry of Alabama complained that Davis "apparently expected Congress to do what he deemed best for the interests of the Confederacy."[97] Rather, one suspects that the president failed to act because his secretary of the treasury had refused to make an issue of the tax question before late 1862.

In view of the rampant inflation, Secretary Memminger's January 1863 tax proposals were lamentably unambitious. Although freely admitting that more than $400 million of treasury notes were outstanding—the equivalent of four times the normal currency of the country—he was still not prepared for a comprehensive tax system. Excises, stamp duties, licenses, and "other like taxes," he dismissed as unworthy of consideration because they required "machinery vexatious in its character, and expensive in its operation." Instead, the fiscal needs of the Confederacy were to be met through a $35 million property tax.

The secretary did not disclose how, in the absence of a census, this tax could be apportioned among the states. Nor did the Permanent Constitution make provision for any alternative method of levying direct taxes. Yet, in view of the manpower shortage and the invasion of the country, a census was impossible. It was only on March 17,

1865, that Congress passed a joint resolution declaring a census to be impracticable. A simple declaration, four years earlier, that the 1860 census was valid for the Confederacy would have been more to the point.[98]

As the second part of his fiscal package, Memminger proposed a 10 percent gross income tax. In choosing to tax gross income, Memminger tacitly recognized that a net income tax would work only if citizens were prepared to disclose their private affairs to the government with reasonable honesty. But that required habits of personal accounting that the average Southerner could not form overnight. Yet, while admitting that so easily evadable tax "would furnish an insecure resource," Memminger still calculated that it would yield $28 million. This, combined with the $35 million from direct taxes, would provide about $63 million for the government.[99]

Coinciding with Memminger's explicit request for substantial fiscal revenues was public recognition that taxes were a necessary evil. "If something is not done, we shall have to pay $27,000 for a barrel of flour," wrote the Assistant Secretary of State William M. Browne. He went on to add "they [Congress] are afraid to pass a good tax bill and nothing else can save us from ruin." As a Georgian editor noted, "The error in the beginning was in not taxing heavily and severely enough to have kept prices down to a specie standard. The Congressman who is afraid of taxing the people is and ought to be regarded as a public enemy."[100]

The Confederates had reason for this change of heart. With prices skyrocketing, they realized that it was better to have Congress distribute taxes on a rational basis rather than be taxed haphazardly through inflation. Moreover, the alleged tyranny of taxation was a mere bagatelle compared with the arbitrary exactions of the invading Unionists or the Confederate Army Commissary Department. Reflecting and inciting public outrage, the press demanded that the burden of supporting the army should cease to fall exclusively on those luckless farmers unfortunate enough to live within reach of the military impressment officers, who were seizing food at prices well below the market price. These demands were reinforced by mounting evidence that inflation and general economic distress were destroying civil and military morale. The editors and the treasury correspondents therefore exhorted the secretary and Congress to take action without delay.[101]

Impressments, together with the ubiquitous currency inflation, were the government's only effective method of taxation. But market prices and the rates paid for impressed goods varied sharply. For example, in July 1863, the impressment price for corn was merely 70 percent of the market price, but by July 1864 impressment prices had fallen to only 20 percent of market price. Quite obviously, this price differential constituted a highly discriminatory tax, which constituted almost 16 percent of the government's revenue.[102]

As Robert G. H. Kean, chief clerk of the War Department, observed:

> March 7 [1863] . . . Farmers are making preparations for only so much corn as will suffice for their own use. They resent the Secretary's [Seddon's] schedule prices which are often 50% below the market or neighbourhood price. The instant impressment of flour, corn, and meat as soon as they are brought to any of the inland towns to be put in the market, is causing universal withholding of surplus—secreting and nonproduction. The Army will be starved and famine will ensue in the cities unless the Secretary changes his policy and buys in the market for the best price. The Government will have to outbid the traders, else neither will get anything of the present scanty stock, and no future stock will be produced.[103]

Kean's views were confirmed by the price commissioners, who confessed that they were having to raise their prices to induce sellers to place their grain on the market.[104]

Moreover, as a note-issuer, the Confederacy was committed to a money economy. To finance its needs by impressing goods at less than market value was a retrogression to a barter economy. The Confederacy, therefore, had to lay unevadable property taxes payable in money in order to prevent the farmers from returning, albeit temporarily, to a subsistence economy. In short, as Robert Toombs himself put it: "[Taxes in kind] should never be resorted to when the currency is redundant, but with all its faults may be a necessary evil whenever there is a great deficiency in the circulation medium."[105] Because the only economic evil the Confederacy was not suffering from was a "deficiency in the circulating medium," a tax in kind was clearly not what was needed. Yet Congress had already levied a tax in kind by passing the Act of April 24, 1863.

Although it was a bitterly contested law, little is known of the legislators' thinking; most of the infighting was done in secret session. Nevertheless, from the printed bills, newspaper reports, and congressional speeches, it is clear that the Congressmen, like their successors today, were far more interested in protecting the special interests of their constituents than in developing a well-articulated tax program. Far from being the simple two-part tax scheme that Secretary Memminger had envisaged, the final product was instead an income tax, amalgamated with a tax in kind and a miscellany of excise taxes.

The first part of the act was a graduated income tax levy, payable each year on January 1. Persons with unearned incomes of $500–$1,500 were taxed 5 percent (those with incomes under $500 were exempt); people with incomes of $10,000 and higher paid 15 percent. Corporations paid a flat 10 percent rate, and earned incomes were lightly taxed at only 1 percent of the excess over $1,000, 2 percent of the excess over $1,500.

In spite of the treasury's urgent need for revenue, a proposal was rejected that this tax should be payable on July 1, 1863 for the year 1862. Such a rejection presumably reflected the desire of the legislators to avoid imposing taxes in advance of the election set for November 1863; that this was not based on a wish to avoid any suggestion of ex post facto taxation is clear enough because just such a levy was imposed on the 1862 profits of speculators who sold clothing and shoes.[106]

But the income tax was not the most productive part of the final legislative package. Early in April, just before the act was passed, Secretary Memminger sent a special message proposing a 10 percent tax payable in kind. Such a tax, he felt, would afford abundant subsistence to the army, would distribute provisions all over the country, and would end the need for impressment, which had roused such discontent. It would also short-circuit the profiteering of speculators by taking the government out of the market, thereby enabling individuals to purchase at lower rates. The trend toward lower prices would, he hoped, be augmented by a decline in government note issues needed to pay its bills. Finally, the tax revenues themselves would be more productive because evasion would be difficult and the income derived from the tax certain in its value. His estimate of the potential yield from this tax was $84 million.[107]

This idea was not invented by Memminger; the Senate had already been discussing such a measure before the secretary's message arrived.[108] Accordingly, Congress followed its own whims in the matter by granting each farmer exemptions of fifty bushels of sweet and Irish potatoes, a hundred bushels of corn or fifty bushels of wheat, and twenty bushels of peas and/or beans. The Confederate government was to take 10 percent of all other agricultural produce, including staples and meat. On paper, this might yield 28 million bushels of corn, 2.2 million bushels of wheat, 40,000 bales of cotton, and other produce.[109]

Under the Act of April 24, 1863, the Congress also levied an ad valorem tax of 8 percent on a variety of agricultural and luxury products on hand on July 1, 1863. A 1 percent tax was placed on currency, bank notes, and solvent credits not used in any business. Funds held abroad were taxed at their current exchange rate in Confederate treasury notes, or 12 percent on October 1, 1863. Nor did Congress stop there. License taxes of $50, $100, $200, or $500 were placed on a wide range of professions and businesses, including bankers, auctioneers, brokers, dealers, pawnbrokers, distillers, innkeepers, entertainers, doctors, and lawyers. The more profitable the calling, as Congress saw it, the higher the license fee and the same for the attached income taxes of 2.5, 5, 10, or 20 percent. Thus a banker paid a $500 license and also a 20 percent tax on gross income, while a druggist paid a $50 fee and 2.5 percent of his gross income.

Deficiencies of the Act of April 24, 1863

The deficiencies of the act were several and substantial. As has been earlier noted, the Permanent Confederate Constitution did not permit property taxes without a census-based apportionment, with the absurd result that strict constructionists were able to prevent the taxation of real estate, livestock, and slaves.

A decisive clash of conflicting ideas on the topic occurred in the House of Representatives on March 11, 1863. Garnett of Virginia conceded that the government did not have the constitutional power to levy direct taxes unless in proportion to the census, but because the census of 1860 was, he asserted, a census within the meaning of the Confederate Constitution, the Congress could use that to levy direct taxes on property. Willis Machen of Kentucky, a strong administration backer, then moved to strike out Garnett's resolution with an amendment which denied the need for a census so long as the taxes levied were "uniform." Augustus Garland of Arkansas tried to table the motion but was defeated by 21–53. The House then approved the Machen amendment, 36–35. An effort on March 14 to reconsider the Machen amendment was defeated 34–47, and a bill including a provision for property taxes was forwarded to the Senate. That body, however, chose to adopt a strict constructionist view and torpedoed all direct taxes.[110]

The inability to levy direct taxes worked a gross inequity in that the slaveholders were enabled to evade contributing to a new nation established for their special benefit. Even so, it should not have been beyond Congress's ingenuity to devise a slaveholders' license fee requirement or some similar evasion of the Constitution, had the will to do so existed. But about 40 percent of Congress's membership consisted of planters, who had no intention of contributing their appropriate share to the Confederacy.

Even the revenue sources Congress authorized were lightly employed. Although the House had taxed incomes over $10,000 at 24
percent, the Senate trimmed the rate to 15 percent. Nor was the tax
on merchandise and agricultural produce heavy enough to make it
unprofitable to withhold goods from the market. A picayune 8 percent
tax payable in 1863 notes was not sufficient to persuade a speculator
or prudent investor to disgorge inflation-proof assets during an 86
percent inflation. A tax of 50 percent would clearly have been required.
As William Gregg, a prominent textile manufacturer in Graniteville,
South Carolina, wrote: "There are plenty of planters who abound in
provisions, have no call for money, and refuse to sell at all. . . . A
heavy Confederate tax would serve to stir up all such."[111] That Congress had felt required to regulate impressments proved that stern
measures were needed to force goods on to the market.[112] A heavy
property tax might have achieved that goal by compelling cash sales;
a produce tax merely created more problems than the treasury could
handle.

In criticizing the Confederate Congress's adoption of the produce
"tithe" tax, one finds it easy, with the wisdom that comes from know-
ing the end of the story, to point out that the measures Secretary
Memminger advocated were foredoomed to failure. Yet even in his
own day Memminger's actions contravened the best economic views
of the time. As has been pointed out in chapter 1, the works of the
nineteenth-century economist Jean Baptiste Say were widely read and
respected in the South. Say had expressed clear views on produce
taxes; in fact, Memminger listed the arguments in favor of a produce
tax in the same order as Say. Yet, if Memminger had read Say, he had
neglected to read him carefully; Say emphatically declared that a tax
in kind was "of all others, the most inequitable; for it makes no
allowance for the advances in the course of production, but is taken
upon the gross, instead of net profits." The Confederate Congress had
partially cured that defect by providing exemptions, but Say had
further objections: the tax was difficult and expensive to collect, it
required a host of agents and provided the dishonest with boundless
opportunities for peculation. Finally, such a tax, Say observed, required a vast number of storehouses if the government were to avoid
heavy loss from spoilage or hasty sales at distress prices.[113]

To Say's objections must be added others. For example, as one
newspaper suggested, "if the Confederacy will furnish the people
with a sound currency, the government will at all times be able to
purchase such supplies as the army may need. . . ."[114] This view

reflected the public disenchantment with a government that compelled its creditors to receive treasury notes, but which itself refused to receive them for "all public dues" as had been promised.

A later analyst, Eugene Lerner, has pointed out that tithe taxes can be highly inflationary. A money tax (presuming that government spends all it receives) only changes the distribution of real goods. A tithe tax, on the other hand, generates inflation by reducing the quantity of goods for sale without reducing the money supply. Using the printing press simply diminishes the quantity of goods available while augmenting the money supply.[115] Yet, although complaints poured in, the tax was continued until the end of the war. No one could devise any other means to compel the dominant agricultural interest to make some contribution to the war effort.[116]

The Last Clear Chance: The Act of February 17, 1864

As might have been expected, collections from the new tax act were slow to be realized. Only $27 million had been received by February 1, 1864, while the government had to wait until May 1, 1864, before receiving a total of $66 million.[117] But the slowness of collections was not the only problem faced by Thompson Allan. In a report, he complained bitterly about the tax evaders in the distillery industry and the frauds perpetrated by farmers who had their grain reduced to alcoholic form, then disposed of it without paying tax. Moreover, graziers avoided paying the bacon tithe by having their animals slaughtered by others.

Far more important than these abuses were certain built-in defects in the tax system. Although favoring exemptions for the poor, Allan argued that anyone who produced more than the reserved minimum should be required to pay the full tax rather than 10 percent on the surplus. This would have substantially augmented the revenue while protecting the less fortunate members of the community. He also favored abandoning the tithe tax altogether in favor of cash collections, as a double tithe on corn and bacon inhibited bacon production.

Differing from Memminger, under whose authority he operated, Allan urged that the currency be scaled by a 25 percent tax and that incomes over $5,000 be taxed 25 percent and incomes over $10,000 at 50 percent. In addition, he proposed a 50 percent levy on corporate incomes after deducting 25 percent of net earnings as dividends to the stockholders.[118]

Secretary Memminger, for his part, was particularly dissatisfied with the lack of property taxes. "The land and the negroes in the

Confederate States constitute two-thirds of the taxable values, and if [apportionment is required], it would establish a surprising conclusion that all the States which ratified the Constitution . . . excepted from the contribution to maintain that war the very property for which they were contending. . . ."[119] The secretary went on to say that in the absence of census, the fiscal uniformity clause should be used, which would be fairer because taxpayers would be levied upon for their own property alone, and not for that under enemy occupation.

Congressional Action

Even when faced with the fading of the Confederate hopes, Congress felt no need to take incisive action in fiscal matters. Indeed, the next tax legislation, the Act of February 17, 1864, was so distorted by planter pressures that, in spite of increased rates, it was even more difficult to administer than its predecessor.[120] Its principal defects can be summed up in five aspects.

First, the produce, income, and property taxes were all riddled by new exemptions. Under the guise of providing relief for the poor, Congress permitted taxpayers to deduct sums paid on one tax from amounts due on the others, which made the tax collectors' task of computing the amounts due virtually impossible. Second, Congress failed to renew the tax on produce retained on the farm, thus leaving the hoarders undisturbed. Third, since the 4 percent funding certificates were made tax-receivable, people naturally used them to pay taxes instead of treasury notes. The result was largely to dissipate any benefit derived from the funding and tax programs, insofar as they related to the currency.

Fourth, the commissioner of taxes had reported that the banks could discharge the 10 percent specie tax on their coin by tendering treasury notes worth only 4 to 5 cents on the dollar.[121] Congress, therefore, provided that the banks must pay a levy in kind on their coin. Thus, a banker holding $10,000 in specie would be required to turn over to the government $1,000 in coin. The discriminatory nature of this tax appeared in even sharper relief when compared with the property tax. Unless sold after 1863, real estate was assessed at the 1860 gold valuation. Thus, a farm worth $10,000 in 1860 was, at the beginning of 1864, worth something over $200,000 in treasury notes. Yet its assessed tax was only $500 in paper, worth something like $20 in coin. Manifestly, real estate taxation was not keeping up with inflation. Fifth, if special interest deductions had been eliminated, the yield from the tax of February 17, 1864 would have been about 300 percent higher than what was actually collected, a fact that many observers recognized at the time.[122]

By November 1864, Tax Commissioner Allan had become disgusted with the selfishness of the planters. In a letter to Secretary Trenholm (who had succeeded Memminger in July 1864) he pointed out that Congress had so drafted the tax laws that farmers paid only 1⅓ percent on their income as against 5 percent for urban dwellers. Worse still, Congress refused to alter a policy that had brought on economic collapse, and along with it the ravaging of the South by federal armies.

The Last Period: The Tax Act of June 14, 1864

In any event, Memminger was clearly unhappy with the tax legislation and its consequences. It was not what he wanted; his views had been callously disregarded. By May 1864 he was a discredited figure to whom the Second Confederate Congress paid little attention. Thus, Congress ignored his requests that the tax credits be repealed, that taxes be assessed on the basis of current values, that corporations not be double-taxed, and that, finally, the complicated rules and regulations governing taxes be overhauled.[123]

To be sure, the bankers compelled Congress to repeal the tax on bank deposits, shifting it instead to the depositors, while the need to raise military salaries forced Congress to add a 20 percent surtax to all taxes and a 30 percent additional tax on all profits realized in trading, buying, and selling between February 17, 1864, and July 1, 1864. Meanwhile, the suspension of property tax collections until the yield from the tithe could be ascertained delayed collections at a most inopportune time. Finally, in lieu of the tax on specie and foreign exchange, Congress permitted banks to pay either in kind or in Confederate money, at a ratio to be decided by the secretary of the treasury. This placed the government in the anomalous position of depreciating its own currency.[124] After this, Congress was content to ignore taxation until March 1865, when several inoperative tax laws were passed before Congress's adjournment.[125]

The Consequences of Confederate Tax Policy

As Toombs put it in 1863, bitterly reflecting with the hindsight of two years' experience: "The first great error was in attempting to carry on a great and expensive war solely on credit—without taxation. This is the first attempt of the kind ever made by civilized people. The result of the experiment will hardly invite its repetition. During the first year of its existence the Present [First] Congress neither levied nor collected a single cent of taxes, and postponed the collection for those levied for the second year to a period too late to support our currency."[126]

Actually, the problem was worse than he described it, for the period of lassitude and indifference began in August 1861, and when, after twenty-one months Congress provided a belated tax program in April 1863, it was far too late. Even that legislation was marred by slackness in concept and execution, an excessive preoccupation with constitutional niceties, and a pervasive conviction that taxation was an avoidable evil. Little wonder that the action fell far short of the requirements of a rapidly deteriorating economy.

Secretary Memminger had made the critical error at the outset. He had failed to comprehend the importance of fiscal revenues in a program of deficit financing. But although Memminger, Denegre, Forstall, and DeBow all realized the need for internal taxes, the Confederacy constantly deferred the requisite action. There were too many inhibiting factors: an optimistic president who paid little attention to the problem, an inexperienced secretary of the treasury unable to assert himself with the Congress or the president, and a public that had not been conditioned to make the necessary sacrifices. One can understand, without excusing, the lethargy of 1861.

What is less pardonable is the way in which Secretary Memminger wasted his own and Congress's time by expatiating at length about customs dues, which, by his own admission, would furnish little, if any, revenue. To be sure, he faced serious difficulties in executing a successful Confederate fiscal program, but many difficulties were of his own making. Although a lawyer, Memminger failed to seek the measures necessary to perpetuate the direct taxing powers Congress had provided the provisional government. He did not take the elementary precaution of obtaining the statistics of the 1860 census (which were available) or, failing that, insert the old federal proviso distributing taxes on the basis of each state's House seats in the absence of a census.

Even when he had been operating under the more liberal Provisional Constitution, Memminger's management of fiscal policy had been far from astute. Although he should have known that the blockade would reduce customs revenues to a minimum, he never explicitly justified his war tax proposals on that basis. Nor did he present his proposals adroitly; he failed to secure the backing of the president and his fellow cabinet members by prior consultation. As a result, the secretary embarked on his struggle for a war tax without the support of a strong presidential message or the backing of his divided and confused ministerial colleagues.

A more dexterous secretary would have consulted the Finance Committee in advance and come before Congress with the facts and figures necessary to justify a detailed proposal. At the very least he might have requested the acceptance of the principle of direct taxes, even if the details required further study. That request might have included a plea for the immediate authority to recruit and compensate an adequate force of collectors and appraisers.

Then in July 1861, when the Provisional Congress reassembled, the secretary would have had in hand the information necessary to suggest a specific tax rate and the items to be taxed. At the minimum, he should have asked for two property levies, one due in 1861, the other early in 1862 (before the Provisional Constitution expired), equal to at least $160 million, to which would be added a variety of license, sales, and excise taxes. Instead, the secretary settled for a modest one-time program that could not pay even the peacetime expenses of the government or the interest on the debt beyond a year. Moreover, he was lamentably slow in setting up his tax collection machinery, with the result that deadlines were ignored and payments deferred until mid-1862. Finally, he ruined what little merit his program had by letting the states assume the tax on a discounted basis and without any real collections.

It seems clear in retrospect that the secretary should have been adamant in requesting more taxes at the earliest possible day. Instead, his initial report to the First Congress contained no specific proposals and no counsel indicating that taxation was a matter of any importance. Once again, the secretary did not enlist the president's aid; indeed, it was not until October 1862 that he belatedly tried to sell an ill-conceived forced loan scheme to his chief. Thus, there was no effective administration pressure for taxes until January 1863, by which time the tax machinery had fallen into desuetude and valuable time was lost recreating it. So, because tax collections were postponed until October 1863 and even later, by early 1864 only $27 million in bona fide taxes had found their way to the treasury. The inadequate measures taken in 1864 merely confirmed the administration's lack of leadership and the disinclination of Congress to cross the planters on an issue of central importance.

Nor in the actual event did the president seek to make Congress's life any easier by efforts to win over the public to the need for heavy taxes. If the Union Congress could levy heavy taxes unaided by the executive branch, then the Confederate Congress, assisted by well-planned executive actions, should have been able to do better. But they could only do better if the president and the secretary of the treasury furnished them with the justification needed for an effective program. Of all the Confederacy's financial problems, fiscal policy was the hardest nut to crack. That was in part organic, for the Southern states had come together out of deep conviction on only a single subject, and the Confederacy that administered their common affairs was always on probation.

Southern planters instinctively accepted the wisdom of Burke's epigram about American taxation a century early that "To tax and to please, no more than to live and be wise, is not given to man." A stiff program of internal taxes at the beginning of the war would, as they saw it, put undue strain on the fragile fabric of the Confederacy. Only time could teach the imperative need for balanced monetary and fiscal measures—but then, of course, it was too late. When Confederate leaders at last realized the validity of Marcus Cicero's remark that "Taxes are the sinews of the state," the treasury was bankrupt, the currency debauched, and the economy, the army, civil morale, and the foreign credit of the Confederacy alike beyond redemption.

NOTES

1. Anonymous, *A Plan of the Provisional Government for the Southern Confederacy* (Charleston: Evans and Cogswell, 1861), pp. 1–6.

2. Charles Robert Lee, Jr., *The Confederate Constitutions* (Chapel Hill: University of North Carolina Press, 1963), pp. 60–81.

3. Lee, *Confederate Constitutions*, pp. 82–112.

4. Ibid., pp. 155–58.

5. James D. Richardson, comp., *A Compilation of the Messages and Papers of the Confederacy etc.*, 2 vols. (Nashville: United States Publishing 1906), vol. 1, p. 35.

6. Lee, *Confederate Constitutions*, p. 95.

7. Ibid., pp. 95–96.

8. Richardson, comp., *A Compilation*, p. 95; Henry Cleveland, *Alexander H. Stephens in Public and Private* (Philadelphia: Philadelphia National Publishing, 1866), p. 719.

9. Julius Hillyer to Howell Cobb, February 9, 1861; Gazaway B. Lamar to Howell Cobb, February 9 and February 22, 1861, in "The Correspondence of Robert Toombs, Alexander H. Stephens and Howell Cobb," in *Annual Report of the American Historical Association 1911*, ed. Ulrich B. Phillips (Washington, D.C.: Government Printing Office, 1913), vol. 2, pp. 538–40, 545. Hillyer opposed free trade and direct taxes; Lamar favored them.

10. *War of the Rebellion: Armies*, ser. IV, vol. I, p. 101; see also Act of

February 9, 1861, in *The Statutes at Large of the Provisional Government of the Confederate States of America from the Institution of the Government February 8, 1861, to Its Termination, February 18, 1862 Inclusive*, ed. James B. Mathews (Richmond: R. M. Smith, 1864), p. 27.

11. *Bankers Magazine* 9 (September 1859):220–21. Out of $53.2 million in duties paid in fiscal year 1860, $34.9 million was collected in New York: see U.S. Bureau of the Census, *Statistical Abstract of the United States 1952* 72nd ed. (Washington, D.C.: Government Printing Office, 1951), pp. 853–54, table no. 996; *The Merchant's Magazine and Commercial Review* 44 (January 1861):84–85.

12. Raphael P. Thian, *Reports of the Secretary of the Treasury of the Confederate States of America 1861–1865* (Washington, D.C.: Privately published 1878), p. 17.

13. Acts of February 18, 20 and March 4, 1861, in *Statutes*, ed. Mathews, pp. 27, 38, 69.

14. Joseph Dorfman, *The Economic Mind in American Civilization 1606–1865*, 2 vols. (New York: Viking Press, 1946), vol. 2, pp. 850–51; *DeBow's Review*, April 1861, pp. 551–52.

15. Act of May 21, 1861, 2d sess. in *Statutes*, ed. Mathews, pp. 129–35 (95 percent of the increases were removals from the free list). See also U.S. Congress, *Tariff Acts Passed by the Congress of the United States from 1789–1909 etc.* House of Representatives, 61st Cong., 2d sess., doc. no. 671 (Washington, D.C.: Government Printing Office, 1909), pp. 162–81.

16. Thian, *Reports*, pp. 6a–6v; see also W. J. Magrath to Memminger, March 1861, in *Correspondence with the Treasury Department of the Confederate States of America 1861–5*, Part 5: *1861–2*, ed. Raphael P. Thian (Washington, D.C.: Privately published, 1880–81), Appendix 9, pp. 28–29, which makes the secretary's estimates look high; *DeBow's Review* (April 1861):565. Debow observed that the cost of patrolling this thousand-mile-long frontier would be ruinous besides necessitating measures that would arouse public displeasure.

17. Ibid., pp. 9–11.

18. Charleston *Courier*, April 4–5, 1862.

19. C. H. Stevens to Memminger, May 21, 1861, in *Correspondence with*, ed. Thian, p. 110. Stevens reported that the USS *Niagara* had closed Charleston Harbor.

20. This report was part of the Confederate attempt to prove the blockade was ineffective (chapter 2). The early days of the blockade seemed to have been rather relaxed, see William Howard Russell, *My Civil War Diary 1861–2* (London: Hamish Hamilton, 1954), pp. 114–16. The ships captured were released at least until the sixty-day deadline ran out.

21. A. B. Noyes (collector, St. Mark's, Florida) to Memminger, October 18, 1861, and W. F. Colcock (collector, Charleston) to Memminger, October 22, 1861, both in *Correspondence with*, ed. Thian, pp. 389–91.

22. Register's Office, November 19, 1861, Report of December 10, 1861, Report of January 13, 1862, and Report of March 14, 1861, all in Thian, *Reports*, pp. 39, 43–44, 61.

23. Reports of March 14, 1862 and December 7, 1863, ibid., pp. 61, 171.

24. *Journal of the Congress of the Confederate States of America 1861–5* (Washington, D.C.: Government Printing Office, 1904–5), vol. 1, p. 22; see also Lee, *Confederate Constitutions*, p. 61.

25. Original Draft of the South Carolinian Exposition on the Tariff, December 1828, in *The Writings of John C. Calhoun*, ed. Richard K. Cralle (New York: D. Appleton, 1854–59), vol. 6, p. 21.

26. "Taxation and Tariffs," *DeBow's Review*, April 1861, pp. 558–66. Wilkinson's article is quoted as part of DeBow's. Yet Cordozo and the accumulated stock of cotton goods in Europe proved the contrary.

27. *Journal of the Congress*, vol. 1, pp. 87–92.

28. Thian, *Reports*, May 1, 1861, pp. 4–5.

29. Thian, *Reports*, April 7, 1863, pp. 161–62. Assuming a three-million bale crop at five hundred pounds per bale, the one-eighth-cent tax would yield only $1.875 million.

30. Thian, *Reports*, December 10, 1861; March 14, 1862; August 18, 1862; January 10, 1863; December 7, 1863; May 2, 1864; November 7, 1864; pp. 39, 177, 257, 383, 446. There are no records from February 18, 1862 to December 31, 1862, or from October 1, 1864 to the end of the war. I estimate $5,000 for the former period and $3,000 for the latter at the utmost.

31. Frank Owsley, *King Cotton Diplomacy: Foreign Relations of the Confederate States of America* (Chicago: University of Chicago Press, 1931), pp. 553–57; see also Stanley Lebergott, "Through the Blockade: The Profitability and Extent of Cotton Smuggling, 1861–1865," *Journal of Economic History* 41 (December 1978):880–83.

32. A. B. Noyes (collector at St. Marks, Florida) to Memminger, January 6, 1864 in *Correspondence with*, ed. Thian, p. 250; speech of April 6, 1816, in *Works*, ed. Cralle, vol. 2, pp. 165–67.

33. Albert Gallatin, *The Writings of Albert Gallatin*, ed. Henry Adams, 4 vols. (Philadelphia: J. B. Lippincott, 1879), vol. 3, Appendix 1, p. 537.

34. Letter of February 22, 1861, in "Correspondence," ed. Phillips, p. 546.

35. Thian, *Reports*, p. 63, March 14, 1862.

36. Adam Smith, *An Inquiry into the Nature and Causes of the Wealth of Nations*, ed. Edwin Cannon (New York: Modern Library, 1937), pp. 860–63, 873–78; Adams, ed., *The Writings of Albert Gallatin*, vol. 3, Appendix 1, pp. 537–45.

37. Thian, *Reports*, March 14, 1864, p. 61; January 10, 1863, p. 100; December 28, 1863, p. 177; Robert E. Gallman, "Gross National Product in the United States, 1837–1909," in *Output, Employment and Productivity in the United States after 1800*, National Bureau of Economic Research Inc., *Studies in Income and Wealth* (New York: Columbia University Press, 1965), vol. 30, table 2, pp. 27, 46–47; Robert W. Fogel and Stanley L. Engerman, eds., *The Reinterpretation of American Economic History* (New York: Harper and Row, 1971), pp. 335–36.

38. Thian, *Reports*, pp. 29–30; December 10, 1861, p. 39.

39. Ibid., March 14, 1862, January 10, 1863, pp. 63, 99.

40. *Journal of the Congress*, vol. 1, May 14, 1861, pp. 220–21. Postmaster General John M. Reagan, Howell Cobb, and Robert Barnwell, who was on the Finance Committee, were opposed.

41. Memminger to George W. Mumford (Virginia secretary of state), June 26, 1861 (in re. state taxes), in *Correspondence of the Treasury Department of the Confederate States of America 1861–5*, Part 4, ed. Raphael P. Thian (Washington, D.C.: Privately published, 1849), p. 128.

42. Caleb B. Smith, secretary of the interior to Governor Letcher of Virginia, April 2, 1861, Virginia State legislature, Richmond, is typical of such letters. The Confederate House of Representative had its seats arbitrarily apportioned in the Constitution on the Provisional Congress.

43. *Journal of the Congress*, vol. 1, p. 286. A resolution was offered by Staples of Virginia on July 27, 1861, but died in committee; July 29, 1861, ibid., p. 291. See also *Report of Committee on Claims* (Montgomery: n.p. [Shorter and Reid], 1861), pp. 1–2. The Congress should have paid them contingent upon getting the report.

44. *Congressional Globe*, 37th Cong., 2d sess., Part 1, p. 525 (Washington, D.C.: J. C. Rives [Congressional Globe Office], 1862).

45. Thian, *Reports*, pp. 19–21; see also Lee, *Confederate Constitutions*, p. 155.

46. *War of the Rebellion: Armies*, ser. 4, vol. 1, p. 912; Act no. 385 in *Statutes*, ed. Mathews, 4th sess., pp. 72–73; Richmond and Danville Railroad, *Fourteenth Annual Report of the Richmond and Danville Railroad Company* (Richmond: G. W. Gary, 1862).

47. Mary Boykin Chesnut, *A Diary from Dixie*, ed. Ben Ames Williams (Boston: Houghton, Mifflin, 1900), pp. 119–49, 259; Harrison A. Trexler, "The Opposition of Planters to the Employment of Slaves as Laborers by the Confederacy" *Mississippi Valley Historical Review* 27 (1940–41):211–24; Lawrence M. Keitt to Hammond, February 13, 1861, Hammond Papers, MSS Division, Library of Congress.

48. Thomas B. Alexander and Richard E. Berenger, *The Anatomy of the Confederate Congress: A Study of the Influences of Member Characteristics on Legislative Voting Behavior, 1861–1865* (Nashville: Vanderbilt University Press, 1972), pp. 223–24, tables 8–4, 8–5.

49. Thian, *Reports*, pp. 21–22.

50. Montgomery *Daily Mail*, April 29, 1861; recounts the proceedings of the Railroad Convention at Montgomery.

51. Thian, *Reports*, pp. 21–22.

52. Letters of May 4 and 11, 1861, in *Correspondence with*, ed. Thian, pp. 86–90, 95.

53. Forstall to Memminger, May 9, 1861, ibid., pp. 91–94; Russell, *My Civil War Diary*, p. 141. Russell was the *Times* correspondent.

54. *Journal of the Congress* 1 (July 25, 1861):282.

55. Ibid., p. 328 (yea: Louisiana, North Carolina, and Texas; nay: Arkansas, Florida, and Georgia; divided: Alabama, Mississippi, and South Carolina). Vice-President Stephens, Ex-President Tyler, Postmaster General Reagan, and Kenner all favored this crippling amendment.

56. Charleston *Courier*, 23 January, 21 April 1862; Thian, *Reports*, p. 109 (January 10, 1863). However, the Confederate judge (Magrath) in South Carolina declared state bonds to be tax-exempt.

57. *Journal of the Congress*, vol. 1, pp. 331–48.

58. "Taxation and Tariffs," *DeBow's Review*, April 1861, pp. 557–58.

59. Matthews, ed., *Statutes*, 3d sess., chap. 23, pp. 177–83.

60. The Confederate tax would be at a 2.5 percent rate. The Confederates could not know the exact yield of the tax; the figures given in table 22 would have been different in 1861.

61. "An Act to Amend the Revenue Laws of This State," approved November 8, 1862, in *Laws of Alabama*, p. 5.

62. W. N. Evands to Thomas Ruffin, April 7, 1863, Ruffin Papers, MSS Division, University of North Carolina.

63. Asheville, North Carolina, *News*, August 20, 1861, p. 2.

64. Quoted in the Salisbury, North Carolina, *Watchman*, August 19, 1861, p. 2. Since the sheriffs in most states were making very little effort to collect taxes, the essence of this view was that no taxes should be paid.

65. Alexander H. Stephens, Speech of July 11, 1861, *Appleton's Annual Cyclopedia and Register of Important Events* (New York: D. Appleton, 1862), p. 143; Wilmington *Journal*, April 9, 1863.

66. London *Times*, 23 April 1862.

67. Salisbury *Watchman*, August 25, 1861, p. 2, August 26, 1861, p. 1.

68. Richmond *Dispatch*, August 27, 1861, p. 1.

69. Richmond *Enquirer*, August 21, 1861, p. 2.

70. W. B. Burton (Eureka, Texas) to Memminger, October 27, 1861; Alexander Clayton (Ward County, Mississippi) to Memminger, October 29, 1861, both in Incoming Correspondence, Record Group 365, National Archives; J. O. Harrison to Stephen Brown, forwarded to President Davis June 28, 1861, in *Correspondence with*, ed. Thian, pp. 171–72.

71. "Taxation and Tariffs," *DeBow's Review*, Article 6 (April 1861):551.

72. "The War Tax," *DeBow's Review*, Article 13 (September 1861): 436–42; for Calhoun's program, see chapter 2.

73. Mathews, ed., *Statutes*, 3rd sess., pp. 177–83.

74. Thian, *Correspondence of*, pp. 189–90. Gallatin had suggested that a secretary should have a list of collectors ready in advance, a piece of advice that Memminger did not follow. Gallatin, *Writings*, vol. 3, p. 539; Circular in Reference to the Qualification of Tax Collectors, ibid., p. 204; ibid., p. 238.

75. Thian, *Reports*, pp. 115–16.

76. Acts of November 27, 1861, no. 5 in *Acts of the Second Called Session of the First Regular Annual Session of the General Assembly of Alabama, held in the City of Montgomery, etc.* (Montgomery: Montgomery Advertiser Book and Job Office, 1862), pp. 8–9. Alabama was cooperative enough to provide "that no tax collector or tax assessor in this state shall be disqualified from holding the office of tax collector or tax assessor under the Government of the Confederate States." Act of November 28, 1861, no. 4. ibid., p. 8.

77. Acts of October 8, 1862, in *Public and Private Laws,* ed. Mathews, p. 70. $111,174.69 was refunded to North Carolina, ibid., pp. 69–70; Louisiana got $70,000.

78. Bureau of the Census, *Agriculture of the United States in 1860,* 8th census (Washington, D.C.: Government Printing Office, 1864), pp. 128–29; Pope to Memminger, April 10, 1862, in *Correspondence with,* ed. Thian, pp. 513–21.

79. Memminger to D. D. Ferebee (commissioner of North Carolina), December 11, 1861, in *Correspondence of,* ed. Thian, pp. 237–38.

80. Thompson Allan to Memminger, January 6, 1863, Thian, *Reports,* pp. 115–23, see p. 123 for Allan's suggestions.

81. A. B. Moore to the Alabama Senate and House of Representatives, October 28, 1861 in *War of the Rebellion: Armies,* ser. 4, vol. 1, p. 693. Moore was overruled, however, by his legislature (see note 75).

82. Act no. 3, February 8, 1861, in *Acts of the Called Session of the General Assembly of Alabama, Held in the City of Montgomery, Commencing the Second Monday in January 1861* (Montgomery: Shorter and Reid, 1861), pp. 7–8; Act no. 1, December 10, 1861, in *Acts of the Second Called Session, 1861 of the First Regular Annual Session of the General Assembly of Alabama,* p. 3; ch. 1, 268 (no. 11), approved December 13, 1861, in *The Acts and Resolutions Adopted by the General Assembly of Florida, at Its Eleventh Session, Begun and Held at the Capitol, in the City of Tallahassee, on Monday, November 18, 1861* (Tallahassee: Office of the Floridian and Journal, 1862), pp. 15–16; Act no. 75, approved December 11, 1861, in *Acts of the General Assembly of the State of Georgia Passed in Milledgeville, at an Annual Session in November and December 1861* (Milledgeville: Broughton, Nisbet and Barnes, State Printers, 1861), p. 78; Act no. 108, approved January 23, 1862, in *Acts Passed by the Sixth Legislature of the State of Louisiana, at its First Session, Held and Begun in the City of Baton Rouge, on the 25th Day of November, 1861* (Baton Rouge: Tom Bynum, State Printer, 1862), p. 79; *Laws of the State of Mississippi Passed at a Regular Session of the Mississippi Legislature, Held in the City of Jackson, November and December 1861 and January 1862* (Jackson: Cooper and Kimball, State Printers, 1862), ch. 136, p. 146, approved December 20, 1861, and ch. 139, p. 164, approved January 28, 1862.

83. Jacob W. Schuckers, *The Life and Public Services of Salmon P. Chase* (New York: D. Appleton, 1874), p. 332; see also Albert Sidney Bolles, *The Financial History of the United States from 1861–1865* (New York: D. Appleton, 1886), pp. 162–68.

84. Bray Hammond, *Sovereignty and an Empty Purse: Banks and Politics in the Civil War* (Princeton: Princeton University Press, 1970), pp. 93, 266–68. The bankers in the North, headed by James Gallatin, were as ardent for taxes as those in the South.

85. Editorial, *Journal of Commerce,* April 9, 1862; New York *Herald,* January 17, April 13, May 7, June 24, 1862. Most of the enthusiasm for such taxes came from those who thought someone else—the rebels—would have to pay.

86. *Congressional Globe,* 37th Cong., 2d sess., July 23, 1862, pt. 1, p. 2877, pt. 2, p. 2891.

87. Bolles, *Financial History,* pp. 170–76; William J. Shultz and M. R. Caine,

Financial Development of the United States (Englewood Cliffs: Prentice-Hall, 1937), p. 303.

88. Richardson, comp., *A Competition,* vol. 1, p. 139.

89. Report of November 20, 1861, in Thian, *Reports,* pp. 34–35.

90. Report of March 14, 1862, ibid., pp. 59–66.

91. Message of August 18, 1862, in *A Compilation,* comp. Richardson, vol. 1, p. 235; Report of August 18, 1862, Thian, *Reports,* pp. 73–77.

92. Memminger to Davis, October 6, 1862, ibid., pp. 93–94.

93. Richmond *Examiner,* September 23, 1862.

94. Eli M. Bruce, *Speech of Hon. E. M. Bruce of Kentucky on the Financial Policy of the Government, October 2, 1862* (Richmond: Published privately, 1862), p. 2, 14–15.

95. *Journal of the Congress,* House, 5 (October 6, 1862):498–99. The vote was 49–15.

96. Message of President Davis to Congress, January 12, 1863, in *A Compilation,* comp. Richardson, p. 293.

97. Edwin A. Alderman and Armstead C. Gordon, *J. L. M. Curry: A Biography* (London: Macmillan, 1911), p. 164.

98. Joint Resolution 174, March 14, 1865, in Charles W. Ramsdell, *The Laws and Joint Resolution of the Last Session of the Confederate Congress, November 6, 1864–March 18, 1865: Together with the Secret Acts of Preceding Congresses* (Durham: Duke University Press, 1941), p. 138.

99. Thian, *Reports,* p. 108 (January 10, 1863).

100. William M. Browne to Howell Cobb, February 21, 1863, Howell Cobb Papers, MSS Division, Duke University; see also Augusta, Georgia, *Daily Chronicle and Sentinel,* April 3, 1863.

101. Richmond *Enquirer,* February 17, 1863; Charleston *Courier,* January 20, March 14, 1863; Charleston *Mercury,* March 26, April 1, 1863; Richmond *Examiner,* March 9, 16, 17, 21, 26, April 15, 1863; see also *Correspondence with,* ed. Thian, pp. 5, 39, 40, 43, 75–76.

102. Eugene Lerner, *Money, Prices and Wages in the Confederacy 1861–5* (Chicago: Privately mimeographed, 1954), p. 63a; Alexander and Beringer, *Confederate Congress,* p. 206.

103. Edward Younger, ed., *Inside the Confederate Government: The Diary of Robert Garlick Hill Kean* (New York: Oxford University Press, 1957), p. 41.

104. Report of the Price Commissioners, Richmond *Enquirer,* August 2, 1864, p. 1.

105. Phillips, *Correspondence,* p. 626, Toombs to the editor of the Augusta *Constitutionalist,* August 12, 1863.

106. "An Act to Levy Taxes for the Common Defence and Carry on the Government of the Confederate States," approved April 24, 1863, in *Statutes,* ed. Mathews, pp. 115–26.

107. Thian, *Reports,* pp. 159–60 (April 7, 1863).

108. W. W. Harris, Silver Hill, North Carolina, to President Davis, January 5, 1863, in *Correspondence with,* ed. Thian, p. 5; Richmond *Examiner,* April 3, 6, 1863.

109. This produce (based on one-third deductions from the 1860 figures and the substantial exemptions) would have been worth about $250–$300 million on the open market.

110. *Journal of the Congress,* House, vol. 6, pp. 173–79.

111. Letter of March 4, 1863, in *Correspondence with,* ed. Thian, p. 40.

112. Act of March 21, 1863, in *Statutes,* ed. Mathews, 1st Cong., 3d sess., pp. 102–4.

113. Jean Baptiste Say, *A Treatise on Political Economy or the Production, Distribution and Consumption of Wealth,* trans. C. R. Prinsep (Philadelphia: J. Grigg, 1830), pp. 438–40.

114. Petersburg *Express,* November 9, 1863.

115. Lerner, *Money,* p. 16.

116. Richard Cecil Todd, *Confederate Finance* (Athens: University of Georgia Press, 1954), pp. 141–42; see also North Carolina *Standard,* September 8, December 4, 1863.

117. Report of Commissioner of Taxes T. Allan to Memminger, February 1, 1864; Memminger to Speaker Bocock, May 2, 1862, in Thian, *Reports,* pp. 253, 257.

118. T. Allan to Memminger, November 1863, ibid., pp. 195–213.

119. Report of December 7, 1863, Memminger to Speaker Bocock, ibid., pp. 178–86.

120. Matthews, ed., *Public and Private Laws,* pp. 204–9, 1st Cong., 4th sess., ch. 64, 66, and 67.

121. Thian, *Reports,* pp. 195–213.

122. John C. Schwab, *The Confederate States of America, 1861–65: A Financial and Industrial History of the South during the Civil War* (New York: Charles Scribner's Sons, 1901), pp. 299–300; Report of October 28, 1864, Thian, *Reports,* pp. 318–84.

123. Report of May 2, 1864, ibid., pp. 263–67.

124. Todd, *Confederate Finance,* pp. 151–52.

125. Act of March 11, 1865, no. 134 (regular taxes); Act of March 13, 1865 no. 145 (tithe), in Ramsdell, *Laws,* pp. 101–7.

126. Phillips, *Correspondence,* p. 622; quoting Toombs's letter of August 12, 1863 to the editor of the Augusta *Constitutionalist.*

CHAPTER SIX

A More Effective Financial Policy

The death rattle of the Confederacy had scarcely ceased when the silence was shattered by bitter words of reprehension and recrimination. But although, in Memminger's words, most critics followed "the ancient example of our forefather Adam, in casting the fault of a general calamity on some other person . . .,"[1] they by and large avoided any serious analysis of the Confederate government's civil policies. Military operations were more visibly related to the missed opportunities for victory than the mundane problems of operating a wartime economy; and, besides, after four years of war everyone was a self-appointed Clausewitz.

This distorted emphasis was a reflection of the South's culture and temperament. Yet that does not mean that economic affairs were ignored totally. Ex-President Davis certainly alluded to the subject when he told his doctor confidentially at Fortress Monroe: "South Carolina placed Mr. Memminger in the Treasury and while he respected the man, *the utter failure of Confederate finance was the failure of the cause.* Had Mr. Memminger acted favorably on the position of depositing cotton in Europe and holding it there for two years as a basis for their currency, their circulating medium might have maintained itself at par to the closing day of the struggle; and that in itself would have ensured victory."[2] Davis, of course, had forgotten that he had disapproved Memminger's proposal for the acquisition of a shipping line to move cotton out of the South, and later he was honest enough to admit that Memminger was not entirely to blame. The situation, he conceded, had been without precedent and no one had foreseen the course of events. Key opportunities had, therefore, been allowed to slip away.[3]

When writing his public defense, Davis was conspicuously circumspect. In *The Rise and Fall of the Confederate Government,* he blandly avoided blaming anyone for the disaster in public finance and limited his comments to a jejune rehash of his own messages and those of Secretary Memminger. Nowhere was the radioactive topic of cotton exports even discussed. He declared that the program to maintain the value of treasury notes by making them fundable into bonds with coupons payable in coin had failed because there had been a specie payments suspension, but he avoided pointing out that the treasury had overlooked several opportunities to accumulate a coin reserve from the existing stocks.

Davis said little in regard to fiscal policy, other than to reiterate his prewar opposition to the tariff and its effect in encouraging extravagance. He correctly noted that "the popular aversion to internal taxation by the General Government had so influenced the legislation of the several States that only in South Carolina, Mississippi, and Texas were the taxes actually collected from the people." But he did not try to put full responsibility on Memminger for the public aversion to taxes; whatever may have been Memminger's sins of omission, Davis had failed to push for effective taxes until January 1863.[4] Davis had failed even more seriously when, although a former secretary of war, he ignored ample warnings and neglected to see to it that Memminger made payments on time to the army, and particularly to the Trans-Mississippi forces to provide them the means to procure food, arms, and clothing. Nor, in spite of his former military responsibilities, had he even addressed himself to the problem of maintaining army morale by assuring that relief was granted to the families of soldiers, either at the Confederate state or local levels.

But if Davis failed to foresee the dangers of his actions or failure to act, Vice-President Alexander H. Stephens proved even less prescient. From the safety of hindsight, and goaded by an aversion for Davis that transcended his qualified loyalty to the Lost Cause, he joined in bemoaning the failure to ship cotton abroad.[5] And even though he had been a vociferous opponent of the Confederate monetary and fiscal measures passed on February 17, 1864, he devoted less than a quarter of a page to the whole subject of Confederate finance in his official apologia.[6] How he expected the treasury to pay the government's bills, in the face of his own adamant opposition to export duties and direct taxes on property without a resort to printing press inflation, he carefully did not disclose.

Wisdom, derived from contemplation after the fact, showed remarkable consistency. Although in his memoirs, General Joseph E. Johnston took Secretary Memminger to task for failing to ship cotton abroad, he muddled his criticism by confusing the 1860 crop, most of which had been shipped by early 1861, with the 1861 crop, which never got out of the country. Like Davis and Stephens before him, Johnston conveniently forgot the public clamor for a cotton embargo which had made cotton shipments politically difficult. Yet, he was on firm ground in his view that the Confederacy had collapsed primarily because financial embarrassment had created military weakness. His colleague, General P. G. T. Beauregard, showed more passion than charity when in his "Epitaph of the Confederate States" he charged Davis with murdering the country aided and abetted by, among others, Memminger.[7]

Edward Pollard, a persistent detractor of both Davis and Memminger, noted in 1866 that cotton might indeed have been harnessed to finance the war effort, if the politicians had not been blinded by the King Cotton doctrine.

> But the government was too grossly ignorant to see it. The purchase of the cotton to the government was denied by Mr. Memminger, as a scheme of "soup-house legislation," and the new government was started without a basis of credit; without a system of revenue; on the monstrous delusion that money might be manufactured at will out of paper, and that a naked "promise to pay" was all sufficient for the wants of war. . . .
>
> Of all the features of maladministration in the Confederacy, which we have unwillingly traced, that of the currency was certainly the most marked, and perhaps the most vital.[8]

One of the shrewdest witnesses at the inquest was undoubtedly Robert Garlick Hill Kean, chief clerk of the Bureau of War, who, in July 1865, listed what he felt were the sources of Southern defeat. The first item on his list was "a bankrupt Treasury." From this flowed the public's refusal to part with valuable goods in exchange for worthless Confederate paper, which, in turn, drove up prices exacted for supplies. Because the government paid its soldiers tardily in a debauched currency and failed to provision them adequately, the desertion rate was high, and the army had to procure supplies by impressment, which in turn discouraged production. In the end, financial policy failed, so Kean insisted, because the Confederate leadership foolishly put their faith in a short war and because the First Congress, the president, and Memminger were ill-equipped to deal with a "very large subject."[9]

Kean's view that the demoralization of the army resulted from all the consequences of a bankrupt treasury was amply confirmed by no less an authority than General Lee himself, who wrote that "insufficient food and non-payment of the troops have more to do with the dissatisfaction than anything else. All commanding officers concur in this opinion."[10]

A later observer, Charles W. Ramsdell, who devoted his life to Confederate research, concluded that the Confederacy's defeat came about chiefly because the Southern people and their government were unprepared to solve quickly enough economic problems that they had failed to anticipate. The result was a weakened and demoralized civilian population disabled from giving the Confederate armies the kind of homefront support they required during the crisis years of 1863–64.[11]

The root of these economic difficulties, as Ramsdell saw it, lay in the finances of the government. The irredeemable paper money "weakened not only the purchasing power of the Government but also destroyed economic security among the people." Although Ramsdell noted the urgent need for a sound currency, ample production, an adequate transportation system, and the need to keep the government's finances as much as possible on a specie basis, he did not place heavy emphasis on the absence of adequate taxation. He evidently viewed the economy as too depressed to furnish much support for the treasury.[12]

While Ramsdell modestly declined to suggest what might have been done better and graciously ascribed Confederate misfortunes (he shuns the word "failure") to an understandable inability to see into a mist-clouded future, his defense is in effect a damning indictment of Confederate leaders. The problems that they failed to resolve in a timely manner were, as Ramsdell correctly summarized them, all patently apparent by October 1, 1861 at the latest. This can be proven by merely listing the facts known to the Davis administration.

The cabinet knew all that was necessary about the trade and cotton questions. It knew that there was little direct trade with Southern ports and that the merchants' trade stocks were at low ebb. It also knew that a blockade had been declared, that it was unlikely foreign powers would break it, and that if cotton were not sold, the already depressed economy would be threatened with collapse. It had also learned from inquiries that the blockade was inhibiting trade, diminishing the customs receipts, and depriving the country of the foreign exchange needed to pay for vital military imports.

Nor was there any lack of information regarding currency problems. Secretary Memminger was under no delusions regarding the inadequacies of the printers. He knew of the need for coin to pay the interest on the public debt and that bank suspensions had made both the financiers and the public reluctant to part with their specie. Finally, he had been warned about the proliferation of rival currencies and the need for voluntary or coercive means, if necessary, to create a national monopoly of the currency.

Tax troubles wre equally apparent. Secretary Memminger was not only apprised of the shortage of customs revenues but also had been strongly urged to resort to additional fiscal means to meet the government's obligations and reduce its dependence on the printers.

Yet in the face of these incontrovertible prods to action, what did the government do? There is no evidence that anyone did serious long-range planning; rumors of hoped-for foreign intervention or peace were credulously accepted; no systematic Confederate government actions were ever addressed to the problems of acquiring coin, curtailing rival currencies, or ensuring the relief of soldiers and sailors. Other matters were allowed to drift for two or three years while Memminger dithered, contradicted himself, or took refuge in trivia and legalisms. It is difficult to find a plausible defense against Pollard's charge of maladministration levied against Davis and Memminger.[13]

Maladministration, particularly with respect to economic affairs, goes far to explain the extraordinary collapse of Confederate resistance in the winter of 1864–65. Faced by privation and a long string of defeats, the public's growing lack of confidence in its government was expressed in a burgeoning opposition to a regime whose actions belied its nominal principles. The South's morale, and at last its willingness to prolong an odious war, were exhausted; with them departed the disposition to resist. The surrender of General Lee simply provided the signal needed by those who were seeking a plausible justification to quit.

Many had looked forward to continued resistance by guerrillas, an event that had been openly feared by federal forces. The country after all was too vast to be held down except at tremendous cost. In Northern Virginia, an area less than two thousand miles square, Lieutenant Colonel Mosby and six hundred regulars tied down forty thousand federal troops who seldom had the better of their frequent clashes. Yet in 1865, the guerrillas also capitulated, enabling the U.S. army to hold the South until 1877 with a comparatively small force. In spite of the rigors of Reconstruction, no effort was ever made to revive the Confederacy, a sure sign that the very idea of an independent nation was so discredited that no one was willing to repeat the experiment.

A Comparison of Union and Confederate Finance

Given this outcome, one can recall Richard Nelson Current's remark "that it is hard to believe, and impossible to prove, that the Southerners did a worse job with economic affairs than the Northerners would have done in the same circumstances." Is this really true? Obviously, the South confronted the blockade, which the North did not. Yet in the matter of currency management and taxation both combatants dealt with similar difficulties. A brief comparison of the policies pursued in these areas will suggest an answer to the question.

The Union, as was seen, established a legal-tender currency in February 1862, which two years later had sunk to about 40 cents per dollar in gold. To sustain its value, the federal Congress from 1862–65 suppressed private scrip notes, city notes, and then state bank notes and substituted in their stead a currency whose denominations ran from 3 cents to $10,000. As a second step in its currency support program, the federal Congress decreed that notes would be fundable into bonds whose interest was payable in coin. In order to assure that there was no default in such payments, customs dues were put on a specie basis only, and Secretary Chase given funds and told to accumulate a coin stockpile from the public. Finally, a substantial tax program was inaugurated, thereby forcing citizens to acquire and pay over such notes to the treasury, thereby limiting the quantity in circulation.

The Confederacy's management of its currency is in marked contrast with that pursued by the Union. The Confederate Congress authorized a currency a year earlier than the Union's, but did not issue notes of $1 and $2 denomination until 1862 and fractional currency until 1863. Secretary Memminger made no effort to suppress rival currencies or even to induce their voluntary withdrawal. Like the federal currency, that of the South was also fundable into bonds, whose interest was payable in coin. But Secretary Memminger made no effort to accumulate a substantial coin reserve, and Congress waited until 1864 to establish a wholly inadequate specie revenue base. Finally, the Confederacy, although it started its currency program nine months earlier than the Union, waited until nine months later to set up anything other than the most trifling of tax programs. And this despite the fact that the Union started with a $60 million a year customs dues base. Was it any wonder, then, that the Union currency in February 1864 was worth 40 cents in gold or that the Confederate currency was worth only 4 cents?

So far as taxation is concerned, not only did the Union start nine months earlier to levy internal revenue, but the program involved more comprehensive dues and higher rates of taxation. Even in the minor areas of avoiding default on its obligations, the Union showed to advantage. Not only was coin systematically procured to assure specie interest payments, but when the demand notes of 1861 could not be paid in coin, they were made a legal tender for all dues including customs, thereby making them the equivalent of gold. The Confederates did practically nothing to sustain coin payments and defaulted. Then, when confronted by the May 16, 1861 Act's two-year notes, instead of doing what could be done to compensate the holders for non-payment, Congress tried to legislate the problem away to the holders' disadvantage.

Given these discrepancies in action and approach, the contrast exhibited in table 23 between the Union's and the Confederacy's management of their finances cannot come as a surprise. The Union taxed more and borrowed less. And what it borrowed, it generally kept out of circulation. Finally, it kept the currency share of its expenditures down to a modest 13 percent of total revenues.

The South on the other hand derived more than half its revenue from non-interest-bearing treasury notes and only 8 percent of its revenue from taxes. Its efforts to borrow at interest proved, on the whole, significantly less successful (not surprisingly) than those of its counterpart. But then, outside the forced funding acts, Southerners had fewer positive or negative incentives to buy bonds.

Could the South Have Done Better?

Yet, in view of the environment in which the Confederacy evolved, might one have expected anything better? It is a difficult—perhaps even a sterile—question, because the answer involves not only unprovable assumptions but also speculation strongly affected by subjective judgments. Still, the exercise is probably worth undertaking, if not to provide final answers, at least to stimulate further research. Thus, consider a hypothetical scenario based on Calhoun's programs

Table 23. Summary of Total Revenue*

Source of Revenue	The Union		The Confederacy	
	Revenue	% of Revenue	Revenue	% of Revenue
Fiscal				
Customs, Taxes, misc.	$ 667.2	20.1	$ 217.9	8.2
Monetary				
Long-term loans	1,044.6	31.4	577.0	21.8
Interest-bearing notes	890.3	26.8	130.3	4.9
Non-interest-bearing notes	458.1	13.8	1,433.3	54.1
Temporary and short-term loans	262.6	7.9	290.9	11.0
Total	$3,322.8	100.0	$2,649.4	100.0

Sources: Thian, *Reports*. Also Davis R. Dewey, *Financial History of the United States* (New York: Longmans, Green, 1934).
* All figures in millions.

of 1816 and 1837. One might assume that the Confederate Congress, at its sessions following the outbreak of hostilities in April 1861, had adopted the following far-reaching financial and economic program:

1. As soon as war broke out, specie was mobilized by an intensive effort. All banks that had not already done so were required (with stiff criminal penalties for noncompliance) to suspend specie payments and to lend their coin and foreign exchange holdings to the Confederacy in exchange for 8 percent bonds or promissory notes (for sums under $50) on which both the principal and interest would be repayable in coin. The banks would remain suspended until the loan was paid off and their specie reserves restored to them. As a result, the government might have borrowed from the banks and public at least $40 million of coin and $15 million of foreign exchange. It could then have floated other bonds with interest payable in coin at 6 percent, while interest-bearing treasury notes might have been emitted paying 1 or 1.5 cents per day per $100 (3.65 or 5.475 percent). In addition, it could have authorized call certificates bearing 4 percent interest for those held under six months and 5 percent if held longer. The interest on the notes and call certificates would be payable only in treasury notes. Through these means and through land sales, customs, and export dues (payable only in specie) the government could have mobilized and retained for its debt service program all available specie, including the coin and bullion acquired from the mints and the federal government.

2. The Confederate government could then have entered the market in relief of the planters and bought $100 million of produce (approximately 2.5 million bales of cotton at 7 cents per pound with other staples in proportion), half with 6 percent bonds, and the other half with special, stationer-printed, or handwritten receipts that were tax receivable before July 1, 1862 and thereafter would be interest-bearing certificates of indebtedness. Because of heavy taxation, the bulk of these would have been paid into the treasury for taxes by mid-1862.

3. The scenario of tax policies follows that spelled out in table 20. The government would have imposed a 2.5 percent ad valorem tax on slaves imposed in the form of a specific sum per slave, according to age, sex, and physical condition, and a 1.25 percent tax on other property, which, after deductions, should have yielded $82.8 million. To this one might add another $30 million that would presumably have come from a variety of income and sales taxes, license fees, and stamp duties. The scenario hypothesizes a double property levy ($165.6 million) for the period November 1, 1861–February 18, 1862 (payable November 1 and February 1).

Thereafter, a rate of 2 percent might have been charged on property and 4 percent on slaves for 1863 and 1864 (payable at the beginning of each year). Property acquired up to 1861 would have been assessed at its prewar value payable either in gold or its value adjusted for treasury note depreciation (payable in treasury notes). Only property bought since January 1, 1862 would have been payable in treasury notes at par. These taxes would have yielded approximately $600 million by early 1865, a sum roughly 20 percent of the South's gross national product for the years 1861–64.

4. Conjointly with its cotton acquisition program, the Confederate government could also have conducted extensive foreign operations. It could have placed in Europe the $15 million of foreign exchange reserves it had borrowed to prime the pump, while through its authorized agent, it might have negotiated a $25 million, twenty-year, 8 percent loan. Like the Erlanger loan, that issue could have been amortized over a twenty-year period. With these funds, the government could have obtained military hardware, a fleet of blockade-runners, and a surplus stock of merchandise for sale in the Confederacy. From time to time, surplus balances that accumulated abroad from the sale of cotton would be transferred to the Confederacy, either in the form of gold coin or foreign exchange that would be sold for treasury notes or matured specie-paying bond coupons. Sterling bills would also have been exchanged for domestic coin in order to enable the government to meet its interest payments. Legislation could have been enacted regulating imports, prohibiting luxury goods, and authorizing the government to commandeer for official use half of all non-state-owned outgoing cargo space.

5. A corps of tax assessors and collectors would have been recruited by the treasury to enforce the laws while several hundred depositories and produce loan agents were hired to carry out commodity and monetary policies. Having established outside Richmond a government-owned, unified Treasury Note Bureau headed by an officer armed with full powers, the treasury would have been in a strong position to execute an effective Confederate financial policy.

6. As an essential part of these programs, the Confederate government would have had to disseminate presidential messages addressed to the Southern people outlining the dangers to the country, the reasoning behind the government programs, and the impracticality of pursuing other proposed lines of policy, particularly in the matters of trade and taxation. Great emphasis might have been laid on the dangers arising from the potential confiscation and emancipation of all slave property, together with other property losses that invasion

would entail. These messages, supplemented by regular presidential tours, would have sought to induce public support for the needed sacrifices and to translate those feelings into pressures on the congressmen to enact Davis's program.

The advantages of pursuing such a scenario as against the erratic, belated, and the roughly similar inferior course actually followed can obviously not be quantified with precision. Still, some rough estimates can be made. Certainly the government's nominal expenditures would have been reduced, but by how much?

As Wesley Mitchell pointed out, when governments purchase commodities and services, commodity prices have buried within them some provision for the cost of labor. He thus broke the government's expenditures into three categories: expenditures for government salaries and interest, which do not rise as rapidly as inflation; expenditures for commodities; and expenditures that necessarily include payments for both commodities and civilian labor.[14]

The Confederate government's wage bills moved within relatively narrow limits throughout the war. For example, the basic pay of a private in the army was $11 a month; it was not until June 1864 that this was increased to $16 a month. Government clerks fared worse or barely as well, getting raises of 20–50 percent.[15]

By analyzing the whole series of appropriations, it is possible to ascertain that approximately 36 percent of the Confederate government's expenses were fixed, either interest payments or salaries; 29 percent were payments for commodities, in which salaries played only a small role, and 35 percent of all expenditures involved a substantial mixture of goods and services. Confederate expenditures can then be broken down into four categories: War Department, Navy Department, the civil government, and the treasury (table 24). This discloses that the Confederacy expended $2,586.1 million, after adjustments for exchanges of treasury notes and call certificates for other securities, leaving $450 million of accumulated arrearages unpaid at the Confederacy's demise.

In order to compare what might have happened with what in fact did happen (see Appendixes E–H), I have broken government revenues and expenditures into categories. In computing the counterfactual budget I found it necessary to make quite a large number of assumptions as to the scope and character of this fictitious system of public finance. I had, for example, to adjust accounts for depreciation differentials, to estimate both the effects of a wise policy on foreign and domestic-made goods, and the prospects of shipping goods in and out through the blockade (table 25).[16] So far as the arrearages in

Table 24. Confederate Expenditures*

Date	Department			Public[†] Debt	Total
	War	Navy	Civil		
Feb. 18, 1861–Feb. 18, 1862 (1 year)	$ 152.8	$ 7.6	$ 5.1	$ —	$ 165.5
Feb. 18, 1862–Jan. 1, 1863 (10.5 months)	390.0[‡]	20.6	13.7	18.0	443.3
Jan. 1, 1863–Oct. 1, 1863 (9 months)	478.0[‡]	38.4	11.6	32.2	559.2
Oct. 1, 1863–Oct. 1, 1864 (1 year)	684.9[‡]	26.4	16.0	120.8	848.1
Oct. 1, 1864–Mar. 31, 1865 (6 months)	475.0[‡]	14.0	10.0	75.0	570.0
(Estimates only)	$2,180.7	$107.0	$56.4	$246.0	$2,586.1

Sources: Raphael P. Thian, *Reports of the Secretary of the Treasury of the Confederate States of America 1861–1865* (Washington, D.C.: Privately published, 1878), Reports dated March 14, 1862, January 10, 1862, April 11, 1863, May 2, 1864, November 7, 1864, pp. 61, 99, 177, 257, 353.
* All figures in millions.
† Excludes cancellation of treasury notes funded into bonds; including interest on the public debt and redemption of call certificates, due bonds, note issues, and the like.
‡ Includes cumulative arrearages of $50 million in 1862; $100 million in 1863, $200 million in 1864, and $313 million in 1865.

treasury payments reported by Secretaries Memminger and Trenholm were concerned, there is no way of ascertaining what part of these were undrawn because of an insufficiency of funds as opposed to the impossibility of procurement. These arrearages were distributed between the War and the Navy Departments in proportion to their overall actual expenditures. Curiously, the counterfactual figures are for much larger sums than the actual ones when paper dollars are converted into their coin value.

This, at first sight, seems paradoxical. Yet the actual figures conceal the revenue from impressments, the failure to feed, clothe, and pay the troops, and other deferred expenses. Treasury note depreciation was an important variable. I estimated the costs by comparing the total circulation with the price index. Then, by applying the price indexes to each of the three categories into which the government's expenses fell, I was able to compute the counterfactual expenses. To the adjusted actual figures I added the arrearages (treated in the same manner), which produced the figures indicated in Appendix F.

It will also be noted that, in addition to the actual and counterfactual

Table 25. Cumulative Blockade Runs and Captures:
All Ports of Confederacy

	1861	1862	1863	1864	1865	1861–65
Steamers						
Vessels engaged*	68	86	118	127	50	449
Attempts	572	205	545	474	108	1,904
Captures in	3	42	50	47	12	154
Captures out	1	11	23	29	6	70
Total captured	4	53	73	76	18	224
% captured	1	26	13	16	17	12
Total successful	568	152	472	398	90	1,780
% successful	99	74	87	84	83	88
Sail						
Vessels engaged*	728	391	310	181	39	1,649
Attempts	2,169*	655	458	249	45	3,576
Captures in	81	155	112	64	18	430
Captures out	28	85	87	62	14	276
Total captures	109	240	199	126	32	706
% captured	5	37	43	51	71	20
Total successful	2,060	415	259	123	13	2,870
% successful	95	63	57	49	29	80
Totals						
Vessels engaged	796	477	428	308	89	2,098
Attempts	2,741	860	1,003	723	153	5,480
Successful	2,628	567	731	521	103	4,550
Captured	113	293	272	202	50	930
% successful	96	66	73	72	67	83

Sources: Marcus W. Price, "Ships that Tested the Blockade of the Carolina Ports, 1861-1865," *American Neptune* 8 (July 1948):196–241; "Ships that Tested the Blockade of the Gulf Ports, 1861–1865," *American Neptune* 11 (October 1951):262–90; 12 (January 1952):52–59; 12 (April 1952):154–61; 12 (July 1952):229–38; "Ships that Tested the Blockade of the Georgia and East Florida Ports, 1861–1865," *American Neptune* 15 (April 1955):97–132.
* Number overstated; many vessels operated in more than one year.

revenue and expenditure accounts, Appendixes G to K also show the counterfactual government's specie holdings, foreign accounts, debt position, and balance sheets. These appendixes cast doubt on Schwab and Todd's assumption of foreordained defeat. For example, by the end of October 1863, the counterfactual Confederacy would have been roughly in the same condition (at least so far as the currency was concerned) as was the real Confederacy eighteen months earlier in April 1862. The October 31, 1864, figures are even more revealing. At that time, the counterfactual Confederate circulation would have had a face value of $90 million worth about 80 cents on the dollar ($72 million); the putative Confederate debt would have been, nominally, almost $2,000 million less than that of the real Confederacy.

Even if one assumes a roughly similar debt maturity scheduling between the real and the counterfactual Confederacy's, the latter would have retired all maturing debt in treasury notes and paid all interest in coin up to the end of 1864. Moreover, there would still have been $18.9 million in coin on hand. Thus, avoiding past errors and employing the knowledge current in that era, the Confederacy had the means of saving itself. What it lacked was the plan, the prudence, and above all, the will to achieve that goal.

Moreover, it might have substantially alleviated economic decay over a four-year period by importing $132.8 million of merchandise with the government's fifty-steamer blockade-running fleet, while bolstering the treasury and the currency by the revenues from the sale of goods (wholesale) that could be bought only with specie or treasury notes.

The programs I have outlined would have improved the South's prospects by reducing economic dislocation and a decline in civilian morale. That morale would have been further sustained by remittances from promptly paid troops to their families and also by furnishing aid for their families at the Confederate, state, or local government levels. The cumulative effect would have meant greatly reduced desertions and an increase in the forces available to repel the enemy. A materially larger army would have reduced territorial losses (with their concomitant desertions), would have won more victories in the field, and would have left the South in the fall of 1864 in fighting trim. Under these circumstances, it is unlikely that the South would have been bisected along the Mississippi River, and the people would probably have been able and willing to continue the struggle.

Such an improvement in Southern morale would have meant a commensurate decline in morale in the North. In spite of two and a half years of steady progress toward victory, there was growing dissension and defeatism in the Union's ranks, and it is a legitimate question whether confronted by no more favorable conditions than those achieved by the end of 1862, the Northern voters would have been willing to retain the Republicans in power. Had the Democrats won in 1864, the Confederates might have achieved independence. Historians would be able to write books and articles proving, as eloquently as they now prove the contrary, "how the South won the Civil War."

Why Did the Southern Economic Program Fail?

In view of the fact that several modern historians and many of the Confederates themselves thought that a bankrupt treasury played an important role in the Union's victory; in view also of the demonstration that effective planning and the efficient execution of programs based on then contemporary economic knowledge might have allowed the South to avoid or at least put off defeat and, finally, taking account of the horrendous costs (Appendix L) suffered by white Southerners as a result of their failed experiment in rebellion, one inevitably comes back full cycle to Charles Wesley's question about why the Confederacy was unable to mobilize its resources more effectively.

Perhaps one can begin to find an answer to this problem by drawing together the elements that contributed to the Union's success. Lincoln and the Republican party stood for two objectives: abolition and the maintenance of the Union. Victory was indispensable if even the Unionist part of their agenda was to be achieved, while the fact that failure posed a serious threat to the survival of the Republican party was a powerful goad to rigorous action.

Lincoln, as a frontiersman, was as ignorant of public finance as Davis and undoubtedly (at least initially) knew far less than Davis about the operations of the War Department and armies in the field. Yet Lincoln, despite his errors (and he made plenty of them), proved to be more successful than Davis. A preeminent pragmatist, he was interested in what would work, and he never allowed a doctrinaire interpretation of his political beliefs to get in the way of achieving his goals. Thus, although he was an abolitionist, he did not permit himself the luxury of adopting the Radical Republican program of immediate emancipation. He never forgot that his primary goal was the preservation of the Union; with slavery if he must, without it if he could. He was too shrewd a politician not to know that the Radical program would drive border-state slaveholders into the Confederacy's arms; that it would galvanize the old Whig slaveholding aristocracy into abandoning their passive or lukewarm support of the Confederacy and instead incite them to vigorous resistance. Immediate abolition would thus assist the Confederate leaders, without any effort on their part, to unite all Southerners in a do or die resistance to the Union. So Lincoln sagely adopted a totally pragmatic, ambiguous policy that confused friend and foe alike about his precise intentions while he consolidated his own position and reenforced Unionist support in the border areas. By the time he dared to issue his Emancipation Proclamation and clarified his abolitionist intentions, the Union had gained the upper hand, and pro-Southern sentiment in the border areas had been effectively neutralized.

In executing his program, particularly in the dramatic days between Fort Sumter and the convening of the federal Congress in Washington on July 4, 1861, Lincoln took a series of semidictatorial or extralegal actions that vastly expanded executive powers and even impinged upon the powers of Congress and the rights of individuals. Lincoln justified these actions on the plain need to preserve the Union and the Constitution:

> It became necessary for me to choose whether, using only the existing means, agencies and processes which Congress had provided, I should let the Government fall at once into ruin or whether, availing myself of the broader powers conferred by the Constitution in cases of insurrection, I would make an effort to save it, with all its blessings, for the present age and for posterity.
>
> In other words, when confronted by a crisis one may be truer to the intent of the Constitution by violating one or more of its provisions in order that the Nation and its fundamental law might ultimately survive, than by rigidly adhering to the strict letter of the law.[17]

Lincoln's doctrines found ready support both in the views and actions of the Republican-controlled Congress. A wide range of "war measures," including legal-tender notes and heavy taxation, were enacted because it was recognized that these were actions deemed indispensable for the maintenance of the Union. And, in undertaking these programs, the Republicans in Congress were prepared to go much further than Secretary Chase, whose views were deemed far too timid to deal with the exigencies of that critical hour.

The Southern intellectual milieu was exactly the opposite. Calhoun's doctrines of states' rights, nullification, and secession were all part of an elaborate system for protecting a Southern minority within the Union, if possible, or for providing a legal justification for withdrawal if the South's rights were violated. In advancing his views, however, Calhoun never lost some measure of his sense of American nationalism, of which he had been a prime exponent in the War of 1812. And when those feelings faded, he had transferred his nationalist feelings to the South.

Those who followed him lost sight of the critical nationalist element in Calhoun's program. Confronted by the need to justify secession, they ignored the right of revolution based on abolitionist raids, Northern hatred for the South, and Northern economic exploitation. Instead, the Confederates were satisfied with the legalistic doctrine of secession. And although arguments to support secession displayed considerable ingenuity, their appeal was purely intellectual. There was nothing in them to lift hearts or generate a feeling of urgency or a sense of nationalism. For many people it was enough to reassure themselves that, since what they were doing was perfectly legal, the North could not oppose their withdrawal from the Union.[18] Few thought of unified action by the Southern people; the emphasis on states' rights deflected any feelings of patriotism to the local level and thwarted any sense of collective nationality.

These attitudes were reflected in South Carolina's Declaration of Independence on December 24, 1860, listing the causes of her dissaffection. Even President Davis, in his inaugural, confined himself largely to a constitutional justification of the Southern position and declared that "it is by abuse of language that their [the sovereign states'] act has been denominated a revolution." The Southerners thus reduced their position to the claim that secession was justified because the North had misinterpreted and misapplied the powers granted in the federal Constitution. And particularly as the war progressed, that raised questions about whether the South's formal complaints justified war and the dissolution of the Union.

This taste for legal technicalities, and the shunning of anything smacking of revolutionary fervor, soon had the Confederacy in trouble. Public policy was hampered by the belief that it was possible to wage a war, in which the very life of the nation and the fundamental basis of Southern society were at stake, by following the well-trod path of business as usual. This in turn implied that there was no necessity for change or speed in the dispatch of public affairs. As Kean described the situation in his diary, there was "a total absence of vigor; all the revolutionary vigor is with the enemy, in legislation and execution. With us timidity, hair-splitting, and an absence of all *policy.*" He also complained that programs were not formulated with their likely outcomes in mind; that is—in today's jargon—they were not goal-oriented.[19]

Implicit in the practice of hair-splitting were two dangers. The first was a tendency to become buried in detail; the second was a preoccupation with whether a proposed course of action was legal or not. This not only produced acrimony and delay, but also blinded the Southerners about the practical reality that however annoying Davis's alleged "tyranny" might be, defeat by the Union was bound to be much worse. As a result of their absorption with minutia and inconvenient legalisms, few had any time for effective planning or action.

These deficiencies suggest clear defects in the quality of Southern leadership. The Southern people did not lack in intelligence or a capacity to work toward practical, utilitarian goals. What they lacked was a leadership prepared to jolt them out of their complacency by telling them candidly of the troubles that lay ahead. Unfortunately, Southern leaders had sold secession to the public as not only a legal, but also a peaceable remedy. To admit, at the beginning, that secession meant war risked the loss of public support.

The failure to appeal effectively to public opinion and to induce the Southern people to make sacrifices in turn reflected the ambiguity of the Southern leadership's attitude toward the Confederacy. Their actions certainly do not disclose any signs that they themselves were prepared to sacrifice everything for the cause—hence their inability to get others to do so. Even after war inevitably came and the South was swept by feelings of inchoate nationalism, sectional pride, and animosity, the leadership still saw little need for extraordinary actions at variance with their prejudices. Indeed, many Southerners thought that if changes became necessary, they could be addressed when the situation required. But if their goal was to keep their options open, then they clearly failed to understand that the passage of time forecloses options. As Pierre Mendes-France, the French Fourth Republic premier, was wont to say, "To govern is to choose."

The Southern lack of a practical plan was of a piece with the ardent acceptance of comforting and unexamined beliefs wholly at variance with realities. So too was the Southern leaders' incapacity to look at matters from more than one perspective. This found further reflection in Southerners' unstructured, casual, and rather opportunistic approach to business matters in general. Northerners tended to be more systematic in their methods and to plot out their decisions carefully. Southerners, on the other hand, viewed such cold-blooded calculations with disdain. Thus while planters might write indignant letters to newspaper editors, complaining about Southern dependence on the North for daily necessities, nothing could induce them, or Southern mercantile and financial groups, to curtail accustomed investments in cotton in order to promote local manufacturing enterprises or to encourage such firms as did exist by purchasing their products.[20] In encapsulating the whole problem, it seems that there was an unreflected dichotomy between what was said and what was done.

President Davis and his colleagues in the cabinet and the Congress seldom, if ever, understood that they faced a very real chance of being defeated and that vigorous and prompt measures were needed to avoid catastrophe. Nothing so neatly illustrates this mindset than the incredulous attitude evinced by President Davis to the reverses suffered in early 1862. Yet given the weakness of the South and the power of the North, should Davis have expected anything but defeat and retreats as the Union launched its initial offensive?

It may also be questioned whether Confederate leaders had the will to do what they knew needed to be done. All the evidence of this narrative, both theoretical and practical, proves conclusively that they could and should have known what actions were required. Yet, President Davis and Secretary Memminger either dithered in agonies of indecision or else immersed themselves in irrelevancies or trivia (which they at least felt able to cope with) while leaving more serious matters unattended to. They were small men in positions too big for them, and the psychological pressures on Davis, with his psychosomatic illnesses, must have been crushing in their intensity.

Finally, there can be no doubt that Southerners' narrow, legalistic approaches to every problem, their resistance to change and fear of innovation in any form, were insuperable impediments to effective executive action. Their unyielding belief in the superiority of private rights over the public interest, when combined with a pathological fear of centralized power, was fatal. A jealous distrust of their own central government, their inability to realize that the Confederate regime was a friend, not a foe, the refusal to abandon narrow parochial concerns in favor of giving consideration to the welfare of the nation as a whole proved equally crippling. Many Confederates were unwilling to address Lincoln's classical dilemma of how governments could avoid being too strong for the liberties of their people yet powerful enough to ensure their own survival.

Confronted by unpleasant realities, the Confederates' first reaction was to dismiss out of hand any proposals that did not accord with their principles. Thus, President Davis indignantly castigated Lincoln's suspension of the writ of habeas corpus in November 1861.[21] Yet, confronted shortly thereafter by crisis within his own jurisdiction, Davis proceeded to suspend the writ repeatedly. That at least demonstrated Davis's belated capacity to grow and adapt to circumstances. The same could not be said for Vice-President Stephens and the extreme states' rights faction, who opposed Davis at every turn.

Stephens and his colleagues were correct when they asserted that principle is an indispensable element in politics and in the administration of a nation. Their original sin was their excessive attention to the metaphysics of principle. In devoting so much time and effort to the morality and legality of what was being done, they lost sight of the need to vindicate by practical results their larger principles. By the time Davis and the more sensible elements in the Confederacy were willing to recognize the existence of a middle ground and act accord-

ingly, Stephens and his associates had irretrievably alienated particu-
larist sentiment by castigating the apparent hypocrisy of a regime that
seemed to proclaim its allegiance to one set of principles and yet acted
on another.

Moreover, one cannot overlook the debilitating effect that Davis's
actions and manner had on the Southern people. His rigidity, his
incapacity, and indeed disinterest in cultivating the personal touch,
coupled with his largely self-imposed isolation, turned him into a
distant and unsympathetic figure. Nor was he able through his messages to communicate his ardent devotion to the cause or inspire
similar feelings in others, who he assumed, without examination,
shared his views. Still worse, he was seen as the man who vetoed laws
for the benefit of prisoners of war and deceased soldiers' families.[22] The
hyperinflation was also charged to his account because of his perceived
inaction, as were the operations of the impressment officers with their
licensed system of robbery and extortion. No wonder then that from
1863 on, confidence in the regime fell off until by 1865 no one was left
who was prepared to heed Davis's call for continued resistance.

The final fruits of the Confederacy's financial policies were a suitable monument to a tragically mistaken order of priorities. States'
rights and a myopic preoccupation with strict construction of the
Constitution were misleading pretexts for deferring or torpedoing
legislation that impinged upon the profits of special-interest groups.
Thanks to the misguided indulgence accorded to their representations,
the slaveholders and the agricultural interest were enabled to shift a
disproportionate amount of the tax burden onto the shoulders of the
urban population; the bankers were permitted to squander their specie
and foreign exchange reserves while blocking aid for the planters; and
the blockade-runners were given carte blanche to import luxuries and
to deny the treasury cargo space needed for its cotton. In short,
flagrant selfishness triumphed over not only common-sense but also
the commonweal.

The root cause of these disasters was a complete absence of effective
executive management and leadership. President Davis was grossly
negligent in not looking after his civilian responsibilities and especially
in not supervising and assisting the treasury in its operations. Secretary Memminger was delinquent in not using his early cordial relationship with the president to talk out his problems and procure Davis's
aid for his programs.[23] He seems never to have understood the full
magnitude of his problems or the need for precautionary measures.
His legalistic and negativistic mental attitude led him to accept the
frustration of his plans without adequately exploring alternate means

to the same goals. Moreover, the secretary never seemed to get his priorities right. For him, the "rights" of the planters, the blockade-runners, the bankers, and the printers, however much they might cripple his plans, always exceeded in importance the treasury's duty to furnish the Confederacy with the means for its survival. And even when he was at last compelled to abandon his misplaced scruples, his measures were too late and marked by unwarranted timidity.

The sad truth is that the South had the resources and programs to succeed in its bid for independence—or at least to achieve a less ignominious result than in fact occurred. But victory and independence were out of the question with men governed by such principles. Instead of doing its duty both to itself and to the South's citizens, the Davis administration improvidently and feebly conducted the economic affairs of a brave and civilized people in a manner reminiscent of the irresponsible, transient rulers of a bankrupt banana republic. Its actions provide further proof that the survival of any nation depends on an administration with the foresight to do and say what is needed and a legislature with the courage to provide what is required.

NOTES

1. Memminger to the Editor, Charleston *Courier and News*, March 28, 1874.

2. John Joseph Craven, *The Prison Life of Jefferson Davis etc.* (New York: Carleton, 1866), p. 155, emphasis added. Davis later denied the statements attributed to him.

3. Craven, *The Prison Life*, p. 158.

4. Jefferson Davis, *The Rise and Fall of the Confederate Government*, 2 vols. (1881, repr. New York: Thomas Yoselloff, 1958), pp. 490–95, 504.

5. Alexander H. Stephens, *Recollections, His Diary, Kept When Prisoner at Fort Warren, Boston Harbor, 1865, etc.* (New York: Doubleday, Page, 1910), pp. 64–65.

6. "Speeches on the State of the Confederacy," March 16, 1864, in Henry Cleveland, *Alexander H. Stephens in Public and Private with Letters and Speeches, Before, During and Since the War* (Philadelphia: National Publishing, Co., 1866), p. 765; Alexander H. Stephens, *A Constitutional View of the Late War Between the States etc.*, 2 vols. (Philadelphia: National Publishing, 1868–70), vol. 2, pp. 428, 568–70.

7. General Joseph E. Johnston, *Narrative of Military Operations Directed during the Late War between the States* (New York: D. Appleton, 1874), pp. 421–22; Thomas L. Connelly and Archer Jones, *The Politics of Command: Factions and Ideas in Confederate Strategy* (Baton Rouge: Louisiana State University Press, 1973), p. ix.

8. Edward A. Pollard, *Southern History of the War* (New York: Charles B. Richardson, 1866), vol. 2, pp. 184, 186.

9. Entry of July 7, 1865, in *Inside the Confederate Government: The Diary of Robert Garlich Hill Kean*, ed. Edward Younger (New York: Oxford University Press, 1957), pp. 243–44.

10. General Lee to the Secretary of War, January 7, 1865, in *War of the Rebellion: Armies* (Washington, D.C.: Government Printing Office, 1880–1901), ser. 1, vol. 46, Part 2, p. 1143; see also Bell Irwin Wiley, *The Life of Johnnie Reb: The Common Soldier of the Confederacy* (New York: Bobbs-Merrill, 1943), pp. 134–37.

11. Charles W. Ramsdell, *Behind the Lines in the Southern Confederacy* (Baton Rouge: Louisiana State University Press, 1944), pp. vi–vii.

12. Ramsdell, *Behind the Lines*, pp. 85, 116, 120.

13. Edward A. Pollard, *The Lost Cause: A New Southern History of the War of the Confederates* (New York: E. B. Treat, 1867), pp. 228–29.

14. Wesley C. Mitchell, *A History of the Greenbacks etc.* (1903, repr. Chicago: University of Chicago Press, 1960), pp. 406–12.

15. James M. Mathews, ed., *The Public and Private Laws of the Confederate States of America Passed at the First and Second Congress 1862–64* (Richmond: R. M. Smith, 1864), 3d sess., pp. 94–97, ch. 4.

16. Eugene Lerner, *Money, Prices and Wages in the Confederacy, 1861–65*, (Chicago: Privately mimeographed, 1954), pp. 52, 52a, 165–82.

17. Clinton Rossiter, "Our Two Greatest Presidents," in *A Sense of History: The Best Writings from the Pages of American Heritage* (Boston: Houghton Mifflin, 1985), pp. 108–11.

18. Their grandfathers, during the Revolution, had been under no such delusions and fully recognized that their acts exposed them to execution at the hands of the British. Fortunately, the Radical Republicans did not propose to bestow martyrs' crowns upon the discredited Confederate leaders. Moreover, given the Constitutional requirement that defendants be tried in the vicinage of their alleged crimes, and the possibility that the erstwhile rebels might have their cases dismissed on the ground that secession was legal, one can see why the cases were ultimately dismissed. Thus even the erstwhile Confederate president suffered nothing worse than two years' imprisonment.

19. Entry of August 26, 1863, in *Inside the Confederate Government*, ed. Younger, p. 101.

20. Barbara Jean Fields, "The Advent of Capitalist Agriculture: The New South in the Bourgeois World," *Essays on the Postbellum Southern Economy* (Austin: University of Texas Press, 1985), pp. 73–75. Fields quotes William Faulkner's view of Yankee capitalism in *The Hamlet* (1956). See also Larry Schweikert, *Banking in the American South from the Age of Jackson to Reconstruction* (Baton Rouge: Louisiana State University Press, 1987), pp. 248–54.

21. Message of November 18, 1861, in *A Compilation of the Messages and Papers of the Confederacy*, 2 vols., ed. James D. Richardson (Nashville: United States Publishing, 1906), p. 140.

22. Message of April 19, 1862, in *A Compilation,* comp. Richardson, pp. 216–17. In his first message, Davis vetoed a congressional act calling for the paying of the prize money due to sailors taken prisoner to their wives (thus leaving them destitute) on the ground that only the men involved could determine how their funds should be disbursed. Similarly, he vetoed the bill paying over the pay and allowances of deceased soldiers to their widows and orphans, on the ground it interfered with either the soldiers' wills (most didn't have one) or with the state laws distributing the assets of intestate persons. In this case also, the families were left destitute while the lawyers haggled over the assets.

23. Thomas E. Schott, *Alexander H. Stephens of Georgia: A Biography* (Baton Rouge: Louisiana State University Press, 1988), p. 330.

Appendixes

Possible Alternative Strategy

Had the Confederate leaders possessed a clearer vision of the future, they would have recognized, like George Washington before them, that they could win a war against superior Northern power only by keeping their armed forces intact. Consequently, they might have formulated the following plan.

First, they would form a regular army and navy placed directly under Confederate command that would absorb the West Point and other professional military men.

Second, these forces would not be expected to defend the entire Confederacy; they would concentrate on covering only those key districts where supplies and railroad trunk lines existed. They would pursue a policy of delaying actions, intended to draw Union forces ever deeper into the South, exposing their communications to attack. Offensive actions would be directed at forces at the ends of their supply lines or fractional portions of the Union army.

Third, the Confederate government would serve notice on the public through the mails and newspapers that the border states and other districts, especially those around waterways, were exposed to Union attack. The government would recommend that slaves be removed from vulnerable districts and offer to hire slaves from those regions for the duration of the war, with appropriate insurance and other safeguards for the owners.

Such a step was vital. The border areas needed to be cleared of slaves, since they were a potential Fifth Column for the enemy. Moreover, the Confederate regime needed a labor force for military projects in the interior.

Fourth, the Regular Army could support Confederate guerrilla forces in the border lands by mounting cavalry raids into those areas and furnishing supplies. The four-hundred-thousand-man regular army would cover the main Union invasion routes into the South via the Trans-Mississippi region, the Mississippi River Valley, central and eastern Tennessee, and northern Virginia. Another hundred thousand men would be kept in reserve, deployed to hold key ports, perform training duties, keep track of those who were recuperating from wounds or were on furlough, and round up deserters.

Fifth, as an important element in the program to promote states' rights sentiment and support, an irregular militia ("partisan rangers"), under the command of the governors, would be created and armed by a collaboration of the states with the central government. That portion of this force located in the border areas would engage in guerrilla warfare against the federal forces. The Confederacy would accord them priority of training and arming after the regular army, and their leaders would be appointed by the governors or elected by local personnel.

Freed from the conventional wisdom and prejudices of the West Pointers who habitually disapproved of bushwhacking operations,[1] the guerrillas could have tied up the invaders' forces in garrison duties and compelled all convoys to travel with large escorts, thus diverting thousands of federal troops to local operations. Thus by the time a federal army had penetrated any distance into the Confederacy, the guerrillas might have so reduced the force available to confront the main Confederate army in the area that the Confederates, on the tactical offensive, would have found themselves at a considerable advantage.

As Jefferson Davis himself belatedly put it on April 4, 1865, freed from General Lee's fallacious advice,

> Relieved from the necessity of guarding cities and particular points, important but not vital to our defence, with our army free to move from point to point, and strike in detail the detachments and garrisons of the enemy; operating in the interior of our own country, where supplies are more accessible, and where the foe will be far removed from his own base, and cut off from all succor in case of reverse, nothing is now needed to render our triumph certain, but the exhibition of our own unquenchable resolve. Let us but will it, and we are free. . . .[2]

Yet to be effective, such a strategy had to be put in a context that would make it work. For example, Confederate propaganda emphasized the defense of the soldiers' homes. Yet the retirement of the regular troops left many men's families exposed and, as it turned out, frequently caused an exodus from the retiring forces. Confederate leaders had to emphasize that such retirements were a temporary expedient, preliminary to the execution of the South's tactical plan. Their failure to inform the troops had a deleterious effect on the cause. For example, when General Polk retired from Columbus, Kentucky, his troops misinterpreted a tactical retreat as a defeat, became demoralized, and nearly half the command deserted. Without such desertions, Polk's forces would have provided the extra reserve needed by Beauregard to deliver a knock-out blow to Grant at Shiloh.

Simultaneously, with the other listed options, the Confederacy desperately needed 1) to rationalize the transportation system and particularly the railroads; 2) to import equipment to manufacture war goods; and 3) to set up plants to make weapons, clothing, boots, and other equipment. To operate at full plant capacity, they needed key raw materials. These actions were all vital if any armed force was to be kept in the field.

Similarly, Confederate leaders should have paid due attention to maintaining army and civilian morale. This required sensitivity to the special problems created by the conscription of married men with families. Given the absence of a family allowance system, the Confederate government might well have considered proposing to the state and local governments a system of county and state relief to soldiers' families with a view to obviating hardships at that level. Prompt payment by the Confederate treasury of the soldiers' enlistment bonuses would also have furnished each family with funds to deal with contingencies.

The Confederate government could have promoted friendly relations with the states by providing payments for military expenses incurred and allocating funds for the state-aid program to soldiers' families. Yet there is no evidence that the Confederate government concerned itself directly with such matters. Nor did it even provide for a system of annual leave from the army for soldiers to look after their families.

Even while it was doing what it could to place its armed forces on a sound footing, still other sensible measures were required. A prime desideratum for the Confederate regime was the need to foster a sense of nationality. President Davis needed to tour the entire country on a regular basis heartening the people and focusing their loyalty upon himself and the Confederate cause. By creating and exploiting personal popularity, he could have greatly facilitated the passage of Administrative measures by the Congress.[3]

To further that enterprise, he needed to concentrate on those themes that commanded wide public support. Obviously, slavery with its underlying belief that the South was "a white man's country" would touch a responsive chord, as would an emphasis on states' rights and opposition to federal aggression. He needed to reiterate other Southern grievances such as the abolitionists' vitriolic incitation of hatred for the South[4] and the economic exploitation of the South through the protective tariff and Northern banking and exchange charges.[5] Such speeches would have focused Southern animosity and patriotism against a common foe and fostered resistance to the North.

NOTES

1. Richard S. Brownlee, *Grey Ghosts of the Confederacy. Guerrilla Warfare in the West, 1861–1865* (Baton Rouge: Louisiana State University Press, 1958), pp. 77, 111. President Davis and such commanders in the Trans-Mississippi Department as Major General "Granny" Theophilus Holmes, Lt. General E. Kirby-Smith et al. opposed the use of guerrillas on the grounds of their irregular character and their bad effect on Confederate sympathizers. Generals Sterling Price and Thomas C. Hindman, on the other hand, were well aware of the persecution of pro-Southern people and encouraged the guerrillas, who tied down 120,000 troops and Unionist state guards in Kansas and Missouri.

2. Dunbar Rowland, *Jefferson Davis, Constitutionalist: His Letters, Papers, and Speeches* (Jackson: Mississippi Department of Archives and History, 1923), vol. 6, p. 530.

3. *New York Times*, November 10, 1863, p. 1, reported Davis's one tour and its bolstering effect on Southern morale.

4. Dwight Lowell Dumond, *The Secession Movement 1860–1* (New York: Macmillian, 1921), pp. 115–16, 126–27.

5. Thomas Prentice Kettell, *Southern Wealth and Northern Profits* (1860, repr. University: University of Alabama Press, 1915), pp. 89–99. Kettell estimated that the North got a rake-off on $500 million worth of Southern produce.

Call Certificates

1. *Act of May 16, 1861 as Amended June 14, 1864,* Funding Loan
Terms:
   a. Amount: $20 million.
   b. Denominations: $100 and up in stock or bonds.
   c. Maturity: Ten years after date, but holders might convert their "bonds" back into treasury notes any time before July 1863.
   d. Interest rate: 8 percent.
   e. Total issued:

1. Coupon bonds	$ 3,344,000
2. Registered bonds	8,128,100
Total	$11,472,100

2. *Act of December 24, 1861 as Amended April 12, (18) 1862,* Funding Loan
Terms:
   a. Amount: $80 million of call certificates.
   b. Denominations: Treasury regulation set minimum at $500, or in multiples of $50 above that.
   c. Maturity: "six months after the ratification of a treaty of peace between the Confederate States and the United States. . . . "
   d. Interest rate: 6 percent payable when certificate redeemed.
   e. Total issued: $70,729,030.[1]

3. *Act of March 23, 1863,* Funding Loan
Terms:
   a. Amount: Unlimited.
   b. Denominations: $500 and above.[2]
   c. Maturity: "six months after the ratification of a treaty of peace," at the pleasure of Congress.
   d. Interest rate: 5 percent on notes date stamped less than a year before; 4 percent on notes dated December 2, 1862 or notes date stamped more than one year after issue.
   e. Any certificate not funded within six months of purchase automatically became a thirty-year bond.
   f. Total issued:

5 percent	$72,074,100
4 percent	1,825,000
Total	$73,899,100

4. *February 17, 1864 (Section 7)*
Terms:
   a. Amount: None specified.

  b. Denominations: None specified, but $100 to $100,000.
  c. Maturity: Payable on demand.
  d. Interest rate: 4 percent
  e. Total issued: $135 million.

NOTES

1. Amount listed as redeemed, Secretary's Report, November 7, 1864. Thian, *Reports*, p. 354.
2. Denomination required by Secretary Memminger.
Figures based on *Statutes at Large*, Thian's *Register*, and Ball collection.

Confederate Treasury Notes[1]

Interest-Bearing Notes

1. *Act of March 9, 1861, as Amended August 3, 1861*
Terms:

    a. Amount: $2 million.

    b. Denominations: $50 to $1,000.

    c. Maturity: One year from date, but interest to run for another sixty days.

    d. Payable: To order and transferable by endorsement only.

    e. Interest rate: 3.65 percent payable with principal.

    f. Total issued: $2,021,100.

2. *Act of April 17, 1862*
Terms:

    a. Amount: Up to $165 million in lieu of the April 12, (18) 1862 bonds.

    b. Denomination: $100 or higher.

    c. Maturity: Six months after peace.

    d. Interest rate: 2 cents per day per $100.

    e. Total issued: $128,241,400.

General Currency

1. *May 16, 1861*
Terms:

    a. Amount: $20 million

    b. Denominations: $5 to $100

    c. Maturity: Two years after date (July 25, 1861)

    d. Payable to bearer.

    e. Fundable in ten-year coupon bonds on stock of $100 denomination of higher convertible at the pleasure of the holder back into treasury notes of this act.

    f. Total issued: $17,347,955.

2. *August 19, 1861 as Amended December 24, 1861, April 17, 1862 and September 23, 1862*
Terms:

    a. Amount: $78 million, plus additions of $50 million, $60 million, and finally an unlimited issue privilege.

    b. Denominations: $5 to $100

    c. Maturity: "Six months after a Ratification of a Treaty of Peace between the CSA and USA."

    d. Payable to bearer.

    e. Fundable in 8 percent bonds payable from January 1, 1864 to July 1, 1881.

    f. Total issued: $291,961,830

3. *Act of April 17, 1862, as Amended September 23, 1862*

Terms:

    a. Change bills (i.e., $1 and $2 bills) authorized to the sum of $5 million, later raised to $10 million.

    b. Total issued: $5,600,000

4. *Act of October 13, 1862*

Terms:

    a. Unlimited amount issuable.

    b. Notes dated "December 2, 1862" were made exchangeable for 7 percent bonds until August 1, 1863; then only 4 percent bonds.

Amount Issued:

a. Change bills ($1 and $2 notes):	$ 2,344,800
b. $5 to $100:	$138,056,000

5. *Act of March 23, 1863*

Terms:

    a. Amounts issuable: $50 million per month (April 1863–February 1864).

    b. Fundable in 6 percent bonds until one year after stamped date, then 4 percent bonds.

    c. Exchangeable for 5 percent call certificates.

    d. Payable two years after peace.

    e. Change bill issues extended to $15 million; a 50 cent note ordered. The new change bills were not fundable.

Total Issued:

a. Other notes ($5 to $500):	$514,032,000.00*
b. Change bills ($1 and $2):	3,023,520.00*
c. Fractional notes (50 cents):	915,758.50*
Total	$517,971,278.50

6. *Act of February 17, 1864*

Terms:

    a. No amount specified, but issue was to be limited to $250 million.

    b. $500 denomination approved.

    c. No fixed funding provisions, but a variety of bonds and certificates were available for investment.

    d. Maturity: two years after a ratification of peace.

    e. Tax receivability could be limited by Congress.

    f. Total issued: $460,000,000 (est.)

NOTE

1. Figures based on *Statutes at Large*, Thian's *Register*, and numismatic collections examined by the author.

Confederate Loans 1861–65[1]

Bonds

1. *Act of February 28, 1861,* Specie Loan
Terms:
    a. Amount: $15 million.
    b. Denominations: $50 or higher in stock or bonds.
    c. Maturity: Ten years (September 1, 1871); callable after five years.
    d. Interest rate: 8 percent, bonds to be sold at par in coin. Coupons receivable for export dues.
    e. Total issued: $15 million.

2. *Act of August 19, 1861,* Funding and Produce Loan
Terms:
    a. Amount: $100 million.
    b. Denomination: $50 and above in bonds (stock authorized by the Act of August 27, 1861).
    c. Maturity: various dates, July 1, 1864–July 1, 1881.
    d. Interest rate: 8 percent bonds in lieu of those authorized by the Act of May 16, 1861 above.
    e. Total issued:

1. Coupon bonds	$74,422,700
2. Stock	25,147,850
Total	$99,570,550

3. *Act of April 12, (18) 1862*
Terms:
    a. Amount: $165 million in stock or bonds.
    b. Denominations: $100 and up.
    c. Maturity: Ten years after date, but Congress could extend the loan up to thirty years on same terms.
    d. Interest rate: 8 percent loan to be effected at home or abroad for specie, foreign exchange, or treasury notes.
    e. Total issued:

1. Bonds	$3,839,600
2. Stock	404,450
Total	$4,244,050

4. *February 20, 1863,* Funding Loan
Terms:
    a. Amount: Unlimited.
    b. Denominations: $100 and up in stock or bonds.

    c. Maturity: Five years, but Congress could defer payment up to thirty years at same rate of interest.

    d. Interest rate: 8 percent bonds to be sold to April 21, 1863, and the 7 percent bonds until August 1, 1863.

    e. Total issued:

1. 8 percent stock		$14,912,800
8 percent bonds		81,668,100
	Total	$96,580,900
2. 7 percent stock		$12,758,100
7 percent bonds		54,183,100
	Total	$76,941,200

5. *March 23, 1863*, Funding Loan

Terms:

    a. Amount: Unlimited.

    b. Denominations: $100 and up.

    c. Maturity: Thirty years, but callable after five years

    d. Interest rate: 6 percent and 4 percent, depending upon whether notes were dated April 6, 1863 or December 2, 1862.

    e. Total issued:

1. 6 percent stock		$ 4,278,100
6 percent bonds		16,740,300
		$21,018,400
2. 4 percent bonds		22,300
	Total	$21,040,700

6. *April 30, 1863*, Funding Loan

Terms:

    a. Amount: $100 million.

    b. Denominations: $1,000 only, in coupon bonds.

    c. Maturity: Twenty years, not callable.

    d. Interest rate: 6 percent payable in coin or one five-hundred-pound bale of cotton (cotton at 12 cents per pound).

e. Total issued		$8,393,000
Premiums paid		4,285,000
	Total Yield	$12,678,000

7. *February 17, 1864 (Section 2)*, Funding Loan

Terms:

    a. Amount: Unlimited.

    b. Denominations: $100 to $5,000.

    c. Maturity: Twenty years, not callable.

    d. Interest rate: 4 percent.

    e. Total issued:

1. Bonds		$ 10,183,900
2. Certificates		350,800,000
	Total	$360,983,900

8. *Februray 17, 1864 (Section 6)*, General Expenses
Terms:
    a. Amount: $500 million.
    b. Denominations: $100 to $10,000.
    c. Maturity: Thirty years after date.
    d. Interest rate: 6 percent
    e. Total issued:

1. Amount sold	$60,000,000
2. Premiums paid	20,000,000
Total	$80,000,000

9. *February 17, 1864 (Section 12)* amended June 19, 1864 to fund state held notes.
Terms:
    a. Amount: Unlimited.
    b. Denominations: None specified, but $100 to $1,000.
    c. Maturity: Twenty years.
    d. Interest rate: 4 percent and 6 percent
    e. Total issued:

1. 6 percent bonds	$6,000,000
2. 4 percent bonds	4,000,000
Total	$10,000,000

10. *February 17, 1864 (Section 14)*, General Loan
Terms:
    a. Amount: Unlimited.
    b. Denominations: None specified, but $100 to $10,000.
    c. Maturity: Two years after peace.
    d. Interest rate: 6 percent tax free.
    e. Total issued: $57,392,200 to March 29, 1865[2]

11. *March 17, 1865*
Terms:
    a. Amount: $3 million.
    b. Denominations: None specified.
    c. Maturity: Two years after peace.
    d. Interest rate: 6 percent payable in coin.
    e. Total issued: No bonds issued, but $300,000 seized from the banks on a pledge of bonds.

Total Bonds Issued:	c. $835,000,000

NOTES

1. Figures based on Thian's *Register* and numismatic collections examined by the author.

2. Real sales unknown; amount sent to depositories.

APPENDIX E

I. Erlanger Loan, 1863

Account	Actual Amounts Realized	Face Value of Bonds
1. Sale of bonds at 72	£2,160,000	£3,000,000
2. Repurchase of bonds at average cost of 90	1,234,785	1,388,500
Net Proceeds	£ 926,215	£1,611,500
3. Sale of bonds at 90	23,438	26,000
4. Sale of bonds at 65 average	233,000	358,500[1]
5. Payment of debts to Isaac Campbell & Co.	267,225	300,000
6. Payment of interest, Sept. 1, 1863	(80,360)	—
7. Interest received	8,800	
Net proceeds received	£1,458,678	£2,296,000[2]
Bonds held by the government		£ 704,000

1. Judith Fenner Gentry, "A Confederate Success in Europe: The Erlanger Loan," *Journal of Southern History* 36 (May 1970): 157–58, says only £270,000 face value of bonds were sold for £213,600.
2. Net bonds outstanding.
Sources: Schwab, *CSA*, pp. 35–41, and *O.R.*, 4, vols. 2 and 3; also National Archives Record Group 365, entries 320, 323.

II. Erlanger Loan 1864–65

Transactions	Actual Cash Receipts (Disbursements)	Face Value of Bonds
Carried over from 1863	£1,458,678	£2,296,000
1. Sale of bonds	90,000	195,000
2. Erlanger forfeiture £100,000 cash in lieu of £140,000 of bonds	100,000	—
3. Pledge of bonds to Gillert & Co., etc.	150,000[1]	241,000
4. Redeemed by cotton warrants[2]	—	(148,000)
5. Interest and principal, March 1, 1864 [3]	(137,885)	(50,700)
6. Redeemed by cotton warrants to Sept. 1, 1864	—	(192,100)
7. Interest and principal, Sept. 1, 1864[4]	(127,206)	(51,200)
8. Redeemed by cotton warrants to Oct. 1, 1864	—	(30,000)
Net proceeds	£1,798,678 $8,741,575	£2,019,000[5]

1. Government bond holdings were £473,100–241,000 pledged or £232,000 net.
2. Most cotton warrants were never presented for payment.
3. Less interest on government bonds (£509,000 principal) £17,815 and £20,600 of bonds redeemed.
4. Less interest on government bonds (£488,400 principal) £17,094 and £15,300 of bonds redeemed.
5. Net debt outstanding.

I. Confederate Budget: February 4, 1861–February 18, 1862
(figures in millions)

Actual		Counterfactual	
Revenues		*Revenues*	
Treasury notes	$ 93.7	Treasury notes	$ 97.8
Int.-bearing notes	2.1	Int.-bearing notes	5.0
Call loans	9.8	Call loans	20.0
Specie loans	15.0	Specie loans[3]	45.0
Other funded debt	16.2	Other funded debt[4]	65.0
Unpaid requisitions	26.4	Tax receivable Certificates[5]	50.0
Customs and export dues	1.3	Customs and export dues[3]	2.0
Internal revenue	0	Internal revenue[6]	110.1
Sundry revenue[1]	1.0	Sundry revenue[1] [3]	2.0
Total	$165.5	Total	$398.4
Expenditures		*Expenditures*	
Civil	$ 5.1	Civil	$ 7.5
Public debt	0	Public debt[5]	54.3
War	152.8	Produce purchase	100.0
Navy	7.6	War[7]	190.2
		Navy[7]	10.0
Total	$165.5[2]	Total	$360.3[8]

1. Includes seizure of coin in the mints.
2. $26.4 million of requisitions due, but not paid.
3. Funds paid into the treasury in coin or foreign exchange, principal and interest payable in coin.
4. Funding loans, bonds used for produce purchases, principally payable in treasury notes, the interest in coin.
5. Paid in the form of crudely printed tax certificates paid for produce and receivable in the years 1861–62. Certificates retired as paid in.
6. Total tax revenue would be $160.1 million, $50 million taken in the form of tax receivable produce certificates.
7. About $15 million paid out in foreign exchange abroad.
8. Domestic cash expenditures are balanced at $347.1 million. The treasury holds $30.5 million in coin. See specie account, the foreign account, and the balance sheet.

II. Confederate Budget: February 18–December 31, 1862
(figures in millions)

Actual		Counterfactual	
Revenues		*Revenues*	
Treasury notes	$215.5	Treasury notes	$ 27.2
Int.-bearing notes	96.3	Int.-bearing notes	4.1
Call loans	69.0	Call loans	50.0
Specie loans	3.0	Specie loans[3]	2.0
Other funded debt	47.8	Other funded debt	40.0
Unpaid requisitions	50.0	Unpaid requisitions	0
Customs and export dues	.3	Customs and export dues[3]	1.5
Internal taxes	16.7	Internal taxes[4]	175.0
Sundry revenue	2.3	Sale of goods in CSA[5]	84.0
		Sale of foreign exchange	3.0
Total	$501.4[1]	Total	$394.9
Expenditures		*Expenditures*	
Civil	413.7	Civil	$ 10.2
Public debt[2]	46.7	Public debt[6]	21.0
War	366.0	War[5]	334.1
Navy	22.0	Navy[5]	20.8
Unpaid requisitions	50.0	Unpaid requisitions	0
Total	$498.4[1] [7]	Total	$386.3[7]

1. Difference held in Louisiana bank gold.
2. Redemption of call certificates $10.6 million; interest $5.9 million; redemption of notes $30.2 million.
3. Duties and loans payable only in coin.
4. Includes $70 million from 1861. $30 million from 1862 deferred to 1863, $55 million uncollectable due to invasions.
5. See foreign accounts, $15 million of army and navy bills paid abroad.
6. $8.7 million paid in coin or foreign exchange, $10 million in call certificates redeemed in interest paid on call loans and interest-bearing treasury notes.
7. Real Confederate currency worth 33 cents; putative currency probably worth about 80 cents. Domestic cash flow balanced at $362.4 million. Domestic coin reserve about $29.9 million.

III. Confederate Budget: January 1–October 31, 1863 (figures in millions)

Actual		Counterfactual	
Revenues		*Revenues*	
Treasury notes	$383.4	Treasury notes	$ 14.1
Int.-bearing notes	8.2	Int.-bearing notes	71.9
Call loans	23.5	Call loans	30.0
Specie loans	0	Specie loans[3]	2.0
Other funded debt	154.8	Other funded debt[4]	30.0
Unpaid requisitions	75.0	Unpaid requisitions	0
Customs and export dues	.9	Customs and export dues[3]	1.8
Internal revenue	4.1	Internal revenue	151.8
Sundry revenue[1]	26.5	Sale of goods in CSA	62.6
		Sale of foreign exchange	5.0
Total	$676.4	Total	$369.2
Expenditures		*Expenditures*	
Civil	11.7	Civil	$ 11.5
Public debt[2]	156.2	Public debt[4]	23.9
War	378.0	War[5]	318.1
Navy	38.4	Navy[5]	30.7
Unpaid requisitions	75.0	Unpaid requisitions	0
Total	$659.3[6]	Total	$384.2[6]

1. Includes $24.5 million of repayments by disbursing officers.
2. Includes $32.2 million public debt and $124.6 million note cancellations
3. Payable only in coin, or interest paid in coin.
4. $9.3 interest, payable in coin; $14.6 principal, in paper, $3.25 million of which
   was in interest, the balance in redemptions.
5. $15 million paid for abroad.
6. Notes in actuality worth 20 cents; counterfactual value 70 cents. Domestic cash
   balance expenditures, $369.2 million

IV. Confederate Budget: November 1, 1863–October 31, 1864
(figures in millions)

Actual		Counterfactual	
Revenues		*Revenues*	
Treasury notes	$ 543.3	Treasury notes[2]	$132.3
Int.-bearing notes	0	Int.-bearing notes	25.0
Call loans	61.2	Call loans[3]	50.0
Specie loans	10.7	Specie loans[3]	2.0
Other funded debt	302.5	Other funded debt[4]	342.7
Unpaid requisitions	225.0	Unpaid requisitions	0
Customs and export dues	.5	Customs and export dues	2.0
Internal revenue	117.7	Internal revenue	148.0
Sundry revenue[1]	70.7	Sale of goods in CSA	85.2
		Exchange of sterling for coin	5.0
Total	$1,331.6	Total	$792.2[7]
Expenditures		*Expenditures*	
Civil	$ 16.0	Civil	$ 15.0
Public debt	557.2	Public debt[5]	337.3
War	485.0	War[6]	442.2
Navy	26.5	Navy[6]	23.3
Unpaid requisitions	225.0	Unpaid requisitions	0
Total	$1,309.7	Total	$826.0[8]

1. Included $62.9 million of repayments by disbursing officers.
2. $60.4 old issue; $72 new issue.
3. $30 million old issue; $20 million new issue.
4. Forced funding of $199.5 of currency and $100 million in call certificates.
5. $19.5 million in coin interest paid; $8.3 for redemption of due debt and call certificates; $10.1 million of paper interest; $299.5 conversion of debt.
6. $20 million paid abroad.
7. Cash disbursements balance at $475.5 million.
8. Currency worth between 40 cents and 80 cents for the new issue.

Specie Account (figures in millions)

Counterfactual

February 4, 1861–February 18, 1862

Receipts		*Expenditures*	
1. Specie loan[1]	$45.0	1. To credit of agents abroad (foreign exchange)	$15.0
2. Customs dues	2.0	2. Interest on the domestic debt	3.5
3. Seizures and post office	2.0		
Total	$49.0	Total	$18.5
Closing Balance	$30.5		

February 18–December 31, 1862

Receipts		*Expenditures*	
1. Opening balance	$30.5	1. Interest on the public debt	$ 8.7
2. Specie loans	2.0		
3. Customs receipts	1.5		
4. Shipped from Europe	5.0		
Total	$38.6		$ 8.7
Closing balance	$29.9		

January 1–October 31, 1863

Receipts		*Expenditures*	
1. Opening balance	$29.9	1. Interest and principal on the public debt	$ 9.3
2. Specie loans	2.0		
3. Customs receipts	1.8		
4. Sale of exchange for coin	2.5		
Total	$36.2	Total	$9.3
Closing Balance	$26.9		

(Continued)

November 1, 1863–October 31, 1864

Receipts		*Expenditures*	
1. Opening balance	$26.9	1. Interest on debt	$22.0
2. Specie loans	2.0		
3. Customs receipts	2.0		
4. Coin purchased with exchange, etc.	15.0		
Total	$40.2	Total	$22.0[2]
Closing Balance	$18.9		

1. Includes receipt of bills of exchange, worth about $15 million.
2. Balance $18.9 million, a sum sufficient to pay the interest on the debt with normal loans and specie income of $6 million in coin until after July 1, 1865. Curiously, President Davis refused to allow purchases of needed supplies through the land blockade at the end of 1862 because he thought that the federal government was going to be bankrupt (suspend specie payments) on January 1, 1863. Why Davis thought the Union would have to give up the war because of a specie payments suspension, when the Confederates had continued with one, is not reported. See Richard D. Goff, *Confederate Supply* (Durham, N.C.: Duke University Press, 1969), p. 116.

Foreign Account (figures in millions)

Counterfactual

February 4, 1861–February 18, 1862

Receipts		Expenditures	
1. From CSA in bills	$15.0	1. Purchase of ships[2]	$10.0
2. From foreign loan	25.0	2. Military purchases	9.0
3. Sale of produce[1]	0	3. Purchase of civil goods[3]	9.0
		4. Ship operating expense	4.5
Total	$40.0	Total	$32.5

Balance $7.5 million

February 18–December 31, 1862

Receipts		Expenditures	
1. To balance	$ 7.5	1. Purchase of ships[2]	$ 3.0
2. To sales of produce net[1]	63.0	2. Military purchases	15.0
		3. Purchase of civil goods[3]	40.0
		4. Shipment of coin to CSA	5.0
		5. Interest and principal of debt	3.2
		6. Sale of exchange	1.5
Total	$70.5	Total	$67.7

Balance of $2.7 million

January 1–October 31, 1863

Receipts		Expenditures	
1. To balance	$ 2.7	1. Purchase of ships[6]	$ 2.0
2. Sales of produce[4]	47.3	2. Military purchases	15.0
		3. Purchase of civil goods	24.0
		4. Interest and principal of debt	3.2
		5. Sale of exchange	5.0
Total	$50.0	Total	$49.2

Balance $.8 million

(Continued)

November 1, 1863–October 31, 1864

Receipts		*Expenditures*	
1. To balance	$ 0.8	1. Purchase of ships[6]	$ 2.0
2. Sales of produce[5]	81.0	2. Military purchases	20.0
		3. Purchase of civil goods	40.0
		4. Interest and principal of debt	3.0
		5. Sale of exchange	5.0
		6. Transmittal of coin	10.0
Total	$81.8	Total	$80.0

Balance $1.8 million

1. Ninety thousand bales of five hundred pounds shipped in 1861–62; 360,000 more bales shipped to the end of 1862. Sales: four hundred thousand bales at 32 cents per pound (includes a one-time sale of long staple sea island cotton).
2. Ships to be purchased or leased to run the blockade, $200,000 each.
3. Items to include railroad equipment, factory parts, clothing, shoes, and other necessities; goods shipped to the Confederacy and held until early 1862 for sale.
4. 300,000 bales sold (270,000 shipped); price 35 cents per pound.
5. 360,000 bales sold (340,000 shipped); price 45 cents per pound.
6. Assumes more ships have to be bought to replace those captured or lost.

APPENDIX I

I. Confederate Government's Balance Sheet (figures in millions)

Counterfactual

February 4, 1861–February 18, 1862

Assets		Liabilities	
1. Coin in hand	$ 30.5	1. Treasury notes	$ 97.8
2. Goods in hand[1]	9.0	2. Int.-bearing notes	5.0
3. Ships owned[1]	10.0	3. Call certificates	20.0
4. Produce held[1]	100.0	4. Domestic funded debt	110.0
5. Cash held abroad	7.5	5. Foreign debt	25.0
Total	$157.0	Total	$257.8

Net Debt: $100.8 Million

Assets		Liabilities	
1. Coin in hand	$ 29.9	1. Treasury notes	$125.0
2. Goods in hand[1] [3]	2.3	2. Int.-bearing notes	9.1
3. Ships owned[2]	10.6	3. Call certificates	70.0
4. Produce held[1] [3]	69.4	4. Domestic funded debt	152.0
5. Cash held abroad	2.7	5. Foreign debt	23.8
Total	$114.9	Total	$379.1

Net Debt: $264.2 Million

January 1–October 31, 1863

Assets		Liabilities	
1. Coin in hand	$26.9	1. Treasury notes	$139.1
2. Goods in hand[4]	.3	2. Int.-bearing notes	81.0
3. Ships owned[5]	11.2	3. Call certificates	100.0
4. Produce held[6]	47.2	4. Domestic funded debt	184.0
5. Cash held abroad	.8	5. Foreign debt	22.5
Total	$86.4	Total	$526.6

Net Debt: $440.2 Million

(Continued)

November 1, 1863–October 31, 1864

Assets		*Liabilities*	
1. Coin in hand	$ 18.9	1. Treasury notes	$ 72.0
2. Goods in hand	1.0	2. Int.-bearing notes	121.9
3. Ships owned[7]	10.0	3. Call certificates	20.0
4. Produce held[8]	36.2	4. Domestic funded debt	526.7
5. Cash held abroad	1.8	5. Foreign debt	21.3
6. Tax arrears and interest	100.0		
Total	$167.5	Total	$761.9

Net Debt: $594.4 Million[9]

1. At cost.
2. Presumes 1 percent losses in 1861; 10 percent, 1862; 14 percent, 1863; 18 percent, 1864.
3. The value of the cotton would be about $173.5 million, and the real debt therefore $158.2 million.
4. Goods worth about $.7 million.
5. One ship in seven captured.
6. Produce worth $165.2 million
7. One ship in six captured.
8. Worth $140.4 million.
9. The actual net indebtedness would be $490.2 million.

II. Actual Accumulated Confederate Indebtedness
(figures in millions)

To: January 1, 1863
1. Treasury notes	$ 288.7
2. Interest-bearing notes	121.8
3. Call certificates	62.7
4. Funded debt (8 percent)	82.6
5. Arrears in payments	50.0
Total	$ 605.8[1]

To: January 1, 1864
1. Treasury notes	$ 688.6
2. Interest-bearing notes	102.5
3. Call certificates	89.2
4. Funded debt (8 percent)	223.2
5. Funded debt (7 percent)	63.6
6. Funded debt (6 percent)	11.1
7. Arrears in payment	150.0
8. Foreign debt	11.5
Total	$1,339.7

To: October 31, 1864
1. Treasury notes	$ 608.1[2]
2. Interest-bearing notes	100.5
3. Call certificates	56.9
4. Funded debt	738.3
5. Arrears in payments	350.0
6. Foreign debt	8.7
Total	$1,862.5

1. The government's only available asset was $35 million of produce, most of which was subsequently destroyed.
2. After forced funding act.

Counterfactual CSA Merchandise Account (in coin; figures in millions)

		Coin Sales Price
January 1, 1862–March 31, 1862		
1. Purchases to 1/1/62	$ 9.0	
2. Purchases to 3/31/62	11.3	
3. Less sales (retail)	(12.0)	$19.2
4. Merchandise balance	8.3	
April 1, 1862–June 30, 1862		
1. Carry forward	$ 8.3	
2. Purchases to 6/30/62	10.0	
3. Less sales (retail)	(12.0)	$20.4
4. Merchandise balance	6.3	
July 1, 1862–September 30, 1862		
1. Carry forward	$ 6.3	
2. Purchases to 9/30/62	10.0	
3. Less sales (retail)	(12.0)	$21.6
4. Merchandise balance	4.3	
October 1, 1862–December 31, 1862		
1. Carry forward	$ 4.3	
2. Purchases	10.0	
3. Less sales (retail)	(12.0)	$22.8
4. Merchandise balance	2.3	
January 1, 1863–March 31, 1863		
1. Carry forward	$ 2.3	
2. Purchases	8.0	
3. Less sales (retail)	(9.0)	$18.0
4. Merchandise balance	1.3	
April 1, 1863–June 30, 1863		
1. Carry forward	$ 1.3	
2. Purchases	8.0	
3. Less sales (retail)	(9.0)	$18.9
4. Merchandise balance	.3	
July 1, 1863–September 30, 1863		
1. Carry forward	$ .3	
2. Purchases	8.0	
3. Less sales (retail)	(8.3)	$18.3
4. Merchandise balance	–0–	

(Continued)

October 1, 1863–December 31, 1863

1. Carry forward	$ –0–	
2. Purchases	10.0	
3. Less sales (retail)	(9.7)	$22.3
4. Merchandise balance	.3	

January 1, 1864–March 31, 1864

1. Carry forward	$ .3	
2. Purchases	10.0	
3. Less sales (retail)	(9.3)	$22.3
4. Merchandise balance	1.0	

April 1, 1864–June 30, 1864

1. Carry forward	$ 1.0	
2. Purchases	10.0	
3. Less sales (retail)	(10.0)	$25.0
4. Merchandise balance	1.0	

July 1, 1864–September 30, 1864

1. Carry forward	$ 1.0	
2. Purchases	10.0	
3. Less sales (retail)	(10.0)	$26.0
4. Merchandise balance	1.0	

APPENDIX K

Counterfactual Confederate Produce Purchase Accounts

1861: **Purchase Accounts**
    1. Cotton purchases ($95 million)   1,900,000 bales
    2. Tobacco, etc.   ($ 5 million)
  Shipments and Losses
    1. Foreign shipments   90,000 bales
    2. Losses on ships, burnt, etc.   20,000 bales
                           110,000 bales
          Total Left   1,790,000 bales

1862: **Purchase Accounts**
    1. Leftover   1,790,000 bales
    2. Produce loans, tax receipts   50,000 bales
                         1,840,000 bales
  Shipments and Losses
    1. Foreign shipments   360,000 bales
    2. Losses on ships, burnt, etc.   92,000 bales
                         452,000 bales
          Total Left   1,388,000 bales

1863: **Purchase Accounts**
    1. Leftover   1,388,000 bales
    2. Produce loans, etc.   50,000 bales
                         1,438,000 bales
  Shipments and Losses
    1. Foreign shipments   360,000 bales
    2. Losses on ships, burnt, etc. 144,000 bales
                         504,000 bales
          Total Left   884,000 bales

1864: **Purchase Accounts**
    1. Leftover   884,000 bales
    2. Cotton purchases and produce 100,000 bales
  loan
                         984,000 bales
  Shipments and Losses
    1. Foreign shipments   270,000 bales
    2. Losses on ships, burnt, etc.   90,000 bales
                         360,000 bales
          Total Left   624,000 bales

What Defeat Cost the South

Only rarely in the annals of nations do mistaken economic policies result in such swift and condign punishment. The defeat of the Confederate bid for independence cost the South the flower of its manpower. To this must be added the white Confederates' psychological trauma of defeat, occupation, and the rule of the loathed carpetbaggers. In its train, Reconstruction also brought even more extensive corruption and waste than might otherwise have occurred, and the Republicans did saddle the South with unfair economic policies that inhibited economic recovery for decades thereafter.

In 1925, James L. Sellers attempted to ascertain the direct cost of the Civil War to the South. He concluded that Confederate expenditures from taxes, loans, and treasury notes came to approximately $522 million. To this he added the value of produce collected by taxes (he made no provision for impressments) and $67 million of repudiated state debts (actually nearer $90 million if city and county obligations are included) which he valued at 60 cents on the dollar. This gave a total of $572 million in gold, or $102 per capita for the free population. By contrast, he calculated the average cost to the North at $140 per capita.[1]

In any inflationary period it is customary to look for income and property redistribution and to ascertain who benefited and who suffered. In this case, the only obvious beneficiaries were emancipated slaves. Holders of all Southern property, whether real or personal, suffered heavily in the loss of their slaves, the devastation of real property, the collapse of the banking system, the repudiation or scaling of state bonds, and the collapse of corporate security prices. Only those who prudently withdrew their capital from the South could have avoided the general ruin.

In monetary terms, the 1860 census had estimated the value of Southern property at approximately $7.2 billion, of which $2.4 billion was in the form of slaves. While it is fashionable today to exclude the slaves from property loss valuations, that practice seems to me misleading because slaves formed a valuable source of income and provided, like other movable property, a source of limited liquidity to the Southern economy.

In 1870, after emancipation, the net value of all Southern property had sunk to a real, as opposed to appraised, value of $2.05 billion. Because values were expressed in greenbacks worth approximately eighty cents on the dollar in gold, total Southern losses can be estimated at an appalling $5.56 billion, or almost 76 percent of Southern gross worth in 1860. If one couples with this the further attrition during Reconstruction, it is amazing that the South managed to produce even 10 percent of the U.S. Gross National Product by 1880.[2]

In an article in the *Journal of Economic History*, Claudine Golden and Frank Lewis have tried to quantify all Southern losses from the Civil War. Some figures suggest, depending on three variables, a total of anywhere from $7.8 billion to $8.5 billion.[3] But regardless of the amounts settled upon, the cost was enormous, and slaveholders clearly foolish in their refusal to pay taxes and to back the Confederacy to the utmost extent of their means.

NOTES

1. James L. Sellers, "An Interpretation of Civil War Finance," *American Historical Review* 30 (October 1924–July 1925):282–97.

2. James L. Sellers, "The Economic Incidence of the Civil War in the South," in Ralph Andreano, *The Economic Impact of the American Civil War* (Cambridge: Schenkman Publishing, 1967), pp. 98–106. Originally published in *Mississippi Valley Historical Review* 14 (1927):179–91.

3. Claudine D. Golden and Frank D. Lewis, "The Economic Cost of the American Civil War: Estimates and Implications," *Journal of Economic History* 35 (June 1978):299–326.

Bibliography

I. Primary Sources

A. Manuscripts

The bulk of the Confederate archival records are now deposited at the National Archives Building in Washington, D.C. These records, divided between those acquired by the War Department and those purchased by the treasury, are broken into a multiplicity of record groups, each with overlapping materials. Basically, the treasury records consist of correspondence (incoming and outgoing) to and from the various offices and bureaus, vouchers, account books, records of War, Navy, and treasury warrants, books for entering the issues of notes and bonds, and ledgers for entering tax revenues.

Each record group's contents fall into two categories: loose papers either wrapped up in bundles and envelopes or held in boxes; and records kept in bound volumes. Particularly useful were Record Groups 56 (100 boxes and 132 manuscript volumes), Record Group 109 (several hundred volumes), and Record Group 365 (primarily loose correspondence). Items in the following list labeled "chapter 8" refer to Miscellaneous Correspondence with the Treasury Department (although less than half are that), and items labeled "chapter 10" are treasury records per se.

R. G. 36: War Department. Collection of Confederate Records (Register of civil warrants, March 28, 1861–June 20, 1864). National Archives, Washington, D.C.

R. G. 56: Treasury Department. Archives of the Confederate Treasury Department. National Archives, Washington, D.C.

Boxes 23–24: Louisiana, cotton transactions (DeBow's).
Box 45: Texas, Cotton Bureau 1864–65 papers.
Box 89: Partial lists of Confederate depositories.
Box 90: Foreign correspondence: Erlanger loan papers.
Box 91: Foreign correspondence relating to building of war vessels in Europe.
Boxes 92–93: Miscellaneous correspondence to secretary of treasury relating to finance, printing of notes, bonds, auditor's certificates, cotton, etc.
Boxes 94–95: Confederate papers relating to sales of cotton in Europe.
Box 96: Confederate papers relating to Erlanger cotton loan; building Confed-

erate cruisers in France; Fraser, Trenholm & Co.; letters to C. J. McRae, Memminger, Erlanger, S. A. Duncan, et al.

Box 99: Confederate papers relating to petition of Richmond banks for return of captured gold; reports of F. E. Spinner and Loomis on same.

No. 46: Texas. "Records" containing organization and transactions of Texas Cotton Bureau in 1863. Col. W. J. Hutchins, chief of bureau.

No. 62B: Confederate treasurer . . . at New Orleans.

No. 103: Record of miscellaneous warrants. Treasury Department, March 29, 1861–April 6, 1864.

No. 111B: Record book of copies of letters of secretary of treasury, March 1, 1861–October 12, 1861.

No. 115F: Record book of copies of letters of secretary of treasury, October 17, 1864–March 31, 1865.

No. 121A: Letters addressed by Lewis Cruger, comptroller of the currency, March 23, 1861–December 16, 1861, comptroller's office; letter book B., United States Depository. New Orleans/A. J. May 14, 1853–May 11, 1865; letters from secretaries to comptroller's office, January 10, 1862–June 11, 1863; press copies of letters, restricted intercourse, June 1–30, 1865. Treasury Dept.; telegrams of the Confederate Treasury Department, February 27, 1861–July 30, 1864. Telegram messages, Treasury Dept.

R. G. 93: War Department Collection of Confederate Records. Congressional papers, speeches, and reports (loose documents), including hand drafts of the reports of the secretaries of the treasury to Congress. National Archives, Washington, D.C.

R. G. 94: Miscellaneous documents including printed drafts of legislative bills or amendments to bills.

Chap. 8, vol. 323: Miscellaneous correspondence with Confederate Treasury Department.

Chap. 8, vol. 325: "Cato on Constitutional Money and Legal Tender." In twelve numbers from the Charleston *Mercury*, 1862.

Chap. 10, vol. 99: Register of treasury notes.

Chap. 10, vol. 118: Correspondence of the register of the treasury.

Chap. 10, vol. 125–54: Journals of transferable stock and coupon bonds, Acts of February 28, May 16, August 19, 1861, February 20, 1863.

Chap. 10, vol. 163: Letters and telegrams of the secretary's office, February 23, 1861–July 3, 1861; May 2, 1862–October 11, 1862.

Chap. 10, vol. 164: Collector's correspondence, secretary's offices, March 21, 1861–January 29, 1862.

Chap. 10, vol. 165: Letters and telegrams of the secretary's office, Treasury Department, 1861–63.

Chap. 10, vol. 189: Loan lists.

Chap. 10, vol. 191: Record Book B, office of commissioner of taxes.

Chap. 10, vol. 207: Accounts of receivers under sequestration act, register's office.

Chap. 10, vol. 221: Record of civil and miscellaneous warrants of the fiscal years 1861–62.
Chap. 10, vol. 252: Record of civil warrants of Confederate Treasury, February 23, 1861–December 31, 1861.
Chap. 10, vol. 257: Record of civil warrants, January 1, 1863 and December 31, 1863.
Chap. 10, vol. 261: Record of civil warrants, January 1, 1864–April 30, 1864.
Chap. 10, vol. 264: Orders and circulars of Treasury Department.
R. G. 135: Archives of the Confederate Treasury Department 1861–65. Treasury Department, National Archives, Washington, D.C.
Chap. 10, vol. 103: Register of miscellaneous warrants.
Chap. 10, vol. 165: Correspondence of the secretary, January 30, 1862–October 29, 1862.
Chap. 10, vol. 175: Register of call certificates and bonds issued, June 1, 1863–January 1865. (Part of this information is also to be found in Vol. 179.)
Entry 8: Letters received by the secretary of the treasury, 1861–65 (now Microcopy M–499). 26 boxes loose papers.
Entry 323: Records relating to Erlanger loan, Box 96.

B. Papers

The utility of the manuscripts outside those held by the Archives and the Library of Congress is limited. Most of Secretary Memminger's personal correspondence was destroyed in the burning of Columbia in 1865; the papers that are left are of limited value. I was, however, fortunate enough to be able to consult with the Erlanger family papers, which tell a great deal about that family's warm relations with Slidell. Unfortunately, at the time of the Erlanger merger with Hill Samuel, Ltd., Leo Erlanger's nephew burned a substantial portion of the company records. The two books covering the Erlanger loan did show that Fraser Trenholm handled all transactions but the loan. Efforts to consult the Baring Papers for a possible connection with the Confederacy proved abortive, as they were closed pending a multivolume history of the firm.

British Foreign Office Papers. America. Dispatches (vol. 781, part ii).
Campbell-Colson Papers. MS. Division, University of North Carolina, Chapel Hill.
Clark, Micajah H. "The Last Days of the Confederate Treasury and What Became of Its Specie." Southern Historical Society Papers. 38 vols. January–December, 1881, vol. 9. Clark was the acting treasurer in May 1865.
Howell Cobb Papers. MS. Department, Duke University, Durham, N.C. Confederate Note and Bond Album. Confederate States of America Collection. MS. Division, Library of Congress, Washington, D.C. A similar album is in MS. Dept., Duke University.

Jefferson Davis Papers. MS. Department, Duke University, Durham, N.C.
James D. B. DeBow Papers. MS. Department, Duke University, Durham, N.C.
Erlanger (family and business papers of), in possession of Leo D'Erlanger.
William A. Graham Papers. MS. Division, University of North Carolina, Chapel Hill.
James H. Hammond Papers. MS. Division, Library of Congress, Washington, D.C.
Charles C. Jones, Jr., ed. Autograph letters and portraits of the signers of the Constitution of the Confederate states. MS. Department, Duke University, Durham, N.C.
Christopher Gustavus Memminger Papers. MS. Department, Duke University, Durham, N.C.
Christopher Gustavus Memminger Papers. MS. Division, University of North Carolina, Chapel Hill.
John T. Pickett Papers. MS. Division, Library of Congress, Washington, D.C.
Ruffin Papers. MS. Division, University of North Carolina, Chapel Hill.
Raphael P. Thian, comp., Confederate notes with description of emblems, 1861–64. MS. Department, Duke University, Durham, N.C.
———. Confederate States of America. Treasury Department notes and bonds, 1861–65. MS. Department, Duke University, Durham, N.C.
George A. Trenholm Papers. MS. Department, Duke University, Durham, N.C.
———. vol. 1 (1853–66):1510. MS. Division, Library of Congress, Washington, D.C.

C. Primary Materials in Print

Undoubtedly the most important of these, from the viewpoint of utility, are the four volumes by Raphael P. Thian. Examination of the original records from which Thian drew his materials (now deposited in the National Archives) has shown a high degree of accuracy. For this reason, even though I may have seen the original reports, letter, or ledger entries on note issues, I use the Thian books for ease of citation. Archival letters are used only when unavailable in Thian.

The Thian works consist of a complete summary of the bound volumes relating to the issues of notes and bonds (*Register*), all of the secretaries' reports and those of their chief subordinates (*Reports*), and more than 2,500 letters to and from the Treasury Department and its officers (*Correspondence of* and *Correspondence with*). Arranged by date, these latter volumes permit the reader to follow Secretary Memminger's line of reasoning and programs with regard to the advice being given to him. They also contain the thinking of many important people in the Confederacy, including cabinet members and other Confederate officials, state officers, and prominent citizens.

Alabama, Controller of. *Biennial Report of the Controller of Public Accounts, etc.* Montgomery: Shorter and Reid, 1861.

Alabama Legislature. *Acts of the Called Session of the General Assembly of Alabama, Held in the City of Montgomery, Commencing on the Second Monday in January, 1861.* Montgomery: Shorter and Reid, 1861.

————. *Acts of the Second Called Session of the General Assembly of Alabama, Held in the City of Montgomery, Commencing on the 27th day of October and Second Monday in November, 1861.* Montgomery: Montgomery Advertiser Book and Job Office, 1862.

————. *Acts of the Called Session 1862, and of the Second Regular Annual Session of the General Assembly of Alabama Held in the City of Montgomery, Commencing on the 27th day of October and Second Monday in November, 1862.* Montgomery: Montgomery Advertiser Book and Job Office, 1862.

Benton, Thomas H., ed. *Abridgement of the Debates of Congress from 1789 to 1856 from Gales and Secton's Annals of Congress.* 16 vols. New York: D. Appleton, 1860.

Blair and Rivers, ed. *The Congressional Globe Containing Sketches of the Debates and Proceedings . . . 1834–1865.*

Bureau of the Census. *Agriculture in the United States in 1860.* Eighth Census. Washington, D.C.: Government Printing Office, 1864.

————. *Historical Statistics of the United States, Colonial Times to 1957.* Washington, D.C.: Government Printing Office, 1960.

————. *Manufacturers of the United States in 1860.* Eighth Census. Washington, D.C.: Government Printing Office, 1865.

————. *Population of the United States in 1860.* Eighth Census. Washington, D.C.: Government Printing Office, 1864.

————. *Statistics of the United States (Including Mortality, Property, etc.) in 1860.* Eighth Census. Washington, D.C.: Government Printing Office, 1866.

Bureau of the Mint. *Report of U.S. Director of the Mint.* Washington, D.C.: Government Printing Office, 1862.

Clark, Walter, ed. *The State Records of North Carolina.* 26 vols. Goldsboro: Nash Bros., 1905.

Calhoun, John C. *The Writings of John C. Calhoun.* Edited by Richard K. Cralle. 6 vols. New York: D. Appleton, 1854–59.

————. *The Papers of John C. Calhoun.* Edited by Robert L. Merriwether. 6 vols. Columbia: University of South Carolina Press, 1959–72.

Cleveland, Henry. *Alexander H. Stephens in Public and Private with Letters and Speeches, Before, During and Since the War.* Philadelphia: National Publishing, 1866.

Congress. *Tariff Acts Passed by the Congress of the United States from 1789–1909. Including All Acts, Resolutions, and Proclamations Modifying or Changing Those Acts.* H. of R. 61st Cong., 2d sess., doc. no. 671. Washington, D.C.: Government Printing Office, 1909.

————. *Miscellaneous Documents.* H. of R., 36th Cong., 2d sess., no. 20. Washington, D.C.: Government Printing Office, 1861.

Davis, Andrew MacFarlane, ed. *Colonial Currency Reprints 1682–1751*. 4 vols. Boston: Prince Society, 1910–11.

Davis, Jefferson. *Jefferson Davis, Constitutionalist: His Letters, Papers, and Speeches*. Edited by Rowland Dunbar. 10 vols. Jackson: Mississippi Department of Archives and History, 1923.

Florida Legislature. *The Acts and Resolutions Adopted by the General Assembly of Florida, at Its Eleventh Session, Begun and Held at the Capitol, in the City of Tallahassee, on Monday, November 18, 1861*. Tallahassee: Office of the Floridian and Journal. Printed by Dyke and Carlisle, 1862.

Franklin, Benjamin. *The Complete Works of Benjamin Franklin etc*. Edited by John Bigelow. 10 vols. New York: G. P. Putnam's Sons, 1887–88.

Gallatin, Albert. *The Writings of Albert Gallatin*. Edited by Henry Adams. 4 vols. Philadelphia: J. B. Lippincott, 1879.

Gallatin, James. *Two Letters to the Hon. S. P. Chase, Secretary of the Treasury*. New York: Hosford and Ketcham, 1861.

Garrison, George P., ed. "Texas Diplomatic Correspondence." *Annual Report of the American Historical Association*. 3 vols. Washington, D.C.: Government Printing Office, 1908–11.

Georgia Comptroller General. *Annual Report of the Comptroller General of the State of Georgia Made to the Governor, October 16, 1862*. Milledgeville: Broughton, Nisbet and Barnes, 1862.

———. *Annual Report of the Comptroller General's Office, October 17, 1864*. Milledgeville: Broughton, Nisbet, Barnes and Moore, State Printers, 1864.

Georgia Legislature. *Acts of the General Assembly of the State of Georgia, Passed in Milledgeville, at an Annual Session in November and December, 1861*. Milledgeville: Broughton, Nisbet, and Barnes, State Printers, 1862.

———. *Acts of the General Assembly of the State of Georgia, Passed in Milledgeville, at an Annual Session in November and December, 1862; Also Extra Session of 1863*. Milledgeville: Broughton, Nisbet, and Barnes, State Printers, 1863.

Green, Duff. *Facts and Suggestions Relative to Finance and Currency Directed to the President of the Confederate States of America*. Augusta: J. T. Paterson, 1864.

Hamilton, Alexander. *Papers on Public Credit, Commerce and Finance*. Edited by Samuel McKee, Jr. New York: Columbia University Press, 1934.

Hamilton, Joseph Gregoire de Roulhac, ed. *Papers of Randolph Abbott Shotwell*. Raleigh: North Carolina Historical Commission, 1929.

Hindman, Thomas C. *Report of Major General Hindman of His Operations in the Trans-Mississippi District*. Richmond: R. M. Smith, 1864.

Huntington, A. T., and Robert J. Mawhinney, comps. *Laws of the United States Concerning Money, Banking and Loans, 1778–1909*. Sen., 61st Cong., 2d sess., doc. no. 480. Washington, D.C.: Government Printing Office, 1910.

Israel, Fred L., ed. *The State of the Union Messages of the Presidents 1790–1860*. New York: Chelsea House Publishers, 1967.

Journal of the Congress of the Confederate States of America, 1861–1865. 7 vols. Washington, D.C.: Government Printing Office, 1904–5.

Jefferson, Thomas. *The Writings of Thomas Jefferson.* Edited by Paul L. Ford. 10 vols. New York: G. P. Putnam's Sons, 1897.

Louisiana Legislature. *Acts Passed by the Sixth Legislature of the State of Louisiana, at Its First Session, Held and Begun in the City of Baton Rouge, on the 25th Day of November, 1861.* Baton Rouge: Tom Bynum, State Printer, 1861.

Manarin, Louis A., ed. *Richmond at War, Minutes of the City Council 1861–5.* Chapel Hill: University of North Carolina Press, 1965.

Marshall, John. *The Writings of John Marshall Late Chief Justice of the United States upon the Federal Constitution.* Boston: James Munroe, 1839.

Martin, Thomas T., ed. "Correspondence of William Gregg," *Journal of Southern History* 2 (August 1945):414.

Mathews, James M., ed. *Public Laws of the CSA, Passed at the Third Session of the First Congress, 1863.* Richmond: T. M. Smith, 1863.

———. *Public and Private Laws of the Confederate States of America, Passed at the First and Second Congresses, 1862–64.* Richmond: R. M. Smith, 1864.

———. *The Statutes at Large of the Provisional Government of the Confederate States of America, from the Institution of the Government, February 8, 1861, to Its Termination; February 18, 1862, Inclusive. Arranged in Chronological Order Together with the Constitution for the Provisional Government, and the Permanent Constitution of the Confederate States, and the Treaties Concluded by the Confederate States with Indian Tribes.* Richmond: R. M. Smith, 1864.

Mississippi Legislature. *Laws of the State of Mississippi Passed at a Regular Session of the Mississippi Legislature, Held in the City of Jackson, November and December 1861 and January 1862.* Jackson: Cooper and Kimball, State Printers, 1862.

Moore, Frank, comp. *The Rebellion Record.* New York: G. P. Putnam's Sons, 1861–63.

Nicolay, John G., and John Hay. *Complete Works of Abraham Lincoln.* 10 vols. New York: Francis G. Tardy, 1905.

North Carolina Convention. *Ordinances and Resolutions Passed by the State Convention of North Carolina, at Its Several Sessions in 1861–62.* Raleigh: John W. Syme, Printer to the Convention, 1862.

———. *Treasurer's Report* Raleigh: John Spelman, Printer to the State, 1865.

Official Records of the Union and Confederate Navies in the War of the Rebellion. 31 vols. Washington, D.C.: Government Printing Office, 1894–1927.

"Petition of William B. Isaacs & Co., of Richmond, Representatives for Certain Banks in Richmond, Praying for the Restoration of Certain Coin Belonging to Them Now in the Treasury of the United States." H. of R. 45th Cong., 2d sess., doc. no. 5. Washington, D.C.: Government Printing Office, 1878.

Phillips, Ulrich B., ed. "The Correspondence of Robert Toombs, Alexander H. Stephens, and Howell Cobb." In *Annual Report of the American Historical Association.* Washington, D.C.: Government Printing Office, 1913.

———. "The Correspondence of Robert Toombs, Alexander H. Stephens, and Howell Cobb." In *Annual Report of the American Historical Association 1911.* Vol. 2. Washington, D.C.: Government Printing Office, 1913.

Proceedings of the Bank Convention of the Confederate States Held at Richmond, Va., July 24th, 25th and 26th 1861. Charleston: Evans and Cogswell, 1861.

Ramsdell, Charles W., ed. *The Laws and Joint Resolutions of the Last Session of the Confederate Congress November 6, 1864–March 18, 1865. Together with the Secret Acts of the Preceding Congresses.* Durham, N.C.: Duke University Press, 1941.

Report of the Committee on Postal Affairs. Montgomery: Barrett, Wimbish, February 16, 1861.

Report of the Special Senate Committee on the Currency. Richmond, January 1864. Record Group 93. National Archives, Washington, D.C.

Richardson, James D., comp. *A Compilation of the Messages and Papers of the Confederacy: Including the Diplomatic Correspondence, 1861–1865.* 2 vols. Nashville: United States Publishing, 1906.

———. *A Compilation of the Messages and Papers of the Presidents 1798–1897.* 10 vols. Washington, D.C.: Government Printing Office, 1897.

Scott, E. H., ed. *The Federalist and Other Contemporary Papers on the Constitution of the United States.* New York: Scott, Fresman, 1894.

South Carolina Legislature. *A Compilation of All the Acts, Resolutions, Reports and Other Documents, in Relation to the Bank of the State of South Carolina, Affording Full Information Concerning That Institution.* Columbia: A. S. Johnston and A. G. Sumner, 1848.

———. *Acts of the General Assembly of the State of South Carolina, Passed in December, 1861. Printed by Order of the Legislature, in Conformity with the Statutes at Large, and Designed to Form a Part of the Thirteenth Volume, Commencing with the Acts of 1861.* Columbia: Charles P. Pelham, State Printer, 1862.

———. *Reports and Resolutions of the General Assembly of the State of South Carolina, Passed at the Annual Session of 1862.* Columbia: Charles P. Pelham, State Printer, 1862.

———. *Reports and Resolutions of the State of South Carolina, Passed at the Annual Session of 1863.* Columbia: Charles P. Pelham, State Printer, 1863.

———. *The Bank Cases Voted by Order of the State Legislature, December 19, 1843.* Charleston: James Leystock Walker, 1843.

South Carolina Senate (Committee on Finance and Banks). *A Bill to Punish Persons or Corporations for Sale or Purchase of Bills of Any of the Local Banks of Any State in the Confederacy at a Premium.* Columbia: Charles P. Pelham, State Printer, 1862.

Southern Historical Society, *Proceedings of the First and Second Confederate Congresses.* Vols. 44–52. Richmond, 1923–59. Last three volumes published by the Virginia Historical Society, into which the Southern Historical Society was merged in 1952.

Tansill, Charles C., ed. *Documents Illustrative of the Formation of the Union of the American States.* H. of R., 69th Cong., 2d sess., doc. no. 398. Washington, D.C.: Government Printing Office, 1927.

Thian, Raphael P. *Reports of the Secretary of the Treasury of the Confederate States of America 1861–1865.* Appendix 3. Washington, D.C.: Published privately, 1878. Only two original copies known of Appendixes 3–5. Books are on film.

————. *Register of the Confederate Debt.* Edited by Douglas B. Ball. Boston: Quarterman Publications Inc., 1972. Originally published in 1879 as Appendix 2 to the Thian series.

————. *Correspondence of the Treasury Department of the Confederate States of America 1861–65.* Appendix 4. Washington, D.C.: Published privately, 1879.

————. *Correspondence with the Treasury Department of the Confederate States of America 1861–6.* Appendix 5. Parts 1 and 2. Washington, D.C.: Published privately, 1880.

Tucker, George. "The Currency." *Hunt's Merchant's Magazine and Commercial Review* 6 (May 1842).

United States War Department. *War of the Rebellion: A Compilation of the Official Records of the Union and Confederate Armies.* 70 vols. in 128 parts. Washington, D.C.: Government Printing Office, 1880–1901.

U.S. Naval War Records Office. *War of the Rebellion: A Compilation of the Official Records of the Union and Confederate Navies.* 30 vols. Washington, D.C.: Government Printing Office, 1894–1927.

Vandiver, Frank E., ed. *Confederate Blockade-Running through Bermuda, 1861–65.* Austin: University of Texas Press, 1947. Letter Books of John Tory Bourne and Major Smith Stansbury, CSA; also the cargo manifests of the Bermuda blockade-runners.

Virginia Convention. *Journal of the Acts and Proceedings of a General Convention of the State of Virginia, Assembled at Richmond, on Wednesday, the Thirteenth Day of February, Eighteen Hundred and Sixty-one.* Richmond: Wyatt M. Elliott, Printer, 1861.

Virginia Legislature. *Acts of the General Assembly of Virginia, Passed in 1861 in the Eighty-fifth Year of the Commonwealth.* Richmond: William F. Ritchie, Public Printer, 1861.

————. *Documents. Called Session, 1862, and Adjourned Session, 1863.* Richmond, 1862–63.

Walker, Robert J. *Jefferson Davis and Repudiation.* London: William Ridgeway, 1863.

D. Newspapers

Asheville *News,* Atlanta *Chronicle and Sentinel,* Atlanta *Intelligencer,* Atlanta *Register,* Atlanta *Southern Confederacy,* Atlanta *Register,* Augusta *Constitutionalist,* Augusta *Daily Chronicle and Sentinel,* Charleston *Courier,* Charleston *Courier and News,* Charleston *Mercury,* Charlotte *Bulletin,* Charlottesville *Chronicle,* Columbia *South Carolinian,* Columbia *Southern Guardian,* Columbus *Sun,* Columbus *Times,* Columbus, Miss., *Republic,* Danville *Dispatch,* Edgefield *Advertiser,* Fayetteville *North Carolinian,* Fayetteville *Observer,* Greensboro, Ala., *Beacon,* Greensboro, N.C., *Patriot,* Houston *News Bulletin,* Jackson *Mississippi 1837–1865,* London *Index 1862–65,* London *Times,* Lynchburg *Republican,* Lynchburg *Virginian,* Macon *Confederate* (merged with *Telegraph* 1863), Macon *Telegraph,* Marietta *Rebel,* Memphis *Appeal,* Memphis *Argus,* Mobile *Advertiser and Register,* Mobile *Evening News,* Mobile *Evening Telegraph*, Mobile *Register*, Mobile *Tribune*, Montgomery *Adver-tiser and Daily Mail*, New Bern *Progress*, New Orleans *Bee*, New Orleans *Crescent*, New Orleans *Delta*, New Orleans *Louisiana Sugar Planter*, New York *Herald*, New York *Journal of Commerce*, Petersburg *Register*, Petersburg *Express*, Raleigh *Confederate*, Raleigh *Progress*, Raleigh *State Journal*, Raleigh *Weekly Standard*, Richmond *Star* (1810), Richmond *Dispatch*, Richmond *En-quirer* (1825), Richmond *Examiner*, Richmond *Sentinel*, Richmond *Times*, Richmond *Whig*, Salisbury *Watchman*, Savannah *News*, Savannah *Republi-can*, Selma *Reporter*, Wilmington, N.C., *Journal*, Wytheville, Va., *Dispatch*, *Yorkville Enquirer*

E. Periodicals

The Bankers Magazine and Statistical Register (1843 to 1861), *DeBow's Review* (1847, 1857, 1861–65), *The London Economist*, *The Merchant's Magazine and Commercial Review (Hunt's Merchant's Magazine)*, *The Numismatist*, *Westmin-ster Review* (1838–60)

II. Secondary Sources

Alderman, Edwin A., and Armstead C. Gordon. *J. L. M. Curry: A Biography.* London: Macmillan, 1911.

Alexander, Thomas B., and Richard E. Beringer. *The Anatomy of the Confederate Congress: A Study of the Influences of Member Characteristics on Legislative Voting Behavior 1861–1865.* Nashville: Vanderbilt University Press, 1972.

"A National Currency." *The Bankers Magazine and Statistical Review* 4 (December 1849): 421–29.

Appleton's Annual Encyclopedia and Register of Important Events etc. Vol. 1. New York: D. Appleton, 1862.

Aristides (Isaac Bronson). *A Letter to the Secretary of the Treasury on the Commerce and Currency of the United States.* New York: C. S. Van Winkle, 1819.

Arnold, Robert Arthur. *The History of the Cotton Famine from the Fall of Sumter to the Passing of the Public Works Act.* London: Saunders, Otley, 1864.

Baldwin, Joseph G. *The Flush Times of Alabama and Mississippi.* New York: Sagamore Press, Inc., 1957.

Balinsky, Alexander. *Albert Gallatin's Fiscal Theories and Policies.* New Bruns-wick: Rutgers University Press, 1958.

Ball, Douglas B. *Confederate Interim Depositary Receipts and Funding Certificates Issued at the Commonwealth of Virginia 1861–1865.* Hampton: Multiprint Press, 1972.

Bateman, F., J. Roust, and J. Weiss. "Profitability in Ante-Bellum Southern Manufacturing." April 1973. Unpublished mss.

Bemis, Samuel Flagg. *A Diplomatic History of the United States.* New York: H. Holt, 1936.

Beringer, Richard E., Herman Hattaway, Archer Jones, and William N. Still, Jr. *Why the South Lost the Civil War.* Athens: University of Georgia Press, 1986.

Berkey, William A. *The Money Question: The Legal Tender Paper Monetary System of the United States.* Grand Rapids: W. W. Hart, 1876.

Bigelow, John. *Recollections of an Active Life.* 5 vols. New York: Baker Taylor, 1901–13.

Black, Robert C., III. *The Railroads of the Confederacy.* Chapel Hill: University of North Carolina Press, 1952.

Blumenthal, Henry. "Confederate Diplomacy: Popular Notions and International Realities." *Journal of Southern History* 32 (May 1966):157–71.

Bolles, Albert Sidney. *The Financial History of the United States from 1861–1885.* New York: D. Appleton, 1886.

Bollmann, Justus Erick. *Plan of an Improved System of the Money Concerns of the Union.* Philadelphia: W. Fray, Printer, 1816.

Brantley, William H. *Banking in Alabama 1816–1860.* Vol. 1. Birmingham: Birmingham Printing, 1963.

A British Merchant. *Currency, Self-Regulating and Explained in a Letter to His Grace the Duke of Argyll, etc.* London: Longmans, Brown, Green, 1855.

Bruce, Eli M. *Speech of Hon. E. M. Bruce of Kentucky on the Financial Policy of the Government, Delivered in the House of Representatives, October 2, 1862.* Richmond: Published privately, 1862.

Bruce, Katherine. *Virginia Iron Manufacture in the Slave Era.* New York: Century, 1931.

Bulloch, James D. *The Secret Service of the Confederate States in Europe.* 2 vols. New York: J. Putnam Sons, 1884.

Butler, Pierce. *The Life of J. P. Benjamin.* Philadelphia: G. W. Jacobs, 1907.

Cairnes, John E. *On the Best Means of Raising the Supplies for a War Expenditure.* Dublin: Hodges and Smith, 1854.

Caldwell, Stephen A. *A Banking History of Louisiana.* Baton Rouge: Louisiana State University Press, 1935.

Capers, Henry D. *The Life and Times of C. G. Memminger.* Richmond: Everett Waddey, 1893.

Cardozo, Jacob N. *The Plan for Financial Relief, Addressed to the Legislature of Georgia and Confederate States Congress as Originally Published in the Atlanta Southern Confederacy.* Atlanta: J. H. Seals, 1863.

Carpenter, Jesse T. *The South as a Conscious Minority 1789–1861: A Study in Political Thought.* New York: New York University Press, 1980.

Caruthers, Neil. *Fractional Money: A History of the Small Coins and Fractional Paper Currency of the United States.* New York: John Wiley and Sons, 1930.

Chase, Phillip H. "Confederate Treasury Notes: The First Hoyer and Ludwig Notes and the Origin of their Varieties." *The Numismatist* 81 (June 1968):707–30.

Chastellux, Francois Jean (Marquis de). *Travels in North America.* 3 vols. New York: White, Gallagher & White, 1827. Reprint. Chapel Hill: University of North Carolina Press, 1963.

Chesnut, Mary Boykin. *A Diary from Dixie.* Edited by Ben Ames Williams. Boston: Houghton, Mifflin, 1949.

Cleveland, Henry. *Alexander H. Stephens in Public and and Private with Letters and*

Speeches, Before, During and Since the War. Philadelphia: National Publishing, 1866.

Coddington, Edwin B. "The Activities and Attitudes of a Confederate Businessman: Gazaway B. Lamar." *Journal of Southern History* 9 (February 1943).

Colwell, Stephen. *The Ways and Means of Payment: A Full Analysis of the Credit System with Its Various Modes of Adjustment*. Philadelphia: J. B. Lippincott, 1859.

Connelly, Thomas L., and Archer Jones. *The Politics of Command: Factions and Ideas in Confederate Strategy*. Baton Rouge: Louisiana State University Press, 1973.

Coulter, Ellis Merton. *The Civil War and Readjustment in Kentucky*. Chapel Hill: University of North Carolina Press, 1926.

———. "Commercial Intercourse with the Confederacy in the Mississippi Valley, 1861–1865." *Mississippi Valley Historical Review* 5 (March 1919):377–95.

———. *The Confederate States of America 1861–5*. Baton Rouge: Louisiana State University Press, 1950.

Crandell, Marjorie Lyle. *Confederate Imprints: A Check List Based Principally on the Collection of the Boston Athenseum*. 2 vols. Boston: Boston Athenseum, 1955. Vol. 1, *Official Publications;* Vol. 2, *Unofficial Publications*.

Craven, John Joseph. *The Prison Life of Jefferson Davis*. New York: Carleton, 1866.

Criswell, Grover C. *Confederate and Southern States Currency*. St. Petersburg Beach, Fla.: Criswell Publications, 1964.

Cullop, Charles P. *Confederate Propaganda in Europe 1861–1865*. Coral Gables, Fla.: University of Miami Press, 1969.

Current, Richard N. "God and the Strongest Battalions." In *Why the North Won the Civil War*. Edited by David Donald. Baton Rouge: Louisiana State University Press, 1960.

Dallas, George M. *The Life and Writings of Alexander James Dillon*. Philadelphia: J. B. Lippincott, 1871.

Davis, Jefferson. "Lord Wolseley's Mistakes." *North American Review* 149 (October 1889):472–82.

———. *The Rise and Fall of the Confederate Government*. 2 vols. 1881. Reprint. New York: Thomas Yoseloff, 1958.

Davis, Varina Howell. *Jefferson Davis: A Memoir by His Wife*. 2 vols. New York: Bellford, 1890.

Dewey, Davis R. *Financial History of the United States*. New York: Longmans, Green, 1934.

Dietz, August, Sr. *The Postal Service of the Confederate States*. Richmond: Dietz Publishing, 1929.

Donald, David. "Died of Democracy." In *Why the North Won the Civil War*. Edited by David Donald. Baton Rouge: Louisiana State University Press, 1960.

Dorfman, Joseph. *The Economic Mind in American Civilization 1606–1865*. 2 vols. New York: Viking Press, 1986.

Eaton, Clement. *Jefferson Davis*. New York: Free Press, 1977.
————. *The Freedom-of-Thought Struggle in the Old South*. New York: Harper Torch Books, 1964.
————. *A History of the Southern Confederacy*. 1st ed. New York: Macmillan, 1959.
————. *The Mind of the Old South*. Baton Rouge: Louisiana State University Press, 1967.
Ellison, Mary Louise. *Support for Secession; Lancashire and the American Civil War*. Chicago: University of Chicago Press, 1972.
Elmore, Franklin Harper. *Defense of the Bank of the State of South Carolina: In a Series of Letters to the People of South Carolina*. Columbia: Palmetto State Banner Office, 1850.
Escott, Paul D. "The Failure of Confederate Nationalism: The Old South's Class System in the Crucible of War." In *The Old South in the Crucible of War*. Edited by Harry P. Owens and James J. Cooke. Jackson: University of Mississippi Press, 1983.
Farrard, Max. *The Making of the Constitution*. New Haven: Yale University Press, 1913.
Ferguson, E. James. "Currency Finance: An Interpretation of Colonial Monetary Practices." *William and Mary Quarterly* ser. 3, 10 (1953):153–80.
Fields, Barbara Jean. "The Advent of Capitalist Agriculture: The New South in the Bourgeois World." *Essays on the Postbellum Southern Economy*. Austin: University of Texas Press, 1985.
Fitzhugh, George. *Cannibals, All—or Slaves without Masters*. Edited by C. Vann Woodward. Cambridge: Harvard University Press, 1960.
Fogel, Robert W., and Stanley L. Engerman, eds. *The Reinterpretation of American Economic History*. New York: Harper and Row, 1971.
————. *Time on the Cross: The Economics of American Negro Slavery*. Vols. 1 and 2. Boston: Little, Brown, 1974.
Franklin, John Hope. *The Militant South 1800–1861*. Cambridge: Harvard University Press, 1956.
Freeman, Douglas S., ed. *A Calendar of Confederate Papers, with a Bibliography of Some Confederate Publications*. Richmond: Confederate National Society, The Confederate Museum, 1908.
Fuller, Claude E. *Confederate Currency and Stamps 1861–5*. Nashville: Parthenon Press, 1949.
Gallatin, James. *Two Letters to the Hon. S. P. Chase, Secretary of the Treasury*. New York: Hosford and Ketcham, 1861.
Gallman, Robert E. "Gross National Product in the United States, 1837–1909." In *Output, Employment and Productivity in the United States after 1800*. National Bureau of Economic Research Inc. *Studies in Income and Wealth*. Vol. 30. New York: Columbia University Press, 1965.
Garrison, R. L. "Administrative Problems of the Confederate Post Office Department." *South Western Historical Quarterly* 19 (1915–16):222–47.
Genovese, Eugene V. *The Political Economy of Slavery: Studies in the Economy and Society of the Slave South*. New York: Pantheon Books, 1966.

Gentry, Judith Fenner. "A Confederate Success in Europe, the Erlanger Loan." *Journal of Southern History* 36 (May 1970):157–88.

Goff, Richard D. *Confederate Supply.* Durham: Duke University Press, 1969.

Golden, Claudine D., and Frank D. Lewis. "The Economic Cost of the American Civil War: Estimates and Implications." *Journal of Economic History* 35 (June 1978).

Gouge, William M. *The Fiscal History of Texas; Including an Account of Its Revenues, Debts and Currency from the Commencement of the Revolution in 1834 to 1851–2 with Remarks on American Debts.* Philadelphia: Lippincott, Grambo, 1852.

———. *A Short History of Paper Money and Banking in the United States.* New York: B and S Collins, 1835.

Gray, Louis Cecil. *History of Agriculture in the Southern United States to 1860.* 2 vols. Carnegie Institution of Washington. Publication 430. Washington, D.C.: Waverly Press, 1933.

Green, George D. *Finance and Economic Development in the Old South, Louisiana Banking 1804–1861.* Stanford: Stanford University Press, 1972.

Griffiths, William H. *The Story of American Bank Note Company.* New York: American Bank Note Co., 1950.

Hammond, Bray. *Banks and Politics in America from the Revolution to the Civil War.* Princeton: Princeton University Press, 1957.

———. *Sovereignty and an Empty Purse: Banks and Politics in the Civil War.* Princeton: Princeton University Press, 1970.

Harlow, Ralph V. "Aspects of Revolutionary Finance, 1775–1783." *American Historical Review* 35 (October 1930).

Hawtrey, R. G. *A Century of the Bank Rate* (London: Longmans, Green, 1938.

Hendrick, Burton J. *Statesmen of the Lost Cause: Jefferson Davis and His Cabinet.* New York: Literary Guild of America, 1939.

Hepburn, A. Barton. *History of Currency in the United States.* New York: Macmillan, 1915.

Hirst, Francis W. *Gladstone as Financier and Economist.* London: Ernest Benn, 1931.

Hofstadter, Richard. *The American Political Tradition and the Men Who Made It.* New York: Vintage Books, 1948.

Holden, Branston Beeson. "Three Banks of the State of North Carolina 1810–1872." Master's thesis. University of North Carolina, 1934.

Homer, Sidney. *A History of Interest Rates.* New Brunswick: Rutgers University Press, 1963.

Huse, Caleb. *The Supplies for the Confederate Army; How They Were Obtained in Europe and How Paid for.* Boston: T. R. Marvin and Sons, 1904.

Jenkins, Brian A. *Britain and the War for the Union.* Vols. 1 and 2. Montreal: McGill-Queen's University Press, 1980.

Jenks, Leland Hamilton. *The Migration of British Capital to 1875.* London: Thomas Nelson and Sons, 1963.

Johnson, Allen, and Dumas Malone, eds. *Dictionary of American Biography.* 22 vols. London: Oxford University Press, 1928–40.

Johnson, Ludwell. *Red River Campaign; Cotton and Politics in the Civil War.* Baltimore: Johns Hopkins University Press, 1958.

Johnson, Robert, and Clarence S. Buel, eds. *Battles and Leaders.* New York: Century Company, 1884–88.

Johnston, Joseph E. *Narrative of Military Operations Directed during the Late War Between the States.* New York: D. Appleton, 1874.

Jomini, Baron de. *The Art of War.* Translated by G. H. Mendell and W. P. Craighill. Philadelphia: J. P. Lippincott, 1973.

Jones, Archer. *Confederate Strategy for Shiloh to Vicksburg.* Baton Rouge: Louisiana State University Press, 1961.

Jones, John Beauchamp. *A Rebel War Clerk's Diary.* 2 vols. Philadelphia: J. B. Lippincott, 1866. Reprint. New York Hermitage Bookstore, 1935.

Kerby, Robert L. "Why the Confederacy Lost." *Review of Politics* 35 (July 1873).

Keynes, John M. *A Tract on Monetary Reform.* London: Macmillan, 1923.

Kirkland, Edward C. *History of American Economic Life.* New York: F. S. Crofts, 1932.

Knox, John Jay. *History of Banking in the United States.* New York: B. Rhodes, 1903.

Larson, Henrietta Malin. *J. Cook, Private Banker.* Cambridge: Harvard University Press, 1936.

Law, Thomas. *Report of the Proceedings of the Committee Meeting in Washington on April 2, 1829 and Its Memorial to Congress Praying for the Establishment of a National Currency.* Washington, D.C.: Way and Gordon, 1824.

Lebergott, Stanley. "Through the Blockade: The Profitability and Extent of Cotton Smuggling, 1861–1865." *Journal of Economic History* 41 (December 1981).

———. "Why the South Lost: Commercial Purposes in the Confederacy, 1861–1865." *Journal of American History* 70 (June 1983):69–70.

Lee, Charles Robert. *The Confederate Constitutions.* Chapel Hill: University of North Carolina Press, 1963.

Lerner, Eugene. *Money, Prices and Wages in the Confederacy 1861–5.* Ph.D. diss. Chicago: privately mimeographed, 1954.

Lester, Richard I. *Confederate Finance and Purchasing in Great Britain.* Charlottesville: University of Virginia Press, 1975.

Lonn, Ella. *Desertion during the Civil War.* New York: Century, 1928.

Lorant, Stefan. *The Presidency: A Pictorial History of Presidential Elections from Washington to Truman.* New York: Harper and Row, 1952.

Luraghi, Raimondo. *The Rise and Fall of the Plantation South.* New York: New Viewpoints, 1978.

Madeleine, M. Grace. *Monetary and Banking Theories of Jacksonian Democracy.* Philadelphia: Dolphin Press, 1943.

McCord, Louisa C. "Justice and Fraternity." *Southern Quarterly Review* 15 (July 1949).

McCulloch, Hugh. *Men and Measures over Half a Century: Sketches and Comments.* New York: Charles Scribner's Sons, 1888.

McKitrick, Eric. "Party Politics and the Union and Confederate War Efforts." In *The American Party Systems*. Edited by William N. Chambers and Walter Dean Burham. New York: Oxford University Press, 1967.

McWhiney, Grady, and Perry D. Jamison. *Attack and Die: Civil War Military Tactics and the Southern Heritage*. University: University of Alabama Press, 1982.

Memminger, Christopher G. *Book of Nullification*. Charleston: n.p., 1830.

———. *A Plan of the Provisional Government for the Southern Confederacy*. Charleston: Evans and Cogswell, 1861.

Mill, John Stuart. *Principles of Political Economy with Some of Their Applications to Social Philosophy*. London: Longmans, Green, 1909.

Miller, Andrew. *Our Currency: Some of Its Evils and Remedies for Them by a Citizen of North Carolina*. Raleigh: John W. Syme, Printer to the State Convention, 1861.

Miller, Helen Hill. *The Case for Liberty*. Chapel Hill: University of North Carolina Press, 1965.

Mints, Lloyd W. *A History of Banking Theory in Great Britain and the United States*. Chicago: University of Chicago Press, 1945.

Mitchell, Wesley C. *A History of the Greenbacks, with Special Reference to the Economic Correspondence of Their Issue: 1862–65*. 1903. Reprint. Chicago: University of Chicago Press, 1960.

Monaghan, Jay. *Civil War on the Western Border*. New York: Little, Brown, 1955.

Moore, Frank, comp. *The Rebellion Record*. 12 vols. New York: G. P. Putnam, 1861–63; Van Nostrand, 1864–68.

Morgan, James F. *Greybacks and Gold: Confederate Monetary Policy*. Pensacola: Perdido Bay Press, 1985.

Morrill, James R. *The Practice and Politics of Fiat Finance, North Carolina in the Confederation, 1782–1789*. Chapel Hill: University of North Carolina Press, 1969.

"National Currency, A." *The Bankers Magazine and Statistical Review* 4 (December 1849):421–29.

Nichols, James L. *Confederate Engineers*. Tuscaloosa: Confederate Publishing, 1957.

———. *The Confederate Quartermaster in the Trans-Mississippi*. Austin: University of Texas Press, 1964.

Oates, Stephen B. *Confederate Cavalry West of the River*. Austin: University of Texas Press, 1961.

Oberholtzer, Ellis P. *Jay Cooke, Financier of the Civil War*. 2 vols. Philadelphia: G. W. Jacobs, 1907.

O'Conner, Richard C. *Ambrose Bierce: A Biography*. London: Victor Gollanz, 1968.

Owens, Harry P., and James J. Cooke. *The Old South in the Crucible of War*. Jackson: University of Mississippi Press, 1983.

Owsley, Frank L. *King Cotton Diplomacy: Foreign Relations of the Confederate States of America*. Chicago: University of Chicago Press, 1931.

———. *States Rights in the Confederacy*. Chicago: University of Chicago Press, 1925.

Parks, Joseph H. *General Edmund Kirby-Smith CSA*. Baton Rouge: Louisiana State University Press, 1954.

Patrick, Rembert W. *Jefferson Davis and His Cabinet*. Baton Rouge: Louisiana State University Press, 1961.

Pollard, Edward A. *The First Year of the War*. Richmond: West and Johnson, 1862.

———. *The Second Year of the War*. New York: Charles B. Richardson, 1864.

———. *The Third Year of the War*. New York: Charles B. Richardson, 1865.

———. *The Lost Cause: A New Southern History of the War of the Confederate etc.* New York: E. B. Treat, 1867.

———. *Life of Jefferson Davis, with a Secret History of the Scenes in Richmond, Containing Curious and Extraordinary Information of the Principal Southern Characters in the Late War, in Connection with President Davis, and in Relation to the Various Intrigues in His Administration*. Chicago: National Publishing, 1869.

———. *Southern History of the War*. New York: Charles B. Richardson, 1868.

Potter, David M. "Jefferson Davis and the Political Factors in Confederate Defeat." In *Why the North Won the Civil War*. Edited by David Donald. Baton Rouge: Louisiana State University Press, 1960.

Powell, Lawrence N., and Michael S. Wayne. "Self-Interest and the Decline of Confederate Nationalism." In *The Old South in the Crucible of War*. Edited by Harry P. Owens and James J. Cooke. Jackson: University of Mississippi Press, 1983.

Pratte, Fletcher. *Civil War on Western Waters*. New York: Henry Holt, 1956.

Price, Marcus W. "Ships that Tested the Blockade of the Carolina Ports, 1861–1865." *American Neptune* 8 (July 1948):196–241.

———. "Ships that Tested the Blockade of the Gulf Ports, 1861–1865." *American Neptune* 11 (October 1951):262–90; 12 (January 1952):52–59; 12 (April 1952):154–61; 12 (July 1952):229–38.

———. "Ships that Tested the Blockade of the Georgia and East Florida Ports, 1861–1865." *American Neptune* 15 (April 1955):97–132.

Ramsdell, Charles W. *Behind the Lines in the Southern Confederacy*. Baton Rouge: Louisiana State University Press, 1944.

Ramsey, Davis. *Ramsey's History of South Carolina from Its First Settlement in 1670 to the Year 1808*. Charleston: David Longworth, 1809.

Raymond, Wayte, ed. *The Standard Catalogue of the United States Coins from 1652 to Present Day*. New York: Wayte Raymond, 1947.

Reagan, John M. *Memoires with Special Reference to Secession and the Civil War*. Edited by Walter F. McCaleb. New York: Neal Publishing, 1906.

Redford, Arthur. *The Economic History of England 1760–1860*. London: Longmans, 1960.

Ricardo, David. *The Works of David Ricardo*. London: John Murray, 1888.

Richards, George K. *Two Lectures on the Funding System and on the Different Modes of Raising Supplies in Time of War*. London: James Ridgeway, 1855.

Ringold, Mary Spencer. *The Role of the State Legislatures in the Confederacy.* Athens: University of Georgia Press, 1966.

Rowland, Dunbar, ed. *Jefferson Davis, Constitutionalist: His Letters, Papers, and Speeches.* Jackson: Mississippi Department of Archives and History, 1923.

Russell, William Howard. *My Diary, North and South.* 2 vols. London: Bradbury Evans, 1863.

———. *My Civil War Diary 1861–2.* London: Hamish Hamilton, 1954.

Ryan, Carmelita S. *Preliminary Inventory of the Treasury Department Collection of Confederate Records.* National Archives Publication 68-3. Washington, D.C.: Government Printing Office, 1967.

Say, Jean Baptiste. *A Treatise in Political Economy or the Production, Distribution and Consumption of Wealth.* Translated by C. R. Prinsep. Philadelphia: J. Grigg, 1830.

Scherber, Henry N. "The Pay of the Troops in the Trans-Mississippi." *Arkansas Historical Quarterly* 18 (Winter 1959):352–53.

Schlesinger, Arthur M., Sr. *The Colonial Merchant in the American Revolution, 1763–1776.* New York: Frederick Ungar, 1957.

Schott, Thomas E. *Alexander H. Stephens of Georgia: A Biography.* Baton Rouge: Louisiana State University Press, 1988.

Schuckers, Jacob W. *The Life and Public Services of Salmon P. Chase.* New York: D. Appleton, 1874.

Schultz, William J., and M. R. Caine. *Financial Development of the United States.* Englewood Cliffs: Prentice-Hall Inc., 1939.

Schwab, John Christopher. *The Confederate States of America 1861–65: A Financial and Industrial History of the South during the Civil War.* New York: Charles Scribner's Sons, 1901.

Schweikert, Larry. *Banking in the American South from the Age of Jackson to Reconstruction.* Baton Rouge: Louisiana State University Press, 1987.

Sears, Lewis Martin. *Jefferson and the Embargo.* Chapel Hill: University of North Carolina Press, 1927.

Sellers, James L. "The Economic Incidence of the Civil War in the South." *Mississippi Valley Historical Review* 14 (October 1927):179–91.

———. "An Interpretation of Civil War Finance." *American Historical Review* 30 (October 1924, July 1925):282–97.

Singer, Charles Greg. *South Carolina in the Confederation.* Philadelphia: Privately printed, 1941.

Smith, Adam. *An Inquiry into the the Nature and Causes of the Wealth of Nations.* Edited by Edwin Cannon. New York: Modern Library, 1937.

Smith, Ernest Aston. "A History of the Confederate Treasury." *Southern History Association Publication* no. 5 (1901):1–34, 99–150, 188–227.

Smith, Walter B. *Economic Aspects of the Second Bank of the United States.* Cambridge: Harvard University Press, 1953.

Spaulding, Elbridge, G. *History of the Legal Tender Paper Money Issued during the Great Rebellion.* Buffalo: Express Printing, 1869.

Stephens, Alexander H. *A Constitutional View of the Late War Between the States.* 2 vols. Philadelphia: National Publishing, 1868–70.

————. *Recollections, His Diary, Kept When Prisoner at Fort Warren, Boston Harbor, 1865.* New York: Doubleday, Page, 1910.

Strode, Hudson. *Jefferson Davis, American Patriot 1808–1861.* New York: Harcourt Brace, 1955.

Sydnor, Charles S. *Slavery in Mississippi.* New York: Appleton Century, 1933.

Thomas, Emory M. *The Confederacy as a Revolutionary Experience.* Englewood Cliffs: Prentice-Hall, 1971.

Thompson, Samuel B. *Confederate Purchasing Operations Abroad.* Chapel Hill: University of North Carolina Press, 1935.

Todd, Richard Cecil. *Confederate Finance.* Athens: University of Georgia Press, 1954.

Trexler, Harrison A. "The Opposition of Planters to the Employment of Slaves as Laborers by the Confederacy." *Mississippi Valley Historical Review* 27 (1940–41):211–24.

Turner, George E. *Victory Rode the Rails.* New York: Bobbs-Merrill, 1953.

Vandiver, Frank E. *Ploughshares into Swords: Josiah Gorgas and Confederate Ordnance.* Austin: University of Texas Press, 1952.

————. *Rebel Brass: The Confederate Command System.* Baton Rouge: Louisiana State University Press, 1956.

Wallace, David D. *The History of South Carolina.* New York: American Historical Society, 1934.

Watts, John. *The Facts of the Cotton Famine.* London: Grimpkin Marshall, 1866. Reprint. New York: Augustus M. Kelly, 1970.

Weber, Thomas. *The Northern Railroads in the Civil War, 1861–1865.* New York: Kings Crown Press, 1952.

Wesley, Charles E. *The Collapse of the Confederacy.* Washington, D.C.: Russell and Russell, 1934.

Wiley, Bell Irwin. *The Life of Johnnie Reb: The Common Soldier of the Confederacy.* New York: Bobbs-Merrill, 1943.

Williams, T. Harry. "The Military Leadership of North and South." In *Why the North Won the Civil War.* Edited by David Donald. Baton Rouge: Louisiana State University Press, 1960.

Woolfolk, George Reubler. "Texas and Slavery in the Ante-Bellum South." *Journal of Southern History* 26 (May 1960).

Wright, Gordon. "Economic Conditions in the Confederacy as Seen by the French Consuls." *Journal of Southern History* 7 (May 1941):195–214.

Yearns, Wilfred Buck. *The Confederate Congress.* Athens: University of Georgia Press, 1960.

Younger, Edward, ed. *Inside the Confederate Government: The Diary of Robert Garlich Hill Kean.* New York: Oxford University Press, 1957.

Index